Matthew within Sectarian Judaism

THE ANCHOR YALE BIBLE REFERENCE LIBRARY is a project of international and interfaith scope in which Protestant, Catholic, and Jewish scholars from many countries contribute individual volumes. The project is not sponsored by any ecclesiastical organization and is not intended to reflect any particular theological doctrine.

The series is committed to producing volumes in the tradition established half a century ago by the founders of the Anchor Bible, William Foxwell Albright and David Noel Freedman. It aims to present the best contemporary scholarship in a way that is accessible not only to scholars but also to the educated nonspecialist. It is committed to work of sound philological and historical scholarship, supplemented by insight from modern methods, such as sociological and literary criticism.

John J. Collins
General Editor

THE ANCHOR YALE BIBLE REFERENCE LIBRARY

Matthew within Sectarian Judaism

JOHN KAMPEN

 Yale
UNIVERSITY
PRESS

NEW HAVEN
AND
LONDON

Published with assistance from the Mary Cady Tew Memorial Fund.

Yale University Press books may be purchased in quantity for educational, business, or promotional use. For information, please e-mail sales.press@yale .edu (U.S. office) or sales@yaleup.co.uk (U.K. office).

Set in Adobe Caslon type by Newgen North America.
Printed in the United States of America.

Library of Congress Control Number: 2018957149
ISBN 978-0-300-17156-3 (hardcover : alk. paper)

A catalogue record for this book is available from the British Library.

This paper meets the requirements of ANSI/NISO Z39.48-1992 (Permanence of Paper).

10 9 8 7 6 5 4 3 2 1

To Carol

Contents

Acknowledgments

Work on this book began with an NEH fellowship at the Albright Institute of Archaeological Research in Jerusalem. In addition to financial support, this institute has provided a base for my research and study in Israel for many years. Its directors, Seymour Gitin and now Matthew Adams, have been supportive as well as helpful with advice and contacts. Colleagues resident at the Albright have been valuable conversation partners. The support of the National Endowment of the Humanities has been essential for this research and is gratefully acknowledged.

Research leaves from the Methodist Theological School in Ohio (MTSO) made this work possible. MTSO has been a good home for my continuing research, and I thank its presidents, Norman Dewire and Jay Rundell, for providing for this support as well as for an environment which values this academic work.

Students at MTSO contributed to the completion of this work. Katya Broadbeck and Joel Wildermuth, talented and diligent student assistants, made significant contributions. There are more students who labored through my Matthew seminars than I can name. These seminars were one of the contexts in which the ideas of this volume developed. I thank them for their willingness to listen to these ideas (as if they had a choice) and for their comments.

Academic colleagues in the International Organization of Qumran Studies have heard many papers on the subjects covered in this volume. Readers will understand why and how scholars of the study of the Dead Sea Scrolls were significant conversation partners in a work on Matthew. Colleagues in both the Qumran and Matthew sections of the Society of Biblical Literature also provided valuable feedback to the many papers that were delivered on the topics discussed.

Research for this volume rested on the support of libraries and librarians. Paul Burnam and David Powell at MTSO not only worked diligently to provide access to the necessary materials, they also made necessary acquisitions to support this research. Expanding the library's holdings in Qumran studies assisted the work on this volume, as well as work in this area by the students of MTSO. The Athenaeum of Ohio in Cincinnati also facilitated access to required materials on a regular basis. The cooperation of these libraries in the OPAL and OhioLINK networks makes my work possible. The libraries and librarians of the Klau Library of Hebrew Union College–Jewish Institute of Religion in Cincinnati have supported my research for the past forty years. This remarkable collection is a scholar's dream. The librarians respond to all suggestions to help ensure the comprehensiveness of the collection. Dr. David Gilner, its recently retired director, supported this project, as he has all of my research projects.

The staff of Yale University Press has been a generous, supportive, and patient presence throughout the research, writing, and production of this volume. From Jennifer Banks, the editor who first contracted the volume, to Heather Gold, the editor who saw it through to final production, the combination of professionalism and support has been extraordinary. It has been a delight to work with Heather Gold. The work of production editor Susan Laity and copyeditor Debra Corman was extraordinary. Their diligent attention is greatly appreciated.

I express deepest gratitude to the editor of the Anchor Yale Bible Reference Library, John Collins. From the development of the initial proposal to his assistance in producing a clear and concise manuscript, John's analytical abilities, mastery of the field, literary skill, and careful editorial work contributed greatly to the present work.

Academic work is demanding in terms of time and commitment. I have been fortunate to have siblings scattered across the provinces of western Canada who have been supportive while recognizing the need for me to be elsewhere, frequently preoccupied with research and deadlines. They are a generous, loving lot.

My wife of twenty years, Carol Lehman, came into the midst of my academic life and nurtured its continued growth. On a daily basis she provides the support necessary to continue this work. Her encouragement certainly helped in the completion of this manuscript. Her interest in the research, the many lectures she has attended, and her company, whether traveling for research or ensconced in my home study, help retain the joy and pleasure to be found in academic labor. I am fortunate that this accomplished woman shares her life with mine. To her this book is dedicated.

Abbreviations

All abbreviations for citations from ancient literature are found in chapter 8, "Abbreviations," in the *The SBL Handbook of Style*, 2nd ed. (Atlanta: SBL Press, 2014). This includes references from biblical and classical sources as well as other literature of Second Temple Judaism including the Dead Sea Scrolls and the Pseudepigrapha.

AASOR	Annual of the American Schools of Oriental Research
AB	Anchor Bible
ABD	*Anchor Bible Dictionary.* Edited by David Noel Freedman. 6 vols. New York: Doubleday, 1992.
ABR	*Australian Biblical Review*
AcBib	Academia Biblica
AGJU	Arbeiten zur Geschichte des antiken Judentums und des Urchristentums
AJEC	Ancient Judaism and Early Christianity
ANRW	*Aufstieg und Niedergang der römischen Welt: Geschichte und Kultur Roms im Spiegel der neueren Forschung.* Part 2. *Principat.* Edited by Hildegard Temporini and Wolfgang Haase. Berlin: De Gruyter, 1972– .
ASOR	American Schools of Oriental Research
ASR	*American Sociological Review*
ATANT	Abhandlungen zur Theologie des Alten und Neuen Testaments
ATR	*Australasian Theological Review*
AYBRL	Anchor Yale Bible Reference Library

BA	*Biblical Archaeologist*
BAR	*Biblical Archaeology Review*
BASOR	*Bulletin of the American Schools of Oriental Research*
BASORSup	Bulletin of the American Schools of Oriental Research Supplements
BBR	*Bulletin for Biblical Research*
BETL	Bibliotheca Ephemeridum Theologicarum Lovaniensium
BibInt	*Biblical Interpretation*
BJRL	*Bulletin of the John Rylands University Library of Manchester*
BJS	Brown Judaic Studies
BZNW	Beihefte zur Zeitschrift für die Neutestamentliche Wissenschaft
CBQ	Catholic Biblical Quarterly
CD	Damascus Document manuscripts from the Cairo Genizah
CEB	Common English Bible
CHJ	*Cambridge History of Judaism.* 4 vols. Cambridge: Cambridge University Press, 1984–2006.
ConBNT	Coniectanea Biblica: New Testament Series
CRINT	Compendia Rerum Iudaicarum ad Novum Testamentum. Minneapolis: Fortress, 1984– .
CSCO	Corpus Scriptorum Christianorum Orientalium
CurTM	*Currents in Theology and Mission*
D	Manuscripts of the Damascus Document
DCLS	Deuterocanonical and Cognate Literature Studies
DJD	Discoveries in the Judaean Desert. 40 vols. Oxford: Clarendon, 1955–2010.
DSD	*Dead Sea Discoveries*
DSSEL	*The Dead Sea Scrolls Electronic Library.* Edited by Emanuel Tov. Rev. ed. Leiden: Brill, 2006.
ECC	Eerdmans Critical Commentary
ECDSS	Eerdmans Commentaries on the Dead Sea Scrolls

EDEJ	*Eerdmans Dictionary of Early Judaism.* Edited by John J. Collins and Daniel C. Harlow. Grand Rapids: Eerdmans, 2010.
EDSS	*Encyclopedia of the Dead Sea Scrolls.* Edited by Lawrence H. Schiffman and James C. VanderKam. 2 vols. New York: Oxford University Press, 2000.
EJL	Early Judaism and Its Literature
EncJud	*Encyclopaedia Judaica.* Edited by Fred Skolnik and Michael Berenbaum. 2nd ed. 22 vols. Detroit: Macmillan Reference USA, 2007.
ExpTim	*Expository Times*
FRLANT	Forschungen zur Religion und Literatur des Alten und Neuen Testaments
HB	Hebrew Bible (Old Testament)
HdO	Handbuch der Orientalistik
HTR	*Harvard Theological Review*
HUCA	*Hebrew Union College Annual*
HUCM	Monographs of the Hebrew Union College
ICC	International Critical Commentary
IEJ	*Israel Exploration Journal*
Inst.	John Calvin, *Institutio Christianae Religionis*
Int	*Interpretation*
JAAR	*Journal of the American Academy of Religion*
JAJ	*Journal of Ancient Judaism*
JAJSup	Journal of Ancient Judaism Supplement Series
JBL	*Journal of Biblical Literature*
JBLMS	Journal of Biblical Literature Monograph Series
JBR	*Journal of Bible and Religion*
JJS	*Journal of Jewish Studies*
JQR	*Jewish Quarterly Review*
JSJSup	Journal for the Study of Judaism Supplement Series
JSNT	*Journal for the Study of the New Testament*
JSOT	*Journal for the Study of the Old Testament*

JSOTSup	Journal for the Study of the Old Testament Supplement Series
JSSR	*Journal for the Scientific Study of Religion*
KJV	King James Version
LCL	Loeb Classical Library
LEC	Library of Early Christianity
LNTS	Library of New Testament Studies
LXX	Septuagint
MMT	*Qumran Cave 4: V. Miqṣat Maʿaśe Ha-Torah.* Edited by Elisha Qimron and John Strugnell. DJD 10. Oxford: Clarendon, 1994.
MS(S)	manuscript(s)
MT	Masoretic Text of the Hebrew Bible
NIB	*The New Interpreter's Bible.* Edited by Leander Keck. 12 vols. Nashville: Abingdon, 1994–2004.
NIDB	*New Interpreter's Dictionary of the Bible.* Edited by Katherine Doob Sakenfeld. 5 vols. Nashville: Abingdon, 2006–9.
NJPS	New Jewish Publication Society Translation
NovTSup	Supplements to Novum Testamentum
NRSV	New Revised Standard Version
NT	New Testament
NT	*Novum Testamentum*
NTL	New Testament Library
NTM	New Testament Message
NTOA	Novum Testamentum et Orbis Antiquus
NTOASA	Novum Testamentum et Orbis Antiquus: Series Archaeologica
NTS	*New Testament Studies*
PAM	Palestinian Archaeological Museum Photograph Number of museum plates holding collections of fragments of the Dead Sea Scrolls
RB	*Revue biblique*
RBL	*Review of Biblical Literature*

RevQ	*Revue de Qumran*
RHPR	*Revue d'histoire et de philosophie religieuses*
S	Manuscripts of the Community Rule
SBEC	Studies in the Bible and Early Christianity
SBL	Society of Biblical Literature
SBLDS	Society of Biblical Literature Dissertation Series
SBLSCS	Society of Biblical Literature Septuagint and Cognate Studies
Schürer-Vermes	Schürer, Emil. *The History of the Jewish People in the Age of Jesus Christ (175 B.C.–A.D. 135)*. Revised and edited by Geza Vermes, Fergus Millar, and Martin Goodman. 4 vols. Edinburgh: T & T Clark, 1973–87.
SCJ	Studies in Christianity and Judaism
SJLA	Studies in Judaism in Late Antiquity
SNTSMS	Society for New Testament Studies Monograph Series
STDJ	Studies on the Texts of the Desert of Judah
StPatr	Studia Patristica
StPB	Studia Post-biblica
Str-B	Strack, H. L., and P. Billerbeck. *Kommentar zum Neuen Testament aus Talmud und Midrasch*. 6 vols. Munich: Beck, 1922–56.
SymS	Symposium Series
TDNT	*Theological Dictionary of the New Testament*. Edited by Gerhard Kittel and Gerhard Friedrich. Translated by Geoffrey W. Bromiley. 10 vols. Grand Rapids: Eerdmans, 1964–76.
ThSt	*Theologische Studiën*
TSAJ	Texte und Studien zum Antiken Judentum
USQR	*Union Seminary Quarterly Review*
VTSup	Supplements to Vetus Testamentum
WBC	Word Biblical Commentary
WLAW	Wisdom Literature from the Ancient World
WUNT	Wissentschaftliche Untersuchungen zum Neuen Testament

A Note on Texts

Quotations from the Hebrew Bible are NJPS and from the New Testament are NRSV unless noted otherwise. Citations of texts from the Dead Sea Scrolls found in the vicinity of Qumran are from *The Dead Sea Scrolls Electronic Library* (*DSSEL*), which means they are usually based upon their DJD publication. For the Thanksgiving Hymns, see Stegemann with Schuller, *Qumran Cave 1: III* (DJD 40). Translations of the wisdom texts from the Qumran corpus are from Kampen, *Wisdom Literature,* unless noted otherwise. The use of [ ] in these texts indicates that the letter or word(s) have been reconstructed, often upon the basis of readings from other MSS.

Matthew within Sectarian Judaism

Introduction

Our perceptions of the history of Judea and Galilee have been in constant
revision for the past half-century. Each decade yields significant new arti-
facts for consideration, sometimes textual, sometimes physical, with even
greater shifts in the perspectives from which they are evaluated and the
methodologies employed in that process. The participants in this interpretive process also keep changing. As only a few of the earliest wave of historians, archaeologists, and critical readers of texts are still active participants
in the debates, the field has yielded to their students, who now are regarded
as the senior scholars in the field, and a third generation of academics,
who are asking questions and employing methods not even dreamed of
when this revolution began. This can be documented for the methodologies employed by the historians of late antiquity, the sophistication of the
archaeologists presently engaged in the continuing exploration of Galilee,
the creative generation of scholars now employed in the next level of evaluation of the Dead Sea Scrolls, the critical readers of the New Testament
who now integrate other early Christian literature into their research in a
more holistic manner, and the students of rabbinic literature now employing methods of textual analysis not even imagined by earlier generations.
New perspectives on the Roman East continue to be advanced.

It is within this context that a volume on Matthew within sectarian
Judaism is a necessary addition to the academic conversation on the development of Judaism in late antiquity and the origins of Christianity. The
changing perspectives on the manner in which Christianity and Judaism as
established religions separated from one another, or didn't, and other developments in our understanding of the history of both movements make

1

such a reevaluation necessary. This academic work opens the way for a new
and remarkably different reading of the first gospel from those developed
on the basis of earlier understandings of Jewish and Christian life in late
antiquity.

This volume has its academic roots in some of the social scientific approaches to the study of the first gospel centered in the 1990s. This study
particularly builds upon the attempts to utilize those methods to examine the social history associated with the material of Matthew. As demonstrated in the first chapter of this volume, this approach resulted in a new
understanding of Matthew as the product of Jews of the first century CE.
In the opinion of many of these recent scholars, Galilee became the preferred provenance for the composition of the gospel. Since that time there
have been significant developments in our understanding of the many aspects of study relevant for the examination of this composition. Certainly
our perceptions of the origins of Qumran and the development of the literature from the Dead Sea have been evolving into a form no longer recognized in the early debates over this literature and its provenance. Methods
of social scientific analysis applied to the literatures and cultures of late
antiquity have continued to advance, particularly in the utilization of sect
theory as applied to new religious movements and in the application of
theories describing the development of social identity. Literary analysis associated with these questions also found further development in its application to these cultures and their literatures. The same could be said for our
understanding of the development of Rabbinic Judaism and its literature.
The evaluation of the remains of the physical culture of Galilee and Judea
has revealed more complex realities at play in this history, exceeding the
expectations of those who did the groundbreaking archaeological work in
the 1960s and 1970s.

Since our understanding of the history of Galilee and greater Syria has
continued to evolve in the past thirty years, this volume produces a very
different portrait of the first gospel from the portraits those studies did
and results in a very distinctive reading of that text. Significant changes in
our understanding of apocalyptic literature, wisdom literature, and sectarian literature, and in particular of the relationships among them, yield an
altered perspective on how a Jewish reader might understand a sectarian
composition in Galilee at the end of the first century CE.

As has become apparent in the literature of the past few decades, determining the relevant nomenclature is also difficult.[1] More detailed analyses

of some of these issues can be found within the present volume. We continue to struggle with the use of terms rooted in contemporary religious conceptualization to describe phenomena in late antiquity that had a different understanding of what we term "religion." For example, it is not clear that we can speak of something called "Judaism" in the first century CE in the same way that we speak of a Judaism or Christianity today, in which we compare systems of belief with some attention to resultant practices. I do not, however, think that the attempts prevalent in the 1990s to talk about "Judaisms" adequately resolved the problem for the analysis of Jewish history, since they simply assumed that there are multiple systems of belief. At the heart of the matter, as discussed in this volume, the debate is over practices and affiliation rather than belief and theology: Whose temple do you enter? Whose assemblies do you frequent? What practices do they have that you observe, and what is the rationale behind them? So in this volume I will use the term "Judaism" infrequently, and when I do it refers to the collective experience of the Jewish people in late antiquity without assuming a coherent ideology or even a consistent way of life behind it. Nor do I assume that it is in all aspects the same as the Judaism that evolves from the creative work of the rabbis. The discussion of the common experience is an important issue in the ongoing academic considerations. In other words, I use the term to recognize a commonality that was present but for which we are not fully capable of providing adequate definition or comprehensive description.

A second issue in the use of nomenclature concerns the word "Jew." There has been ample research discussing the difficulties involved in translating the Greek *Ioudaioi* as "Jews" or "Judeans." In this case the debate is whether the term represents a geographical orientation and persons connected with it or whether some other religious or theological commonality is to be presumed. Of course, since the majority of these Jews are dispersed around the Mediterranean and the Near East, this question of definition becomes quite complicated. The translation of the term and its utilization to represent a group of people in late antiquity is limited and somewhat deceptive if solely translated as "Judean." In my own evaluation I fail to come up with a more adequate term to represent these non-Christian successors to Israel than "Jew." I again admit the difficulties of providing an adequate definition or description, but I also am convinced that other alternatives are even less satisfactory. So I will use the term "Jew" in singular and plural in this volume to designate the members of this collective entity.

Some readers of this volume will recognize the manner in which it has been influenced by my research on the Dead Sea Scrolls. This is one of the features that distinguishes this volume from earlier works that approached the gospel of Matthew utilizing the methodologies of the social sciences. I want to clarify at the outset that the central focus of my argument is not that the author(s) of Matthew was (were) dependent upon the texts we now call the Dead Sea Scrolls. It is rather that the scrolls have provided the best material ever possessed by modern academics to understand some first-century Jewish sects, hence furnish the basis for our most advanced understanding of sectarianism, its functioning and development, during that era. This makes it possible to examine the reading of Matthew as the literary artifact of a Jewish sect and understand it in significant new ways.

This is not to suggest that the argument for the utilization of the Dead Sea Scrolls in the study of Matthew rests solely on theoretical considerations. The rationale for the inclusion of these materials in this volume rests on content, even though not necessarily on demonstrated literary dependence. Similarities in the treatment of the law, authority, and communal legislation between the Sermon on the Mount and the scrolls can be identified. The treatment of wisdom betrays remarkable similarities, even though the complex nature of its development in Second Temple literature defies simplistic comparisons. Communal discipline in Matthew finds a context in the sectarian legislation of the Qumran corpus. With the exception of the materials in the trial and execution narratives, the topics treated here point to identified connections with the finds from Qumran. It is these similarities in content that require explanation. They are explored within the context of the social, political, literary, intellectual, and religious developments within the Jewish world of the Second Temple era, the environment shared by Matthew and the corpus of texts from the vicinity of the Dead Sea.

This approach to the material has also determined the sections of the first gospel that are the focus of attention in this study. Presuming the use of Mark as one major source for the composition, the reader will note that most chapters of this study center on material not present in that composition. Other material appears in a very different form in Matthew. The same could be said about content in Matthew similar to that in Luke, that which is basic for the consideration of a Q document. Note particularly the sections on the Sermon on the Mount, the attention to wisdom in Matt 11, and the topic of communal discipline in Matt 18. The treatment of Matt 21–27 highlights material not present in those earlier sources as well. An analysis of this material peculiar to Matthew, at least in literary structure and formation if not also in content, places the sectarian nature of the composition in more distinctive focus. In many instances the literary sections peculiar to Matthew are those which betray the most similarities with material attested in the fragments from Qumran. More significantly, the comparisons provide a manner of reading which permits a greater understanding of how Matthew would have been read and understood as a sectarian Jewish composition at the end of the first century CE.

1 Matthew and the First-Century Jewish World

The development of sectarianism within the people of Israel is particularly marked during the latter half of the Second Temple era, its seeds evident already in the immediate post-exilic period. Many efforts directed toward the reform or renewal of Israel at this time are best understood from this perspective.[1] The significance of this phenomenon became most apparent with the discovery of the texts in the Qumran caves. This evidence is important because of not only the unprecedented snapshots of sectarian life that it provides but also the light it sheds on literary, ideological, theological, and social developments among the Jewish people during this period. This more fully developed portrait of sectarianism provides the context for a more adequate understanding of the origins of the Jesus movement in the first century CE and some of the literature it spawned. It is the argument of this volume that we find in Matthew the work of a writer who is advocating a distinctive Jewish sectarianism, rooted in the Jesus movement, probably in Galilee toward the conclusion of the first century.[2] Such a sectarian reading of the gospel of Matthew is informed by the content of these texts from Qumran and by our shifting perceptions of the development of sectarian Jewish movements in the late Second Temple era. It is to be distinguished from both the other early writings of the followers of Jesus and the competing groups present within Jewish communities at the end of the first century CE, such as the Pharisees and the Sadducees.

The composition is also the product of neither "Christianity" as it came to be known through the formulations of a trinitarian theology nor "Judaism" in the form now familiar to the modern world through its formulation in the rabbinic corpus. The use of the term "Judaism" when applied to the

Second Temple era is not without complexity and controversy. Discussion of its usage is interwoven with the debate on whether the translation of the term *Ioudaioi* should be "Jews" or "Judeans." Opinions range from the case advanced by Steve Mason that the term "Jew" should not be used in the translation of this term in Second Temple literature to the arguments of Amy-Jill Levine and Adele Reinhartz that the avoidance of the term in these translations constitutes one more attempt to erase Jews from the historical record.[3] Mason proposes that the translation "Judean" more accurately represents the geographical and ethnic dimensions of the employment of the term in this literature. Furthermore, language related to practice and observance, even conversion, is to be encompassed within an ethnic perspective rather than understood as a religious phenomenon.

A consideration of the range of possibilities for the translation of *Ioudaioi* has been advanced by Shaye Cohen. He proposes three possibilities: geographical (Judean), religious/cultural (Jew), and political (citizen or ally of the Judean state).[4] The geographical meaning is the early and only designation before about 100 BCE. However the extensive diaspora presence of these Judeans complicates this picture, so its ethnic component gradually comes to the fore. According to Cohen, it is in the diaspora that this ethnic component gradually transitions to a religious definition, that is, the worship of the God whose temple is in Jerusalem. Steve Mason and Daniel Boyarin argue that the transition to a religious definition occurs only after Constantine.[5] For them, the category of religion as a meaningful descriptor of the human experience should only be used to describe post-Constantinian societies. Of some significance is the observation that Cohen's category of "Judean" is a function of either birth or geography. This definition means that the term "Judean" also encompasses an ethnic identification. This perspective is legitimately critiqued by Daniel Schwartz, who notes that the common English usage of the term "Jew" includes the latter.[6] For him the move from a geographical identification "Judean" to "Jew" as a cultural and religious meaning is evident in a contrast between the geographical sense in 1 Maccabees and the use of *Ioudaismos* (Judaism) in 2 Maccabees, or in Josephus's geographical usage of the term in *The Jewish War* and the religious and cultural identification in *Antiquities*, which was written after Josephus had spent substantial time in Rome. Seth Schwartz problematizes the discussion by indicating that there is evidence of an ethnic identification even before 200 BCE and that "Jew" retains that meaning right up until the present day: "It seems clear that by a certain date, certainly before the Hasmonean period, what was called Judaism or the Jewish religion *was* an *element* in the national culture of the Jews. It was furthermore an unusually integrated and concentrated element."[7] Applying the term "Judaism" to this Second Temple literature is necessary if we accept the validity of the use of religion as an analytic and descriptive category. What must immediately also be noted, however, is that this study is not one primarily of belief but rather of practice, a topic that will receive further attention below.[8]

While Matthew has sometimes been advanced as a Jewish Christian composition, such a characterization results in an attempt to create a synthetic hybrid rather than capturing the very particular dynamic of a Jewish sectarian viewpoint in the late Second Temple era. I rather consider Matthew to be a Jewish composition that originated among the later followers of Jesus a generation or so after the disciples as they are portrayed in the New Testament. It is when the work is examined in such a context and from such a viewpoint that we advance our understanding of what it might have meant for those members of a Jesus movement to advocate for their understanding of Jewish history and their proposals for Jewish life at the end of the first century CE.

This sectarian reading of the first gospel uncovers a late first-century composition that is making a unique claim within the Jewish community(ies) of which it was a part. Using the accounts already available among the followers of Jesus, that is, at least Mark and Q, the author in this composition sought to challenge the authority structures of the community in the wake of the destruction of the temple in Jerusalem. Both Matthew and the sectarians of the Qumran compositions advanced a vigorous critique of the leadership of the temple, that structure which had formed the center of Jewish life. Similar critiques are also present in other apocalyptic literature. A variety of groups were competing for popular support as these Jewish communities sought to find their way within a more vigorous Roman hegemony at the macro level and a less coherent power structure for the Jewish community at the micro level. This is apparent in the heightened polemic of the accounts in the first gospel when compared with the other synoptic gospels. It is in the sections peculiar to Matthew that the polemic is most ardent.

In order to advance this analysis of Matthew as a sectarian composition, it is necessary to focus attention on those portions of the text that either in content or literary structure are unique to Matthew within the synoptic gospels. The Sermon on the Mount, to receive extensive treatment in Chapter 3 below, is a substantive statement of this particular author, not present in Mark, except for limited parallels to particular sayings. While more literary parallels can be demonstrated with Luke and the Q source, its distinctive literary structure and rhetoric are not present there either. The Sermon's placement near the beginning of the composition marks its importance for identifying major emphases integral to the composition as a whole. Some of these same emphases reappear with particular force in Matt 23, setting the context for the climactic account of the trial. The distinctive treatment of Jesus as wisdom in Matt 11 impels an examination of the first gospel within the context of the development of wisdom traditions in Palestinian Jewish literature of the late Second Temple period. They will be discussed further in Chapter 4. The distinctive treatment of the Torah, when compared with the other NT gospels, identifies Matthew as the product of the sensitivities reflected in the literature of Palestinian Jews. The treatment of specific issues within the context of Torah is a distinctive feature of this composition, evident throughout the Sermon on the Mount and other passages of a paraenetic character.

This sectarian analysis permits an exploration of concrete communal expectations. Such a perspective also provides a basis for differentiating the Jewish way of life prescribed for the followers of Jesus in Matthew from that of the Jewish community as a whole. Groups such as the Pharisees, the Sadducees, the Essenes, revolutionary groups, and followers of Jesus all are minority groups, each of which distinguish themselves from one another and from the "common Judaism," a topic to be explored later in this chapter. Such an approach also permits the identification of the features of the formation of social identity that distinguished a particular body of Jews from those around them.

The higher level of conflict with contemporary groups depicted in the first gospel when compared with the other synoptic accounts requires careful examination. The Pharisees in particular have a very prominent role in the composition. The scribes also receive repeated mention, and the Sadducees are significant. Hypotheses about these groups, particularly the Pharisees, have played a crucial role in the study of the first gospel for two millennia. Some historians now recognize that the evidence for the connection of the Pharisees with the later rabbinic movement is at best inconclusive. Hence their treatment should rest only on the Second Temple evidence. This changes our understanding of their role in Matthew as primary opponents of the Jesus sect. They were a competing force in the Jewish community of which Matthew was a part, with their own claims for the priority of their viewpoints and with greater access, in the opinion of the author of the first gospel, to the local power structure. In first-century Galilee after the destruction of the temple, this local power structure will have been characterized by its random and arbitrary character within the context of Roman hegemony, wherein the real power rested.

A similar case is to be made for the use of the synagogue in Matthew. The nature of this institution, which was plagued for almost two millennia by the same amount of misinterpretation as the Pharisees, is very different in the evidence of first-century Jewish life from the role ascribed to it in later centuries, when it became central for Rabbinic Judaism. Its role as a central public institution for local Jewish life provided a context for conflicts within the Jewish communities of Galilee in which these rival groups could compete and make their claims. In this case the designation as "public institution" indicates a place more akin to the Hellenistic *bouleuterion*, which served political, religious, and social functions for the community.[9] Particularly after the destruction of the temple and the growth of an aggressive Roman hegemony, the functions and impact of the synagogues will have been localized without the broader impact attributed to them in later Jewish history. As will be demonstrated in Chapter 5, the picture of a localized institution at the center of communal Jewish life is consistent with its portrayal and utilization by Matthew. The sectarian argument of this composition receives depth and context in the description of the "others" as well as the institutions and the power structure in which it is located.

Most of the literary evidence from the Qumran caves precedes Matthew by almost a century, so it does not constitute direct evidence of a contrasting contemporary sectarian Jewish group. But the material from the shores of the Dead Sea does constitute the best direct evidence available of a sectarian group or groups not directly associated with the Jesus movement in the latter portion of the Second Temple era. In some cases, similarities in texts and viewpoints between Matthew and these sectarian compositions can be identified; of even greater significance are direct points of contact in practice or ideology. Study of the texts from Qumran has also permitted the identification of some aspects of sectarian viewpoints and the communities associated with them. The analysis of Matthew in this volume is informed by these perspectives.

The purpose of this sectarian analysis is to produce the basis for a reading of Matthew congruent with what can be known about a late first-century Jewish context. The polemical nature of the text itself justifies the utilization of such a methodology. Such a procedure attempts to identify the particular areas of Jewish life of concern to this sectarian group, this new religious movement, the manner in which it approached these issues, and its supporting rationale. As in the case of the sectarian lifestyles reflected in the Qumran compositions, the Jewish way of life discussed in Matthew is an integral part of its polemic. In both literatures, the manner in which these sectarians distinguished themselves from other Jews is central for gaining an understanding of their identity within Second Temple Jewish life.

Antique Perceptions of Matthew

Prior to the critical post-Enlightenment study of biblical materials and its resultant assertion of Marcan priority, Matthew tended to be regarded as the translation of a Hebrew or Aramaic original. This lent authority to its status as the "first gospel." Of course, these claims do not constitute evidence for such a Semitic version. Its apparent origins as a work emanating directly from the first-century Jewish experience in Syro-Palestine was part of the claim for a certain type of authenticity. This argument for an original Semitic version demonstrates the extent to which Matthew was viewed as a distinctive composition within the Christian tradition, a viewpoint that held sway for many centuries. The argument for a sectarian reading of the first gospel based upon historical and methodological considerations is an attempt to gain a deeper understanding of this distinctive character recognized by these early exegetes.

The earliest reference to Matthew known to us is by Papias, bishop of Hierapolis (circa 130–140), as attributed to him by Eusebius: "Now Matthew collected the sayings in the Hebrew language, and each translated them as best he could."[10] It is very doubtful that this would have been a Semitic version of the text as we know it, since "sayings" constitute an important but very incomplete portion of the Greek composition. Speculation about whether this consisted of some type of handbook, or even the Sayings Source "Q," which many think existed first in an Aramaic version, is amply attested. Beyond speculation based upon the presence of the word *logion* (saying or oracle), there is limited evidence to support this connection.[11]

The quotation from Papias did provide the basis for the widely held belief that Matthew was the earliest gospel because it originally had been written in Hebrew or Aramaic and then translated into Greek. It was assumed that this Semitic composition would have preceded the other Greek versions of the life of Jesus. Whether this very limited claim of Papias was accurately interpreted by later writers such as Irenaeus or Eusebius can be debated, but to dismiss the entire claim of Papias as sheer fabrication also appears to be a hasty judgment.[12] While limited, it provides a hint that Matthew was regarded as different from the other gospels due to its Semitic linguistic provenance. This linguistic claim points to a tradition which considered Matthew to have a different relationship to its Jewish context than the other gospel traditions did. It should not escape notice that this early identification of "sayings" with Matthew brings to the forefront the observation already noted above, that the sayings portions of Matthew, such as the Sermon on the Mount, constitute the major blocks of "added" material when compared with the narrative of Mark and the sayings of Q, assumed to be its principal sources.

The earliest claim that Matthew was the first gospel to be written is attributed to Origen by Eusebius: "With reference to the only gospels which are accepted . . . without controversy in the Church of God, I have learned from tradition: The gospel according to Matthew, who was first a tax collector and later an apostle of Jesus Christ, was the first to be written: it was written in the Hebrew language for the believers from Judaism."[13] A similar declaration is attributed to Irenaeus.[14] To this information Jerome added that it was composed in Judea and preserved in the Caesarean library.[15] This claim for the existence of a Hebrew copy provides evidence for the early, widely held opinion that it was directed to believers who were Jewish. Beyond the argument for precedence, Matthew here is singled out as a special composition based upon its relationship to Judaism.[16]

Moving ahead through Christian history, Judaism and Christianity took on a more formal and institutional form. The connection with Matthew as a book initially written for Jewish followers of Jesus became less significant. With the ascendancy of Christianity to a position of power, the issues took on a very different tone. What became most significant about the Jewish character of Matthew is its role in the interpretation of the law for Christian theology and practice and the issue of "blood guilt" with regard to Jews and Judaism.

The immediate connection with Judaism was very quickly lost in this interpretive theological tradition. The argument advanced by early commentators that the book was addressed to Jewish Christians to justify the gentile mission acquired other meanings as the actual Jewish presence in the Christian movement receded into the background. These arguments for the gentile mission were turned into a justification for the exclusion of Jews. Once such a case was in the hands of a different body of Christian adherents—those in the majority within designated political jurisdictions and for the most part with access to power—these texts were used to dispossess Jews of their rights and status within the new Christian world. Throughout this period the gospel of Matthew retained its status as the primary authoritative gospel based upon its distinctive status as a Hebrew gospel, the closest to the original Jewish experience of the immediate followers of Jesus.

The sensibility of these early exegetes regarding the first gospel provides a very different perspective on its character from that produced by modern historical criticism. While not accepting all of his conclusions regarding a first-century reading of Matthew, I consider the viewpoint of David Sim instructive on this question when he argues that Matthew became very important to the Christian church but the heart of its argument in its original context disappeared rather quickly from that same tradition. The Christian Judaism portrayed in Matthew faded from history and was absorbed by the gentile church. Some of the anti-Pauline tendencies identified in Matthew could be found in the later law-observant Christian heresies.[17] Significant is the widely shared belief in those first centuries that Matthew was rooted in the Jewish experience in ways that are not true for the other gospels and other compositions that make up the New Testament. In this study I argue that it is not anti-Pauline tendencies that mark the treatment of the law in this composition but rather disagreements with other groups present in the first- and second-century Jewish communities about the teachings and application of the law. If Matthew is a composition intended to address issues in the Jewish community, then it is the particulars of the legal requirements and their justification rather than the status of the Torah itself that is at issue. The examination of Matthew's Jewish sectarian perspective is of particular significance for advancing such a proposition. The basis for such an approach is outlined in Chapter 2.

The Composition of This Gospel

The identification of the time and place of the Jewish community in which this gospel originated is not a simple matter. A variety of locations for the composition of the first gospel have been proposed.[18] Included in this list, among others, are Alexandria, Caesarea Philippi, Capernaum,[19] Caesarea Maritima, Transjordan, Damascus, Phoenicia, and Edessa.[20] None of these has been found particularly convincing by a broader range of scholars. The most widely accepted location in modern research has been Antioch, sometimes more by default than conviction.[21] Some of the scholars who from the late 1980s to the present day have applied the methodologies of the social sciences to the study of Matthew have favored a Galilean locus, usually Sepphoris or Tiberias.[22] Among those scholars was Alan Segal, who, while very amenable to the arguments for Galilee, proposed that Galilee and Syria should be considered one geographical area, particularly from the standpoint of the development of Jewish and Christian hostility.[23] Highlighting the similarity to apocalyptic literature such as Enoch, Frederick Grant pointed to northern Palestine or as far north as into Syria as the environment in which this literature developed.[24] The wide spectrum of these proposals regarding provenance demonstrates the difficulties involved in making this determination. There is no conclusive evidence in the text pointing to a specific location. This means that speculation on location of composition is integrally connected with interpretation. In this volume I am building on the work of scholars of the social scientific approach, many of whom were inclined toward a Galilean provenance. More significantly, here I will advance what I consider four important characteristics of the first gospel that should be considered when discussing the question of the provenance of this gospel.

The most obvious point is that Matthew is a Greek composition. While we have the allusions to a Hebrew text in the early Christian literature mentioned above, there is no definitive evidence which points to the present text of Matthew as originally a Hebrew or Aramaic composition.[25] The Hebrew text of Matthew that appears in *Even Boḥan* (The Touchstone), a fourteenth-century Jewish polemical tractate by Shem Tov ben Isaac ben Shaprut, preserves textual and linguistic features that predate the fourteenth-century manuscript. The editor and translator of this text argues that it contains readings that agree sporadically with early Jewish and Christian writings.[26] He suggests that the evidence points to a Shem Tov type of Hebrew text that goes back to sometime in the first four centuries of the Christian era, when some of its motifs are reflected in Jewish Christian works. There is no extant copy of that text. That a Hebrew version of this text from the Second Temple era can be recovered is very doubtful.

It certainly does not provide evidence of a Hebrew original for the first gospel from which the present Greek text could have been translated. A Middle Egyptian text from the fourth century is a relatively free version of Matthew that in the opinion of Ulrich Luz is not related to an earlier Hebrew or Aramaic version, since it does not bear evidence of the tendencies found in Jewish Christian texts of the second and third centuries.[27] The assumption that this is a Greek composition composed by and for the inhabitants of a Jewish community(ies) is a significant indicator of its provenance. But the interest evidenced in Hebrew versions of the composition betrays a connection with Jewish literature not as apparent for other NT compositions.

The multilingual nature of Judea and Galilee has been adequately documented in recent research.[28] After the Roman conquest of the Levant, Greek remained the "international" language of the Near East, while Latin was used in the western portions. This is clear in some of the admittedly limited literary compositions from the first and second centuries such as the Old Greek bible and revisions of the LXX. More remarkable are the large number of inscriptions in Greek in the public buildings of Judea and Galilee, including the inscriptions in the synagogues of Galilee. It comes as no surprise that the larger portion of the inscriptions in Greek come from the urban areas such as Sepphoris and Tiberias. Unfortunately, the provenance of literary compositions cannot be identified with the same degree of specificity as that of inscriptions.

The provenance of this Jewish composition in Greek, reflecting sensibilities we equate with the literary production of Jewish Palestine, is found within the complex cultural world of Roman Syria, renamed Syria Palaestina after the Bar Kokhba revolt when Judea and Galilee were integrated into that same Roman jurisdiction. The location of central authority for the region in Syria is recognized throughout the early Roman period. Josephus places the revolts in Galilee and Judea following the death of Herod the Great during the time when Quintilius Varus was governor of the province of Syria. Varus already is present at the trial of Antipater, charged with a plot to poison his father, Herod.[29] He also directs the response to the revolts in Jerusalem, Judea, Idumea, and Galilee upon the death of Herod, sending troops to defend Sabinius in Jerusalem and burning the city of Sepphoris.[30] When Nero becomes concerned about events in Judea, he appoints Vespasian to take command of all of the armies of Syria and then collects his troops in Antioch, from where he launches his expedition to Jerusalem, beginning with Galilee.[31] The Romans regarded Judea and Galilee as part of Syria.

The context of the province of Syria is recognized in Matt 4:24, "So his fame spread throughout all Syria, and they brought him all the sick, those who were afflicted with various diseases and pains, demoniacs, epileptics, and paralytics, and he cured them." All of the places mentioned in the following verse would have been part of that province: "And great crowds followed him from Galilee, the Decapolis, Jerusalem, Judea, and from beyond the Jordan." The first verse is without parallel in the gospels. In fact, the only other mention of Syria is found in Luke 2:22 in the birth narrative with reference to Quirinius as governor of Syria. Mark 3:7 // Luke 6:17 constitutes a partial parallel to the second verse, but the latter has a different orientation concentrating on the sections of Syria that would have been of greater significance for the Jewish population than Tyre and Sidon mentioned in Mark and Luke. Of greater significance is the parallel of Matt 4:23 found in Mark 1:39 and of Matt 8:1 in Mark 1:40. Assuming some literary dependence upon Mark, Matthew places the entire Sermon on the Mount including the introduction in 4:24–25 between Mark 1:39 and 1:40. The first major didactic section of the composition is located explicitly in the Roman province of Syria, in portions most familiar to a Jewish audience. The inclusion of these verses in the account of the Sermon is explicit in the outline of the material by Kurt Aland in his *Synopsis,* where the first pericope is defined as 4:24–5:2.[32] The explicit identification of the Syrian provenance distinguishes the first gospel from its contemporaries in the New Testament.

The editor of a recent set of essays on the question of the cultural character of Galilee concludes his introduction: "Ancient Galilee, it seems, reveals its secrets the more one is prepared to see it as [*sic*] dynamic region in constant interaction and transition where ethnicities and identities are no static monoliths but gain their contours in continuous movement."[33] This dynamic interplay is true of Syria more generally. Andrade notes that there is not sufficient evidence to discuss a significant "Syrian culture" independent of the Greek traditions of the area following the Hellenistic empires. Some Syrian cultures did exist, but they were never uniform and unitary but rather constantly shifting. Already in the early Roman period, where client kings were used to support the empire's provincial structure (31 BCE–73 CE), local ethnic groups were integrated into Greek polities in such ways that they assumed Greek civic identifications, interweaving

"Greek, Roman, and Near Eastern idioms into new expressions of Greek-ness and Syrianness."[34] Within an environment of such cultural hybridity, ethnic Greeks, Syrians, Phoenicians, and "Arabs" all increasingly shared in a Greek civic structure and symbolic system so that gradually the Greek *boulē* became the defining characteristic of Greek civic life in Roman Syria.[35] This is true for many of Syria's greatest cities, including Antioch, Apa-mea, Gerasa, Palmyra, and Dura-Europos. Tiberias and Sepphoris could be cited as examples of these developments as well.[36]

Within Jewish life, this era is characterized by cultural hybridity and shifting identities. This also is the period of the imposition of direct Roman rule: quasi-autonomous local rulers such as the later Herods were replaced by Roman officials, direct taxation was imposed, and "judges" made deci-sions based upon an ad hoc mixture of Roman, Greco-oriental, and local law.[37] Imperial support for the temple, its functionaries such as the priests and the scribes, and its constitution as a way of organizing and regulating Jewish life came to an end. The Greco-Roman urban culture just described now became significant for the Jews of Galilee in places like Tiberias and Beth She'arim where the evidence suggests the population was largely Jew-ish. This was not developed through imposition, but rather through the response of the urban elites to the changes in the manner of direct Roman rule. By entering into the cultural world of the eastern Roman Empire, Jewish leaders were able to find their place in this new reality. The nature of that culture can be found in the largely pagan character of the material remains of Tiberias or the abundant presence of Jewish symbols and pa-gan iconography at Beth She'arim. Evidence for the rise of the patriarchs such as Judah I, described in the rabbinic materials as wealthy and a large landowner as well as responsible for the compilation of the Mishnah, is not forthcoming in a significant manner in the remains of the material culture of the period. In the case of both the patriarchs and the rabbis, their power and influence are limited since they rely totally upon the consent of the Jews of Galilee. The patriarchs appear to rely on the diaspora for financial support.[38]

These shifting identities in Syrian culture were also the basis for ethnic conflicts. That Jews were one of the ethnic groups that at times resisted some of these impulses is evident. Examples of literature that demonstrate such a Jewish response include 4 Ezra and 2 Baruch. This is most apparent in 4 Ezra 11:36–12:39 and 2 Bar. 36–40, where the four-kingdom schema familiar from Dan 2 and 7 is now recast with Rome as the fourth and final worldly kingdom. Whether any of the impact of the rebellion of Jews in Alexandria and Cyrenaica in 115–17, with apparent repercussions in Mesopotamia, reached Palestine or Syria is a matter of conjecture.[39] The evidence suggests that the Roman legion at Legio was established within a few years of the beginning of the reign of Hadrian in 117. It is in this Syria that is emerging at the end of the first century CE that the provenance of a Jewish composition of conflict and resistance written in Greek with Palestinian sensibilities is most likely to be located. In the Greek world of the eastern Roman Empire, it was customary for a variety of cultural and ethnic representations to find expression in the Greek language.

The use of the Greek language for Matthew points to a second feature already identified in the previous discussion, the urban character of Matthew. An urban environment must be identified since it is presumed in the gospel. What exactly is meant by "an urban environment" is subject to interpretation. It does not necessarily mean only the larger metropolitan areas such as would be presumed of a city such as Alexandria or Antioch. Smaller concentrations of a population in a center of some commercial or administrative importance to its surrounding area should also be included. Such a possibility is apparent from the use of the term *polis* (city) within Matthew itself. It appears much more frequently and with greater significance in this composition than in Mark, the work used as a primary source.[40] For example, while in Mark 6:6 Jesus "went about among the villages [*kōmas*] teaching," in Matt 9:35 he "went about all the cities and villages, teaching in their synagogues." The author of the first gospel drops the reference to the villages of Caesarea Philippi in Mark 8:27 and refers to its *merē* (regions) in Matt 16:13. When Jesus commissions the disciples, in Mark 6:10–11 their instructions are dependent upon "whatever house" they enter into, while in Matt 10:11–12 they concern the "city or village." Later in that chapter they are instructed, when they are persecuted in that *polis,* to flee to another, a theme also picked up in Matt 23:34. In Matt 11:1 Jesus went on to teach and preach "in their cities," that is, the cities of Galilee. Finally, to the statement in Mark 3:24–25 that a kingdom or a household divided against itself cannot stand, Matt 12:25 adds a city. Of course, we also recall the interesting parable of the wedding banquet in which the king burned "the city" of those who had killed the slaves he had sent to summon them to the celebration.[41]

The urban portrait characteristic of this composition is rather consistent. These "cities" are within the storyline of events in Galilee and do not betray hints of the metropolises of the Roman Empire such as Rome or the religious center of Jerusalem, but they do reflect a consistent addition to the story of Mark. Emerging "urban" contexts of Galilee are the most likely explanation for these additions in the Matthean rendering of the story of Jesus. Furthermore, when we add the layer of the repeated stories of conflict with Jewish functionaries listed as scribes, Pharisees, and Sadducees, which include appearances in the streets and marketplaces, we also are convinced of an urban context. The initial portrayal of the Pharisees in the denunciations of Matt 23 include references to the *agorai* (markets), as well as "banquets" and "assemblies" (*sunagōgai*).[42] The same can be said for Matt 6:2, all of these references reflecting a particular Matthean orientation. An urban context with a more stratified social structure provides a more likely context for the particular portrayal of the conflicts developed with Jewish leadership groups throughout the work.

The third significant requirement for determining a location for the composition of Matthew is the pronounced level of conflict with other Jewish groups represented in the text. When compared with the other synoptics, it is hard to imagine that the polemical character of the first gospel does not indicate a distinctive social location vis-à-vis its Jewish context. The conflicts with the scribes, Pharisees, and Sadducees, on the one hand, and with the chief priests, the elders, and the high priest, on the other, demonstrate the manner in which the followers of Jesus related to Matthew were at odds with an existing Jewish community of some complexity in its social structure. Of course, the conflicts with the local Roman hierarchy are also represented. However, Matthew is characterized by the increased attention given by the author to the conflicts with the other Jewish "religious" groups, particularly the scribes and the Pharisees, but also the Sadducees. Matthew is the only synoptic gospel in which the Pharisees are brought into the trial scenes, present along with the chief priests in the representation to Pilate (Matt 27:62). The scribes, closely aligned with the Pharisees in the diatribes of Matthew 23, join the elders and the chief priests in mocking Jesus while on the cross (Matt 27:41). The attention given to the Pharisees in the two distinctive compilations of the Sermon on the Mount (Matt 5–7) and the diatribe against the scribes and Pharisees of Matt 23 signal an engagement on issues within the Jewish community of which it is a part. The followers of Jesus represented in Matthew live in an environment in which the Pharisees have emerged into a central position of leadership. Some background on these groups in first-century Judaism will provide a context for the more extensive discussion of Matthew and sectarianism in the subsequent chapter.

While presumed in the previous discussion and in some of the scholarship on Matthew, the Jewish nature of the first gospel requires mention as the fourth of its characteristics. The particular nature of the argumentation central to the first gospel and described in this volume demands a substantive Jewish community as a setting. This gospel is *not about Jews* or even *about Jewish issues.* It is the argument of this volume that *it is addressed to Jews about substantive questions relevant to Jewish life immediately after the destruction of the temple.* In the discussion of the evidence related to the "great commission" in the final chapter of this volume, it will be demonstrated that gentiles or a gentile mission is not the author's primary concern. Matthew rather was writing for a type of renewal movement within the Jewish community, as were other Jewish writers and scholars throughout the time of the early and middle eras of the Roman Empire. This is not the occasion for a debate as to the extent to which this feature distinguishes Matthew from other NT and early Christian writings. Rather the case to be made is that the composition of this gospel was within the Jewish community.

These four characteristics of the composition permit us to hypothesize the nature of the provenance of the first gospel and provide the basis for the sectarian analysis to follow. The gospel of Matthew demands a provenance that was Jewish and included representatives of some of the sectarian groups found in the Jewish communities at the end of the first century or their successors. That Jewish community was located in an urban environment, most likely somewhere in Galilee in the Roman province of Syria, since that is the area which would have had the most proximity to the kinds of sectarian groups mentioned in Matthew and present in Judea in the first century, particularly as they are described in Josephus. The use of the Greek language also points to an urban environment and to a significant role for that Jewish community within it. The author presumed not only an immediate circle of devotees but a wider circle of Jewish readers and hearers.

The time of composition for the first gospel is a less complicated matter. The acceptance of the two-source theory establishes the date of composition of the gospel of Mark as a terminus a quo. This is most frequently dated to the destruction of the temple in 70 CE, just before or more likely within a few years after that event. This leaves 80–90 CE as the most common default position for the composition of Matthew.[43] We do find an emphasis on the delay of the parousia in certain passages (Matt 24:48;

25:5, 19); presumably related is the assurance of the continuing divine presence through Jesus after his death and resurrection (1:23; 18:20; 28:20). Of greatest importance is the insertion, only by Matthew, of the destruction of the thieves and the burning of the city into the parable of the wedding feast (22:7). Whether the tearing of the temple curtain in Matt 27:51 should be seen as an allusion to the end of the temple is debated. In contrast to Mark 15:38, the Matthean account also speaks of the rocks being split, pointing to the destruction of the building in addition to the torn curtain, even if in apocalyptic language. Some of the other evidence provided for this dating such as the separation of the church from the synagogue is less convincing given the nature of the synagogue at the conclusion of the first century CE, a subject to be addressed in Chapter 5 below.

The utilization of Matthew by Ignatius, bishop of Antioch, in writings dated between 100 and 118 CE is also cited as evidence for its dating. There are four passages which come up for consideration. In Ign. *Eph.* 19:1–3 we find an articulation and description of the virgin birth and its significance including the imagery of the star that betray some similarities to Matt 2:1–12. Schoedel correctly indicates that Ignatius's use of the star imagery, while betraying similarities to Matthew, goes back to a more mythological version of the account. The context for the incarnation appears to be in apocalyptic thought.[44] In Ign. *Phld.* 3:1 we find a reference to the evil plants which Jesus Christ does not cultivate, taken by some as an allusion to the parable of the wheat and the weeds (KJV, "tares") in Matt 13:24–30. In Ign. *Magn.* 9:1 we find a reference to the abandonment of the Sabbath and adoption of the Lord's day, presumably by disciples who abandoned Judaism and began to keep Sunday as their holy day, in reaction to the Judaizers. This reference is too general to point primarily to Matthew. The most significant potential allusion to the first gospel is in Ign. *Smyrn.* 1:1 where, after mention of Jesus's divinity and virgin birth, it is said that he was "baptized by John that all righteousness might be fulfilled by him."[45] We note that the similarity to Matt 3:15 is striking, particularly with the inclusion of the term *dikaiosunē* (righteousness), not common in Ignatius, however a significant leading term in Matthew.[46] But it is not a direct quotation since the passive voice is employed in Ignatius. This is the only place where the particular text of Matthew appears to be evident, but as noted by Helmut Koester this could be due to oral transmission.[47]

Even if there is a citation of Matthew in the writings of Ignatius, it may not indicate as early a date of composition as previously believed. Based upon arguments that the letters of Ignatius may be dated later than previously thought, Sim has argued that the date of composition for Matthew could be advanced to the beginning of the second century CE.[48] If these compositions are not the direct product of the hands of Ignatius, but dated to the middle of the second century or later, then the evidence for the Antiochian context of Matthew from the writing of Ignatius becomes less significant.[49] It is also necessary not to overlook the obvious. The arguments of Ignatius in which heresy is connected with Judaism was not an indication of continuity with Matthew, even if this gospel is understood within the context of a gentile mission. The relationship between Matthew and the compositions of Ignatius would not be a matter of simple appropriation.[50]

The apocalyptic orientation of a good deal of the paraenetic literature in this gospel suggests an era similar to that proposed for 2 Baruch and 4 Ezra, also between the destruction of the temple and the Bar Kokhba revolt of 132–135 CE, in the land of Israel.[51] As we consider the relevant issues related to the development of Jewish life in Galilee, we will find that such a possibility has considerable merit. Sim notes that the earlier we date the composition of the gospel, the less likely it is that the critiques of the scribes and Pharisees reflect a real conflict. The growing Roman military presence in Judea and Galilee after the first revolt as well as the building projects and enhanced Roman imperial presence also fit the beginning of the second century more adequately than the first decade after the destruction of the temple. The work is advanced within the context of a Jewish community that is engaged in the struggle for identity and direction after the destruction of the temple and the subsequent imposition of a more vigorous Roman hegemony. A date of composition at the conclusion of the first century more adequately fits this portrait of Jewish life. Central to the gospel of Matthew are interactions with a variety of groups present within the Jewish community at the time of its composition.

Pharisees, Sadducees, and Scribes

An attempt to identify the nature and significance of these groups at the end of the first century is difficult. Particularly formidable is establishing their relationship to the subsequent development of the rabbinic movement. But since the Pharisees receive such prominent treatment in the gospel of Matthew itself, their identity is of paramount significance in establishing the socio-religious location of the composition.

More traditional Jewish historiography identified the origins of the Pharisees with the "men of the Great Assembly" in m. 'Abot 1:1, considered to be the 120 elders who came up from exile with Ezra.[52] This early development is described as the growing division after the exile between the priestly and lay scribal circles over the interpretation of the Torah. The origin of the Pharisees is to be found in those lay scribal circles, also called the ḥăkāmîm (sages).[53] A good deal of recent scholarship on the Pharisees has been more inclined to admit a lack of evidence regarding origins. Their first appearance in the sources acknowledges their visibility and role as a political force during the Hasmonean revolt. In *The Jewish War* Josephus mentions a significant role for them during the reign of Salome Alexandra (76–66 BCE), indicating both their popularity and their power.[54] In his later *Antiquities* he attributes significant power to them already during the time of John Hyrcanus (134–104 BCE), as he describes the conflict which he claims had John switch his allegiance to the Sadducees.[55] Whether this testimony to their popularity should be ascribed to the early period of John Hyrcanus (135–104 BCE) has been questioned.[56] Josephus's initial reference to the "sects" in *Antiquities* located already in his narration of the events related to Jonathan (160–142 BCE) points to an earlier origin for the group,[57] but their total absence from the accounts of 1 and 2 Maccabees suggests otherwise. The Pharisees are understood to be major players in Hasmonean politics, a portrait that finds good support in the record of Josephus, even if the claims made on the basis of that evidence are sometimes overstated.[58]

With no mention of the Pharisees during the time of Herod (37–4 BCE) in *The Jewish War*, Josephus's first account of this period, and limited references in *Antiquities*, the assessment that they dropped out of active political engagement shortly after Salome Alexandra is an accurate reflection of the evidence: "Evidently the end of the Pharisaic political party came with Aristobulus, who slaughtered many of them, and was sealed by Herod who killed even more."[59] E. P. Sanders agrees with this identification of the trajectory of Pharisaic involvement and activism, that is, they were in control under Salome Alexandra and actively sought that position throughout the late Second Temple period.[60] He sees a consistent though low-level role for them, as they were not part of the high priestly aristocracy favored by the Romans but a body of dissent who offered resistance at opportune moments.[61] One might infer from Josephus that the Pharisees (and the Sadducees?) were a religio-political group throughout the last centuries of the Second Temple period who took the opportunity to have an impact on national policy under the Hasmoneans when the opportunity was available, that is, when there was some level of self-government within the Judean population of Palestine. Only with the return to an internal conflict within Jewish leadership leading up to and during the revolt does Josephus again record instances of the Pharisees' influence and power. Throughout the late Second Temple period they are a significant group within Palestinian Judaism, but their political engagement is neither their defining nor their dominant characteristic.

Worthy of attention for our purposes is the increased attention given by Josephus to the Pharisees in *Antiquities* and *The Life* during the same period in which the gospel of Matthew was written, that composition within the New Testament which contains the largest number of references to the Pharisees and to the Sadducees.[62] In contrast to the other gospels, their role is continued in Matthew even into the description of the events of the trial of Jesus. One of the characteristics of the portrait in Josephus is the manner in which the Pharisees are portrayed as popular, influential, and accurate interpreters of the law. In contrast to other explanations we should at least contemplate the most obvious point derived from this evidence, that they actually were influential in Palestine, including Galilee,[63] during that period of time immediately after the destruction of the temple.[64] The evidence for their presence in Syria beyond Galilee is more limited, as are other details of Jewish life and social structure. But, as noted by Alan Segal, perhaps the distinction between Galilee and Syria should not be overemphasized.[65] The most frequent evidence cited for Pharisaism in the diaspora is the apostle Paul.[66] However those references are less than convincing. It is in speeches in Acts 21:39 and 22:3 that he claims to be from Tarsus in Cilicia. We know that these speeches in written compositions, as those in a historian such as Josephus, were constructed on the basis of rhetorical principles, rendering them unreliable with regard to historical detail. The same could be said for the claim in Acts 22:3 that he received a strict education in ancestral law at the feet of Gamaliel. So when in 23:6 and 26:5 he refers to his Pharisaic credentials, Acts would seem to be arguing that they were acquired in Jerusalem. The reference in his own words to his Pharisaic credentials in Phil 3:5 does not suggest anything different; in fact the letters make no mention of his diaspora birth. Paul's claims for his Pharisaic credentials are similar to what we would expect of other Palestinian Jews such as Josephus.

Stemberger argues against drawing any conclusion that the Pharisees would have been influential, but his concern is the argument for the continuity between the Pharisees and the rabbis, a topic to be considered shortly.[67] While in many instances the portrayal of the Pharisees in Matthew as an influential group has been viewed as anachronistic, the evidence of Josephus suggests otherwise. In both cases the authors of the compositions had to come to terms with the group's apparent influence and power. Josephus accomplishes this in his later writings through a negative assessment of that influence with regard to the welfare of the Jews, in light of the power of Rome, a factor which in his opinion was evidence of divine favor. In the case of Matthew this is accomplished by making them the leading voice in opposition to the life and teaching of Jesus Christ.[68]

While Josephus does not make mention of Pharisees in Galilee, it is obvious that as important adversaries of Jesus they are routinely located there in the gospels. We note that this is true for almost all of the references to the Pharisees in the gospel of Mark and also of Luke.[69] In Matthew we find in addition significant interchanges between Jesus and the Pharisees within the temple precincts in Jerusalem following the transition verse to the final section in Matt 21:1. After the parables in that chapter, we find only in Matthew the conclusion that "when the chief priests and the Pharisees heard his parables, they realized he was speaking about them."[70] The debate intensifies in the next chapter, immediately followed by the denunciations of the scribes and Pharisees in chapter 23.[71] Then they appear in the account of the trial itself. Nowhere else in the synoptic gospels do the Pharisees come as close to the center of power (and responsibility?) as in Matthew.[72]

A similar social structure is implicit in the description of the team sent out from Jerusalem to investigate the charges against Josephus in Galilee. The four-person body appointed by Ananus the High Priest and Simon son of Gamaliel was to comprise persons of diverse social backgrounds but similar in education. Accordingly we find therein two "commoners" who were adherents of the Pharisees, one Pharisee of priestly stock, and one member from the high priestly families. This description appears only in *The Life*, probably Josephus's last work. The composition of this group coheres with the description of the principals involved in the consultation at the outbreak of the war.[73] Simon son of Gamaliel is described as a Pharisee in this account in *The Life*, a feature neglected in the earlier *Jewish War*.[74] In these latter compositions of Josephus, dated to the 90s of the first century CE, significant leadership rests with the chief priests and the Pharisees, in a way very similar to the portrayal in Matthew. Both authors provide evidence that the Pharisees were a body with some power in Palestine in the concluding decades of the first century CE.

This evidence suggests that the sociological category of "denomination" proposed by Runesson is well-informed.[75] This category was added to the original categories of "church" and "sect" proposed by Weber and advanced by Troeltsch, by H. Richard Niebuhr, who was attempting to understand the character of American religious development with particular attention to the after-life of sects.[76] In this case, Niebuhr proposed that sects had a short life span and one of the options was to reduce the level of tension with the surrounding society by becoming what he termed "denominations."[77] As will be seen in Chapter 2 below, this characteristic helps provide a sociological basis for the distinction between the Pharisees at the conclusion of the Second Temple period and the Matthean community.

The Sadducees also make a more frequent appearance in the gospel of Matthew than any other NT composition. Like the Pharisees, their first mention in Josephus is an insertion about the "schools" in the description of the time of Jonathan (160–142 BCE).[78] In this passage they are said to deny the possibility of fate, claiming that human beings are responsible for their own well-being, that all things are within their power. A similar statement in the extended excursus on the sects in *The Jewish War* attributes to them the denial of a belief in the persistence of the soul after death and of penalties or rewards in the underworld,[79] comparable to the denial of the resurrection attributed to them in the New Testament.[80] We have already noted their role in the governance of John Hyrcanus, as described in *Antiquities*.[81] In the first gospel, with the exception of the reference just mentioned concerning the resurrection, the Sadducees are allies of the Pharisees, paired in stories in which "many" from both groups come to John for baptism and lose verbal contests with Jesus. The injunction to the disciples is to beware of the "leaven" of both groups.[82] As in *Antiquities* these are parallel groups with some philosophical differences, with the Pharisees having a much more substantive role in the narrative.

The relative lack of the mention of the Pharisees and the Sadducees is immediately apparent in the Mishnah, the earliest collection of Tannaitic literature. The most significant and well-known passage is from m. Yad. 4:6–8 in which the viewpoints of the two groups are compared on a variety of purity issues including the handling of scriptural texts, touching the bones of the dead, the nature of the *niṣṣoq* (unbroken stream of liquid), legal responsibility for the actions of slaves, and the inclusion of the date according to the secular ruler on the bill of divorce.[83] Elsewhere there are texts that address positions the Mishnah ascribes to the Sadducees, such as a reference to the denial of the after-life in m. Ber. 9:5.[84] Another question of ritual purity is addressed in m. ʿErub. 6:2. Additional issues receive mention such as the date of Pentecost,[85] the meaning of the phrase "life for life" in the context of witnesses in capital cases,[86] and the handling of the purification of the priest in the instance of the red heifer.[87] These cases as well as the instance of niṣṣoq mentioned above are of interest because they all receive mention in major legal sections of the Dead Sea Scrolls, an observation that led Lawrence Schiffman to equate the Sadducees with the authors of the sectarian legislation in that corpus of literature.[88] Whether the resulting historical reconstruction is accurate can be questioned. What he has demonstrated in establishing that connection is a consistent set of issues and stances that characterized one party of Jews during the Second Temple era or at least a set of issues concerning which the Pharisees had opponents.[89] Jack Lightstone advances the argument that the Pharisaic identity in these rabbinic texts is constructed in opposition to a Sadducean "other." The real purpose of these texts in the second and third centuries is to provide the Pharisaic "roots" of the rabbinic movement and simultaneously to construct a view of their "other." He notes that we cannot find a consistent principle of interpretation in these texts, such as "oral" versus "written" law, or "more literal/plain" versus "less literal" interpretations. In other words, the body identified as the Sadducees is distinguished in these texts by being the opponents of the Pharisees, not by an interpretive method or philosophy.[90]

The evidence for the Pharisees in the Talmud is complicated. Pərûšîm (to be separate) would apply to the passage in m. Ḥag. 2:7 where the "separated ones" rank between the common people and those connected with the priesthood in regard to the requirements for ritual purity. Commenting on m. Sotah 3:4, which lists the "plagues of the Pharisees" as one of the things that destroy the world, b. Sotah 22b includes a list wherein seven types of Pharisees are described in a less admirable light in terms suggesting exaggerated acts of humility, impure motives for acts of piety, and hypocrisy, in some cases similar to characterizations found in Matt 23. Both of these stereotypical descriptions could apply to religious sectarians as viewed by poorly informed outsiders or opponents. Since it is very difficult to determine where the Hebrew term is employed as a proper noun formally designating the group, this talmudic reference betrays either a historical remembrance of a group with this name or uses it as a common adjective without attributing much significance to the name. The first explanation is more likely, even though it may be rather dim and imprecise. In any case, this passage does not provide evidence that these rabbis held up the Pharisees as their heroic founders.[91] We will return to the discussion of the rabbis later in this chapter.

The scribes appear to be treated within this text on an equal level to the other groups already discussed above. The combination of "Pharisees and scribes" appears throughout the composition, most notably throughout Matt 23.[92] When compared with the Marcan source, however, it is apparent that in the confrontations with Jesus, the scribes have become primarily the Pharisees in Matthew.[93] We note instances in which the author of Matthew has replaced "scribes" in the Marcan source with "Pharisees."[94] When the total number of references to scribes in the two compositions is compared with those to the Pharisees, the change is apparent.[95] We also note the fewer references in Matthew where scribes are linked to the chief priests, or even the chief priests and elders, in the narratives surrounding the crucifixion.[96] Of some significance is the disappearance of certain elliptical references such as "the scribes of the Pharisees" in Mark 2:16. We also find only one reference to the Sadducees in the second gospel. These references may be some indication that the author of Mark really was not aware of the particulars of these groups.[97]

What is striking about these references to the scribes is the impression of a more clearly defined body than is apparent in many other sources from the Second Temple period. For example, in Josephus the scribes are not compared to the Pharisees, Sadducees, or Essenes, but rather serve a much broader societal function. Within early rabbinic literature, scribes of the Second Temple era are primarily teachers and copyists.[98] For the most part scribes in the period of the Second Temple are functionaries educated at various levels, some with a fairly high status as portrayed in Ben Sira, others at the village level and viewed more as secretaries-copyists.[99] Within Mark these functionaries of the retainer class are placed primarily in Jerusalem, aligned with the chief priests and elders, but also with the Pharisees in Galilee. Nowhere in the synoptics are they portrayed as a particular *hairesis* (sect, party, philosophy) with a distinct viewpoint. They represent an educated elite opposition to Jesus, a position attributed more exclusively to the Pharisees in Matthew. They are combined with the Pharisees in Matthew 23 to represent the leadership of the Jewish community that is opposed to the followers of Jesus. In other words, the Pharisees were aligned with or supported by the professional scribes in the Jewish community(ies?) in which the composition of Matthew took place.[100]

The influence of the particular groups described by Josephus should not be overestimated. I would agree with the claim of E. P. Sanders that a knowledge of all of these bodies does not give us an understanding of the first century CE as it would have been experienced by most Jews. The population as a whole did not have to make a decision concerning adherence to one of these three groups.[101] Josephus, who tends to exaggerate numbers, claims more than six thousand Pharisees at the time of Herod[102] and four thousand Essenes in the first century.[103] First-century Jews are not the sum of these groups. They need to be evaluated and understood within the social and religious context E. P. Sanders described as "common Judaism." For E. P. Sanders this is defined as "what the priests and the people agreed on."[104] Josephus says that there were more than twenty thousand priests.[105] While the accuracy of any of these numbers can be questioned, we should assume the relative proportions to be more reliable. In that case, the proportion of the population that served in the priesthood was a more significant presence than the membership of the sects. The number suggests a widespread distribution throughout the countryside. As we are reminded by Lester Grabbe in his discussion of the Roman period, "The importance of the temple in the regular practice of religion is frequently overlooked in modern writings."[106] The manner in which temple symbolism is prominently featured in the synagogue mosaics of Galilee over the next few centuries is significant.[107] Of particular importance is the priestly nature of the evidence related to the synagogue at Sepphoris.[108] The evidence suggests an acknowledgment of the continuing role of the priestly dynamic in both the changing social structures and the conceptual world of these Galilean Jewish communities.[109]

While E. P. Sanders finds common Judaism to be centered on the temple, the synagogue, and the home, I would disagree with regard to the second element.[110] The synagogue is not the important religious institution in the first century CE that it comes to be in later Jewish life. The temple and priesthood are dominant forces defining Judaism in the first century. The outline of the work and life of the common priesthood in E. P. Sanders demonstrates the manner in which their work and life were integrated into Judean society.[111] The majority of the priesthood lived outside of Jerusalem; probably many of them served as teachers and magistrates in their local towns and villages. Their limited time of service in the temple certainly did not provide even their food for the year. Whether some held more menial jobs, as was true for some rabbis in a later period, is an open question. When we speak of cult and priesthood as a dominant presence in first-century Judea, the necessity for understanding Torah within that configuration is also self-evident.[112]

Within the gospel of Matthew the sustained attention to disputes with the Pharisees (and the Sadducees and the scribes) points to the ongoing polemical context of some portion of Jewish communities in Palestine at the end of the first century CE.[113] The literary evidence from Josephus and the Mishnah attests to the presence of these groups as an integral part of Jewish life in the first century, including the first few decades after the destruction of the temple. The evidence in Matthew understands these groups to be the major opponents of the sect formed around Jesus of Nazareth. The nonexistent temple and its priesthood are still at the center of Jewish life, but a battle for the hearts and minds within the Jewish community is now under way between the various ideological groups and their views of these central institutions. The extent to which this viewpoint represents a "real" portrait of Jewish communities in Galilee at the end of the first century is certainly up for debate; that this is the viewpoint advanced in Matthew is rather apparent. This younger sectarian entity is engaging in open competition with adherents of groups, each of which had their own critiques of the temple and its functioning in the late Second Temple era as well as their own viewpoints of what was central to Jewish life. But for many NT scholars the references to these groups have been obscured by assumptions about the relationship of the Pharisees to a group of Jews whose name probably does not even receive mention in the gospel of Matthew.[114]

The Rabbis

The relationship of the Pharisees and the rabbis is of importance to the study of Matthew in order to clarify the nature of the Jewish community of which Matthew was a part, and to locate as specifically as possible the major conflicts central to the identity of the followers of Jesus related to this composition. A direct connection between the Pharisees and the rabbis was a mainstay of scholarship on the development of early Judaism throughout a good deal of the nineteenth and twentieth centuries. Significant voices have continued to argue for some understanding of continuity between the Pharisees and the rabbis. E. P. Sanders concluded his chapter on the history of the Pharisees as follows: "After the destruction of Jerusalem, they led the reconstruction of Judaism, giving up their party name, becoming more catholic, and taking the title 'rabbis,' 'teachers.'"[115] Roland Deines has advanced a vigorous defense of this relationship.[116] While this presupposition undergirded the well-known argument of Shaye Cohen concerning the significance of Yavneh, it was not his main point. He did not find any convincing evidence for the connection, but rather concluded that the evidence from Josephus and the New Testament had some collective weight, with the result that "in all likelihood there was some close connection between the post-70 rabbis and the pre-70 Pharisees."[117] He then went on to point out that a definitive connection between the two could not be demonstrated until the medieval scholion to Megillat Ta'anit. This question has received considerable attention since his pivotal article.

The major personalities of Second Temple Judaism considered important for rabbinic history, such as Hillel and Joḥanan ben Zakkai, are not referred to as Pharisees in Tannaitic literature, the early stratum of the rabbinic corpus including the Mishnah and some of the early midrashim. Many of the first-century figures regarded as important by the rabbinic tradition are never called Pharisees in the rabbinic texts and most do not even receive mention in Josephus. In his examination of this question, Sievers found the names of only twelve Pharisees in Josephus and the New Testament scattered over the course of two centuries.[118] The two that would appear to have the greatest connection with the rabbinic traditions are Gamaliel, with whom Paul allegedly studied,[119] and Simon ben Gamaliel, who is said to have been influential in the empaneling of a delegation to investigate Josephus's removal from his post in Galilee.[120] While these are the only two figures actually referred to as Pharisees who also appear in the recital of leading personalities in m. 'Abot 1:16–17, their placement has been questioned since they are not introduced with the traditional formula that would include them as participants in the chain of tradition. This formula includes the Hebrew verbs *qibbēl* (received) and *māsar* (transmitted), the latter only stated in the first verse and implied thereafter, that is, "received the Torah from . . . and transmitted it to." But the formula is applied when we get to Joḥanan ben Zakkai in 2:8. In other words, the formulaic transmission of the tradition jumps from Hillel and Shammai ending in m. 'Abot 1:15 to Joḥanan ben Zakkai in 2:8. Traditions related to Gamaliel and Simon ben Gamaliel are not introduced by that formula, and these figures are not even included in the related text of 'Abot R. Nat. A 14, at which point Joḥanan ben Zakkai follows directly after Hillel and Shammai, nor in 'Abot R. Nat. B 29 (and 31), which does the same thing.[121] Recent scholarship has understood m. 'Abot 1:16–2:7 to be an insertion into an older tradition for the purpose of supporting the dynastic claims of the house of Judah the Prince, usually regarded as the final editor of the Mishnah.[122]

The case for other figures rests on the assumption that the Pharisees were to be related to the sages and/or scribes identified as such in references to the era of the Second Temple.[123] The texts of the Mishnah only attribute to the Pharisees positions on halakic matters, and these references are very limited.[124] They receive even less mention in the Tosefta, remaining completely in the background.[125] The Palestinian Talmud appears similar to the Tosefta; however the Babylonian Talmud contains more *baraitot,* narratives in which opinions are attributed to some of the Tannaim, such as Joḥanan ben Zakkai in b. Menaḥ. 65a–b and b. B. Bat. 115b–116a.[126] It is assumed in contemporary scholarship that the Babylonian Talmud is the last of these collections to be edited into the final form of its extant manuscripts. This evidence suggests that the connection of the Pharisees with the rabbinic movement is a case that was made as the tradition developed and is not apparent in its origins.

The emerging rabbinic movement did not have as much authority in the second century CE as has been attributed to it in earlier scholarship. In a subsequent study of all of the references to the rabbinic figures in the Tannaitic materials, Shaye Cohen notes that there is limited evidence for seeing them as the leading figures of their communities.[127] Their institutions were oriented toward the select few rather than to the common people, sometimes designated *'am hā'āreṣ* (the people of the land). The rabbis were not the leaders of the synagogues. They were identified by their father rather than their teacher, and none of them are portrayed as being poor. While they declared that Torah was to be the province of all Israel, there is no evidence of a system whereby the poor or members of the general population could devote themselves to its study. So their actual role and status in the communities in which they lived in Galilee is somewhat of an enigma. Prior to Judah the Prince (also called Patriarch) they seem to have been based primarily in the villages and towns rather than in more urban centers such as Sepphoris.[128] Recall what has already been established earlier in this chapter. The Romans were in control of the big questions and were prepared to step in to resolve any ambiguity which suggested instability or threatened their control. All the evidence points to the rabbis as a scholastic group in the second century who studied Torah and worked at developing a model for the ideal Jewish life, however without any real power within the Jewish population as a whole: "Between 70 CE and the middle decades of the fourth century, rabbis in Palestine appeared to be a numerically small group of religious experts with limited influence."[129]

The work of Catherine Hezser is instructive for integrating the evidence from the NT texts with the talmudic materials. Citing the NT texts that utilize the term "rabbi," she rejects the rigid distinction that has been made concerning the use of this term in the pre- and post-70 CE evidence.[130] It is in the gospel materials that we find evidence of the pre-70 usage. Its most prominent usage to designate Jesus is found in Mark and John.[131] In Matthew its use for this purpose is more limited, but it also appears in the negative with reference to Jewish leaders.[132] For Hezser the term appears to be used as an informal and unofficial form of address already in the first century. This view receives support from the analysis of the rabbinic evidence, where the title is not used in the Mishnah with reference to the pre-70 sages. Throughout the first to the fifth centuries CE, the general address for a superior in rabbinic literature appears to be *mārî* or *'ādônî* (my master) rather than *rabbî*.[133] In Hezser's research the title *rabbān* is applied to first-century sages such as Gamaliel I and Simon ben Gamaliel, but the term *rabbî* is used first for the students of Joḥanan ben Zakkai, who is designated *rabbān* in m. 'Abot 2:8, in contrast to his disciples.[134] Since no title is given to Gamaliel or his son in Acts or in Josephus, it may be that the terms were applied anachronistically in the rabbinic tradition. Thus Hezser proposes that the title within the rabbinic texts may have been deliberately avoided with reference to the pre-70 sages to highlight the significance and innovations of Joḥanan ben Zakkai and the "Sanhedrin" at Yavneh. She notes that the term *rabbî* is employed for Judah the Prince, perhaps being tied explicitly to the patriarchate rather than the rabbinic tradition.[135]

The evidence suggests that the rabbinic movement in its early stages in the first and second century CE comprised individuals from a variety of backgrounds. While research has tended to focus on the question of the continuity between Pharisaism and rabbinism, it appears that a more adequate picture results if one asks the question more broadly concerning the backgrounds of the persons who entered this movement. The chaotic and conflicted period leading up to the year 70 CE provides justification for such an approach. For example, we note that Josephus claims credit for being from a priestly family, for being of royal lineage (i.e., the Hasmoneans), for being aligned with the Pharisees, and for being commander of the resistance forces in Galilee (i.e., a revolutionary).[136] All in all, a rather complex pedigree. Already noted above is the composition of the delegation sent to investigate Josephus's command in Galilee: two Pharisees of lower-class background, one Pharisee from a priestly family, and a younger member from the high priestly families.[137] While in the changing fortunes of a post-70 Jewish society it can be argued that Josephus makes arguments similar to the Pharisees for the centrality of Torah to Jewish life, he does not identify the leadership of that vulnerable period with the latter and rather seems to identify himself with his more aristocratic background among the priesthood to both his Jewish and Roman readers.[138]

That a substantial number of Tannaim were of priestly background has been noted in earlier research. We have already observed earlier in this study the estimate of the large number of priests scattered throughout Judea and Galilee in the first century CE, when compared with comparable figures for adherents of the various sects. The evidence for the continuing presence, status, and roles of priestly families between the revolts has been collected by Matthew Grey.[139] Included in the list of first-generation Tannaim that were of priestly descent are Rabbi Ḥananiah (sometimes thought to be Ḥaninah) the "chief of the priests," Rabbi Tarfon, Rabbi Ishmael, Rabbi Zadok, Rabbi Eleazar ben Zadok, Rabbi Zechariah ben Hakkazzab, Rabbi Yose the priest, and Rabbi Eleazar ben Azariah.[140] The recognition that at least a third of the Mishnah (also Tosefta and both Talmuds) is composed of prescriptions related to the temple structure and its practices also suggests the continuation of hierocratic interests, even though by itself not direct evidence of priests engaged in the propagation of this legislation. This observation is of even greater significance when we note the more recent argument of Shaye Cohen regarding the origins of Tannaitic law. In an analysis of the legal traditions that constitute the halakah of the Mishnah, he notes that over half of the content of the Mishnah is of interest to priests. While admitting that all of this material may not derive directly from priests, he argues that some of it does.[141] Note that the cumulative effect of the collection of the names of these persons and the legislation is to find evidence for a more significant presence of the priesthood than of the Pharisees among the Tannaim, the early sages of the rabbinic movement. The historical evidence for the relationship of the Pharisees and the rabbis remains tenuous. There is no reason to regard the rabbinic movement itself as a significant force in the immediate post-70 environment of Galilee. Matthew does suggest that the Pharisees were important, and that should remain the focus of scholarly attention in the study of the first gospel.

Yavneh—Jamnia

An area of inquiry demanding attention in this investigation of the origins of the rabbinic movement is "the significance of Yavneh," the title of Shaye Cohen's seminal article already mentioned above.[142] This demands our attention because of its importance in the scholarship on the history of Second Temple Jews and the impact of that work on the study of Matthew.[143] A highly influential work was that of W. D. Davies on the Sermon on the Mount, casting it as a Christian response to Yavneh (also transliterated as Jabneh; Greek, Jamnia).[144] In 1964, the same year as Davies's publication, Jack P. Lewis argued for the significance of Yavneh as the site and occasion for the finalization of the canon of the Hebrew Bible.[145] These studies resulted in great significance being attributed to Yavneh among scholars of the New Testament, a stance already prevalent among historians of the rabbinic movement at that time.

A pivotal passage for this perception is b. Roš. Haš. 31b:

> Correspondingly, the Sanhedrin wandered to ten places of banishment, as we know from tradition, namely, from the Chamber of Hewn Stone to Hanuth, and from Hanuth to Jerusalem, and from Jerusalem to Yavneh, and from Yavneh to Usha, and from Usha [back] to Yavneh, and from Yavneh [back] to Usha, and from Usha to Shefar'am, and from Shefar'am to Beth She'arim, and from Beth She'arim to Sepphoris, and from Sepphoris to Tiberias.

Incidentally, Tiberias is regarded as the low point of this migration. In Song Rab. 8:13 we read, "On another occasion when the sages of Israel were taking a vote in the vineyard in Yavneh—now were they in a vineyard? In fact it means the Sanhedrin, so called because they sat in rows and groups like the plantation of a vineyard." These are the oldest references in the rabbinic materials making a direct connection between Yavneh and the Sanhedrin.[146] This connection is not identified in the Tannaitic materials, even though m. Yad. 3:5 and 4:2 and m. Zebaḥ. 1:3 mention the installation of Rabbi Eleazar ben Azariah as head of the yəšibah (academy), that is, at Yavneh. The traditions relating to the conflicts at Yavneh such as that of Rabbi Joshua and Rabban Simon ben Gamliel in b. Ber. 27b–28a also appear first in the talmudic records.[147] These conflicts are implicit behind the critical issues involved in an analysis of the various versions of the chain of tradition recorded in m. 'Abot 1–2 as well as in 'Abot R. Nat. A and B already discussed above.

In m. Ḥag. 2:2 the designation *nāśî'* (prince) is employed with reference to the five pairs (*zûgôt*) in the chain of tradition of m. 'Abot 1:4–15, the last of whom are Hillel and Shammai. These pairs are identified as "princes and fathers of the court." This title only reappears with reference to Judah the Prince, the title recorded for him in numerous references throughout the Talmud. He clearly is the end point or objective in the chain of tradition as it is recorded in m. 'Abot 2:1–2 but, as already noted above, absent from the same record in 'Abot R. Nat. A. Here we have literary evidence of the self-conscious development of a tradition to establish his authority. The stage of formation of the Mishnah that includes m. 'Abot claims the authority of the pre-70 Sanhedrin for Judah the Prince and incorporates the scholastic developments attributed to Rabban Joḥanan ben Zakkai and his students into that authoritative tradition. While an evaluation of the evidence concerning Judah the Prince's role as patriarch and as responsible for the codification of the Mishnah is important, it is not of great significance for establishing the nature of leadership in the Jewish communities at the end of the first century CE. In the accounts discussed above we learn how the later rabbis understood the basis of their authority. It is their "myth of origins."[148] It does not constitute definitive or even very convincing evidence that Yavneh was actually a significant institution or event in Jewish life at the end of the first century CE. It was remembered as being important to an early group of sages whom the emerging rabbinic tradition considered foundational to their movement. In other words, there is no convincing evidence that it was significant in Jewish life at the time of the composition of Matthew or that it is immediately relevant to a discussion of the Pharisees.

Conclusion

We are left with the conclusion of Amram Tropper regarding the institutional status of the rabbinic movement: "Scattered disciple circles, rather than a functioning, centralized academy characterized the rabbinic social structure in the tannaitic period."[149] The relationship of the Pharisaic movement to this history is shrouded in the obscurity of both the lack of documentation concerning them at the end of the first century and the absence of any definitive evidence for these early phases of rabbinic history. An examination of the origins of Rabbinic Judaism does not result in a holistic or convincing portrayal of Jewish life in Galilee at the time that Matthew was written, nor does it provide an adequate context for understanding the opposition that the author seemed to be railing against. The meager evidence we have about the Pharisees is actually more helpful for this purpose. In this instance, the continuing presence of temple ideologies and hierocratic impulses should play an equal role in determining the admittedly obscure outlines of the socio-religious context for the authorship of the first gospel and the community related to its origins. From Matthew we learn that the Pharisees had some power and influence in this urban community at the end of the first century CE.

What the rabbinic evidence does supply is some verification of the portrait already present from other archaeological and historical evidence concerning the nature of Galilee at the end of the first century CE. Cities with a substantive Roman administrative and military presence are the best location in which to locate a sectarian Jewish composition which reflects an awareness of a gentile presence, apparent in the encounters recorded in rabbinic literature as well as in the depiction of Sepphoris that emerges from the archaeological record. The historical cultural hybridity of the region completes this profile. Here the sectarian gospel of Matthew provides a picture of an apocalyptically influenced community that is both Jewish and multicultural, reflecting the complex character of the administrative and military centers of the eastern Roman Empire, with Roman bureaucrats, military personnel from a variety of backgrounds, a variety of commercial interests, and the complex native populations whose offspring occupied the hinterland of the Roman cities. Within this variegated cultural setting, the author of Matthew portrays the manner in which the future for Jews rests with this group of sectarians who are followers of Jesus. While the future of the world is also implicit in this argument, the author's concern is the Jewish community. The primary opponents of this sectarian body are the local Jewish religious leadership. While analysis by modern scholars demonstrates the likelihood that these leaders had very limited power and that the important decisions rested in the hands of the Romans, Matthew is concerned primarily about what the Jewish community believes about its future and its way of life. This volume is an attempt to examine the Jewish way of life and its expectations that were advocated by this author. In order to do that, we need to take a look at what we mean when we speak of a sectarian Jewish community.

2 Matthew within Jewish Sectarianism

A conference at Southern Methodist University in 1989 marked a major shift in the study of the first gospel. The early results of this new wave of research from the perspective of the social sciences were summarized in the following manner:

1. The Matthean community was situated in an urban environment, perhaps in Galilee or Syria, but not necessarily Antioch.
2. While encompassing gentile converts, the constituency of the Matthean community was ethnically predominantly Jewish Christian.
3. The Matthean community is best thought of as a sect within Judaism.
4. At the time of writing, the Matthean community was encountering severe opposition from Pharisaic, or formative, Judaism.
5. At the center of the quarrel with Pharisaic Judaism was the interpretation and practice of the Jewish law.[1]

This listing signified a remarkable departure from a good deal of previous Matthean scholarship.

A survey of critical scholarship on Matthew from the earlier portion of the twentieth century would demonstrate the extent to which the Jewish context of the first gospel had become less significant in the examination of its historical development. Going from being regarded as an originally Hebrew composition and the oldest (hence most authentic?) of the gospels, it had moved to being dependent upon Mark and Q according to the source critics in the nineteenth century. This was followed by the magisterial work on form criticism by Rudolf Bultmann, who identified layers of text within the development of the early Christian movement but did not relate them in a significant manner to contemporary Jewish literature.[2] The criteria employed tended to emphasize theological developments in early Christianity rather than responses to Jewish life reflected in its literature.[3] After his detailed attention to what could be termed "the microforms," redaction criticism was an attempt to identify the theological stances which each of the gospel writers brought to his appraisal of the significance of Jesus, usually a christological focus.[4] Again, the Jewish experience of the first century was relegated to the background as a primary concern of the interpreters. In the hands of more recent exegetes this approach to an analysis of the text as a whole gradually looked to literary methods for the analysis of the text.[5] Literary criticism was interested in the exploration of the dynamics within the text, frequently with an eye to the text as a mode of communication, rather than to the Jewish world within which the text was composed and read.[6] All of these methods inevitably led to the text being read primarily as a Christian text, with minimal attention to its Jewish context.[7] The possibility that Matthew should be read primarily as a Jewish composition did not come into consideration during the utilization of these methods which were predominant in twentieth-century gospel scholarship.

The new chapter in research on the first gospel was apparent in the volume of J. Andrew Overman, who began his study with a description of the sectarian nature of Judaism in the latter portion of the Second Temple era.[8] His work was informed by archaeological experience in Galilee and the application of social scientific methodologies to the study of the texts of the New Testament. Both formative Judaism and the community of Matthew emerged within a context of factionalism that can be identified throughout the literature of Second Temple Judaism. Between the Jewish war with Rome in 66–70 CE and the Bar Kokhba revolt of 132–135 was a time when the Pharisees and their successors became more dominant. In Overman's view, the Matthean community was in conflict with this formative Judaism for which the Pharisees were emerging as the most viable leadership. Overman proposed Sepphoris as the most likely location in which this particular dynamic could be found because of its central role in the development of formative Judaism.[9] The focus of Matthew was on communal formation rather than world transformation. Little evidence for the presence of gentiles within the Matthean community was to be found in the first gospel, but it represented a community in the process of opening up to gentile participation. In this groundbreaking work we also can identify some of the difficulties which would arise as this methodology was employed in the study of the first gospel.

The broad definition of "sectarianism" employed by Overman and a number of scholars of first-century Jewish history at that time has proved difficult and sometimes deceptive in terms of developing a convincing picture of the context of first-century Judaism. It is not clear that the Pharisees can easily fit the same sociological category as the Matthean community or most of the other groups of which we are aware in first-century Judaism.[10] Such a viewpoint is further confused by the claim that "formative Judaism and the Matthean community may have been roughly equal in size and shape."[11] This appears doubtful. A model which is supposed to help us clarify relationships and relative positions of groups actually winds up leveling them, that is, making them all appear more similar than is warranted by the evidence. It must be noted that the development of Rabbinic Judaism, the contributions of the Pharisaic movement, and the significance of Galilee have only become more complicated historical issues since Overman's book was written.

Anthony Saldarini broadened the methodological lens to include three theoretical approaches to the study of Matthew based in the social sciences: realistic conflict theory, social identity theory, and deviance theory.[12] He devoted the most attention to social identity theory, an area also developed by Philip Esler as well as others in the subsequent decade.[13] This approach stresses the role of cognition in group formation, in contrast to realistic conflict theory, which concentrates on needs and desires (emotions). Social identity theory places an emphasis on self-identity. "It explains the strength and performance of the long-lasting and deeply ingrained group identification which was characteristic of ancient society. . . . Groups ask who they are before they ask whether they need or like other people or things."[14] In Matthew, identity involved being a follower of Jesus, a member of Israel, and a participant in the kingdom of God. This identity leads to conflict as groups compare and contrast their own viewpoints with those of others. Furthermore, "central to the theory is the idea that when a specific social identity becomes salient, self-perception and conduct become stereotypical of the in-group, whereas perceptions of members of other groups become out-group stereotypical."[15] Behavior and understanding respond initially to the norms, values, and beliefs of the group itself, thereby viewing all of those outside the group as similar regardless of the differences in their affiliations and orientations. The important aspect that motivates perceptions of and behavior toward the outside group is precisely that they are outside the group. If this is the case, then to these followers of Jesus, Pharisees and chief priests can appear remarkably similar, even though any other observers would be astounded at the connection.

Saldarini's appropriation of the sociology of deviance as a major methodological tool was informed by the assertion that it is a broader theoretical concept of which sect is a subordinate category.[16] He described the community as well as its spokesperson, the author of the gospel of Matthew, as deviant in the sense that it accepted all the major commitments of first-century Judaism but modified the interpretation or actualization of the law in such a way that it conflicted with other Jewish groups: "Matthew is deviant because he is a minority against the majority and because he recommends a more fundamental reorientation of the tradition than many other Jewish movements."[17] He pointed out that deviance was one of the mechanisms of identity: "What a society rejects is determinative of what it is."[18] Saldarini was not arguing for some notion of a normative Judaism, but rather that the author of Matthew wrote as though the scribes and Pharisees were representative of a parent group which regarded itself as "sitting" in that majority position.

Saldarini's analysis produced interesting results with regard to the question of the "gentiles" in the first gospel. Saldarini pointed to the multiple meanings of the term with important observations about its usage, such as noting that in Matt 21:43 the kingdom of God will be given not to a "nation" but to a "people," in this case the author's own voluntary association or social group that produces the fruits of the kingdom.[19] The multiple uses of the term with both positive and negative connotations suggests that sometimes the term is used to reflect insider-outsider dynamics for the Matthean community rather than the strict Jew-gentile distinction. That community does accept people from the nations who are responsive to Jesus. He concludes, "In Matthew's version of a reformed Judaism, gentiles are peripheral, but firmly present."[20] In contrast to the literary studies discussed above in which justification for a gentile mission was considered central to the purposes of the composition, for both Overman and Saldarini the gentile question was not one of the defining issues of the first gospel.[21] In this stance they are followed by Sim and Runesson.[22]

In his important study David Sim accepted most of Overman's and Saldarini's premises concerning the sectarian nature of the Matthean community, but then argued that this gospel was a significant voice within the tensions concerning the place of Judaism within the early Christian movement at Antioch.[23] He sought to establish that the Christian Judaism reflected in Matthew was the direct descendant of the configuration which emerged after James's victory over Paul for the control of the Christian community in Antioch. This Christian Judaism portrayed in Matthew faded from history and was absorbed later by the gentile church, while evidence of some of its anti-Pauline tendencies could be found in the later law-observant Christian heresies.

It is not clear that we can apply a sectarian analysis of Judaism to Matthew while simultaneously placing it within a literary trajectory of responses to major challenges facing the proto-Christian movement.[24] It is very difficult to see how a sectarian body within Judaism could emerge *after* *and in response to* the proto-Christian gentile mission, as developed by Sim. Admittedly, the picture could be more compelling if Paul was seen as an individual "within Judaism" rather than the anti-legalistic portrait developed by Sim.[25] From the standpoint of sectarian analysis, the "parent body" no longer is Judaism. It is very difficult to see how the anti-Pharisaic vitriol of Matt 23 and the entire tenor of hostility toward the leadership of the Jewish community would be so central to a work that was correcting an anti-legalistic legacy of Paul. The argument that some of Matthew's viewpoints can be found in later law-observant communities that were regarded as heretical by proto-Christian traditions moving toward orthodoxy merits further attention.

Apart from the trajectory of scholarship represented by Overman, Saldarini, and Sim, a significant contribution to the use of sociology in the study of Matthew is found in the work of Graham Stanton, in which he compared Matthew with the Damascus Document.[26] Both works represent groups that are in sharp conflict with parent bodies. Like in CD, the polemic directed within Matthew at the leaders of the dominant group is one way the minority community distances itself from the parent group. The strong arguments for group solidarity in passages such as Matt 7:13–27 or in the explanation of the parable of the weeds in 13:36–43 reflect the internal dynamics of a sect in that they exhibit the hostility that a group in conflict shows toward internal dissent.[27] The legitimation of both groups is based in the claim that the new group is not the innovative one; it is the parent group which has become deviant or gone astray. Notice that in this study the Pharisees and scribes are understood within the gospel of Matthew to be representative of that parent body which has gone astray.

What is interesting for our discussion with regard to Matthew and Judaism is that while Stanton asserts the value of a sectarian analysis for developing an understanding of Matthew, he presumes, in contrast to Overman and Saldarini, that this leads to the establishment of an independent identity: "Both the Damascus Document and Matthew's gospel explain and sustain the separate identity of communities which have parted company painfully with parent bodies."[28] For Stanton, Matthew appears as a result of and after a parting of the ways.[29] Within the history of scholarship on the New Testament, those arguing for a sectarian understanding of Matthew have assumed that their work resulted in a more Jewish portrait of the Matthean community in terms of its identity and affiliation in the first century. Stanton suggests a different orientation. He argues that its sectarian orientation provides the context for the definitive break whereby the early Christian movement becomes a gentile phenomenon, a break already apparent within Matthew. But Stanton may be assuming too linear a progression of the parting of the ways, a continuous trajectory from a Jewish phenomenon to a Jewish Christianity (or Christian Judaism) to a new religion with primarily gentile adherents. It may not be an early form of Christianity as we come to know it in the second century. The lack of evidence for a predominantly gentile orientation for the work will receive more attention below in Chapter 7. The task at hand rather is to determine the nature of a Matthean community which made a break with what it understood to be a Jewish parent, but which was not Christian—defined as we know it primarily from other New Testament and second-century sources—and whose major interest was not the status of gentiles among the followers of Jesus but rather the particular type of Jewish community and its practices they espoused. It is interesting that Stanton is proposing an equal level of tension with the surrounding environment for both Matthew and the Damascus Document, a significant observation for a sectarian analysis.

Establishing himself firmly within the line of scholarship summarized above, with results closer to those of Stanton, is the work of Paul Foster.[30] While he does not explicitly adopt the social scientific methodology of the previous scholarship already discussed, he attempts to build upon the results of that work. He also holds that the Matthean community recently had made a decisive break with the synagogue. His conclusions are based particularly upon his analysis of Matthew and the law and the work's stance with regard to the gentile mission. It is his argument that Matt 5:17–20 sets up a case for understanding Jesus to be the authoritative interpreter of the law to be followed by the antitheses which contradict biblical and contemporary Jewish interpretations of it. These four verses are "to be understood as a pastorally pedagogical piece," which assure the followers of Jesus that he is not destroying the law, as some of his opponents charge.[31] He then notes that in the antitheses, areas of dispute are resolved not by appealing to Mosaic authority (e.g., citing a contrasting biblical verse), but by appealing to the authority of Jesus. The new age and its implications are proclaimed through Jesus.[32] The author of the first gospel did not advocate a wholesale rejection of the Mosaic law, but rather claimed Jesus as a higher authority, the legitimate interpreter and re-definer of Jewish tradition. Further discussion of this topic is to be found in Chapter 3 below. The place of gentiles coming into this new movement is fundamental to the work. Foster maintains that the author also was contradicting traditional Jewish understandings in his advocacy of a gentile mission.[33] The basic tension addressed by the author arose from the presence of recent gentile converts who needed to be incorporated into the community, a topic to be addressed below in Chapter 7.

New directions in advancing a social scientific approach to the study of Matthew are apparent in the work of Anders Runesson.[34] Significant is his critique of Richard Bauckham, who has argued that the gospels were written for the general body of the followers of Jesus rather than each for a specific locale and purpose.[35] Runesson rather has argued that the community in which Matthew originated can be identified with the composition: "that the gospel traditions and texts were transmitted and written down within—and served the needs of—specific communities as these groups interpreted their beliefs in specific cultural contexts and addressed specific problems."[36] Runesson bases his analysis on positing a "Matthean community." He then posits the layers of the development of that community reflected in the text, in my opinion a much more hypothetical possibility. In this volume the text of Matthew will be related to a community that existed at the time of its final composition without positing a prior history to be recovered from the text itself. While it cannot be argued that the literary work includes a description of a community, it is reasonable to posit its connection with a real community containing instruction connected with its actual existence.

This Matthean community emerged out of a split from the Pharisaic "association" for Runesson. To make this argument he proposes a Galilean provenance for the community, probably Sepphoris. Relying on categories of sociology of religion, he classifies the Pharisees as a denomination rather than a sect, based upon a perceived lack of tension with the surrounding society.[37] There were Pharisaic synagogues (e.g., Matt 10:17; 12:9; 23:34).[38] The Matthean group was a sect in relationship to the Pharisees. The Matthean community then was not a sect in relationship to "common Judaism" centered in the temple and cult that continued even in the initial period after the destruction of the temple, but only in response to the Pharisaic associations from which they had separated. I do not find this argument convincing and outline a different approach to the question below. It is at this point where analogies with the sectarian analysis of the Qumran evidence is helpful. On the basis of a sectarian analysis and as is clear from the social identity approach outlined by both Saldarini and Esler, Runesson's portrayal of the Pharisees is too dependent upon the evidence in Matthew, who demonstrated little interest in giving his readers an accurate or even full depiction of the Pharisees and their significance.

Returning to the earlier summary of the results from 1989 of the study of social history related to Matthew from 1989 which began this chapter:

1. The argument for the urban character of a Matthean community was already presented in Chapter 1 above. The Galilean context of greater Syria at the conclusion of the first century was also advanced as the most likely location for its composition.

2. Subsequent research on Jewish history and identity in the late Second Temple period has demonstrated that the designation "Jewish Christian" is not a meaningful category. The early and middle Roman periods are marked by the variety of Jewish and Christian groups attested in the disparate literary sources, which do not provide evidence of an identifiable and significant single body that bears this epithet. It can be demonstrated that Matthew is addressed to a body of persons who were part of a Jewish community, hence an analysis based on social science is an attempt to understand that relationship and its significance. That the gentile interest expressed in the first gospel is rather limited will be argued in Chapter 7 below. The possibility of a committed Jewish group which exists in a social context that is both Jewish and gentile has received further confirmation in the archaeological and historical work of the last two decades, particularly in the further study of Galilean sites such as Sepphoris.

3. There are two aspects of this sectarian analysis which move it beyond that from the 1990s. First, the continued use of the categories of sectarian analysis in Qumran and NT studies in the past two decades permits greater depth in their present application to the study of Matthew and its social world. The ongoing utilization of the categories of Stark and Bainbridge as well as Wilson in the study of a more comprehensive body of texts from the Second Temple era has yielded a more extensive body of comparative literature for further development. Second, the extensive publication of the texts from the Qumran corpus that became available after 1991 has enhanced and often transformed our understanding of literary, intellectual, and religious developments in the Second Temple Jewish experience. These shifting perceptions now inform our understanding of the origin and development of sectarianism during this period and its implications for Jewish society at the time. This volume is an attempt to probe the implications of these developments for the study of Matthew within a Jewish context at the end of the first century CE.

4. As argued in Chapter 1 above, the evidence demonstrating a clear link of continuity between the Pharisees and the later rabbis has proved to be much less certain than was considered the case in 1990. The formation of Rabbinic Judaism as a significant and widespread force in the Jewish community is now regarded by many scholars as a later development in Jewish history, perhaps in the fifth or sixth century CE. So while the Pharisees can be seen to be influential in the Jewish community in the last decades of the first century CE in the evidence from the New Testament and Josephus, the relationship to later developments is unclear, hence the association with a formative Judaism is unattested. The idea that Pharisees and a Matthean community would have been similar in their sectarian character is also hard to maintain on the basis of the extant evidence, particularly the suggestion that they were relatively equal in size and influence. For comparative purposes, a "Matthean community" is to be equated with other much more clearly defined sectarian entities in Second Temple history in order to make meaningful claims related to social history.

5. The move away from a binary approach to the study of law in Matthew was a most welcome advance. The simplistic categories that had been employed in the study of Matthew were intended to determine whether Matthew was a legalist or whether the author was attempting to de-

scribe some ethic that was "beyond the law," that is, centered in Jesus Christ. Did Matthew understand that Jesus superseded the law or made it unnecessary in the same manner as previous scholars understood that Paul had argued that the law was no longer necessary after Christ? The shift in the study of Matthew mentioned here permitted readers to understand that the arguments in Matthew are about the law (Torah), what it says and what it requires of those who choose to follow it. First-century Jews disagreed and argued vigorously about its requirements, but not about its validity. The validity of the law was called into question only when opposing groups observed it differently. The relationship of law and community formation then becomes central to the interpretive task. Our knowledge of the development of Jewish law in the Second Temple period has been greatly enhanced by the materials from the Qumran caves. Matthew and the law will receive substantive treatment in Chapter 3 of this volume.

Defining Sectarianism

Having argued for the value of utilizing a social scientific approach in the study of the first gospel, and having outlined the perspectives on the context of social history, I will now explain the concept of sectarianism underlying this volume. Controversy has surrounded the definitions of sectarianism employed in biblical studies throughout the second half of the twentieth century. Attempts to develop categories adequate for the classification of the new texts available in Qumran studies after 1991 also resulted in attempts to provide greater clarity for the use of this methodology.[39]

Significant in American sociology was the pivotal article by Benton Johnson that moved the discussion from a historical and theological analysis of movements rooted in the Reformation—and developed by Ernst Troeltsch—to a conception that attempted to describe the religious developments of the twentieth century.[40] It is to him that the category of "tension" was attributed by Stark and Bainbridge as they attempted to develop criteria for the description and evaluation of new religious movements. The other paradigm that has most frequently been employed in the analysis of Second Temple Jewish sectarianism is that of Bryan Wilson, also based in the study of new religious movements.[41] In attempting to broaden the discussion of sect within sociology and free it of an ideological bias, he identified a spectrum of responses to evil among groups he considered sects: conversionist,

revolutionist, introversionist, manipulationist, thaumaturgical (and spiritu-
alistic), reformist, and utopian.[42] While his differentiation of these responses
has been an important contribution to the study of social movements in
the Second Temple era, it is not as helpful for differentiating sectarian and
non-sectarian literature in a meaningful manner.[43] An analysis based upon
religious deviance is of greater significance for attempting to understand the
social location of various groups in the first century CE. Toward this end it
is the criteria of Stark and Bainbridge that are of greater value.[44]

While there are a number of analysts who provide similar or related
definitions of "sectarianism," I will adopt that of Albert Baumgarten, who
follows up from Stark and Bainbridge's emphasis on the opposition of these
groups to prevailing views: "a voluntary association of protest, which utilizes boundary marking mechanisms—the social means of differentiating
between insiders and outsiders—to distinguish between its own members
and those otherwise normally regarded as belonging to the same national
or religious entity."[45] While somewhat more focused, this definition repeats
the essential elements of those descriptions advanced by earlier scholars.[46]
In addition to adherence to the same national or religious entity, Cohen
had noted that the sect "asserts that it alone embodies the ideals of the
larger group because it alone understands God's will."[47] Noting that the
conflict has its basis in the claims of the deviant group to represent the ideals or beliefs of the dominant body is important for our comprehension of
this social phenomenon. One of the issues that plagued earlier studies of
sectarianism during this period was the inability to identify with any precision the nature and beliefs of that dominant group. Baumgarten's definition
does not require such an endeavor since it highlights the "boundary marking mechanisms" of the group itself, thereby permitting the analyst to find
the distinction between the group and its opposition within the sectarian
literature rather than basing it upon the description of that larger national
or religious entity. Such an approach accords with social identity theory,
already identified by Saldarini and discussed above, where behavior and
understanding are the result, initially, of the norms, values, and beliefs of
the group itself.

The perspectives of Stark and Bainbridge were brought into Qumran
studies particularly through the work of Jutta Jokiranta, with some ongoing
analysis of the manner in which the category of "sect" has been employed in
the study of that literature.[48] Her careful analysis of the sociological definitions of the term suggested that the best candidates to use as criteria for

sectarianism are the tension with the socio-cultural environment and the tendency to view oneself as uniquely legitimate or to establish boundaries against another.[49] Stark and Bainbridge's understanding of sect formation as a type of subcultural deviance consists of three elements: difference, antagonism, and separation.[50] Difference indicates the extent to which the behaviors and practices of the group vary from the average members of the population or from the standards of the powerful members of the society. In other words, sectarians follow deviant norms of behavior. Antagonism is represented in the attitudes toward other religious groups or society, usually expressed in particularistic beliefs denying the legitimacy of competing groups. This normally results in the sect's rejection by these other groups. Separation concerns the extent to which there is a restriction of social relations to mainly in-group members. Group norms and activities or simply devotion to the group may restrict the social relations of the members so that contacts and relations to outsiders are reduced.[51] These three elements are not to be understood as independent axes or dimensions each capable of separate evaluation, but rather are the interdependent categories by which tension is created and sustained.[52] It will be apparent in the following study of the first gospel that all three of these elements combine to depict a first-century Jewish sect exhibiting a high level of tension with surrounding Jewish co-religionists.

The Dead Sea Scrolls and Sectarian History

The possibility that a Jewish group at the end of the first century CE could be sectarian is rooted in the experiences of the Second Temple era. The Dead Sea Scrolls provide evidence that sectarianism is an integral part of the history of that period. This was recognized by the first scholars to study these materials, and the subsequent seven decades of study and additional discovery have contributed to that picture. Additional research has permitted the development of a portrait of Jewish sectarianism that has roots in perspectives already described in literature from the third century BCE. This portrait includes a widespread movement exhibiting various patterns of social organization scattered throughout the towns and villages of Judea and possibly beyond. The first evidence of explicitly sectarian organization appears toward the end of the second century BCE and is described as a widespread presence in Jewish life of Palestine throughout the first century CE.

The most definitive statement on the origins of a movement associated with the Dead Sea Scrolls and perhaps the site of Qumran is to be found in CD 1:4–11. In a vast collection of texts noted for the absence of identifiable historical references, these lines from the Qumran corpus capture our attention. If taken literally, this would place the origins of the "new covenant in the land of Damascus" (CD 6:19) in 197 BCE, 390 years after the destruction of the temple in 587 BCE. The appearance of the teacher of righteousness is then dated to 177 BCE.[53] The interpretation of chronological references in the literature of antiquity is a widely recognized problem in historical study, so we cannot with any degree of certainty know the dates intended by the ancient author or their relationship to the origins of a movement perhaps attested at the site of Qumran or in other sectarian texts from the corpus. Of interest is the rabbinic reference to the origins of sectarianism in 'Abot R. Nat. A 5, discussing the successors of Antigonus of Sokho: "So they arose and withdrew from the Torah and split into two sects, the Sadducees and the Boethusians: Sadducees named after Zadok, Boethusians after Boethus." In the chronology related to m. 'Abot, the basis of this account, Simon the Just and Antigonus of Sokho would be located between the emergence of the "men of the Great Assembly" (m. 'Abot 1:1), and the "pairs" of the Hasmonean era (m. 'Abot 1:4–11). In other words, the collective memory of the rabbinic tradition placed the origins of these sectarian developments just prior to the Maccabean revolt. Perhaps that was also the intent of the Damascus Document. Josephus's first reference to the Essenes appears in his account of Jonathan (152–142 BCE), the brother of Judah Maccabee. This citation is frequently cited as justification for dating the origins of the movement associated with the Qumran text and site to early in the Hasmonean period.[54] Recent work on sectarian history related to Qumran does not find a high degree of credibility in the acceptance of any of these dates, but the collective memories of different portions of the Jewish tradition point to the period immediately before and after the Maccabean revolt as significant for the origin of Jewish sectarian groups, including those we now identify with the Dead Sea Scrolls.[55]

This evidence assumes additional significance when we consider the historical trajectory related to the fragments of the Dead Sea Scrolls initially charted by Michael Stone and others on the basis of their early analysis of the texts of Enoch and other non-sectarian non-biblical materials as compositions some of which date to the third century BCE.[56] George Nickelsburg and Devorah Dimant developed these perspectives in their treatments of these bodies of literature.[57] Both García Martínez and Boccaccini advanced hypotheses about the origins and history of the Qumran movement incorporating this evidence.[58] In some manner all of these studies recognize a significant body of literary compositions with apparently deviant viewpoints on issues of significance to Palestinian Jewish life and dated prior to the Maccabean revolt. On the assumption that there is some conceptual integrity to the corpus of texts from the caves at Qumran, they bear some relationship to the sectarian literature that forms one portion of this literary corpus. A sociological analysis of the latter texts found below demonstrates the expected high level of tension with the surrounding environment called for in the preceding discussion of sectarianism. The significance of these sectarian groups is attested by the evidence of their broad distribution throughout Judea (and surrounding environs) in the early Roman period. This is not to suggest that they are characteristic of Judean society as a whole.

Well-known is the statement about the members of the new covenant in CD 7:6–7: "But if they live in camps according to the rule of the land, and marry women and beget children."[59] This composition contains extensive legislation regulating divorce, incest, and other aspects of sexual relations. It points to a movement that is dispersed, living according to the law of the land.[60] The extensive rationale for a sectarian way of life developed in the first eight folios of this composition suggests broad engagement rather than a set of regulations for an isolated group. The Community Rule throughout its various versions does not contain references to women or legislation regarding family or sexual issues. Thus it frequently is said to be consistent with a hypothesis that the adherents of the *yaḥad* (community) were celibate, in most cases related to a somewhat isolated or at least independent existence.[61] But any mandates related to requirements of celibacy are absent in these materials. Significantly, there is nothing in the Cave I copy of the Community Rule that would directly point to the sectarian lifestyle proposed there, whether celibate or not, being limited to one site.

The Greek literary evidence describing the Essenes bears mention. Except for the reference in Pliny which occasioned the early identification of the scrolls with the Essene evidence, no other Greek author connects the Essenes with the region of Qumran or even the Dead Sea.[62] Philo notes that they live in villages (*kōmēdon*) rather than in cities (*poleis*) because of the lawlessness (*anomia*) of the latter's inhabitants.[63] "Lawlessness" here refers to the failure to abide by the ancestral traditions, including the Torah, rather than to brigandage or anarchy. Elsewhere, perhaps in a less biased reference, he says they live "in a number of towns [*poleis*] of Judaea, and also in many villages and large groups."[64] Josephus similarly says that "they have not one town, but rather in each [town] many settle."[65] This latter statement particularly stresses their wide distribution in direct contrast to any thesis that would confine them to one location, such as Qumran. Also noteworthy is Josephus's reference to the Essene gate in the western part of the city wall of Jerusalem. The designation may have been derived from the section of the city in which Essenes lived.[66] In any case the name of the gate provides additional evidence of the widespread nature of this group which Philo and Josephus assumed to be a movement dispersed throughout Judea.

A critical evaluation of the compositional history of the multiple copies of the S and D texts points to the complex history of the sectarian movements associated with these texts. The D manuscripts yield a portrait of a group that is based in Torah with a rather strict ethic making excessive demands upon its members but being based in a family system.[67] It demonstrates vigorous critique of some practices of the priesthood in the second century BCE. While showing remarkable differences, the legislation demonstrates connections with the S materials as well as compositions such as the Messianic Rule (1QSa). What does such a process tell us about the nature of the communities in which these copies were produced? For Collins the multiple divergent copies of the S texts and the related but different trajectory apparent in the D MSS point to multiple communities related to one diverse movement. "The *yaḥad*, and still more the new covenant of the *Damascus Rule,* was not an isolated monastic community, as has sometimes been imagined, but was part of a religious association spread widely throughout the land."[68]

In a similar vein, Alison Schofield has provided a related model based upon her analysis of the S texts: "My model reads the S versions as sharing a common core of material but reconstructs them as primarily diverging traditions without the unwarranted assumption that a limited group of scribes at Qumran developed all S traditions."[69] She then concludes that the term *yaḥad* is not limited to any one geographical location. The legal precepts apply to multiple residences and camps.[70] She does not see evidence of a linear chronological development within those traditions. The disparate nature of the communities that wrote, read, and rewrote these texts points to a chronologically and geographically diverse movement(s) behind these compositions.

Some comparison of the sectarian literature and the social structure found therein with Greek and Roman parallels has centered on a discussion of voluntary associations. Foundational for ongoing research on this topic is the influential monograph of Moshe Weinfeld which centered particularly on the penal code in 1QS and CD, compared with contemporary cultic associations, with particular attention to the Iobacchi code.[71] The similarities are evidence of a broader cultural context for these sectarian regulations without arguing for a direct historical or literary dependence of one upon the other. The most significant study to build upon the analysis of Weinfeld is that of Yonder Gillihan.[72]

In his extensive study of the Greek and Roman materials, Gillihan notes the manner in which associations tend to replicate the organizational patterns, laws, and self-descriptive language of the state. This tendency to find state-like features represented in patterns of leadership, councils, initiation procedures, rules for behavior, and discipline central to the life of the voluntary associations was widespread throughout the Roman Empire. Rather than focusing merely upon specifics of organization, Gillihan has a particular interest in the civic ideology underlying the relationships between these associations and the state.[73] What is of significance for the purpose of a sectarian analysis is his identification of the manner in which counter ideologies emerge which contest the claims of the state.[74] It is among these associations with alternate civic ideologies that Gillihan locates the sectarian ideologies of the S and D materials. In so doing he demonstrates the manner in which they critique the state or society as a whole for failing to live up to their stated ideals and offer a corrected interpretation of those themes including an alternative organization and regulations to which its members belong. Three features distinguish "the covenanters" from most of the other political associations of the time. First, they did not write political literature of a speculative or philosophical nature, but rather they "studied Torah and composed numerous legal texts, fully intent on implementing their halaka as the law of Israel."[75] Liturgical texts were oriented toward a restored temple, as were the laws on sacrifice and the festival calendar. The military procedures and prospects of the War Scroll and related texts anticipated real warfare. They were preparing for the rule of the remnant of Israel in an eschatological future. This was an alternative structure to that of the Hasmonean state, presumably based upon the Torah. The second feature that distinguishes the covenanters is that the group organized itself as a state, with preparations for actual governance, as can be seen in the penal codes. Finally, they were "conservative" in that they retained real boundaries between citizens and outsiders. Membership as well as roles and status within the group were carefully defined in the extant literature.[76]

Gillihan's analysis of Jewish sectarianism within the context of voluntary associations coheres with the definition advanced by Albert Baumgarten, already found above: "a voluntary association of protest, which utilizes boundary marking mechanisms—the social means of differentiating between insiders and outsiders—to distinguish between its own members and those otherwise normally regarded as belonging to the same national or religious entity."[77] The development of Jewish sects with a distinctive alternative civic ideology to that of the Hasmonean state and the Jewish aristocracy of its Herodian successors can then be identified within the texts of Qumran. They constitute one example of how some Jewish people attempted to represent their collective and individual identities within the larger cultural milieu of which they were a part.

The sociological dimensions of these sectarian compositions can be explored by evaluating the level of tension with the socio-cultural environment evident therein. Evidence of high tension indicates a heightened sense of sectarianism within the composition.[78] This evaluation is made possible by utilizing Stark and Bainbridge's understanding of sect formation as a type of subcultural deviance, perhaps the sociological equivalent of a distinctive alternative civic ideology, which consists of three elements: difference, antagonism, and separation.[79] All three are evident throughout the S and D materials. Other texts could be evaluated as well, but these two bodies of material are representative of the central features of sectarian representation found throughout the corpus of texts from Qumran.

The deviant norms of behavior evident throughout the S and D material provide adequate documentation of the element of difference. This is evident throughout the Admonition section of CD where particular behavioral expectations rooted in a tradition of biblical legislation are advanced and justified. For example, the citation of Isa 24:17, "Fear and pit and snare are upon thee, dweller in the land," in CD 4:14 leads into an exposition on the ways in which Belial has led Israel astray and which those who enter into the covenant have the opportunity to correct. As CD follows the text of Isa 24:18, these three elements described as the "traps" into which Israel has fallen are identified as *zənût* (fornication), *hon* (material wealth), and *tāme' hammiqdaš* (defilement of the temple). The text then goes on to describe laws prohibiting polygamy and divorce, as well as extending the definition of incest, all departures from biblical law. The prohibition of marriage between an uncle and niece is considered an extension of the biblical law prohibiting the marriage of an aunt and nephew (Lev 18:13). With regard to the temple, "None who have been brought into the covenant shall enter into the sanctuary to light up His altar in vain" (CD 6:11–12). While there is some academic controversy regarding whether this constitutes a total prohibition of temple activity, some restriction is evident. Such limitations are particularly evident in the following lines when the observance of the Sabbath, the feast days, and the day of fasting is mandated "according to the commandments of those entering the new covenant in the land of Damascus" (CD 6:19). This difference is developed throughout the entire code(s) of law found in the B section of CD and in the other D MSS. A similar difference is apparent in the legislative materials of S.

With the covenant renewal ceremony found in 1QS I–III establishing the context for the majority of the S MSS, the sociological feature of difference for all of the resulting legislation and other material has been clearly established.[80] Justification for the difference in legislation is not required since it is established at the outset. Of considerable significance is the legislation of the penal code in which penalties for violations focus upon the prohibition of participation in the *tohorah*, frequently the *tohorat harabbim* (pure food of the many) (1QS VI, 25; VII, 3, 16, 19, 20, 25). The final steps of study and examination result in admission to full participation in the *tohorat harabbim* (1QS VI, 16, 22). The process of initiation, renewal, and punishment with a focus on membership and participation establishes the group's existence and behavior as deviant. The philosophical basis for the distinction is developed in the Treatise on the Two Spirits (1QS III, 13–IV, 26). This difference over against the rest of society is expressed in the latter section of 1QS and corresponding texts with reference to the sectarians as the *mitnaddəbim* (those who volunteer): "This is the rule for all the men of the *Yahad* who volunteer to repent from all evil and to hold fast to all that He, by his good will, has commanded" (1QS V, 1). The sect is made up of those who have voluntarily determined to turn away from the remainder of Israel and turn to God, whose will is revealed within the sect, whose members live in a manner that is pleasing to God, in contrast to the remainder of Israel outside of this group (1QS V, 6, 8, 10, 21, 22; VI, 13; cf. 1QS I, 7, 11).[81]

The level of antagonism between the groups mandated in the legislation of the S and D compositions and the surrounding society is apparent throughout. The opening mandate to the sectarians of 1QS is "to love everything God chose and to hate everything he despised" (1QS I, 3–4 [my translation]). The sage is to teach the sectarians "to love all the children of light . . . and to hate all the children of darkness" (1QS I, 9–10). The distinction between the blessings of the priests for all the members of the sect in good standing is contrasted with the curse of the Levites upon "on all those foreordained to Belial" (1QS I, 16–II, 18). Note, for example, some of the content of the curse: "May the God of terror give you over to implacable avengers; may He visit your offspring with destruction at the hands of those who recompense evil with evil. May you be damned without mercy in return for your dark deeds, an object of wrath licked by eternal flame, surrounded by utter darkness" (1QS II, 5–8). The level of antagonism is established at the beginning of this version of the S texts and meant to be retained throughout. There is no suggestion that this looks different in any of the other S MSS that contain some textual equivalent to 1QS I–IV.

The "othering" of Israel via the role of Belial in leading Israel astray demonstrates the level of antagonism that the sectarian members have against the remainder of their people in the D texts: "During all these years Belial will be set loose in Israel" (CD 4:12–13). As mentioned above, Israel is then ensnared in the three nets of Belial mistaken for three types of righteousness (CD 4:15–17). The primary identification of the antagonism in this composition is through chronological periodization familiar from apocalyptic literature: "But strength, might, and great wrath in the flames of fire [with] all the angels of destruction shall come against all who rebel against the proper way and who despise the law, until they are without remnant or survivor, for God had not chosen them from ancient eternity. Before they were created, He knew what they would do. So He rejected the generations of old and turned away from the land until they were gone" (CD 2:5–9). This description includes present-day non-sectarian Israel. In the explicit description of the covenant, the mandated observances are in contrast to the law of the era of wickedness that resulted in corruption, embezzlement, robbery, and defilement (CD 6:11–7:4). Throughout the remainder of CD 7–8 we find that those who do not keep the commandments of the covenant "will perish" (7:9), "are delivered up to the sword" (8:1), and "are condemned to destruction by Belial" (8:2). The ultimate accusation is that "they did not separate from the people, but arrogantly threw off all restraint, living by wicked customs" (8:8–9). This results in the judgment by the kings of the gentiles and the chief of the kings of Greece, who "comes to wreak vengeance upon them" (8:11–12).

Separation is apparent in the formation of the covenant in the D materials: "according to the commandments of those entering into the new covenant in the land of Damascus" (CD 6:19; cf. 8:21, 19:33). Separation for the purpose of holiness, the avoidance of defilement, and communal maintenance are central to the legislation proposed for these covenanters. The separation from the remainder of Israel is apparent earlier on this page: "None who have been brought into the covenant shall enter into the sanctuary to light up His altar in vain" (6:11–12). Those who enter the covenant have sworn an oath "to return to the law of Moses" (15:2, 9, 12; 16:2, 5). There are regular references to the oath of the covenant and the laws of the covenant throughout the composition, in addition to the consequences for those who violate them.[82] Both "covenant" and the related oath "to return to the law of Moses" feature prominently in the 4QD MSS as well. The members of the covenant have separated themselves in some distinct manner from the remainder of Israel, even if we cannot clearly determine the extent to which this is a physical or geographical reality. The emphasis on the particularistic legislation, already noted above in the discussion of difference, is evidence of its distinctive nature.

The fundamental distinction between the children of light and the children of darkness that characterizes the opening section of 1QS along with its philosophical discussion in the Treatise on the Two Spirits (1QS III, 13–IV, 26) indicates a level of separation from the remainder of Israel that is fundamental for the identity of the yaḥad. This distinction is evident in the emphasis on the voluntary nature of membership: "This is the rule for all the men of the Yahad who volunteer to repent from all evil and to hold fast to all that He, by his good will, has commanded" (1QS V, 1). The translation of mitnaddəbîm as "volunteers" downplays the significance of the commitment being made: "All who enter the Yahad's Rule shall be initiated into the Covenant before God, agreeing to act according to all that He has commanded and not to backslide because of any fear, terror, or persecution that may occur during the time of Belial's dominion" (1QS I, 16–18). This term rather represents the extra commitment of an additional sacrifice or other gift to God. This is what the children of light do. As noted above in CD, here also the initiate "is to enter the covenant in full view of all the volunteers. He shall take upon himself a binding oath to return to the Law of Moses, according to all that He commanded, with all his heart and with all his mind" (1QS V, 8–9). Returning to the law of Moses is integral to these sectarian identities. Included is everything that God has commanded, the legislation intended for those who volunteer to join the *yaḥad*. The separation is related to holiness, for ultimately the sectarians are joined with the angels: "To those whom God has chosen all these has He given them as an eternal possession. He has given them an inheritance in the lot of the Holy Ones. He unites their assembly to the sons of heaven for a council of community. They are an assembly built up for holiness, an eternal Planting for all ages to come" (1QS XI, 7–9). This is not the province of Israel as a whole, the Israel of the past that is still present, but rather the fate of those chosen and who have chosen to join this sectarian body. Their lot is with the angels rather than the remainder of Israel; their place and their fate are as a separate body.

The high level of tension with the surrounding environment is amply identified by illustrations of the features of difference, antagonism, and separation present in both the D and S compositions.[83] As evident at the theoretical level and from the preceding discussion of references, these three categories are not independent and isolated, but rather an interactive complex attempting to describe and evaluate the level of tension evident within these texts. The interrelatedness of these three elements is most evident in their treatment of truth, knowledge, and wisdom. While these texts display a great reluctance to employ the term *ḥokmah* (wisdom), the related terms for truth and knowledge are ubiquitous in both compositions and throughout other sectarian compositions. What is most important about the claims in these texts is that truth and knowledge reside only with the sect, the *yaḥad* of the S texts or the covenant in the D materials.[84] The sectarians must separate themselves from the remainder of Israel to acquire this knowledge; it is of a different nature and mandates differences in the observance of the Jewish way of life. In this process they negate the former way of life of Israel and its present manifestations as being uninformed and the subject of derision in the D materials or subject to the curses of the sectarians in the S compositions. The claim that knowledge is the result of revelation available only to the sect provides the basis for the tension that this literature displays toward the Israel whose mantle the sectarians now claim to possess in an exclusive manner, thus the high level of tension apparent throughout the compositions.

The depth and breadth of Jewish sectarianism within the Second Temple era are apparent. Its origins in deviant viewpoints in the earlier centuries of this period result in the sectarian social formulations in the latter second century BCE. The corpus of sectarian writings from the Qumran caves is representative of these developments, but most likely not the basis for a comprehensive description of their substance, history, or impact. The following reading of Matthew using the sociological criteria assumes that Matthew is to be placed within this sectarian tradition. This does not mean that it should be considered the direct successor of a sectarian group attested in the texts from Qumran. It assumes importance as one representation of developments within the broader swath of literature. Comparison with other sectarian works permits a thicker reading of the text of Matthew.

Sectarianism after 70 CE?

The majority view had the community at Qumran, hence the Essenes, come to an end with the destruction of the site in 68 CE. This view coincided with the hypothesis advanced in the well-known article of Shaye Cohen that sectarianism came to an end in Palestine with the destruction of the temple.[85] Direct evidence of a continuation of a sect related to any of the Dead Sea Scrolls in Galilee and, more particularly for our purposes, after 70 CE is rather limited. But at the time that Cohen wrote his article, sectarianism associated with the Qumran scrolls was still assumed to be confined to that one ancient site and the evidence related to its history. Understanding the sectarian movement(s) associated with the Dead Sea Scrolls to be evidence of a much broader phenomenon in the late Second Temple era suggests that it would not have disappeared as easily or readily as Cohen would appear to have assumed. Note for example the evaluation of Seth Schwartz: "There is no reason to accept Cohen's view that the rabbinic 'agreement to disagree' was a feature of the earliest post-70 figures. Sectarian and priestly self-consciousness may have survived among proto-rabbis longer than Cohen thought."[86] In the wake of this more comprehensive picture of Jewish sectarianism it is not clear that such a hypothesis can be sustained. We face similar problems when attempting to understand the nature of the Pharisees and the Sadducees in Galilee at the end of the first century CE. The limited rabbinic evidence already has been discussed in Chapter 1. The question of the continuation of the sectarian groups attested in the Dead Sea Scrolls is not particular to any one of these groups. It rather is part of the larger issue facing historians concerning the development of Galilee in the last decades of the first century CE.

It is in this context that the claims of Martin Goodman require consideration. In his response to the Cohen article, he asserts, "I have argued that it is a mistake to assume that because rabbinic Jews did not discuss other types of Judaism they therefore did not exist, and that for all we know Sadducees and Essenes might have continued as identifiable groups throughout this period even though there is no clear evidence that they did so."[87] His argument is based more on the negative than the positive, noting the extraordinary selectivity of the rabbinic tradition with regard to what was retained. What distinguishes their limited references to the *minîm* (heterodox or "heretic") is the lack of specificity with regard to who they were and what they taught. The primary injunction to the adherents of the rabbinic tradition is to ignore these "others." Joshua Ezra Burns also has argued that the definition of *minût* is rather diffuse in the Tannaitic literature, including magicians, mystics, Gnostics, and Jewish Christians; only later does the term coalesce around Christianity. He then cites examples from the Mishnah and Tosefta that indicate an awareness of sectarian existence. He cites t. Šabb. 13:5, which criticizes some *minîm* for maintaining private houses of worship where they practiced unacceptable rites; m. Ḥul. 2:9 forbids certain sacrificial practices that the rabbis considered characteristic of the *minîm.* He also cites the calendrical controversies and an overemphasis on ritual purity.[88] Jodi Magness adds to the list, for example, "You strain out a gnat but swallow a camel." The sectarian legislation concerning swarming things in CD 12:12–13 extends the biblical legislation, indicating it to be a disputed legal issue in the Second Temple period. Its continued presence in Matt 23:24 and then in rabbinic literature, wherein the straining of wine or vinegar (t. Ter. 7:11) is regarded as heterodoxy (or heresy?), is evidence of a continuing dispute after 70 CE. A similar issue arises with regard to locusts and fish in which rabbinic literature permits their consumption whether dead or alive (t. Ter. 9:6), while CD 12:13–15 mandates that fish should be torn alive and their blood shed, and locusts should be cooked alive in fire or water prior to consumption.[89]

Furthering the argument of Martin Goodman, Martha Himmelfarb observes that while the evidence for the destruction of the Jewish sects after 70 CE is elusive, it is apparent that Jewish sectarianism continued.[90] The issue at stake in her analysis of Cohen's argument is not the continuation of the influence of the Essenes or the groups associated with the Dead Sea Scrolls, but rather the nature of Rabbinic Judaism. She notes its marked anti-sectarian character in an appeal to the whole "people of Israel" rather than to a "righteous remnant." Pointing to the argument of Daniel Boyarin about the creation of a rabbinic orthodoxy requiring a "rejected other," she notes the use of b. Sanh. 44a, "An Israelite, even if he sins, remains an Israelite."[91] While this certainly does not constitute definitive evidence for the continuity of specific pre-70 sectarian groups into the next era, it does put some of the traditions preserved in the rabbinic literature into a perspective that points to greater continuity with the portrait based upon the pre-70 evidence.

Most frequently cited in the debates about the Qumran texts and rabbinic literature is m. Yad. 4:6–8, already discussed above in Chapter 1. In this passage we find a record of some disputes between the Zadokites (Sadducees) and the Pharisees. In my earlier discussion of these passages I commented on the extent to which the stances on issues of practice resemble or even imitate those attributed to the sectarians attested in the scrolls. There is strong evidence within this early rabbinic literature that the divergent, or sectarian, stances either were present within the communities in which this literature was recorded or had an active place in the memories of those doing the recording. In either case, stances of the sectarian tradition as found in the Qumran scrolls continue.[92] The practices of biblical legislation associated with these sectarians either were being advocated within the Jewish communities in which the first gospel was composed or were within its immediate and very active memory, since these controversies would have been recorded in the Mishnah at least a century later.

The other group mentioned in 'Abot R. Nat. A 5 cited above is the *Baytûsîm* (also called Boethusians, based upon the Greek name of the high priests so designated). This group is attested in Tannaitic texts primarily in connection with calendrical disputes with the sages, a documented area of divergence with the sectarians of some of the scrolls. The dispute concerning the harvesting of the Omer is attributed to the *Baytûsîm* in m. Menaḥ. 10:3. Here the dispute is whether the day after the Sabbath specified in Lev 23:11 refers only to the day after the seventh day of the week or whether the Sabbath is meant to include also the day of the festival.[93] The Pharisees held the latter view. What is at stake is the dating of the festival of Shavuot (Pentecost) fifty days later. The apparent willingness of the *Baytûsîm* to produce false testimony concerning the appearance of the new moon since they did not consider it calendrically significant is attested in m. Roš Haš. 2:1, there attributed to the *mînîm* (heterodox or "heretic"), but to the *Baytûsîm* in t. Roš Haš. 1:15. The relationship of this group to some of the Zadokite (Sadducean) traditions is unclear, with overlapping texts that suggest confused traditions about the two groups. However, in both instances we have groups identified with certain priestly traditions that hold some halakic viewpoints similar to those advocated within the divergent traditions attested in the Qumran scrolls.[94] The treatment of the issues suggests some ongoing controversy with actual opponents in the second century CE, rather than the record of an issue resolved in the distant past prior to the destruction of the temple. As noted in Chapter 1 above, in the rabbinic literature the Sadducees are the "other" against whom the Pharisees are defined. Certainly the *Baytûsîm* play the same role in the literature, hence the overlap in description.

A discussion of the continuation of sectarianism as evidenced in rabbinic literature would be incomplete without reference to the *birkat hamminîm* (blessing of the heretics or "sectarians," hence really a curse) as the twelfth of the Eighteen Benedictions, a central portion of the Jewish daily liturgy. This particular benediction has figured prominently in an evaluation of the references to the exclusion of early followers of Jesus from the synagogue, particularly in the scholarship on Matthew and John.[95] A debate concerning whether there are eighteen or nineteen benedictions is related in b. Ber. 28b–29a. The total of nineteen is attributed to the addition of a benediction against the heretics at Javneh, composed by Simon *happaqûlî* (perhaps "cotton merchant") at the request of Rabban Gamaliel. Apparently the refusal to recite this benediction was a test of whether the person was a *mîn,* which could just as easily be translated as "sectarian" as well as "heretic" and gets interchanged with Sadducees and *Baytûsîm* in some talmudic traditions. The earliest reference to this innovation is found not in the Mishnah, composed at the conclusion of the second century CE, but in t. Ber. 3:25, probably a mid-third-century composition.[96] In the latter text the *mînîm* are equated with the *pərûšîm,* the Hebrew term for "Pharisees" but also meaning "the separated."[97] The term *mînîm* itself is only attested first in the second-century texts. It is doubtful that this blessing appeared in the first century. Of greater significance for our purposes is the inclusion of this benediction a few centuries later, thereby indicating a continuing interest in dealing with sectarianism within the developing rabbinic movement. From the nature of this particular benediction, it is reasonable to infer that there were real sectarians who were the point of concern. The evidence also suggests that in the talmudic period the identification of the *mînîm* with the emerging Christian movement would have grown throughout the talmudic period, suggesting a greater likelihood that earlier references would have included other Jewish groups as well.

Some treatments of the book of Revelation also point to a continuity of sectarianism after the destruction of the temple. David Frankfurter has focused attention on "those who say they are Jews but are not, but are a synagogue of Satan" (Rev 2:9; see also 3:9). In an attempt to identify the "other" in this composition, he suggests that these are proselytes who claim the title of "Jew" but are not "halakhically pure enough to merit this term in its practical sense."[98] The 144,000 who are standing with the lamb on Mount Zion have not defiled themselves with women (Rev 14:4). The off-spring of the woman who bears the male child that will rule all the nations with a rod of iron are described as the keepers of the commandments of God (Rev 12:17; 14:12). It is worthwhile observing that nothing unclean is to enter the temple (Rev 21:27). This has been described as akin to the manner in which sectarian adherents of legislation found in the Qumran scrolls are to act in the holy war camp and in the ideal temple and/or Jerusalem.[99]

The widespread and extended influence of sectarian Judaism after the destruction of the temple may also be apparent in the evidence of the "Jewish Christian" sects. The ambiguity of the term and its usefulness as a descriptor have received extensive discussion in recent years.[100] The material describing these groups is even more diffuse than the rabbinic evidence. For the most part, it relies on the description of the heterodox groups in the patristic evidence. A few examples must suffice for a study that would require a separate monograph. The group that receives the most attention is the Ebionites, based upon the Hebrew term 'ebyôn (poor), found in both singular and plural in the sectarian scrolls from Qumran. The Ebionites are said to keep the Jewish law and customs, just as Jesus did. This includes the requirement of circumcision.[101] Interestingly Epiphanius suggests they were selective with regard to the laws of the Pentateuch, thereby justifying their vegetarianism.[102] He also notes their attention to matters of purity including ritual cleansing and contamination through contact with gentiles,[103] both concerns evident in the Qumran scrolls. Jerome accuses them of continuing to observe the "ceremonies of the Jewish superstition."[104] The most extensive analysis of their connection with the sects of the Qumran materials has been that of Joseph Fitzmyer.[105] In that early but still valued examination of the question, he documents the similarities but rejects any connection between them as well as the possibility that the Ebionites are successors of an "Essene" sect. This question may require reevaluation when set against the evidence of a more disparate and widespread "Essene" movement.

Coincident with the revised understanding of the sectarian move-ment(s) associated with the Dead Sea Scrolls is the body of material on the history of Mani based upon the Cologne Mani Codex initially published in 1970.[106] In the accounts of his life, Mani is said to have been raised with the Elchasites and at some point broke free from them, going his own way and founding what developed into the Manichean tradition. In these ac-counts, the followers of Elchasai are characterized as "those of the law," and those who are not members are *ta ethnē* (the gentiles). They revered tradi-tions regarding purity that were received from their fathers and teachers, particularly concerned with the body and foodstuffs. Reference in these texts is made to the *archēgoi* (leaders) as persons of respect, but that title could well be an anachronism from later Manichean practice. More sug-gestive is the *oikodespotēs* (master of the house), holding a position similar to the *məbaqqer* (overseer). The *presbuteros* (elder) is attested in the New Testament as well as in 1QS VI, 8, where the elders take second place after the priests in the "assembly of the many." This same phrase in Greek, *tou sunedriou tou plēthous,* appears in the trial of Mani within the Elchasite context prior to his departure from this baptist sect. A sectarian Jewish context with some similarities to the "community" of the S texts and the "covenant" of the D materials emerges from this portrait of Mani's life with the Elchasites.

Continuity in the descriptions of the sects in later Jewish materials is summoned by Reeves as evidence of the continuing influence of this literature. The patristic material suggests at a minimum a theological con-cern with the presence of these groups. The presence of medieval copies of the Testament of Levi and of two copies of the Damascus Document in the Cairo Genizah found in 1896–97 attest to a later influence in the Jewish world. Some similarities to Karaite practices and teaching are also noteworthy, particularly as noted in the disputes with the Rabbanites re-corded by Qirqisani. Eusebius mentions that Origen used in his Hexapla a book of the Psalms found in a jar at Jericho.[107] A discovery of biblical and non-biblical MSS receives mention by the Nestorian patriarch Timothy of Seleucia around 800 CE. Reeves suggests "the conclusion seems inescap-able that there existed a 'paper trail' that stretched from Second Temple literary, and especially sectarian, circles to Islamicate Jewry."[108] These ex-amples point to a continuation of Jewish sectarianism after the destruction of the temple. Attempts to document that continuation with any precision are extremely difficult. It is even more difficult to demonstrate direct connections with the sectarian compositions from the Qumran corpus. What is now evident is that the continued existence of sectarian groups in those circles that eventually produce the Christianity of the Roman Empire and the Judaism of the rabbis is a necessary consideration in the discussion of the "parting of the ways."

The demonstrated interest in the gospel of Matthew by some of these groups is a fascinating aspect of these descriptions. Already noted above in Chapter 1 is the manner in which a Hebrew version of this work is considered important among the church fathers and related in some instances to arguments for its priority. However, in the attributions to sectarian beliefs and practices we see that Irenaeus claims that the Ebionites only use the gospel of Matthew.[109] Later Epiphanius also makes the claim for the use of the first gospel by this group.[110] He then notes that they called it "according to the Hebrews," for it is the only one written in Hebrew.[111] However he goes on to suggest that it is not the actual gospel of Matthew, but rather an account "which is not complete but it is falsified and distorted."[112] In his great attempt to collect and synthesize this material he presumably is trying to reconcile the witnesses of Irenaeus with that of Eusebius, who claims that they rejected all of the epistles and used only "the so-called Gospel of the Hebrews."[113] The appeal to the gospel of Matthew as a Hebrew composition is evident in these accounts, whether or not the composition is the same as the text preserved in the canonical traditions. It is apparent that this composition is linked to Jewish sectarianism in the traditions known by these church fathers. Matthew as a sectarian Jewish composition must find its place in the conflicted and complicated developments of the emerging Jewish and Christian worlds of the second century CE and immediately thereafter.

Conclusion

The employment of social scientific methods in the study of the first gospel was an integral part of a reorientation toward the examination of its Jewish context that emerged in the last decades of the twentieth century. This approach coincided with new developments in the study of Jewish history of that era. The results of both archaeological work in Galilee and new critical studies of the literary evidence informed these developments. A resultant social history made it possible to hypothesize a south Syrian or Galilean context with an orientation toward a gentile mission as a minor rather than major concern of Matthew. From such a standpoint the treatment of issues of Jewish law emerges as a major consideration for attempting to determine its location within Jewish religious and intellectual life at the conclusion of the first century CE. The nature of the composition suggested a sectarian orientation within that context.

The treatment of Matthew as a sectarian text relies heavily on comparison with elements of the sectarian compositions found among the Dead Sea Scrolls. This argument does not rest upon a demonstration of direct dependence on the part of Matthew, nor upon concrete evidence in Galilee for the presence of Essenes or other sectarian groups associated with the scrolls. What has been demonstrated is the continuing presence of the type of sectarianism found in the scrolls within Jewish life in Judea, the Transjordan, and Galilee after 70 CE. The sectarian exemplars in the scrolls are the best evidence we have available illustrating in some detail major features of sectarian thought and practice in the second half of the Second Temple era.

The following analysis of selected portions of Matthew departs in a significant manner from the studies of Eyal Regev, who has compared the materials from Qumran and early Christianity with regard to the topic of sectarianism.[114] Since he assumes the early Christian movement as represented in the literature of the New Testament is reflective of a movement and is to be considered in the aggregate, the particular features of the gospel of Matthew do not receive adequate attention.

This setting provides the environment within which it is possible to read Matthew as an example of sectarian literary production at the end of the first century CE. The emergence of sectarian groups in Jewish life beginning in the second century BCE coincides with the appearance of voluntary associations in the Hellenistic and then Roman worlds of that time period. The sects are a manifestation of this phenomenon and are identified as voluntary associations of protest exhibiting a distinctive alternative civic ideology with boundary marking mechanisms to distinguish themselves from the remainder of the Jewish society. Many of the other voluntary associations within Hellenistic society are viewed as an integral part of the societies of which they are a part and play a vital role in their maintenance. Based on sociological criteria developed for the study of new religious movements, sectarian groups can be differentiated on the basis of the level of tension they demonstrate with regard to their socio-cultural environment. These groups tend to view themselves as uniquely legitimate and to establish boundaries against others with the same national or religious identity. Itemized above are the three elements Stark and Bainbridge have identified which can be used to determine the level of tension exhibited by the group: difference, antagonism, and separation. These have been utilized in the study of the materials from Qumran and here will be applied in the study of Matthew as a sectarian Jewish composition from the end of the first century CE.

The development of sectarian groups attested in the scrolls from Qumran not only demonstrates a similarity in social location with material in the gospel of Matthew, but also provides evidence of overlap in subject matter. It is these intersections that form the intellectual center of the material to be explored in the following chapters. The rationale for the inclusion of these materials is based on content but dealt with as intersections rather than as direct evidence of literary dependence. Their treatment rests on demonstrated likenesses in social structure, particularly in relationship to other types of bodies in the Jewish communities of the time period, but begins with similarities in the treatment of the law, authority, and communal legislation. The discussion of wisdom in Matthew rests in part upon the evidence of the Qumran scrolls and the portrayal of wisdom in Second Temple literature that resulted from the study of those texts. The sectarian legislation found in the Rules texts from Qumran provides a context for the treatment of the subject in Matthew 18. The portions of Matthew within which these overlaps are found are not ancillary material. Sections such as the Sermon on the Mount form the literary and intellectual center of the composition and are of central importance for the ideology of the sect related to its composition.

3 The Polemic of the Sermon on the Mount

Historical and archaeological studies of Judea and Galilee in the past half century opened up new possibilities for the examination of the pivotal text, the Sermon on the Mount. Assuming the Galilean provenance, it is reasonable to attempt a reading that is informed by the evidence from the sectarian Jewish disputes of the first century CE and the social environment in which they developed. Such a perspective immediately assumes an orientation different from those presumed in the debates throughout Christian history. Ample evidence is available to demonstrate that Jews of the first century in Galilee and Judea had a variety of interpretations of the law and its requirements that were the occasion for serious disagreements and debate. The first gospel constitutes an argument about how the followers of Jesus at the conclusion of the first century understood the requirements of the law and the rationale for their understanding of its requirements. Outlining such an understanding of the Sermon on the Mount is the objective of this chapter.

It should be no surprise that the Sermon on the Mount has been at the heart of a good deal of the debate about the meaning and significance of the composition regarded as the most "Jewish gospel." Since major topics such as law and righteousness hold a prominent place in the literary structure of these three chapters, it has been a text central to the law-gospel debates throughout Christian history.[1] A different formulation of this issue can be found in the discussion of the relationship of "gospel" to "teaching" surrounding this text.[2] Earlier commentators such as Augustine and Aquinas understood the issue to be the contrast between the old and the new law. Augustine refers to "the greater precepts given through his Son

68

to a people now ready to be freed by love." Aquinas describes the discontinuity between the "law of bondage" and the "law of liberty."[3] The correct interpretation of the law for the church was the concern of the Protestant reformers. For Luther, "Christ not only recites the Law of Moses; he interprets it . . . perfectly."[4] Luther wanted people to know how to keep the law, and Christ's interpretation was necessary for that purpose. For Calvin, "Christ is the 'best interpreter' of the law but not a lawgiver who supplied something that was missing in the Mosaic law."[5] He emphasized the connection between law and gospel. In the antitheses, Jesus protected the decalogue from misinterpretation by the Jews. In order to achieve this objective, Calvin thought defective Jewish interpretations of the laws needed to be critiqued and corrected. The distinction between the old and the new law, already noted in Augustine and Aquinas, received emphasis by the Anabaptist interpreters.[6] Of course, behind these debates were the different assumptions scholars brought to bear on the question of Jews and gentiles in the first gospel. Since the works of Johannes Weiss[7] and Albert Schweitzer,[8] the relation of this text to eschatological expectations was also a significant consideration.

The most significant attempt to develop a first-century Jewish reading of this pivotal text was *The Setting of the Sermon on the Mount* by W. D. Davies.[9] We have already noted that Davies developed a portrait of the sermon as a Christian response to Yavneh. He of course presumed that Yavneh was the site of the crucial initial developments for the foundation of Rabbinic Judaism: "We cannot certainly connect it with the discussion and activity at Jamnia, but the possibility is a real one that the form of the *SM* [Sermon on the Mount] was fashioned under their impact. It is our suggestion that one fruitful way of dealing with the *SM* is to regard it as the Christian answer to Jamnia. Using terms very loosely, the *SM* is a kind of Christian, mishnaic counterpart to the formulation taking place there."[10] As demonstrated in Chapter 1 above, there is limited evidence for the formulations attributed to Yavneh by the later rabbinic traditions. While important in the later rabbinic formulations of their own origins, the evidence does not point to a movement of great significance already in place at the end of the first century CE. Yavneh then cannot be used as a way of designating a significant leadership structure in the Jewish community at that time. This is not to negate the identification of connections with specific formulations in rabbinic literature that may be of significance in determining certain viewpoints held by portions of the Jewish community. Davies's command of this material is to be utilized in the study of the first gospel. We also note that his careful work on these texts led Davies to suggest that portions of Matt 5 betray evidence of a confrontation with the Essenes: "The Sermon reveals an awareness of the sect and perhaps a polemic against it."[11] He attributed the conflict with the Essenes directly to Jesus, as did Kurt Schubert in his very early essay analyzing those statements that suggest a response to Essene ideas.[12] The primary methodology employed in these studies was form criticism, an attempt to identify the literary history of a given statement and thereby its social context.[13] The identification of these "Essene ideas" demonstrates an extensive engagement with the texts. In this analysis they are evidence of Matthew's context rather than that of Jesus.

Davies indicates that his formulation of the Yavneh hypothesis goes beyond the evidence available: "The juxtaposition of it [the Sermon on the Mount] with Jamnia is not a leap into the dark, but into the twilight of available sources. . . . It was the desire and necessity to present a formulation of the New Israel at a time when the rabbis were engaged in a parallel task for the Old Israel that provided the outside stimulus for the Evangelist to shape the *SM*."[14] His hypothesis, on the one hand, is the result of the limits imposed on a work using the methodology of form criticism to identify the larger context of the social location for the work as a whole. On the other hand, his work reflects the prevailing academic understanding of Jewish history available at the time, a viewpoint that endured even for a few decades after its publication. Given those limitations, his work endures as the most significant contribution to the study of the Jewish context of the Sermon on the Mount in the twentieth century.

The Setting

The Sermon demands significant attention due to its particular placement and significance within the composition, a factor that is even more apparent when viewed in comparison with the other synoptic gospels. It is self-evident that the composition as a whole is a biography of Jesus, even though that point has been debated. We note, however, that the essential features of the biography follow Mark, a source apparently available to the author. In fact, Matthew essentially reproduces with occasional paraphrase about 90 percent of Mark's account and then supplements it. Those supplements include the author's version of the birth and early life of Jesus, as well as post-resurrection appearances. The outline of the year's ministry and the time in Jerusalem as well as the account of the crucifixion are remarkably similar to those found in Mark, even though there are significant differences in detail. While there are substantive portions of the parable discourse and the eschatological discourse in Mark, that composition is not structured around the five substantive orations central to the structure of Matthew: Sermon on the Mount (5–7); missionary discourse (10); parable discourse (13); ecclesiological discourse (18); and the eschatological discourse (24–25).[15] While some of the sayings included in these discourses are found scattered throughout both Mark and Luke, these orations are helpful in defining the particular nature of the composition and its message. Furthermore the Sermon is the first of these five orations and is the longest consecutive body of didactic material in the gospels. Along with the prior chapters, it defines for the receptive reader the nature of the biography that is to follow. These three chapters are important, not only because of their significance in Christian history; they are central to the portrayal of Jesus developed by the author of the first gospel.

The complex nature of Matthew's portrait of the setting of this didactic oration is apparent in the final verses leading up to it. The previous chapter concludes with Jesus going throughout Galilee teaching in synagogues, preaching the gospel, and healing diseases. This is followed by the report that these activities spread throughout Syria, the province that would have included Galilee, followed by more healings and exorcisms. Many crowds from Galilee, the Decapolis, Jerusalem, Judea, and the Transjordan followed him (Matt 4:23–25). Then abruptly in 5:1–2, "When Jesus saw the crowds, he went up the mountain; and after he sat down, his disciples came to him. Then he began to speak, and taught them."[16] In other words, it would appear that Matthew is telling readers that the Sermon is addressed to the disciples, or at least that is how commentators have tended to read this line. However, the assumption that this material is addressed only to the disciples does not seem to be warranted. If we look to the end of the sermon, in 7:28–29 we surprisingly read that "the crowds were amazed by his teaching." In other words, he has been teaching them all along. The connection between the crowds and the disciples is also apparent with the use of the word *akolutheō* (follow) with reference to the crowds in 4:25. The first four disciples have just left their boats and nets to "follow" him in 4:18–22. Of course, the rigor of the two-ways passages and the contrast between the wise and the foolish builders concludes the oration (7:13–14, 24–27). So the tension between an inner group and a general audience is built into the literary composition. As is well-known this tension is central to the discussion of the parable of the sower (13:10–17, 36–43) and related sections such as the discussion on tradition and defilement (15:10–20). This literary tension is characteristic of apocalyptic literature, most clearly exemplified in passages such as 2 Esd 14:26, 45–47, a composition dated to roughly the same time period. While the setting in Matt 4:23–5:2 is also capable of other explanations, the literary usage of the multiple settings later in the work supports the analogy to apocalyptic literature and the allure of "hidden" knowledge that is available to all who are willing to make the commitment to join those who are seeking it. The tension between readily accessible knowledge in the invitation to follow and the necessity for commitment in order to attain that which is hidden is integral to preparing the reader for the material in the Sermon on the Mount.

That this composition addresses issues of concern to the Jewish community is evident in the treatment of the figure of Moses in this introductory material. In his argument for the portrayal of Jesus as a new Moses in the first gospel, Dale Allison has collected and examined all the material bearing upon this portrayal.[17] Allison's central argument has been and is subject to debate. The caution expressed by Luz that the abundance of the material related to Moses does not mean that Jesus is therefore portrayed as a second Moses is well-taken.[18] Of significance for our concerns is the observation that the utilization of the figure of Moses is most apparent in the first section of the composition, Matt 1:1–8:1.[19]

Having established in the first chapter the basic claims for the identity of Jesus, the author depicts the childhood of Jesus by employing the typology of Moses. Evidence of features from the stories of Moses in Second Temple literature are apparent,[20] but most obvious is the flight to Egypt to escape the wrath of Herod and his order to kill all of the children two years old and under. The miraculous birth and the delivery from death related to the sojourn in Egypt mark the connection with the Moses tradition. The relationship of the temptation account in Matthew to the biblical depiction of the wilderness experience continues the use of the Moses typology. The particular formulation of the Matthean adaptation of this story contains features such as the temporal setting in Matt 4:2 in which Jesus fasted for forty nights, in addition to the forty days mentioned in Mark, Luke, and presumably Q. This suggests an allusion to Exod 24:18, a description of Moses on Mount Sinai, and then to the same event depicted in Deut 9:9 and 9:18, "Bread I did not eat and water I did not drink," that is, he fasted.[21]

In Matt 4:8 the devil takes Jesus to a very high mountain and shows him "all the kingdoms of the world and their glory." The mention of a mountain is missing from the parallel account in Luke 4:5. The reader would be reminded of the view of "all the land" from Mount Nebo that is given to Moses in Deut 34:2.[22] The author of the first gospel forms a distinct link between Jesus and the story of Moses in the first chapters of this composition.

At the beginning of the Sermon, the reader is taken back to Mount Sinai, the site of divine revelation.[23] The crowds are assembled, and the leader withdraws from the crowd and takes a smaller body with him (as in Exod 24:1–2); however the instruction given is directed to the entire group of people assembled (Exod 24:3; Matt 7:28–29). The statement in Matt 5:1, "after he was sitting," has occasioned debate. There are traditions suggesting that Moses sat at Sinai,[24] and there is archeological evidence of a seat for a teacher or reader in fourth-century synagogues; however it is not clear that either presents a compelling case for connecting this passage with those traditions. In b. Meg. 21a we observe a dispute regarding whether the Torah is to be read (and studied) standing up or sitting down. Any claim that this is a dispute of real consequence or that it applied to this earlier pre-rabbinic period could be questioned.[25] We note the manner in which Jesus sits for a number of major teaching sessions (Matt 13:1–2; 24:3) or when the crowds gather around him (13:1–2; 15:29; 26:55). The most compelling internal reference is Matt 23:2, "The scribes and the Pharisees sit on the seat of Moses."[26] While there is no evidence that the particular act of sitting has an authoritative claim with regard to Moses, the author of Matthew considers it a typical position for an authoritative teacher.

The typology of Moses employed in the portrayal of Jesus in these first chapters, enhanced by the claims for an authoritative level of teaching, sets the stage for the Sermon on the Mount.[27] However, the Moses typology is used along with other literary devices and argumentation, such as accounts of miracles and spreading fame, to set up Jesus as the authoritative teacher, not the new Moses. Since Matthew 1 makes the argument for the divinization of Jesus, that also is part of this portrayal of a person who has authority derived from an enhanced level of access to the Divine. The resultant paraenetic material concerning the best way to live as a Jew is based upon this comprehension of the fundamental nature of the universe derived from a teacher whose authority rests in a particular relationship to divinity. Such an audacious declaration for its founder makes it possible for a sectarian group of Jews to advance their cause in the midst of the competing claims that would have characterized the communal life of fractured Jewish communities in Galilee at the end of the first century CE.

The Beatitudes

The possibility of a different reading of the Sermon is already apparent in the consideration of the opening section, the Beatitudes. Among the materials from Qumran is a Hebrew text which has attracted considerable attention due to its close resemblance to this introduction to the Sermon; 4Q525 (Beatitudes) 2 II + 3, 1–11 is closer in form and structure than any parallels which occasioned discussion prior to this discovery, including Luke 6:20–26. It clearly is a wisdom text, beginning: "which he spo]ke with the wisdom that Go[d] gave to [him . . . [2] . . . to kno]w wisdom and instru[ction], to make insightful . . . [3] . . . to increase [knowledge]."[28] The final beatitude, translated below, identifies wisdom with Torah. A section on wisdom personified is apparent in the fragments beginning at 5, 5. Wisdom here is portrayed in a manner remarkably similar to Ben Sira 14:20–21, which in the Hebrew text reads, "Happy is the person who meditates on wisdom and cultivates understanding, who takes to heart her ways and is immersed in her understanding."[29] Psalm 1 lurks in the background of both of these claims. The connection between wisdom and Torah is noted in the next verse, Ben Sira 15:1, and then developed explicitly in chapter 24. My translation of 4Q525 2 II is as follows:[30]

> [Blessed is he who seeks her][31] [1]with a pure heart, he does not slander with his tongue. Blessed are those who hold fast to her statutes, they do not hold fast to [2]the ways of injustice.
>
> Bles[sed] are those who rejoice in her, they do not spout forth the ways of folly.
>
> Blessed are those who seek her [3]with pure hands, they do not search for her with a deceitful heart.
>
> Blessed is the man who has obtained wisdom. He walks [4]in the law of the Most High and prepares his heart for her ways. He conducts himself according to her discipline and in her corrections he delights daily. [5]He does not leave her unheeded during the afflictions of his distress, in the time of hardship he does not abandon her, he does not forget her in the days of dread [6]and in the affliction of his soul he does not abhor her.
>
> For on her he meditates daily and in his distress he considers [her . . . and througho]ut [7]his living through her [he gains insight and he places her]

before his eyes so as not to walk in the ways of [injustice . . .] [8] . . . together
and he makes his heart perfect toward her. . . .

[9] . . . A crown of pure g]old [she places upon] his [hea]d and with kings
she se[ats him . . . [10]with] his [sc]epter over . . . brothers he shall separ[ate. . . .

While there is always some uncertainty with regard to the reconstruction of fragmentary texts, the basic outline of the passage is clear. Apparent
is a structure of 4 + 1 macarisms for the literary unit.[32] In Matt 5 we have a
structure of 8 + 1 macarisms. In both cases the last macarism consists of an
extended text. The suggestion of George Brooke that the difference between
4 + 1 and 8 + 1 may be an insignificant variation in poetic structure should
be considered. He also notes that two clauses can often be introduced by
the term 'ašrê (blessed), without it being repeated for the second clause.[33]
In this case 4Q525, just as Matt 5:3–12, would consist of eight macarisms.
More doubtful is the addition of four macarisms in the missing section of
col. I, as proposed by Emile Puech.[34] Readers should also note the reconstruction of the last line of the previous column in the above translation, a
proposal for the content of the beginning of the first macarism.

When the Hebrew text of 4Q525 is divided into stichoi (or "lines"), we
see eight prior to and eight following the central opening statement of the
last macarism, "Blessed is the man who has attained wisdom." Thereby its
significance as the interpretive center of the literary unit is highlighted. A
similarity to the lengthy concluding macarism of Matt 5:11–12 is apparent.
In both cases there are allusions to the difficulties involved in following
the wisdom outlined in the earlier macarisms, whether it is the Torah connected with wisdom in 4Q525 with the following allusions to hardship and
distress or the reviling and persecution that comes to the followers of Jesus
in Matthew. This is followed by mention of the rewards, "a crown of pure
gold" upon his head and being seated with kings while holding a scepter in
ll. 9–10 above, while a great reward in heaven is the occasion for rejoicing
in Matt 5:12.[35] Since elsewhere in Matthew—and already in the Sermon
on the Mount—the kingdom of heaven receives frequent mention, the
anticipated futures outlined in the two compositions show a remarkable
similarity.

Ben Sira 14 has already received mention. The extended macarism, or
set of macarisms, begins at 14:20 and continues at least until the end of the
chapter. In this case in the Hebrew version the term 'ašrê only appears at the
beginning of the section and is assumed to apply to all of the macarisms in

vv. 21–27. The remainder of the literary structure is consistent with the form of 4Q525 and others. We note the use of the verb *hāgāh* (meditate) in 14:20 as well as in l. 6 of 4Q525.[36] Also apparent is the similarity of 4Q525 2 II, 4, "who prepares his heart for her ways," to the Hebrew text of Ben Sira 14:21, "who takes to heart her ways," a phrase not evident in earlier biblical materials. The pursuit of wisdom is central and common to both compositions.

We note the presence of two macarisms in the text of another sapiential composition from Qumran, 4Q185 (Sapiential Work) 1–2 II, 8–13 and 13–15.[37] The second instance demonstrates similarities in content and form to both 4Q525 2 II and Matt 5:11–12. In this document the integration of wisdom with accounts of salvation history and the giving of the law reflects a post-biblical development in Jewish wisdom that fits well with the eschatological setting of comparable wisdom compositions. Wisdom is equated with Torah in this composition in a manner similar to Ben Sira.[38] While Torah is never mentioned in the extant text, the usage of language and references from Deuteronomy point to the overlap between wisdom and Torah in the composition. The fragmentary evidence suggests that the composition anticipated judgment as a consequence of not accepting wisdom. There are no hints, however, of a dualistic universe, nor are there any known vocabulary items that suggest sectarian social structures in these fragments. It is thus possible to consider a date of composition in the first half of the second century BCE similar to 4Q525 and the Hebrew text of Ben Sira.[39]

Another extended macarism can be identified in 2 En. 42:6–14, a composition of disputed provenance. This enigmatic text, available only in Slavonic MSS, remains the subject of continuing debate, some regarding it as a first-century composition and others a number of centuries later. The connection of this elusive composition with the gospel of Matthew has been noted by Grant Macaskill.[40]

These texts demonstrate a continuity with biblical wisdom literature as well as the manner in which that tradition is changed and developed in Second Temple Judaism and subsequent literature. It is apparent that the macarism form is associated with wisdom traditions; its presence in apocalyptic literature suggests the overlap between the two genres as presently understood in our fields of study.[41] Also evident is the extent to which Torah becomes identified with wisdom in a number of these texts, particularly Ben Sira, 4Q525, and 4Q185.[42] Given the extensive use of this literary form and the very specific similarities in literary structure in 4Q525 identified above, it is clear that the author of Matthew is placing Jesus in this literary tradition with his very person and teaching assuming the place that Torah, and more broadly wisdom, occupies in these other compositions. This is a remarkable claim by a Jewish author of the first century, which finds its best explanation in the kinds of arguments that are made for exclusive access to knowledge and truth in some of the sectarian expressions of that era.[43] This is the best explanation for the extensive demands for allegiance to the person of Jesus ("on my account") the author of Matthew included in a text such as Matt 5:11. We note of course that 4Q525 does not yield evidence of being a sectarian composition; however it is reasonable to approach it with the assumption that it was valued by sectarian readers.

Significant connections with the sectarian compositions from Qumran can also be identified in the content of the Beatitudes.[44] Matthew 5:3 speaks of the poor in spirit, also evident in 1QH[a] (Thanksgiving Hymns[a]) VI, 14 ('anwê rûaḥ) and 1QM (War Scroll) XIV, 7 ('anwê rûaḥ). David Flusser drew attention to the connection between Matt 5:3–5 and 1QH[a] XXIII, 15–16 with reference to the poor in spirit, the meek, and those who mourn:[45] "in order to [rai]se up the herald of good news according to your truth, [and to tel]l of your goodness, to proclaim good news to the poor according to the abundance of your mercy, [and to s]atisfy from the fount of kn[owledge all the brok]en in spirit and those who mourn (that they may have) eternal joy."[46] He noted the connection of these two passages with Isa 61:1–2 and 66:2.[47] Furthermore, Flusser points to Ps 37:11 in which "the meek shall inherit the earth" and notes that in the sectarian exegesis of the text the "meek" are identified as the "assembly of the poor."[48] Again, in the exegesis of Ps 37:22, "those who are blessed of him will inherit the earth" is interpreted as a reference to the "assembly of the poor."[49] In the same text this body is also called "the assembly of his elect," that is, the members of the sect. The "poor" are also found in multiple references in Pesher Habakkuk, the War Scroll, and the Thanksgiving Hymns. The evidence shows that these sectarian authors understood themselves to be "poor," "meek," and "humble." There are some other terms for "poor" such as *dal* and *reš* used in the Hebrew Bible that are not employed in these sectarian texts from Qumran or Matthew, however attested in other compositions from the Qumran corpus such as Instruction, a non-sectarian wisdom composition. The first three macarisms of the Sermon on the Mount show evidence of vocabulary familiar to us from the sectarian texts of Qumran, in which they are employed in a significant manner for self-designation. These distinctive indicators of sectarian identity serve as boundary marking mechanisms pointing to the members of a particular group, in this case the followers of Jesus. In using these indicators, the author is employing a vocabulary already utilized by previous sectarian groups in Second Temple Jewish life.

Central for an understanding of the macarism concerning those who "hunger and thirst for righteousness" (Matt 5:6) is the recognition that the latter term receives treatment in Matthew unlike any other book in the New Testament. "Righteousness" is one of the terms employed by the author to designate the particular expectations of a Jewish way of life developed in this composition. In the exaltation of wisdom building up to the statement on the correlation of wisdom and Torah in Ben Sira 24:19–21 we find the invitation to "eat your fill of my fruits." Wisdom is so sweet that "those who eat of me will hunger for more, and those who drink of me will thirst for more."[50] While the wisdom analogy at the forefront of this verse may find further explanation in the promises expressed in Ps 107:5–6 and Isa 49:10, the connection between wisdom and Jesus, hence with the Jesus community and righteousness, is the identification the reader is called upon to embrace.[51] To obtain life-giving wisdom the reader is invited to become a part of the followers of Jesus rather than join one of the other groups of Jews calling for their allegiance.

The "merciful" of Matt 5:7 has not received as much attention. "To proclaim good news to the poor according to the abundance of your mercy" is also included in 1QHᵃ XXIII, 15–16, already just mentioned. In Isa 63:7 the hearers are reminded of "all that the Lord has done for us, and the great favor to the house of Israel that he has shown them according to his mercy, according to the abundance of his steadfast love."[52] Within the Thanksgiving Hymns the "abundance of your mercy" is repeated twenty times, this term for "mercy" thirty-five times.[53] Were we to add the term ḥesed (steadfast love), which is the other major Hebrew term that the LXX translates as "mercy," we would find another thirty-five references, frequently also combined with "abundance." These terms are common throughout the MSS of the Community Rule, the Damascus Document, the Messianic Rule, and the War Scroll, also all sectarian compositions. That mercy is important for the Matthean community is evident in the employment of Hos 6:6, "I desire mercy and not sacrifice," in Matt 9:13 and 12:7, a citation not found in the other gospels. In the well-known diatribe against the Pharisees, in 23:23 they are accused of forsaking "the weighty matters of the law, justice and mercy and faith."[54] The use of Hos 6:6 in pivotal locations is also found later in rabbinic literature. In 'Abot R. Nat. A 4, it appears twice in the interpretation of the famous saying by Simon the Righteous: "On three things the world stands—on the Torah, on the temple service, and on acts of loving-kindness."[55] The significance of mercy for the rabbis is apparent with its frequent mention.[56] The evidence suggests that the search for mercy was a significant aspect of Jewish life into the rabbinic period. The author wanted it to be understood that this was a significant value among the followers of Jesus, as it was with the claims made by other sectarian groups, and subsequently in Rabbinic Judaism.

The "pure in heart" of the next verse (Matt 5:8) would be a natural expectation for the lifestyle outlined in the sectarian texts from Qumran, in which the desire to be "clean" or "pure" was a central aspiration. While the phrase finds a possible biblical precedent in Ps 24:4, *bar leb* (pure of heart), this Greek term *katharos* in the LXX is much more frequently a translation of the Hebrew *ṭāhōr* (clean, pure). The latter term is found in the phrase "pure in heart" in 4Q525 (Beatitudes) 2 II, 1 as well as in the wisdom-related composition 4Q435 (*Barkhi Nafshi*[b]) 2 I, 1 // 4Q436 (*Barkhi Nafshi*[c]) 1a+b I, 10. This root "purity" as adjective, noun, verb, and abstract noun pervades the central sectarian texts such as the Damascus Covenant, the Community Rule, the Thanksgiving Hymns, and the War Scroll. The central claim for those who join the new covenant in CD 6:17 and 12:20 is "to distinguish between the impure and the pure." Purity is central to the vision developed in the Temple Scroll (forty-four references to *ṭāhōr*) and fundamental for the legislation outlined in 4QMMT.[57] In this case we see evidence of its importance in the sectarian texts as well as in associated compositions.[58] That "they will see God" is an expectation that we would expect to be associated with cult, that is, purity is what is required in order to be in the presence of the Divine. So it comes as no surprise to find an emphasis on purity in the angelic liturgies of the Songs of the Sabbath Sacrifice. Purity is at the center of the sectarian legislation found in the scrolls as well as in some of the literature retained and presumably valued by them, particularly literature that reflects post-biblical developments in legal literature. The sectarian followers of Jesus addressed in the first gospel are to be understood as a continuation of this trajectory.

The blessing of those who make peace in Matt 5:9 appears to be a very specific designation referring to the followers of Jesus in the Jewish community addressed in the first gospel.[59] While the longing for peace is a common refrain in the Hebrew Bible, here it is employed in a manner that suggests allusions to related texts in the first gospel. We note the last of the antitheses in the same chapter: "But I say to you, love your enemies and pray for those who persecute you, so that you may be children of your Father in heaven" (5:44–45). In both cases, the consequence of "doing peace" is being called "children [or 'sons'] of God." The "children of God [or of 'the kingdom']" are those who have elected to join this sect of Jesus followers who participate in it as a present reality and as a statement about their future eschatological hopes. This would seem to be the intent of the parable of the seed in 13:38, where "the good seed are the children of the kingdom." The author is asserting that one of the marks of this sect is their peacemaking. The argument in 5:43–47 seems to be cognizant of viewpoints held by other Jewish sects, as they are attested in the Qumran evidence. A blessing on those who make peace is also found in 2 En. 52:11–15. The rabbinic tradition attributes a positive role to the peacemaker as well, evident in the traditions attributed to Joḥanan ben Zakkai as well as the statement attributed to Hillel, "Be of the disciples of Aaron, loving peace and pursuing peace."[60] In both cases we have a rabbinic understanding of what was taught and valued in the late Second Temple period. Perhaps Matt 10:34 should be understood as a contradictory emphasis: "Do not think that I have come to bring peace to the earth. I have not come to bring peace, but a sword." It should quickly be pointed out that the simultaneous desire for relief from conflict and for harmonious relationships coupled with the expectation that there will be conflict getting to such a place is not unusual in apocalyptic literature.[61] Whether this self-understanding as peacemaker is distinctive to this group within that Jewish society is impossible to determine. Evidence from both apocalyptic literature and later rabbinic literature makes that doubtful. An argument for its distinctiveness is not necessary to recognize its centrality for the sectarian way of life advocated in the first gospel.

When we come to Matt 5:10–11 we see the manner in which persecution and defamation are the prelude to some greater reward stated in v. 12. The same development has already been identified above in 4Q525 2 II, 5–10. Luz is instructive when he considers the eighth beatitude as redactional, that is, it is constructed by the author of the first gospel to tie together portions of the first macarism (Matt 5:3) with the conclusion (5:11–12) to emphasize key points, the kingdom of God and righteousness. The term *diōkō* (persecute) also is used in a manner peculiar to this composition and to this section of it.[62] Luz suggests Matt 23:34 as a reference to some type of persecution already part of the experience of this particular group of Jews.[63] The frequent appearance of the term *paradidōmi* (deliver up or be-

tray) throughout the composition also bears mention.[64] The particular usage of "righteousness" in the Sermon, also highlighted by Luz,[65] will receive
more extensive discussion below. In Matt 5:9 we already recognize that the
author is employing particular language to refer to and describe the followers of Jesus when he proposed that "they will be called sons of God." This
same feature is evident in v. 10, "for theirs is the kingdom of heaven," as well
as in vv. 11–12, "for my sake." This combination of terms clearly identifies
the recipients and "doers" of this set of macarisms, setting them apart from
other groups of Jews who would make similar kinds of claims. They are
named and identified with a set of distinguishing marks, examples of which
are to follow in the remainder of Matt 5, that serve as "boundary marking
mechanisms . . . to distinguish between [a group's] own members and those
otherwise normally regarded as belonging to the same national or religious
entity."[66] The sectarian identity of the followers of Jesus is clearly established in this introduction to the paraenetic discourse, which sets out the
distinctive manner in which this group is to live within the Jewish world
at the end of the first century. Persecution is included among this list of
identifiers, the link between the eighth and final macarism.

Persecution as part of the Jewish experience in the late Second Temple
era is well-attested in its literature.[67] Its significance is already apparent in
the early apocalyptic literature. In "The Book of the Watchers" (1 En. 1–36)
we find an explanation of the origins of the violence, sin, victimization,
and pollution that characterize the human experience. We presume that
the conditions of violence and pollution that require explanation are those
experienced by the residents of Judea from the early years of the Hellenistic
empires through the reign of Antiochus IV Epiphanes (175–164 BCE).[68]
The most visible evidence that this world is characterized by profound evil
and radical injustice is its total dominance by the rich and powerful who are
foolish and lawless. The place of the righteous is summarized in the final
discourse of this section: "I swear to you that the angels in heaven make
mention of you for good before the glory of the Great One, and your names
are written before the glory of the Great One. Take courage, then, for for-
merly you were worn out by evils and tribulations, but now you will shine
like the luminaries of heaven; you will shine and appear, and the portals of
heaven will be opened for you."[69] The description of their present lot begins
in the following manner: "In the days of our tribulation, we toiled labori-
ously, and every tribulation we saw, and many evils we found. We were
consumed and became few, and our spirits small, and we were destroyed

and there was no one to help us with word and deed; we were powerless and found nothing."[70] These righteous have a remarkable transcendent future in marked contrast to their present situation. The current situation of the righteous and pious is one of tribulation and persecution.[71] A similar portrait of persecution is apparent for the "wise" of Dan 11:33–35 who "shall shine like the brightness of the sky" (Dan 12:3), who are regarded as the group to which the author(s) of the book belonged.[72]

This perception of persecution of a faithful and/or righteous minority becomes a significant point of identification for sectarian groups in Judea in the second century BCE, as attested in some of the scrolls from Qumran. In the LXX the term *diōkō* (persecute) is most frequently a translation of the Hebrew *rādap* (pursue). In the only composition that provides an account of its own sectarian history, the persons who were inspired by the man of the lie "pursued them [i.e., the root plant under the guidance of the teacher of righteousness] with the sword."[73] The root plant consisted of those who later are described as "entering into the new covenant in the land of Damascus" (CD 6:19). Similarly, in 1QpHab XI, 4–6 it is the wicked priest who "pursued the teacher of righteousness to consume him in the heat of his anger at his place of exile." Further support for this understanding of the lot of the teacher of righteousness and his followers is found in 1QpHab VIII, 1–3 in which "all those who keep the law . . . God will deliver from judgment because of their suffering and their faith in the teacher of righteousness." This comparatively specific portrait of the teacher of righteousness and the community betrays connections with the Thanksgiving Hymns. In 1QHᵃ VI, 14–15 we find reference to "the humble [or 'poor'] in spirit, those purified by affliction, and those refined by the crucible."[74] Those portions of the Thanksgiving Hymns are well-known that represent the reflections of an individual leader many regard as the teacher of righteousness, even though that cannot be verified: "The author presents himself as the persecuted and exiled leader of a community that he regards as utterly dependent upon leadership."[75] This portrayal can be found in hymns such as 1QHᵃ X, 22–32, 33–41; XI, 6–19, 20–32; XII, 6–XIII, 6. They provide a model for how a rhetorical development based on the experience of the founder of the sect can be used as a vehicle in the formation of sectarian identity.[76] Persecution, mistreatment, and relegation to outsider status of the leader play a crucial role in this formative process. Whether the author of Matthew was inspired directly by these accounts is questionable, but these examples show that this perception was a significant factor in sectarian identity in Second

Temple Judaism. The perception that the group was persecuted and being dealt with badly by external forces fits this portrayal of a sectarian community. To identify that experience in the life of the leader is a highly effective mode of identity formation.

That persecution becomes an accepted and common theme in apocalyptic and sectarian literature during the latter period of the Second Temple helps establish a context for the references in Matthew. It also complicates a reading of the text since it is hard to distinguish between literary theme and historical occurrence. The earliest broadly attested persecution of Christians is under Nero. Before that, the edict of Claudius may provide a suggestion that members of the Jesus movement in Rome were being regarded as troublemakers.[77] Presumably dated to the latter years of his reign (ca. 49 CE), it may have been a prohibition of assembly fomented by trouble stirred up within the Jewish community by Chrestos (Christ). Whatever its intent, its jurisdiction covered only the city of Rome and applied to the Jewish population as a whole.[78] The edict of Nero against Christians, if actually issued, was limited to Rome and appears to be of very limited duration.[79] The executions of Peter and Paul, not known in any detail, are indicative of problems at Rome, but there is no evidence of a systematic program of persecution in Rome or throughout the Roman Empire in the first century CE.[80] The evidence down to the third century points to sporadic localized persecution. Even the amount of localized persecution appears to be overstated in most of our evaluations.[81] Similarly, the attribution of widespread persecution to the time of Domitian in the scholarship related to Revelation is questioned.[82] What does this mean for Galilee immediately after the destruction of the temple?

It is evident that the author of the first gospel uses the term *diōkō* in a distinctive manner. The gospel of Luke (6:22, 27) uses the term *miseō* (hate) where Matthew uses *diōkō* (Matt 5:11, 44). Luke's usage may reflect the earlier Q version of these sayings. This would indicate that the choice of the term *diōkō* reflects a Matthean perspective on these sayings. The reference in 5:10 is a compelling indicator since it points to the term "righteousness," a key term denoting the particular way of life of the followers of Jesus. In 5:12, this particular expression of Judaism is anchored in the prophetic tradition. The blessed are those who are persecuted because they have decided to live out their lives in the manner advocated by the followers of Jesus as it is developed in the gospel of Matthew. That is what being "persecuted for righteousness' sake" (5:10) means in this composition. Such a perspective is also apparent in the missionary discourse commissioning the twelve apostles, "When they persecute you in one town, flee to the next" (10:23). This verse, not found in any of the other gospels, also reflects this particular Matthean usage. Echoes of the Sermon on the Mount are apparent in the previous verse, "You will be hated by all *because of my name*" (10:22, cf. 5:11). According to Matthew, the sectarian allegiance of the followers of Jesus is the reason for their persecution in the Jewish community.

The pervasive presence of this theme throughout the first gospel stands in contrast to the other canonical compositions describing the life of Jesus. The similarity of Matt 10:23 to 23:34 demonstrates the manner in which key terms and connections found in the Sermon pervade the entire composition: "Therefore I send you prophets, sages, and scribes, some of whom you will kill and crucify, and some you will flog in your synagogues and pursue [or 'persecute' (*diōkō*)] from town to town" (Matt 23:34). The connection is apparent, in both cases including the reference to the *polis* (town or city). The particular usage of "persecution" in this composition points to the perceived social marginalization of the followers of Jesus associated with the Matthean community in the first-century Jewish community. They interpreted their experience within the tradition of rejection that had been attributed to the prophets. They understood themselves to be in this tradition as it had been developed and enhanced within some of the apocalyptic and wisdom traditions earlier in the Second Temple period. By making rather exclusive claims for their own understanding of the Jewish tradition, they adopted the strategy of other sectarian groups that preceded them. However, that also placed them in a marginal position, rejected by the majority of the Jewish population and presumably feeling somewhat isolated and powerless. They perceived that the claims they made about the future of the Jewish people and the stances which they took on contentious issues were rejected by the majority of the community and by those who either were, or claimed to be, in the leadership.

The Beatitudes are identity markers for this sectarian group of Jews who identified themselves as followers of Jesus. Within the rhetorical development of the gospel as a whole, they are the introduction to the first and longest discourse of the work. This major section of the composition addresses the followers directly, indicating who they are or perhaps more accurately whom they should consider themselves to be. Employing terminology used by other sectarian groups, they are identified as "a voluntary association of protest" who claim Jesus alone as their source of wisdom. The author credits him as the source of instruction regarding what it means to be "children of God" (5:9) who are part of the kingdom of God ("heaven" in Matt 5:3, 10). The select nature of the group is reinforced as its adherents are considered "blessed," the recipients of divine favor. The three elements characteristic of sectarian groups are all implicit in this identification: difference in the sense that they will be engaged in activities regarded as deviant by other Jews; antagonism in the expected response of defamation and persecution by other groups; and separation in their claim to the exclusive authority of Jesus as the representative of the will of God to the exclusion of other sources of wisdom from the Divine. As the way of life proposed for this sectarian body is developed throughout the remainder of the sermon, its distinctive features become more apparent and the presence of these three elements can be more specifically identified.

Jesus and the Law

Discussion of the issue of Jesus and the law in the first gospel has rested primarily on the treatment of the Sermon on the Mount, specifically Matt 5:17–48.[83] As identified by Luz, 5:17–7:12 constitutes the major programmatic section of the Sermon, defined by the inclusio of "the law and the prophets" in 5:17 and 7:12. In that outline 5:21–48 and 6:19–7:11 are substantive portions of equal length, while 6:1–18 with the Lord's Prayer at its center represents the theological heart of the sermon.[84] Such an analysis is less than convincing when viewed from the perspective of first-century sectarianism in which law holds a central place. While the argument for the inclusio of "the law and the prophets" is possible, it is much more plausible to consider its literary significance to rest on its repetition, also found in two other signal texts, Matt 11:13 and 22:40. Then it also does not follow that the Lord's Prayer constitutes the literary and thematic center of this literary unit.[85] The first major discourse of Matthew rather provides an orientation to Jewish law from the particular sectarian perspective of Matt 5:17–20,[86] illustrated by six case studies, the antitheses. The Sermon should be understood as an exposition of these three verses for those persons claiming the group identity already established in the Beatitudes.

Christian interpreters most frequently have understood the New Testament to reflect a debate concerning the validity of biblical (and postbiblical) law as a whole, with the exception of kosher food and circumcision, for the early Christian movement rather than specific requirements within it.[87] Even the debates about those two issues concern their applicability as a whole in the communities of the followers of Jesus. This debate would have been very foreign to the authors and readers of the other texts that emerge from within the various circles of Jewish life in the Second Temple period,[88] since the issues reflected within these texts most frequently concern the nature and validity of specific provisions within the law.[89] This acknowledgment is related to the observation that the definition of religion in antiquity has to do with practice rather than belief: "Ancient Judaism had no creeds. The Jews of antiquity devoted much energy to theological speculation and achieved almost unanimous agreement on certain theological principles ... but the boundaries of Jewish communities were not defined by beliefs."[90] This relates both to groups within Jewish communities as well as boundaries between Jews and gentiles. In his evaluation of the use of the category of religion for the study of ancient Judaism, Seth Schwartz also highlights practice. Citing the importance of religion as an analytic category for the study of the ancient Mediterranean and Near Eastern worlds, he notes that "religion can be salvaged as a heuristic category if we mean by it: the practices (including the cognitive ones) which constitute people's relations with their god(s)."[91] Here he is evaluating the claims of Mason and Boyarin that religion is a category that appears with the development of Christian theology. The analysis of religion in antiquity has first and foremost to do with practice. This is very apparent in the study of ancient Judaism.

In the case of Jewish texts of the Second Temple era, these debates about practice are encompassed within the scope of materials understood to be "Torah" in its broader sense. Here we are referring to authoritative interpretations of biblical law and narrative that may include but are certainly broader than the material included in the Pentateuch. Evidence of this broader understanding of Torah finds a distinctive development within the later rabbinic tradition with the concept of the "oral Torah."[92] Within Judaism of the Second Temple era, we know that "Torah" was important when talking about communal structure, identity, and ethics.[93] This trajectory through Second Temple literature is evident in the Qumran literature.[94]

A significant attempt to address Matthew's treatment of law was that of Davies and Allison, who understood the initial section of 5:17–20 as a response to anticipated objections arising from the treatment of the issues in the following antitheses. In their view the two responses designated in this preamble are (1) in these "antitheses" Jesus does not set aside the Torah but upholds it, hence there is no real conflict between Jesus and Moses, and

(2) what Jesus requires of his followers surpasses the requirements normally attributed to the Torah.[95] While taking the Jewish context of this composition seriously, this response is rooted in the supposition that it is addressed to the issues which arise in conflict with a Pharisaic–proto-rabbinic opposition. Since this hypothesis has been called into question, a different approach is called for. In the sectarian context of first-century Jewish life, both Torah and a righteousness that "exceeds that of the scribes and Pharisees" (5:20) demand further examination. In this case I reverse the literary relationship of these two sections, with the "antitheses" functioning as cases that illustrate the implications and method of the legal principle of interpretation that is set out in 5:17–20. To set the stage for such a discussion it is necessary to understand what Torah may have meant at the end of the Second Temple period. An initial observation is in order.

That Matthew has a particular interest in the law unique among the gospel writers is attested by the exclusive use of the term *anomia* (lawlessness). Concluding the Sermon on the Mount, it is the "workers of lawlessness [NRSV—evildoers]"[96] who are not recognized by Jesus and cast out (7:23). This same phrase is applied to those against whom the Son of Man will send his angels in Matt 13:41.[97] The accusation against the "scribes and Pharisees, hypocrites," in Matt 23:28 is that "you also on the outside look righteous to others, but inside you are full of hypocrisy and lawlessness." The juxtaposition of the righteous with lawlessness is also the implication of 5:17–20: "Do not think that I have come to abolish [*katalusai*] the law . . . but to fulfill [*plērōsai*]." In both the Hebrew translation of the New Testament by Delitzsch and in the medieval Hebrew copy of Matthew from Shem Tov the term *hēpēr*, the *hiphil* form of the root *p-r-r* (break, destroy, make useless), is employed to translate the Greek *kataluō*.[98] This Hebrew term is used in contexts such as the annulling of vows in Num 30:9, 13, 14, 16 or the breaking of the covenant in Gen 17:14 and Jer 31:32. In b. Šabb 116b in Talmudic Aramaic is contained the words of "another book," which is usually considered to be a version of Matt 5:17, "I came not to diminish the law of Moses or to add to the law of Moses." In both instances, the Semitic version of the phrase immediately places the discussion within the debates about the keeping of the law and the provisions required to do that in a manner pleasing to God. In v. 20, "unless your righteousness exceeds that of the scribes and Pharisees, you will never enter into the kingdom of heaven," we see what is required to keep the law and to avoid being considered among the "workers of lawlessness" at the conclusion of the Sermon (7:23).

What is required is the kind of life mandated and explained in the intervening sections of this oration.

Finally, in Matt 24:12 it is due to the increase of lawlessness that the love of many of the followers of Jesus will grow cold.[99] While some commentators would suggest that this is a broader reference to events within the Jewish community at the time and its treatment of the followers of Jesus, a more consistent and likely sectarian reading suggests this to be a comment on life within the Matthean community.[100] An awareness that the dualistic nature of the entire creation is present within each individual as well as in societal structures, Israel, and the cosmos is evident in the Treatise on the Two Spirits (1QS III, 13–IV, 26). The extent to which this passage is representative of sectarian thinking is the subject of considerable debate.[101] The extent to which divisions within the movement were central to sectarian history in the second and first centuries BCE also occasions debate.[102] In other words there is ample evidence that sectarian claims resulted in contested histories and charges of lack of faithfulness. Calls for endurance such as in the one in the following verse (24:13) would have been a necessary part of sectarian rhetoric.

Within the literature of Second Temple Judaism the term *anomia* is significant in the controversies of 1 Maccabees, where "lawless" is the most attested adjective describing the opponents of Judah Maccabee and his brothers.[103] In the disputes over the manner in which the law is upheld during this era, the characterization of the opponents as "lawless" is one way of discounting their legitimacy. The significance of the law for Jewish identity is one of the major arguments of 1 and 2 Maccabees, presumably establishing the basis for the legitimacy of Hasmonean rule in the Second Temple era.[104] When there are questions about the proper observance of the law, those which have a variant understanding are quickly branded as "lawless." This tendency to brand the opposition with defamatory titles is particularly marked in sectarian rhetoric, here also evident in Matthew. What would "Torah" have meant to a Jewish reader/hearer at the end of the first century CE?

Hindy Najman has proposed a model for how authority is portrayed and understood in these texts. Her concept of "seconding Sinai" begins from an examination of Deuteronomy ("Second Law"). Rejecting any argument that understands Deuteronomy to be a replacement for the Covenant Code and usurping its authority, Najman views it as the exemplar and earliest model of a continuing Mosaic discourse.[105] Within it we find an expanded role for Moses and the reworking of an earlier text in such a manner that it is regarded as an authentic expression of the law already characterized as a Torah of Moses in the Covenant Code.[106] This tradition of biblical law continues to develop, and these subsequent examples of a Mosaic discourse do not supersede the earlier representation in the Pentateuch. Najman's work makes it possible to claim authoritative status for texts such as Jubilees and the Temple Scroll without having to maintain that they replace the legislation of the Pentateuch. In this reappropriation of the text the readers are transported back to Sinai rather than engaged in a heated debate with the original texts. The significance of a text that "seconds Sinai" is the manner in which it reframes the reader's understanding of the original text.[107] In this experience the authority of the legal text rests with the figure of Moses rather than the specific text itself.[108] Hence the manner in which the author of the first gospel models Jesus after Moses is part of the argument for the authoritative nature of his teaching as a lawgiver. It is this lawgiver who takes the readers back to Sinai.

The work attributed to the lawgiver Moses is called "Torah." The consequence of such a proposal is to begin to recognize that its content is not necessarily coterminous with the first five books of the Hebrew Bible. Works such as Jubilees and the Temple Scroll can be regarded as authoritative on the basis of the claim of Mosaic authorship without justifying the innovative legislation proposed as having been derived from the Pentateuch. Already in the account of the reading of the *sēper Tōrat Mōšeh* (book of the law of Moses) by Ezra in the city gate recorded in Neh 8:1–3 we find material not found in the Five Books of Moses. For example, the priestly courses and the division of the Levites mentioned in Ezra 6:18 are referenced in 2 Chr 35:2–5 rather than in the Pentateuch. The sacrificial procedures related to the festivals detailed in Neh 10:31–40 are more extensive than anything found in the first five books. Other instances could also be cited.[109] The same case can be made when we turn our attention to the sectarian texts. In the compositions covering sectarian legislation, the "law of Moses" is used primarily with regard to the oath "to return to the law of Moses," sworn upon admission to the sect. In CD 15:1–16:5 we see that the idea of "return" is based upon the presentation in Deut 31:12–13 and 31:28–30, which are presented as reenactments of the Sinai event: "They shall install him by the oath of the covenant that Moses made with Israel, his word to return to the law of Moses with the entire heart and the entire soul" (CD 15:8–9). The enhanced figure of Moses looms over a representation at Sinai also using the language of covenant renewal from Ezra and Nehemiah. A similar requirement is specified in 1QS V, 7b–20. What is clear is that this oath is not simply a reference to biblical law as found in the Pentateuch, but to all of the sectarian legislation binding upon the person who takes the oath. The person taking the oath is in the same position as the Israelites at Sinai, but the authority of Moses now includes all of the sectarian legislation as well. This legislation has power, being able to turn away the angel Mastema (CD 16:5), and a violation of it is a defilement of the name of God (CD 15:2). Torah refers to authoritative texts attributed to Moses at Sinai rather than to pentateuchal legislation.[110] It is a much more malleable term used to designate authoritative revelation and legislation rather than a mere set text of codified law found in the Pentateuch.

In the discussion of the Beatitudes we already noted two features of significance for the study of these verses. In the comparison with Qumran texts such as 4Q185 and 525, it is evident that Matthew identifies Jesus with wisdom and Torah. Furthermore, apparent connections with sectarian traditions evident in the Qumran materials can be identified in the Beatitudes. Prior to Matt 5:17–20, Jesus has already been advanced as the pivotal figure for the sectarian identity of his followers within the Jewish community. This is the nature of the Mosaic discourse into which the author of Matthew places the figure of Jesus and provides the context for the statement "Do not think that I have come to destroy the law or the prophets; I have come not to abolish but to fulfill" (5:17). Matthew has placed Jesus within this continuing Mosaic discourse; it is his person who now takes persons back to Sinai to hear the authoritative message God gave to Moses. There is no conflict between that message and Jesus; for Matthew this is the message.

The literary implications of this argument for reading the text of Matthew is the recognition that 5:17–20 is one literary unit. The sectarian author of this composition outlines the manner in which this Jewish community, the followers of Jesus, are not "to abolish the law ... but to fulfill." The latter term, *plērōsai,* does not have the sense of completion or of bringing it to some conclusion. For this sectarian Jewish community, the way that Jesus taught is the only manner in which it can be fully kept or observed. That the reference is to the entirety of the law as taught by Jesus is emphasized in v. 19: "Whoever breaks one of the least of these commandments, and teaches others to do the same, will be called least in the kingdom of heaven; but whoever does them and teaches them will be called great in the kingdom of heaven." The gospel writer here advances a sectarian understanding of the law, causing it to stand out from the competing claims of other Jewish groups, and calling for the full allegiance of the members of the community who have gathered around the figure of Jesus.

Lest the readers miss the point, the full polemical force of this entrée into the Mosaic discourse becomes clear in Matt 5:20: "For I tell you, unless your righteousness exceeds that of the scribes and Pharisees, you will never enter the kingdom of heaven."[111] The term "righteousness" stands out because of its absence in the other gospels.[112] In his study of the social world of the Matthean community, J. Andrew Overman argues that *dikaiosunē* is a term selected to designate "the proper behavior and disposition of the members of his community, in contrast to those with whom the community contends."[113] A number of studies have argued for the essential role of the term in the self-understanding of the literature from the Qumran sect.[114] This is true particularly for the legal literature such as the Temple Scroll (11Q19; 11Q20), Jubilees, the Zadokite Documents (CD), and the Community Rule (1QS).

Jesus as the fulfillment of righteousness has already been established in the introductory act of baptism in Matt 3:15: "for it is proper for us in this way to fulfill all righteousness." That it is a desired characteristic of those participating in the coming kingdom of God is highlighted by its mention twice in the Beatitudes (5:6, 10). That it is the term utilized to describe the claims of Jesus on the lives of the followers and the priority of that specific lifestyle is made clear in the connection between vv. 10 and 11. Both are related to the question of persecution expected (or anticipated) by these Jewish followers of Jesus as described in Matthew. By the time we get to Matthew's declaration that Jesus is a contemporary spokesperson for the Mosaic tradition, the designation of its expectations as righteousness has already been firmly established. The Sermon on the Mount takes the reader/listener back to Sinai to understand what God requires of the people of Israel in the first century CE, placing that revelation in the mouth of Jesus Christ and calling it righteousness. This understanding of the Jewish way of life puts this sect in direct conflict with other authorities and viewpoints in the Jewish community.

While Matt 5:20 serves to bridge the statement on the law with the antitheses that follow by placing them in a more specific context, it also provides a framework for them when linked with the conclusion in v. 48. The requirement "Be perfect" concludes the antitheses, the other side of the bracket.[115] The term is particularly prominent in the Damascus Document (D) and its associated MSS, 4Q274 (Tohorot A), and the Temple Scroll (11Q19; 11Q20). In these texts its usage applies to a much broader range of requirements and behaviors than the cultic applications which are central to its biblical exemplar. It would be no surprise to find in literature attributed to the sectaries at Qumran some legal materials within an inclusio bracketed by righteousness and perfection.

The Antitheses and Their Form

For David Daube, Matt 5:21–48 is an illustration, utilizing six examples (or cases) of the general principle advanced in v. 20.[116] For him each of these cases is made up of two sections. In the antitheses the author initially presents a legal formulation rejected by Jesus, followed by his statement of an alternative principle. The author then provides examples—more accurately called focal instances[117]—for each case to illustrate the point of the saying. The issue of divorce in vv. 31–32 is the exception, with no examples added. Earlier commentators who looked to rabbinic materials for an explanation of this form found in these verses an outline of the *šōmea' 'ănî* syllogism (literally "I might hear" or "I might understand"), the purpose of which was to correct what the rabbis considered to be an incorrect inference from a verse.[118] Daube pointed out that this syllogism is most frequently related to a literal, narrow understanding of the biblical statement and suggests that the use of the term *šāma'* (to hear) is related to *ēkousate* (you have heard) in the antitheses. He did note that Matthew had altered the rabbinic form to suit his own purposes.[119] It is not immediately apparent how Matthew could have derived the form of the antitheses from the formal rabbinic type of argumentation.[120] Other options are available for consideration.

While our sources documenting the relationship between the various Jewish groups of the late Second Temple period are rather limited, we do find in what is available to us some evidence of the disputes between the various Jewish "sects." Both sides of a dispute are noted in m. Mak. 1:6, where the disagreement concerns whether false witnesses in capital crimes are put to death only after the execution of the accused: "False witnesses are executed only after the verdict is complete. For the Zadokites say, 'Until he [i.e., the convicted] has been killed, as it is said, "Life for life" (Deut 19:21).' The sages said to them, 'Has it not already been said, "Then you will do to him as he determined to do to his brother" (Deut 19:19).' Then his brother is still alive." The positions of both the Zadokites (or Sadducees) and the sages in this legal dispute are introduced through the use of the plural verb, and the reply of the sages is addressed to their opponents using the plural pronoun.[121] In this instance the position of the Zadokites emphasizing a literal understanding of "life for life" coincides with the literal interpretation of that phrase found in the Temple Scroll and Jubilees, compositions considered to reflect legal traditions at variance with "mainstream" Jewish teaching of the time.[122]

The conflict between the Zadokites (Sadducees) and the Pharisees in m. Yad. 4:6–8 (already discussed above in Chapter 2) begins: "The Zadokites say, 'We denounce you, Pharisees, for *you say*, "The Holy Scriptures render the hands unclean, but the writings of Homer do not render the hands unclean."'" Note the plural form of the direct speech which characterizes this polemical interaction between these two groups. Of particular interest is the second person plural phrase "for you say." In this vivid portrayal of the differences between the two groups, the Zadokites charge the Pharisees using the words "for you say," with "you" in the plural.[123] Noteworthy is the polemical nature of this form—the accusation as a quotation from direct address to characterize the stance of the opponent. What we have here is not a sophisticated mode of argumentation rooted in a specific set of exegetical principles peculiar to a particular scribal group in Second Temple Judaism, such as a proto-rabbinic movement, but rather a style of vigorous argumentation frequently based on popular appeal rather than logic.[124] Also apparent is the lack of attribution to any individual teacher or sage in either the argument or the counter-argument.[125] Even when in m. Yad. 4:8 the opinion is that of a Galilean heretic,[126] an individual, the quotations are still in the plural. The similarity in the construction of these *mišnāyōt* stands in stark contrast to the major portion of the mishnaic legislation which is cited either in an anonymous manner or attributed to one of the Tannaim. In this case we rather find a particular literary style portraying conflicts between groups of Jews attributed in the Mishnah to the Second Temple period, that is, before the destruction of the temple.

In the well-known account of a rabbinic view of the origin of the sects in 'Abot R. Nat. A 5, an even later text, the opinion of the Zadokites is transmitted via a direct quotation and introduced with the plural verb "they say": "So they arose and withdrew from the Torah and split into two sects, the Zadokites and the Boethusians: Zadokites named after Zadok, Boethusians after Boethus. And they used silver vessels and gold vessels all their lives—not because they were ostentatious; but the Sadducees said, 'It is a tradition amongst the Pharisees to afflict themselves in this world; yet in the world to come they will have nothing.'"[127] This of course suggests the debate about the resurrection and after-life. The point may appear obvious, but for our purposes it is important: when the positions of competing groups from the Second Temple period are presented in rabbinic materials, they use plural nouns and verbs, in contrast to the majority of rabbinic literature which rests on arguments between individual sages and rabbis and is cited accordingly. It appears that the rabbinic authors remember the period of the Second Temple as a time of conflict and contest between rival groups within Judea.

In evaluating the literary nature of the argumentation of the antitheses, MMT ("Some of the Works of Torah"—4Q394–99) is the most significant parallel we find in Second Temple literature. The longer central section of this composition deals with issues of Jewish law using an argumentative formula.[128] At least seventeen different topics are dealt with in these listings, sometimes including multiple stipulations.[129] Included are regulations regarding sacrifices and related matters of purity as well as other legislation on the purity of Jerusalem and the temple. The reconstruction of the full form of the argument is difficult, but its typical structure in the fragments begins, "and concerning . . . we consider" (or "we are of the opinion that" or "we say"), followed by a less frequent but interspersed "and you know," always concerned with what "they" do or "their" actions. In other words, all three persons are utilized in advancing these proscriptions.[130] Since the group whose viewpoint is represented in the composition ("we") states in this address to some related group (the "you" of the composition), "You know we separated from the majority of the people" (4Q397 IV, 7), some kind of separation is apparent.[131] There is no evidence that this separation is directly related to the sectarian lifestyles described in D or S materials or in the Greek descriptions of the Essenes. To place the division within a priestly context makes sense in the era prior to the destruction of the temple since the priestly law would have been the dominant "official" view on matters of Israelite identity in Judea and the diaspora, linked of course with the use of Torah as a primary authority.[132] Groups in Second Temple Judaism argued about issues of practice and observance; the priestly law would have been at the center of that discussion. Of primary consideration were issues related to purity and cultic practice.

One remarkable piece of evidence is to be found in 4Q394 8 IV, 5–8 // 4Q396 1–2 II, 6–9: "And concerning liquid streams [*mūṣāqōt*], we say that they are not pure. Liquid streams cannot provide a separation between pure and [im]pure, for the liquid of the stream and of the [receptacle] which receives it are one liquid." In m. Yad. 4:7, already noted above, we find reference to the same issue. The question is whether a stream of liquid being poured from a pure vessel into an impure receptacle becomes impure. In this instance the stance of MMT agrees with the viewpoint of the Zadokites listed in this significant passage from the Mishnah. As in some other instances, MMT agrees with the stance attributed to the Zadokites and opposed by the Pharisees in the literature of the rabbinic tradition. This does not make it a sectarian text; the criteria for such a consideration have been discussed in the previous chapter. It means that we have better evidence for understanding how Jewish groups with distinct identities argued in the Second Temple period. In the case of 4QMMT, we do have evidence that the text was utilized, hence presumably valued, by a sectarian group. Six copies in the Qumran corpus point to a document of some importance to the group. It is within the context of these inter-sectarian debates of first-century Judaism that the form of the antitheses finds its setting.[133] MMT reflects a mode of Second Temple argumentation that relates specifically and directly to the practice of religious law, focusing frequently on issues of cult and purity.[134] In both MMT and the D materials, topics not covered in the Pentateuch are regarded as Torah. The antitheses of Matthew are one more instance of this type of listing of variant teachings which like CD are justified on the basis of a sectarian treatment of biblical law.

The full formula of the antitheses appears in its first exemplar, Matt 5:21–22. When Matthew places the word "you have heard" in the mouth of Jesus he means, "You, as members of my group, as the adherents of my particular Jewish sect, have heard that. . . ." This context of inter- and intra-sectarian debate follows from the second person plural form utilized in the opening term. The next term in this formulaic expression is *errethē* (it was said). Robert Guelich and Robert Gundry interpret the passive mood of this verb as representing the voice of God which here is speaking through the Hebrew Scriptures.[135] What they fail to note is that the particular form of the verb used consistently in the antitheses, *errethē*, is unique to this section in Matthew.[136] The evidence for the hypothesis that the author is using the formula to cite passages from the Hebrew Scriptures is lacking, particularly in view of the fact that all of the citations do not appear in any known versions of the sacred texts. It is conceivable, however, that the author is attempting to make the text read as though it is appealing to the voice of God. While some passages attributed to God in the Qumran texts prefer the passive *kɔtūb* (it is written) to *šeneʾĕmar* (it was said), there is no doubt that attention is regularly called to God via the passive voice.

The blending of the voice of God with specific claims and stipulations attributed to a Sinai tradition has already been argued above. We now find developed in compositions such as Jubilees and the Temple Scroll major legislative innovations placed in the mouth of God and delivered to Moses "on this mount."[137] It is then possible that this other literature which "you have heard," reflecting authoritative teachings and valued by first-century sectarians associated with Qumran, would have been part of the tradition that concerned the author of the first gospel toward the end of the first century. This would have been particularly the case if the author was making a case for a correct understanding within the sectarian movements that struggled for place and identity after the fall of the Second Temple.

The term *archaioi* (ancient, old) is noteworthy in the passages which introduce the two major sections of this literary unit (Matt 5:21, 33). While some commentators note its use in the classical Greek sources,[138] Gerhard Barth sees this as an allusion to the Sinai generation, but in the context of its rabbinic meaning where a continuous tradition of interpretation and legislation is rooted in the revelation of the law on the mountain.[139] In other words, the ancients are those who received the law from God in the wilderness, but they are mentioned here because the rabbis saw their teachings as being in direct continuity with and a part of that revelation. Kurt Schubert already identified a different possibility. He noted that the Hebrew term *riʾšōnîm* (first ones, ancients) is used in CD 1:4 and 4:10.[140] In CD 4:7–10, as well as other places which can be noted in the work, "first" refers either to the founders of the sect or to its earlier membership.[141] In the Community Rule "first" points to the original or initial legislation pertaining to communal life.[142] Elsewhere in the Qumran literature we can look to the book of Jubilees for uses of this term. In Jub. 1:26, as God speaks to Moses, we read the following: "Now you write all these words which I will tell you on this mountain; what is first and what is last and what is to come."[143] The same idea is found in Jub. 1:4: "Moses remained on the mountain for 40 days and 40 nights while the Lord showed him what had happened beforehand and what was to come."[144] What precisely the author of Jubilees had in mind has been a matter of considerable dispute. What is clear is that in the context of Jub. 1 we are speaking of the authority of an additional Torah (or authoritative composition) which God is giving to Moses, having already written "the book of the first law" which the author refers to in 2:24 and 6:22.[145] Given the attribution of this pseudepigraphic composition, "first" is a reference to the original Torah and/or the Sinai experience. The authoritative claim being made here is that this law which appears to be new was also given to Moses at Sinai, part of the original revelation. How do these usages relate to Matthew's use of "first"?

Commentators on the first gospel have correctly identified this term with the revelation at Sinai.[146] Since the particular legal formulations found in some Qumran literature and in some instances attributed to the sect were considered to be the result of revelation,[147] it is plausible to argue that "the first" had a broader range of potential references by the time of the composition of Matthew, including sectarian predecessors who understood that they had received their law from Mount Sinai.[148] The use of the term "first," as in the Qumran texts, is then deliberate and of some significance.[149] This designation indicates that Matthew is engaged in this continuing debate/discussion in Second Temple Judaism concerning the nature and content of the Mosaic revelation. With an authoritative word from Jesus, the author of this gospel is in dialogue and/or dispute with other Jewish movements, some of greater antiquity.

The audacious nature of the clause "but I say to you" lends credence to this argument. Its nature was already noted by David Daube in his comparison of this section of Matthew with what he characterized as a more scholastic rabbinic form: "The tone is not academic but final, prophetic, maybe somewhat defiant. Nor is there any reasoning."[150] Rather than looking to rabbinic formulations, this claim is much closer to the sectarian arguments in which legal formulations are understood to be the result of revelation. The central vehicle of revelation in Matthew is the figure of Jesus, the authoritative spokesperson of the will of God. The first person is employed in these texts to enhance the figure of Jesus as the one who speaks for God, the author of revelation.[151] When the followers of Jesus attempt to practice and understand the Jewish way of life considered acceptable before God, Jesus is the authoritative representative of the will of God. He is able to proclaim the real meaning of what God has revealed for God's people, in contrast to other groups within Second Temple Jewish life that had made or were making similar claims.

The Antitheses and Their Content

Murder (Matt 5:21–26)

The first case begins with a statement from the decalogue, "You shall not murder."[152] However the remainder of the statement in Matthew does not come from the same source: "and whoever murders shall be liable to judgment." Interpreters have either looked to the rabbinic tradition or assumed that the pronouncement was derived directly from Torah.[153] I would suggest that we can find evidence of a more specific trajectory in which this phrase finds explanation in Jub. 4:31–32:

> At the conclusion of this jubilee Cain was killed one year after him. His house fell on him, and he died inside his house. He was killed by its stones for with a stone he had killed Abel and, by a just punishment, he was killed with a stone. For this reason it has been ordained upon the heavenly tablets: "By the instrument with which a man kills his fellow he is to be killed. As he wounded him so are they to do to him."[154]

Cain is given a just (or righteous) punishment for the murder that he committed. This incident provides legal precedent for the ruling of Jubilees that is assumed to be legislation for some body of persons, whether imagined or real.[155] Later in the same work, the shedding of innocent blood is considered one of the major injustices which, along with uncleanness and sexual impurity, brought the flood upon the earth.[156] In this case, as elsewhere in Jubilees, the biblical prohibitions against the eating of blood are linked with the shedding of blood, a connection not made in the biblical materials themselves.[157] As specified in Jub. 21:19, the problem with accepting payment as atonement for killing is that this does not constitute justice and the earth is not purified from the sin of bloodshed by such action. The significance of these texts is enhanced when we recognize a whole host of offenses which require capital punishment, with an even more extensive list in the Temple Scroll.[158] The legal tradition in Jubilees being discussed here is related to the subsequent consideration of *lex talionis* in Matt 5:38–42 discussed below. A similar outlook also appears to be reflected in the hatred of the enemy in Matt 5:43. The statement in 5:21 that is to be refuted finds explanation in a tradition that has been retained and valued by the sectarians associated with Qumran and the broader movements represented in its literature. The Matthean response follows.

"But I say to you that everyone who is angry with his brother shall be liable to judgment; whoever calls his brother worthless shall be liable to the council, and whoever says, 'You fool!' shall be liable to the hell of fire" (Matt 5:22).[159] Most often the three sections of this verse have been interpreted as standing in an increasing order of severity.[160] Both the severity of the infraction and the harshness of the penalty are seen to increase with each new clause. However, *krisei* (judgment) is found already at the end of v. 21 and could refer to capital punishment in both instances.[161] The rhetorical critique here rather emphasizes the importance of collegial relations among the community of disciples, the followers of Jesus. What prompted the author of this gospel to express it in this manner? Among the sectarian compositions of the Qumran corpus, a premium is placed upon the regulation of communal relationships. This is most apparent in 1QS V, 20–VII, 25 but is evident throughout the penal codes.[162] This legislation provides a list of mandated activities arbitrated by a sectarian hierarchy and reinforced with a dualistic ideology. With the critique of Matt 5:22, Matthew appears to be raising questions about that approach to the issues of sectarian lifestyle, laying out a response in 5:23–26 focused upon the topic of reconciliation.

The curious part of Matt 5:23–24 is that the subject is discussed in the context of an altar. One explanation has been to point to b. Yoma 87a, which speaks of the necessity of being reconciled to one's neighbor on the day of atonement.[163] But is that an adequate explanation? I would suggest that the centrality of temple and cult throughout the latter portion of Second Temple Judaism, including the prominent place they held in the imagination and polemics of various deviant Jewish groups, accounts for the allusions in these verses.[164] Their centrality for the religious life and ideology of the Jewish people did not disappear with its destruction. In the Matthean text we witness the possibility that leaving something at the altar would have been a concrete image in the minds of the hearers/readers, even if not a physical reality. The continuing presence of the temple in the minds of a broad spectrum of the Jewish population at the end of the first century seems apparent.

Equally puzzling are the final two verses in this pericope (Matt 5:25–26). This common bit of wisdom, that it is better to be reconciled with your opponent on the way to court than to lose to him in the courtroom, again raises the question of context. Certainly the resolution of issues in rabbinic courts is a part of the later world recorded in the Mishnah and the Talmuds. But what about the readers for whom the gospel of Matthew was written? The court system is no more likely to have survived the destruction of 70 CE than the temple. However, the author here "sees" the courts in operation. In this instance I again appeal to the texts from Qumran. In the Temple Scroll we find the discussion of court procedures and witnesses in the context of the development of biblical law. This court is composed of twelve leaders (or "princes"), twelve priests, and twelve Levites, acting as a check on the arrogance and actions of the king.[165] The multiples of the number twelve suggest the idealized nature of the construction. The mandate to appoint judges who will not pervert justice or take bribes follows immediately after the injunction stressing the holiness of Israel. Should judges pervert justice or take bribes they shall be put to death.[166] When discussing crimes against the state punishable by "hanging on a tree," biblical laws regarding the nature of the hanging itself and the number of witnesses are brought into play.[167] While there may have been some historical events or practices behind some of this legislation, the strict provisions primarily reflect the author's vision for how biblical law should function in idealized (or utopian?) Israel. The resolution of issues via sectarian courts is discussed in considerable detail in CD B and throughout the remainder of the D materials, as well as in various S MSS. In the mind of this author the court system, just like the temple, continues, perhaps in an idealized or utopian form.

The first of the six antitheses advances the group's understanding of what the commandment against murder means. The real meaning of the commandment is to highlight the value and necessity of reconciliation within this Jewish assembly. On the basis of the sociological analysis advanced in Chapter 2 above, this section highlights the element of difference. The claim is advanced within the context of a Jewish society in which the temple and the court system were still alive within the historical memory, including critiques of those institutions and visions of how they could have been better. The author of the first gospel uses the injunction against murder in the biblical legislation to advance a different understanding of that legislation for the Matthean community, a set of deviant practices. It is reasonable to assume on the basis of the evidence from Qumran that other Jewish groups were doing the same thing, advancing practices that they believed reflected a vision for a Jewish future. In addition to critiques of the traditional Jewish institutions of the Second Temple era, deviant groups were in competition with one another for adherents and for control of their communities. Matthew represents one vision for the followers of Jesus who were part of that competition. A similar pattern of interpretation is then evident in the remaining five examples.

Adultery (Matt 5:27–30)

The second of the antitheses begins with the next (seventh, and in some traditions sixth) commandment from the decalogue, "you shall not commit adultery" (Exod 20:13; Deut 5:17). While there is no additional phrase here indicating the envisaged problem, it is reasonable to postulate that in the opinion of the author there is something amiss in the manner in which it is understood. Initially we note the presence of the verb *epithumeō* (desire) in Matt 5:28, which points to the tenth commandment in Exod 20:14 (20:17, LXX) and Deut 5:18 (5:21, LXX).[168] The use of the term would seem to indicate the intention to provide a different viewpoint on the seventh commandment, possibly in the context of the decalogue as a whole.

The most telling clue to the problem underlying this section is to be found in the observation that Jub. 20:4 uses the principle outlined here in Matthew with regard to sexual impurity: "If any woman or girl among you commits a sexual offense, burn her in fire; they are not to commit sexual offenses [by] following their eyes and their hearts so that they take wives for themselves from the Canaanite women, because the descendants of Canaan will be uprooted from the earth." The prior verses provide the context in which Abraham instructs his offspring to keep the way of the Lord, not deviating to the right or the left from the ways which the Lord commanded: "that we should keep ourselves from all sexual impurity and uncleanness; and that we should dismiss all uncleanness and sexual impurity among us."[169] The legislation itself follows from Lev 21:9; however in that text it concerns only the daughter of a priest who commits a sexual offense, without reference to the Canaanites. In Jub. 20:5–6 the giants and the inhabitants of Sodom and Gomorrah are said to have died because of their fornication and impurity. The legislation concerning sexual impurity (fornication) and holiness is also addressed in the stories of Reuben (Jub. 33:18–20) and Judah (Jub. 41:23–28). In Jub. 25:1–10 the wives of Esau are Canaanite, and the problem with them is their sexual impurity and lust.

This concern about sexual impurity is labeled *porneia* in the next antithesis (Matt 5:32). In an examination of this term I have demonstrated that in the sectarian compositions from Qumran, the term is "employed for the purpose of defining activities contrary to the sectarian lifestyle, . . .

most frequently referring to issues of marriage and sexual relations."[170] The injunctions against sexual impurity in the Qumran texts become integrated into the concerns about exogamy and boundary maintenance. This is evident in the second antithesis as well.

The other two verses of the second antithesis (Matt 5:29–30) find their best explanation within a sectarian context. The author here calls for clear choices to be made with regard to allegiance, since the presence of the offending member (or limb) leads to Gehenna. It is apparent that in these verses the legislation regarding adultery is connected with sectarian communal existence and solidarity. While 5:21–26 had been dominated by the issue of the nature of the relationships within this community of the followers of Jesus, this section is concerned with the question of loyalty, boundary maintenance in sociological terminology. While John P. Meier is correct in noting that the eye and the hand are mentioned in these verses because of their sexual connotation,[171] the implications derived from this discussion of sexual behavior extend much further. Within a sectarian analysis we see evidence in this section of separation in addition to difference. The need for exclusive loyalty on the part of the followers of Jesus, their separation from other Jewish groups with other allegiances, is here placed into the context of the biblical legislation regarding adultery. To desire or covet the wife or property of another is equated to a violation of the single-minded devotion required to be a member of the Jesus group. This connection between the violation of sexual norms and sectarian solidarity is characteristic of sectarian legislation at Qumran and some of its predecessors such as Jubilees as well as the principles here spelled out in Matthew. Such a reading of these verses is evident as well in the third antithesis concerning divorce.

Divorce (Matt 5:31–32)

The prohibition of divorce is found in a number of texts in the New Testament: Mark 10:4, 11–12; Luke 16:18; and 1 Cor 7:10–16; in addition to Matt 5:31–32 and 19:3–9.[172] Such evidence suggests connections between persons related to legislation found in the Dead Sea Scrolls and among the early followers of Jesus, since those are the only places where such legislation is attested in Jewish literature of that era. However, such an observation is inadequate to account for what we find in the first gospel. Peculiar to Matthew is the so-called exception clause, *parektos logou porneias* (except in the case of sexual impurity), also *mē epi porneias* (except for sexual impurity) in 19:9. This clause finds its origin in the phrase in Deut 24:1, *'erwat dābār* (something objectionable [NRSV]; something obnoxious [NJPS]),[173] even though the LXX versions read *aschēmon pragma* (indecent deed).[174] In this case we see that the vocabulary utilized in Matthew reflects a direct translation of the Hebrew word employed in these discussions throughout Second Temple and later Judaism, rather than the linguistic choices reflected in the LXX.

The first issue to be addressed is the meaning of the term *porneia,* a translation of the Hebrew term *zənūt,* which is usually rendered "unchastity" or "fornication" in English versions of the text of Matthew, but which I translated above as "sexual impurity." This term is very significant for a number of Qumran texts. The most well-known reference in CD 4:17 points to *zənūt* as the first of the three nets of Belial which are portrayed as three kinds of righteousness. In the following two folios, this theme is developed pointing to the issues of bigamy, incest, and divorce as *zənūt,* giving it a broad definition. The stipulations for entrance into the new covenant in the land of Damascus are that "no one shall profane the kin of his flesh, by keeping apart from *zənūt* according to the statute" (CD 7:1–2). The breadth of this definition is attested in legislation from other D MSS as well as 4QMMT, the Temple Scroll, and other compositions.[175] As already indicated, my conclusion is that the term is "employed for the purpose of defining activities contrary to the sectarian lifestyle elaborated in the various compositions, most frequently referring to issues of marriage and sexual relations."[176] In other words, to "fornicate" means to do things not approved by the legislation for the sectarian lifestyle. It designates a person or activity that was not in compliance with the demands of God for Israel as they were understood and taught within these Jewish sects.

The interweaving of this antithesis with the previous one is apparent: "anyone who divorces his wife, except on the ground of unchastity [*porneia*] *causes her to commit adultery,* and whoever marries a divorced woman *commits adultery.*"[177] The concern about the offending member in Matt 5:29–30 sets the context for the interpretation of the third antithesis. The variety of relational and sexual behaviors that were regarded as violations of biblical law in sectarian teaching are those taught in the gospel of Matthew rather than the ones identified in the texts from Qumran. That objectionable item in Deut 24:1, for which divorce is permissible, is identified here as the violation of the sectarian norms of the group defined in Matthew as the followers of Jesus. As already noted, the prohibition of divorce had been

established for certain groups in the Second Temple era, including followers of Jesus. Matthew translates the tradition already established among
followers of Jesus into the specific context of the Jewish community in
which he writes and this body of followers is located. In this context of
competing allegiances, group solidarity is an important consideration. Violation of important rulings of biblical law as defined by the sect such as
those concerning sexual behavior was the objectionable circumstance under
which divorce was permitted, presumably because the partner had through
her actions in some manner placed herself outside the group. The sociological element of separation is apparent in this strict extension of biblical law
from violations of the sexual code to include the relationships required by
adherence to the sect composed of the followers of Jesus.

Oaths (Matt 5:33–37)

The second section of the antitheses begins with another full citation
of the polemical formula of introduction already discussed above. The issue
presented for discussion is as follows: "You shall not swear falsely but carry
out the vows you have made to the Lord" (Matt 5:33). Swearing falsely in
this case could mean giving false testimony while under oath (i.e., perjury)
or making a vow that is not kept. The second meaning is more consistent with the second half of the statement.[178] The response for the Jesus
sect, however, suggests that you should not swear at all. This is not without precedent in Second Temple Judaism. That is clearly the preference of
Philo, the Alexandrian Jewish philosopher of the first century: "The first of
these other commandments is not to take the name of God in vain; for the
word of the virtuous man, says the law, shall be his oath, firm, unchange-
able, which cannot lie, founded steadfastly on truth."[179] In this instance
Philo proposes that if you do have to swear an oath, then do it on the
health or happy old age of your father or mother if alive, on their memory
if dead. Ben Sira similarly cautions against swearing of oaths using the
divine name.[180] In his description of the Essenes, Josephus notes the prohibition: "Any word of theirs has more force than an oath; swearing they
avoid, regarding it as worse than perjury, for they say that one who is not
believed without an appeal to God stands condemned already."[181] What is
surprising in this description is the initiation procedures immediately following: "But, before he may touch the common food, he is made to swear
tremendous oaths."[182] The description of these oaths then continues for a

full page! They do not swear by the name of God concerning the veracity of their statements; they do, however, swear an extensive oath of allegiance upon full admission to membership in the sect. A similar stance is to be found in CD 15:1–16:2, where the issue is the use of the name of God in the oath. In 1QS V, 8–11 each member of the covenant "shall undertake by a binding oath to return with all his heart and soul to every command-ment of the law of Moses in accordance with all that has been revealed of it to the sons of Zadok." Perhaps 1QS I, 16–II, 18 provides evidence of the content of the binding oath mentioned in 1QS V, 8, in which case it would be based upon the blessings and curses of Deut 27–29, with material from the priestly blessing of Num 6:24–26. While we can cite various texts from the Hebrew Bible which appear to form the background of Matt 5:33 (e.g., Exod 20:7; Lev 19:12; Num 30:3–15; Deut 23:22–24; Ps 50:14),[183] no one pas-sage seems to capture the essence of this saying, particularly with regard to clarifying what the author considered objectionable. In Matt 5:33, the author brings to mind both the covenant of Deuteronomy[184] as well as the holiness regulations of Leviticus in that opening line (Lev 19:12). In this case the purpose of the injunction to the members of the Jesus group is not to contradict the concern about the use of the name of God in oaths, or the arguments about when oaths and vows can be nullified, but as indicated in the next verse the requirement for swearing oaths of allegiance, presumably by members of other Jewish sectarian groups.

The familiar and significant response follows: "But I say to you, 'Do not swear at all'" (Matt 5:34).[185] The explanation placed on the lips of Jesus in 5:34–35 finds its basis in Isa 66:1: "Thus says the Lord, 'The heaven is my throne and the earth is my footstool. Where could you build a house for Me, what place could serve as my abode?'"[186] Just as in instances already identified such as the offensive body members of Matt 5:29–30, the call for the allegiance of the followers of Jesus is simple: "Let your word be, 'Yes, Yes' or 'No, No'; anything more than this comes from the evil one" (5:37). An oath of allegiance is not desirable; a simple declaration is what is re-quired if you want to be a part of the group within the Jewish community that describes itself as followers of Jesus.[187] From the standpoint of this author any additional requirements come from the evil one; that is, they are rooted in sectarian groups who demand oaths of allegiance but who are misguided and lead people astray. The author appears to consider the oaths to be superfluous and deceptive; the Jewish way of life defined by Jesus is considered desirable by God, and oaths are not required. More significant for understanding the apparent intent of the author is the reliance upon Isa 66.

This chapter in which the apostates are called to account and Jerusalem is consoled and vindicated concludes with the gathering of all of the nations and tongues to behold the glory of the Lord and serve him.[188] As will be demonstrated in Chapter 6 below, this is also the concluding vision of Matthew. The vindication of Jerusalem, a not insignificant claim at the end of the first century, and the gathering of the nations will come about because the people of Israel have chosen to live out their lives consonant with the teachings of Jesus Christ rather than other sectarian leaders who attempted to recruit followers in the same communities.

This fourth case in the discussion of Jewish law yields evidence of the complex sociological environment of this sectarian Jewish body. Its formulation suggests some acquaintance with the practices of other sectarian groups as they are described in the S and D MSS from Qumran. Since the practices of the opponents are described as being of the evil one, this section clearly demonstrates the sociological element of antagonism as well as separation. Difference also is evident since the practice of the oath is distinguished from that required by other groups. The best comparable evidence suggests the opposition is another sectarian group or more than one. In this case the boundary marking mechanisms utilized in these verses function in opposition to other sectarian groups as well as whatever authorities existed within the Jewish community. Those opponents are of the evil one since they are opposed to living the Jewish life that would lead to the defeat of the Roman Empire and permit the rule of God as described at the end of Isaiah to emerge. Separation from the Jewish community as a whole is assumed, and in this case separation from opposing utopian groups is also mandated and antagonism toward them is in evidence. All three elements of sect formation can be identified in this instance.

Retaliation (Matt 5:38–42)

Citing a portion of Deut 19:21, "eye for eye and tooth for tooth," this segment cites the legal principle of *lex talionis* applied in legislation in the Hebrew Bible and some Qumran literature as well as later rabbinic texts. The segment from Deuteronomy is cited in 11Q19 (Temple Scroll[a]) LXI, 11–12, applying it to the same legal problem—the treatment of false witnesses in crimes against the person, apparently including capital punishment.[189]

The application of this principle to levels of compensation in non-capital cases is its primary usage in rabbinic literature and a consideration in Exod 21:23–25 and Lev 24:19–20.[190] In post-biblical materials Jub. 4:31–32 provides an instance where the law is applied exclusively to capital punishment.[191] In both the Temple Scroll and Jubilees the listing of capital offenses is rather extensive.[192] The many MSS of Jubilees and their close relationship to much of the legislation found in the Temple Scroll suggest that these instances of harsh penalties were important for the sectarian authors attested in the Qumran scrolls. Just as the opponents in Matt 5:33–37 appeared to hold to a strict sectarian rule based on oaths of initiation, the author in v. 38 is pointing to a fairly harsh penal code which either in actuality or in its ideology characterized some sectarian codes of community behavior.

The response, placed on the lips of Jesus, is rather arresting: "But I say to you, 'Do not resist the evil one'" (Matt 5:39).[193] Many translations fail to note that the term *ponēros* (evil one) used here is the same as the term just employed at the conclusion of v. 37. In this case it finds explanation in the same text as the protasis of Deut 19:19–20: "Thus you will destroy the evil from your midst; those who remain will hear and be afraid, and they will not again do the evil deed such as this in your midst. Nor must you show pity: life for life" (my translation). The popularity of the use of Deuteronomy throughout the Qumran texts, including in the sectarian legislation, is apparent. In this case, it is easy to understand the manner in which sectarian adherents would have read the text of Deut 19:19, "Thus you will destroy the evil one from your midst."[194] In the dualistic structure characteristic of the sectarian literature, the evil one, who can be called Belial, Mastema, the Angel of Darkness, or designated in other ways, is either the ruler of the realm of darkness and evil or its figurative representative.[195] This statement then has to do with sectarian behavior. "Do not resist the evil one" is an injunction addressed to the followers of Jesus concerning their approach to the members of other Jewish sects in their community. The evidence suggests that a literal and harsh interpretation of *lex talionis* rested with other Jewish sectarian groups at the end of the first century or at least Jews that were influenced by those perspectives. The response with a reference to "the evil one" is consistent with such a reading. As might be expected in the development of legal interpretations, the resultant principle is then extended to cover other instances regarding the relationship of members of the Jesus sect with others outside their group, including other Jewish sectarians, members of the Jewish community, leaders of the Jewish community, and soldiers in the Roman army, who could just as well be from other countries of the Roman east as from Italy.

The complex social construction that had already been demonstrated for the prior antithesis above is much in evidence here as well. Separation is evident in the identification of the problematic element in the apodosis and the response within the protasis. The element of difference is inherent within the literary structure of the argument and a necessary part of the rhetorical response articulated here. The sectarian identity of the addressees has been sufficiently established by this point in this didactic construction that it can be presumed and utilized as part of the rhetorical structure. In this case the construction of the argument rests upon the elements of difference and separation. The absence of antagonism is apparent, but since that very feature is proposed as an integral strategy for the maintenance and survival of the sectarian body, this should not be surprising.

The proposed response for these Jewish sectarians is one of acceptance rather than retaliation. Those modern interpreters who read these verses in the context of strategies of non-violent resistance stress that the approach articulated here is one in which identity and community are preserved, rather than power inadvertently ceded to those external authorities that seek to define and control the sectarian dissenters. Examples are offered, all having to do with the negotiation of power relationships at multiple levels including social class (slapping probably has to do with the action of a superior), at the social level (court activity probably related to seizure of property and assets), and at the imperial level (conscription by a Roman soldier).[196] The followers of Jesus are given a strategy that permits the group to retain and develop its distinctive identity. Of course, we advance this statement with the recognition that we cannot identify very specifically the nature of the power structures of communities of Galilee at the end of the first century.[197]

Love of Enemies and Being Perfect
(Matt 5:43–47 and 5:48)

The injunction to love your neighbor as yourself, based on Lev 19:18, is significant for the author of this gospel. In Matt 19:19, it is included in the list of commandments given to the rich man but not in the parallel accounts in the other synoptic gospels. In 22:39 it is listed as the second greatest commandment (see also Mark 12:31 and Luke 10:27). Matthew's understanding of the redefinition of this biblical injunction by other sec-tarian adherents becomes clearer in the next clause, not part of the earlier biblical verse: "and hate your enemies." While one certainly can find allu-sions to hatred of enemies in the Hebrew Bible, Craig Evans is correct in asserting that these instances are relative, if not hyperbolic.[198]

It is no surprise to find that hatred of enemies is developed in an explic-itly sectarian context in Second Temple Judaism. While Davies and Allison admit the possible allusions to literature from Qumran in this interesting adaptation of biblical law, they argue that it cannot be "a polemical barb aimed right at the Essenes" because "this would make 5.43–48 anomalous" since "none of the preceding paragraphs is (presently) directed against the Essenes."[199] Since we have found the latter not to be the case, the sub-stantive material related to this antithesis is of potential significance. Of particular consequence is the introductory material in 1QS I, 9–11: those admitted to the covenant shall walk perfectly and "love all the Children of Light—each commensurate with his rightful place in the council of God—and to hate all the Children of Darkness, each commensurate with his guilt and the vengeance due him from God."[200] Earlier in the column the unidentified addressee is to instruct them "to love everything He chose and to hate everything He rejected."[201] This, of course, is the introduction to the blessings and curses of the initiation ceremony described in the open-ing columns of the rule.[202] Later in the Community Rule we learn, "These are the rules of conduct for the Master in those times with respect to his loving and hating."[203] What God hates is described as the ways of the sons of darkness.[204] In the marked dualism of the Community Rule and the Zadokite Documents, the correct attitude toward those outside the sect is described as one of hatred.

The contrasting response for those sectarians who considered them-selves followers of Jesus is advanced as follows: "Love your enemies and pray for those who persecute you, so that you may be children of your Fa-ther in heaven" (Matt 5:44–45). This response asserts and provides a more specific context (at least rhetorically) for themes already identified as basic to the identity of this sectarian group. We recall that the peacemakers will be called children of God (5:9) and that the kingdom of heaven belongs to those who are persecuted for righteousness' sake (5:10). The practice ex-pected of the sectarians following Jesus is listed, with the result that they are recognized as the children of God, that is, living a life in accord with what the Divine finds pleasing. This assertion in the response completes the sentence, as has been recognized in the CEB translation. In contrast to the reading of the NRSV, the Greek term *hoti* (for) in v. 45 then introduces a parenthetical sentence explaining the activity of God, rather than an explanation for or result of the followers of Jesus being called "children of your Father in heaven." That phrase already contains the result for a sectarian group. What does God do? "He makes his sun rise on the good, and he sends rain upon the righteous and the unrighteous." The Jewish sectarians are to love their enemies and pray for their persecutors *because* God loves both the good and evil, the righteous and the unrighteous. This response is reinforced in vv. 46 and 47 using the examples of the tax collectors and the gentiles.[205]

As in the previous two antitheses, the sociological element of separation is assumed and the element of difference is advanced in the practice recommended for these sectarian adherents. The element of antagonism is implicit in the apodosis of the opening statement, where the other sectarians are those who live by hate. In the multicultural context of late first-century Galilee, the Jewish sectarian is supposed to recognize the manner in which God has expressed love for all. This attitude stands in contrast to that of the Pharisees and scribes as well as other Jewish sectarians. Lest readers miss the point, he returns to the use of the root *perisseuō* in Matt 5:47, "what *more* are you *doing* than others?" bringing to mind "*exceeds* that of the scribes and Pharisees" in v. 20. By loving their enemies, these sectarians exceed the righteousness of the scribes and Pharisees.

The chapter concludes with the verse on perfection: "Be perfect, therefore, as your heavenly Father is perfect" (Matt 5:48). There is debate as to whether this verse is part of the last antithesis or whether it concludes the section as a whole.[206] While the tie with the Father in heaven in v. 45 is apparent, we already noted that this connects with the Beatitudes (vv. 9, 10) as well. As noted above, the most significant literary feature of this verse is the manner in which it functions as the bracket that concludes this section, the other side of the inclusio indicated by the key term "righteousness" in v. 20—a term also discussed above. *Tāmîm* (perfect) is a very important leading term in the legal and communal discipline texts of the Qumran corpus, appearing primarily in the sectarian compositions, but also common in some other texts such as the Temple Scroll, 4Q525 (Beatitudes), and 4Q510–11 (Songs of the Sage).[207] Perfection is one way of describing the holiness by which the sectarians are set apart in accordance with the divine will. In Matthew the sectarian identity of these followers of Jesus is affirmed utilizing vocabulary used by sectarian movements in the first century. Other sectarian Jews also had their own set of practices, such as the festal calendar at Qumran that led them to observe the festivals at different times. Outlined here is the particular manner in which followers of Jesus gave expression to their understanding of righteousness and perfection.

Conclusion

The Sermon on the Mount is the first of five orations which could be said to give the gospel of Matthew its distinctive character. They certainly are the dominant feature which differentiates it from the other two synoptic gospels. The Sermon is the longest of these orations and the first. Hence it is the key to an understanding of the purpose of the composition. Located toward the beginning of the work, it identifies Jesus as the authoritative spokesperson for the will of God by patterning him after Moses. Thus the Sermon constitutes a claim to be an authoritative statement of what God desires of those who wish to serve God, in this case those sectarian Jews who constituted themselves as followers of Jesus at the end of the first century CE.

The Beatitudes are the opening expression within the Sermon of that sectarian identity. Comparisons with the vocabulary of sectarian identity in the scrolls from Qumran suggest the presence of related traditions in the Matthean community. Comparison with earlier models of macarisms in Second Temple literature, particularly 4Q525, suggests an attempt to identify Jesus as law-wisdom. The sectarian identity of these Jews is clearly established in this initial section of the Sermon. The three elements characteristic of sectarian groups are all implicit in this identification: difference in the sense that they will be engaged in activities regarded as deviant by other Jews; antagonism in the expected response of defamation and persecution by other groups; and separation in their claim to the exclusive authority of Jesus as the representative of the will of God to the exclusion of other sources of wisdom from the Divine.

The place of Torah in Jewish life is a subject that must be addressed by any sectarian Jewish group in the Second Temple era since their allegiance to the Jewish community (and nation?) would have been continuously questioned. Torah as central to the Jewish nation is apparent in the books of the Maccabees, and those who do not support the Hasmonean state are said to be among the "lawless." However it can be demonstrated from the literature of that period that Torah was used to designate the revelation to Moses at Sinai rather than the specific words of the Pentateuch, so legislation found outside of those books is already affirmed as Torah in Ezra-Nehemiah, Jubilees, and the Temple Scroll. Sectarian legislation in the S and D compositions is also given that designation. So the concept of Torah remains a more malleable conception at the end of the Second Temple era than when it begins to develop shortly thereafter within the orthodoxies that ultimately define catholic Christianity and Rabbinic Judaism. The author of Matthew engages Jesus in the process of "seconding Sinai" by putting into his mouth the authoritative practices that should be followed by this sectarian group. The teaching of Jesus permits the sectarians to understand how their manner of Jewish practice is based on authoritative revelation that justifies their departures from the practices of other Jewish groups.

The antitheses of the Sermon constitute the author's attempt to provide "case law" for the authoritative revelation to which this group is privy. In the mouth of Jesus are found principles and instances demonstrating how this group differs from the remainder of the Jewish people (or "nation"—*ethnos*). Within these antitheses we find evidence that the author of Matthew is countering certain practices and attitudes that can be identified within the sectarian compositions of the scrolls from Qumran. There are evident hints of a sectarian assembly that has a more open attitude to interactions with the community(ies?) within which it is located. Examination of the antitheses demonstrates a very complex social construction of the Jewish community in which the author is advancing the claims of the first gospel. All three elements of sect formation identified in the study of new religious movements can be identified. The element of antagonism is the least apparent in this section, perhaps since that has been established already in the fundamental identity of the group exhibited above in Matt 5:10–12. Separation also is already established in the Beatitudes, so the antitheses are that section which develops the element of difference, the manner in which the behaviors and practices of this group differ from the remainder of the Jewish people and groups within it.

4 Sectarian Wisdom

There are only three references to *sophia* in the first gospel.[1] In the LXX this is the Greek equivalent of the term *ḥokmah* (wisdom). This fact alone fails to account for the significance of the figure of wisdom in this composition. The passage usually regarded as the most consequential wisdom statement in the work, Matt 11:25–30, does not even contain the term. In addition, we find two references to the term *sophos* (wise).[2] Its importance as a central theme in the book has been the subject of much dispute. While M. Jack Suggs brought the subject to the center of Matthean studies and argued for its centrality in the composition,[3] the major monograph by Celia Deutsch noted that "use of the Wisdom metaphor is not central to Matthew's thought."[4] Anthony Saldarini suggested that "he leaves wisdom in the background to enrich and interpret his portrait of Jesus."[5] Deutsch and Saldarini accepted the identification of Jesus with wisdom established particularly in chapter 11 but did not regard it as a significant factor in determining the literary or social context for the work as a whole. While it has frequently been argued in recent scholarship that Jesus was identified with wisdom within this composition,[6] some have accepted the identification but argued that it was a minor piece in a larger argument.[7] Such is the case for Dale Allison when he accepts the argument for the identification in Matt 11:19 and 11:25–30 but sees the primary identification for Jesus to be with Moses.[8]

The meaning of wisdom in this composition also has been debated. While some saw it as Torah, others identified it with any of the varieties of hypostatization that were characteristic of the Hellenistic world, sometimes of a more mystical type. Others related it to some elements of

Gnosticism. Of particular significance for our present study of Matthew is the cache of wisdom compositions from the Qumran corpus that became available after 1991 and have been the subject of continuous research since that time. The resultant transformation of our understanding of wisdom in Palestinian texts during the first century CE permits a new reading of this Matthean material.

Wisdom in the Qumran Texts

The relative absence of the term *ḥokmah* (wisdom) in the first Cave 1 texts has frequently been noted. In my survey article on the first fifty years of research on wisdom in the Qumran texts, I pointed to the manner in which it had been regarded as relatively absent from the corpus.[9] When James Sanders published the Psalms Scroll from Cave 11 in 1965, he noted that "no work has been done, to my knowledge, on Wisdom thinking generally in Qumrân literature."[10] This reflected the evaluation attributed to him that "the Sapiential is not a Qumran characteristic."[11] While noting the presence of wisdom vocabulary in some documents such as 1QS and 1QH, he attributed their presence to the continuing impact of liturgical material such as the canonical psalms rather than as evidence of a wisdom tradition. His claims reflected the evaluation of the majority of scholars of Qumran literature concerning the question of wisdom in the corpus at the conclusion of the first two decades of research.

In that same survey I observed that the significance of wisdom and knowledge had been noted in many publications of the first scholars who did the initial translations and analyses of the Cave 1 materials from Qumran. Note, for example, the manner in which Millar Burrows in his extensive survey provides a summary of the use of the term "knowledge" in those first scrolls, including the Damascus Document, Pesher Habakkuk, the Manual of Discipline, and the Thanksgiving Hymns, highlighting both the nominal form and the verb "to know."[12] Earlier he had noted, "'Knowledge' is one of the prominent words of DCD and it is used primarily with reference to the divine law."[13] In his analysis of the use of the word *da'at* (knowledge), W. D. Davies noted eschatology and ethics as features which distinguish the Qumran materials from the perspectives of Gnosticism. He highlighted the connection with law in the Qumran literature, noting that the Gnostics "seem to have placed a greater emphasis upon the concept of knowledge, whatever its exact connotation, than the more strictly Jewish circles, whose literature across the centuries is preserved in the Old Testament."[14] In noting the amount of attention focused on the relationship of this new body of literature to Gnosticism, we must remember that the most frequent translation of "knowledge" in the LXX is *gnōsis*.[15] Both of these early students of these materials distinguished them from Gnosticism upon the basis of a connection with biblical law which they saw demonstrated in the texts.

The study of wisdom in the Qumran corpus went through a transformation beginning in 1991 with the open access to and subsequent publication of all of the fragments held by the Israel Antiquities Authority. The identification of fragments of a number of wisdom compositions not only extended the breadth and scope of the materials available, it also permitted the older materials to be read in a different manner. The study of this material is ongoing. The longest wisdom text with multiple copies attested in hundreds of fragments, which has been at the center of this Qumran research, is Instruction. With this publication, copies of a significant document which regularly used the term *ḥokmah* in a manner familiar to us from the book of Proverbs, but clearly independent of the biblical wisdom materials, was suddenly available. Such a recognition impelled a reexamination of the question of wisdom in the Qumran texts.[16] The unique character of this composition has been adequately described in both scholarly and more popular literature.[17] This extraordinary text contains a combination of instructional material similar to that of wisdom materials found in biblical books such as Proverbs and Ben Sira, and eschatological material rooted in part in Hebrew prophecy, best known to us previously from the books of Enoch. Universal judgment is a theme throughout a number of the fragments. The sons of truth and the people of the spirit of flesh represent the human conflict. The expectation of an epoch of truth is developed in the composition; references to heavenly hosts round out the picture of the cosmos. Gaining an understanding of the nature and lot of humankind is the task of the junior sage who is the object of its instruction. That same junior sage is also given counsel concerning the problems of indebtedness, how to retain your dignity when in the service of someone of higher station, the treatment of your wife, the obligations you have for the reproof of your neighbor, your level of responsibility with regard to pledges made by your wife, and an injunction to honor your parents. Prior to the discovery of these fragments, scholars of the history of Second Temple Judaism did not even consider the possibility of literature of this nature.

At least eight and possibly more copies of this composition can be identified among the Qumran fragments.[18] Such a large number of copies suggests extensive usage, perhaps that this text was regarded as "'authoritative' or even considered 'canonical.'"[19] However, it "does not reflect a specific or closed community like that of Qumran, nor an earlier quasi-sectarian group."[20] Most students of Instruction have proposed a date of composition somewhere in the second century BCE.[21] I am among those who consider an early second century BCE date prior to the Maccabean revolt most likely. Torlief Elgvin posits the first quarter of the second century BCE but also is open to the late third century BCE as a possibility.[22] Note that this places Instruction at the same time as portions of 1 Enoch.[23] Elgvin points to the lack of any hints of the Maccabean crisis or of the eschatological urgency that appears to have emerged as a more prominent element in Jewish life after the events in the reign of Antiochus IV Epiphanes (175–164 BCE) as evidence for a date of composition prior to that era. I concur with this evaluation of the date of composition.

It appears best to regard Instruction as a transitional composition between the biblical wisdom books and the emphasis on wisdom and knowledge found in major sectarian compositions of the Qumran corpus. I employ an examination of vocabulary items concerning wisdom, knowledge, and cognate terms as seen in the following table to begin to describe these developments.

A comparison of the usage of these terms in different configurations provides the very rough outlines of a demonstrable pattern.[24] Over half of the appearances of the term *ḥokmah* in the Hebrew Bible are found in the three wisdom books, Proverbs, Job, and Ecclesiastes. These 88 references suggest its importance for those compositions.[25] Within the entire Qumran corpus of fragments of over seven hundred non-biblical compositions it is found only 60 times.[26] Employing a somewhat arbitrary but very narrow definition of sectarian texts, only 15 references to the term *ḥokmah* appear.[27] When compared with the three other terms analyzed here, the different proportion in the use of this term "wisdom" when compared with "knowledge" and other cognate terms is apparent.

The interest of the early students of the scrolls centered on the term "knowledge."[28] When the same delineation of texts as above is used, only 54 references in the three wisdom books can be identified. However within the whole Qumran corpus there are 172 references, 59 of those in the sectarian texts. So the total number of references is almost three times as many as

Wisdom Vocabulary in the Qumran Texts

Term	Wisdom Texts of HB	Qumran Texts	Sectarian Texts	Instruc- tion and Mysteries	1QS	1QH[a] (Recon)
ḥokmah (wisdom)	88	60	15	18	4	12
da'at (knowledge)	54	172	59	11	18	34
'emet (truth)	13	323	163	49	43	71
sekel (insight)	7	62	32	7	10	16
binah (understanding)	23	93	25	25	2	19

in the wisdom texts of the Hebrew Bible, and a higher proportion are to be found in the sectarian texts. The word "knowledge" has become one of two central terms for the designation of the wisdom and understanding central to sectarian ideology, as noted already by Davies over a half century ago.[29] The most remarkable evidence concerns the other term central to sectarian self-understanding, "truth." It is found only 127 times in the entire Hebrew Bible, but not primarily in the three wisdom books, where it appears only 13 times. The Qumran MSS contain 323 references, 50 percent of them in the sectarian texts. "Knowledge" and "truth" are the two most significant terms used to convey the central concepts of sectarian life and belief. Similar but less dramatic changes in the use of "insight" are apparent. The term "understanding" is more consistent across the spectrum of literatures included above, with some increase in sectarian usage also apparent when compared with "wisdom."

This examination has demonstrated a significant shift in vocabulary from the biblical wisdom texts to the sectarian compositions.[30] Note furthermore that a similar distribution of terms is apparent in 1QS. This is also true for 1QH[a] (Thanksgiving Hymns); however in this case binah (understanding) is more prominent than sekel (insight).[31] The manner in which sekel and 'emet have replaced ḥokmah and to a lesser extent da'at (knowledge) as the major terms for this word group is apparent. The use of the term "replace" in this instance points to the fact that the authors of these compositions lived within a tradition which valued and was quite cognizant of the literature of the Hebrew Bible. It is difficult to determine whether this change was an intentional shift on the part of the authors or reflects the vocabulary current at the time of writing. The question now is whether a broader context for the apparent changes already noted can be identified.

It already has been demonstrated above that Instruction is a major "wisdom" composition within the Qumran corpus. The work most closely identified with Instruction in terms of literary content is Mysteries.[32] If we look at the frequency of the terms just discussed in those two compositions and compare those results with the previous analysis, some interesting trends can be identified. We find 18 references to the term "wisdom" in those two traditions, 30 percent of the total appearances in the entire Qumran corpus. This suggests some continuity with the biblical wisdom works, more adequately represented here than in the sectarian compositions. The other significant indicator, "knowledge," has only 11 references in Instruction and Mysteries, appearing here in a proportion similar to the biblical wisdom texts when compared with "wisdom." However, it appears four times more frequently in the sectarian texts than "wisdom." The most prominent term within the sectarian texts, "truth," appears in Instruction and Mysteries much more frequently than "wisdom." A trajectory can be identified in which Instruction and Mysteries have a connection with the biblical wisdom tradition but also reflect the developments within the semantic range characteristic of these sectarian texts. These earlier compositions in the Qumran corpus form a bridge between the earlier biblical traditions and the manner in which the sectarian compositions deal with the continuation of wisdom.

Within the sectarian texts wisdom—that is, knowledge, truth, insight, and understanding—is available only to the sectarians.[33] The continuing influence of the sapiential tradition can be observed in these texts.[34] Note the introduction to the Treatise on the Two Spirits, a central ideological statement in the Community Rule:

> A text belonging to the Instructor, who is to enlighten and teach all the Sons of Light about the character and fate of humankind: all their spiritual varieties with accompanying signs, all their deeds generation by generation, and their visitation for afflictions together with eras of peace. All that is now and ever shall be originates with the God of knowledge. Before things come

to be, He has ordered all their designs, so that when they do come to exist—at their appointed times as ordained by His glorious plan—they fulfill their destiny, a destiny impossible to change.[35]

The *maskil* (instructor or sage) is to give instruction regarding the nature of world history which was ordained prior to creation. This history is described in terms of the two spirits in which humankind can walk, the spirits of truth and falsehood. All of this originated from the God of knowledge, the earliest known reference to that designation in extant Jewish literature. These two realms are ruled, respectively, by the Prince of Light and the Angel of Darkness. Developed at length are the characteristics of those persons who are ruled by each spirit as well as the consequences of each one's rule. The two spirits are regarded as equals, their contrasting realms are also described using the terms "truth" and "folly." However then, "in His mysterious insight and glorious wisdom God has countenanced an era. . . . Then shall truth come forth in victory. . . . At the time of the appointed judgment truth shall be decreed. By His truth God shall then purify."[36] It is through the language of knowledge, insight, and truth that the dualistic conflict and its inevitable outcome is described in this text. To be wise is to have been among the exclusive recipients of these perspectives: "Thereby He shall give the upright insight into the knowledge of the Most High and the wisdom of the angels, making wise those following the perfect way."[37] Finally in the conclusion of this section, "He has granted them [i.e., the two spirits] dominion over humanity, so imparting knowledge of good [and evil]."[38] To know is to be a member of the group to whom knowledge has been given and to give exclusive attention to that body. A similar viewpoint can be found in the Thanksgiving Hymns.

Expressing gratitude to God for what God has bestowed upon lowly humankind, the Thanksgiving Hymns, using the language of knowledge and insight, describes how to understand the nature of the world and the manner in which it functions. As in 1QS this is rooted in the order of creation. After describing all of this the author states: "In the mysteries of your insight [you] apportioned all these in order to make known your glory. [But how i]s a spirit of flesh to understand all these things and to gain insight in [. . .] great [. . .]?"[39] This viewpoint pervades the composition: "Your compassion is for all of the children of your good favor. For you have made known to them the secret counsel of your truth, and given them insight into your wonderful mysteries."[40] The Damascus Document is addressed to

those who know and understand: "And now, listen, all who know righteousness and understand the deeds of God."[41] Since the composition outlines
the history and explains the stances of the sect on a number of controver-
sial subjects, perhaps they still have a lot to learn. As adherents who have
entered into the new covenant they are in a position to learn: "And now,
children, listen to me that I may uncover your eyes to see and to understand
the deeds of God."[42] Again, membership is necessary in order to acquire the
desired knowledge of the nature of creation and the history of the world,
to penetrate the "esoteric knowledge" given by God. Such is the sectarian
understanding of wisdom.

A similar trajectory is apparent in the development of the figure of the
maskîl (sage or instructor).[43] This term receives limited but significant mention in Instruction, occurring as both noun and participle in that composition. The apprentice nature of the addressee, the "man of discernment," is
highlighted in 4Q417 1 I; in line 25 he is referred to as the "son of a sage." The
sage as teacher is found in 4Q418 238, 1 and 4Q418 81+81a, 17: "Gain greatly
in understanding and from the hand of every sage grasp even more." In this
document the sage is the teacher, essentially the guide into the "mystery of
existence" in which the "son of discernment" gains knowledge of the basic
issues of theology and history. Their mention is rather infrequent in these
fragments, but their role with regard to the instruction of the addressee is
crucial. A similar portrait is evident in 4Q421 (Ways of Righteousness[b]) 1 II,
10, 12. However no authoritative role is evident within these compositions.

The role of the sage is much more definitive in some of the sectarian
texts. In the S texts the sage provides the basic instruction about the nature
of the community, its origins and theology, as outlined in the opening of the
Treatise on the Two Spirits, quoted above. However he also has responsibility for the admission of new members into sectarian membership and the
ranks of the sectarian hierarchy. The role of the "sage" receives emphasis in
1QS IX, 12–X, 5, a section that begins, "These are the statutes for the sage."
As summarized by Carol Newsom, he is "concerned with the formation of
the community, both through his admission and regulation of members
and through his instruction in the knowledge that the community shares
in common, yet that separates it from outsiders."[44] His focus is the life of
the sectarian community: "He should conceal his own insight into the Law
when among perverse men. He shall save reproof—itself founded on true
knowledge and righteous judgment—for those who have chosen the way,

treating each as his spiritual qualities and the precepts of the era require. He shall ground them in knowledge."[45]

Sections of the Thanksgiving Hymns associated with the sage have similarities with the language and themes related to this figure in 1QS, and the speaker of 1QHa VI, 28–32 attributes to himself the same role of establishing the hierarchical order of the community as is ascribed to him in 1QS IX, 14–16.[46] John Strugnell points out that the frequent use of the sage as author in Qumran texts (here he means sectarian texts) and the absence of the sage as author in biblical texts helps to establish the common sectarian provenance of these compositions.[47] This rather general designation of a person who teaches and instructs in Instruction is developed into a specific position and role in sectarian life. The office fills a role consistent with what is outlined in Instruction, but it now has an authoritative place in the sectarian structure. In other words, the description of persons who earlier are described as having the role of mediating wisdom, knowledge, truth, and understanding for those interested in pursuing it changes as the office of the sage is developed into an official instructional and gate-keeper role.

On the basis of an examination of trends in vocabulary usage we have identified a trajectory of wisdom literature within Second Temple Judaism which explains its prominent presence among the sectarian compositions. This demonstrates the importance of wisdom and knowledge for the Judeans of this period as a vocabulary which assisted them to deal with the changes in religio-cultural identity as they encountered the various imperial powers. The extent to which the Hellenistic environment provided the context for the development of these trends is a question beyond the scope of this investigation. An outgrowth of these challenges was the development of sectarian self-understandings, one of which is represented in the texts from Qumran. These options are part of Jewish life at the end of the first century CE, when the gospel of Matthew was written.

Sectarian Wisdom in Matthew

The term *sophia* appears only once in Matt 11, but it is a dominant theme throughout the chapter and culminates in the crucial statements in its conclusion, vv. 25–30.[48] In 11:19 in reply to the charge that the Son of Man is "a glutton and a drunkard, a friend of tax collectors and sinners," Jesus responds with the statement, "Yet wisdom is vindicated by her deeds." This is usually regarded as a Matthean rendition of the statement in Q,

"Nevertheless, wisdom is vindicated by all her children," found in Luke 7:35.[49] Whichever is more original, the Matthean formulation is indicative of the approach to this question found throughout the composition. The identification of Jesus with wisdom is presumed in this passage, but it also connects to the evidence concerning the coming reign of God. Within this chapter the reference to the "deeds" points back to Jesus's response to the disciples of John the Baptist. As reported in Matt 11:2, John has heard of the "deeds" of Jesus. When his disciples are instructed to inquire whether he is the figure to inaugurate the messianic era, they are told to report back what they have seen and heard, that is, the deeds they have witnessed. These are evidence of the beginning of the reign of God (cf. Isa 26:19; 29:18; 35:5–6; 42:18; 61:1).

It is interesting to note that the explicit identification of Jesus with wisdom in Matt 11:19 is made utilizing the title of "Son of Man." Given the context in which the term is used in this chapter with regard to the coming reign of God, it is reasonable to accept Luz's interpretation of the use of the title here as referring to the future role of Jesus as judge, based primarily upon a specific reading and subsequent interpretation of Dan 7:13–14.[50] The coming messianic era—including a decisive role for Jesus within those unfolding events—is here linked with wisdom. Of course, throughout Matthew the figure of Jesus is even more explicitly linked with the title "Son of God," and that identification is also presumed in this verse. As such, he is the authoritative representative of God, here equated with wisdom. The connection between wisdom and deeds can be found in Jewish texts from well before the time of the composition of Matthew.

In the introductory section of Instruction we find repeated reference to deeds (4Q417 [Instruction[c]] 1 I, 3–13):

and consider [the mystery of existence and the deeds of old, for what was and what will be] [4][with them ... for]ever [... for what [5]is and for what will be with them ...] in all[...]every de[ed ...] [6][... day and night meditate upon the mystery of ex]istence and search daily and then you will know truth and perversity, wisdom [7][and foll]y [...] dee[ds] in all their ways with their assignment for all epochs forever and the assignment [8]for eternity. Then you will know the difference between the [go]od and [evil according] to [their] deeds. For the God of knowledge is the base of truth and with the mystery of existence [9]He spread out her foundation and her deeds. [... with all wis]dom and with all ... He fashioned her. The dominion of her deeds [10]is for a[l]l [... He ex]pounded for their under[st]anding all of her d[eed]s, how to walk [11]in [the inclination of] their understanding. He expounded [. . .] and with the disposition for understanding present, [the sec]rets of his intention are made kn[own] [12]with those who walk perfectly [in all] His [d]eeds. These things diligently seek daily and consider carefully [al]l [13]their consequences. Then you shall know the glory of [His] stren[gth with] the mysteries of [His] wonde[rs and the mig]ht of His deeds.[51]

At the outset we notice how the "deeds of old" are equated with the elusive mystery of existence, which encompasses an understanding of the past, present, and future, that is, knowing the deeds of old is to know the past. To know "truth and perversity, wisdom and folly" is to understand the nature and destiny of deeds, hence the ability to discern good and evil. This is not merely human history since the "deeds" encompass the acts of creation and the structure of the universe (ll. 8–10). Based upon an understanding that the deeds of creation establish the structure of the universe, the secrets of the Divine can then be apprehended and humankind then knows how to proceed in life, hopefully to walk in perfection. There is a direct connection between the deeds of creation and the ethical life God desires of humankind. In that sense the fate of these "deeds" in the arena of human activity is predetermined. In the following lines we then see the outcome: "These things diligently seek daily and consider carefully [al]l their consequences. Then you shall know the glory of [His] stren[gth with] the mysteries of [His] wonde[rs and the mig]ht of His deeds" (ll. 12–13). Such a conception is evident throughout the sectarian texts from Qumran, including the Damascus Document, the Community Rule, the Thanksgiving Hymns, and the War Scroll, in which *ma'ăśîm* (deeds) is ubiquitous. Gaining an understanding that a future era of glory in which the wonder and might of the deeds of God will be realized because of the diligent pursuit of these issues—that is, getting the deeds of the human hearer of this message in consort with the deeds of the universe, its structure and fate—is to know that "wisdom is vindicated by her deeds." The deeds of Jesus, Son of Man and Son of God, indicate the coming reign of God. Wisdom is the recognition that this is occurring even though wisdom itself is also related to the agency that brings this about. Of course, the larger portion of the present generation is not wise and does not recognize the "deeds" of the reign of God in either John or Jesus.

The reproach of Matt 11:20–24 begins with the following words: "He began to reproach the cities in which most of his deeds of power had been done." This citation indicates a literary connection to the beginning of the chapter: "he went on from there to teach and proclaim his messages in their cities."[52] Within those two verses, we have already noted the brackets of vv. 2 and 19 with reference to the "deeds."[53] Note that in these two verses the term is *ergon,* whereas in v. 20 it is *dunamis* (mighty act). The discourse on Jesus as wisdom and the reign of God, signaled already by John the Baptist, was directed to and rejected by the cities around the northern edge of the sea of Galilee, the center of Jesus's ministry in Matthew. The cities Chorazin, Capernaum, and Bethsaida[54] are all in close proximity to one another, the apparent homes of a number of the disciples. The "mighty acts" done in those cities may also be a reference back to the accounts of Matt 8–9.[55] In contrast to Matthew, Luke places this saying in the context of the instruction for the seventy who are sent out and can anticipate rejection (10:12–16). The rejection of wisdom is a theme identified in apocalyptic literature. In Bar 3:9–4:4 we find the account of the rejection of wisdom by Israel and its consequences, presumably in an account that would predate the composition of Matthew. This rejection has placed them in the land of their enemies as well as in Hades. In 1 En. 42 wisdom attempted to dwell with humankind but, finding no home, returned to heaven and dwelt with the angels, thereby creating room for iniquity to take her place. James VanderKam suggests this is a negative counterpoint to Ben Sira 24:7–11 in which wisdom finds a resting place in Zion.[56] The rejection of Jesus as wisdom is the point of the Matthean placement of these sayings.

While commentators emphasize the significance of Sidon and Tyre in biblical prophecies of doom for the interpretation of these references, it would appear that this is rather a more contemporary reference to those cities outside of the immediate area of Galilee, still in the Roman province of Syria and the centerpieces of the older Phoenician cultural and commercial enterprises on the Mediterranean.[57] These are cities that still play a jurisdictional role for Hyrcanus and the Judeans at the time of Julius Caesar[58] and which benefited from the largesse of Herod the Great, who extended his goodwill to cities outside of his jurisdiction through building projects.[59] For local Jews in Galilee these cities still would have been symbols of imperial power and perhaps even cultural influence, even if they did not have direct political control over the area. Of course, the biblical references will have provided a framework for the theological interpretation of their present status. Thus they are not simply evidence of a Jewish-gentile division in the book of Matthew as frequently assumed;[60] they are symbols of foreign political and cultural power. The strength of the indictment can be seen in the use of the woe-oracle that is used in the prophetic literature for the condemnation of the wicked and the foolish, as well as the wealthy who oppress the poor and pervert justice.[61] In using them as an example Matthew, through the words of Jesus, is insulting those who would see in Tyre and Sidon the historical symbols of their own oppression and victimization. With such an indictment their lack of knowledge of the true activity of God is contrasted not simply with gentiles but with foreign rule and dominance in contrast to the reign of God. It rather suggests the conversion of Nebuchadnezzar in Dan 4:34–37 as an analogy, when he recognizes who really is sovereign of the world.

In the final six verses of the chapter, Matt 11:25–30, there is no mention of the term, but the utilization of the imagery of wisdom is evident throughout. In vv. 25–27 the words of Jesus are similar to those used elsewhere to describe the reception of wisdom. This reception stands in stark contrast to the rejection of vv. 20–24 already discussed. This section begins, "You have hidden these things from the wise and intelligent and have revealed them to infants [nēpiois]." This is familiar from the biblical wisdom traditions where Proverbs is addressed to the pata'im (simple) and the na'ar (youth).[62] Of course, in Proverbs the goal is to get beyond that state. Here that goal is recast in a manner similar to other Jewish groups which spoke of a wisdom that is not universally accessible and is not acquired through merit or labor.[63] Deutsch makes the connection of "infants" to the 'ānāwîm language, sometimes translated as "poor," as related to the self-identification of Jesus as tapeinos (humble) and praus (meek) in v. 29.[64] An understanding of wisdom as revelation that is available to those who understand themselves as the poor, the humble, and the meek takes us back to the initial macarisms of the Sermon on the Mount (5:3–5) and the other sectarian identifications we have discussed based upon the evidence from the Qumran scrolls.[65] As noted in that prior discussion, this identification as the poor, meek, and humble was significant for the sectaries of the Dead Sea Scrolls as well as for the followers of Jesus in the first gospel. These Jews addressed in Matthew are the "children" that become the object of revelation; in this case they are the ones chosen to "know" the father. It is very difficult to make the case, certainly on the basis of this text, that "it is precisely in his antithesis to the prevailing stream of Jewish piety that Jesus, who contrasts the simple people with the wise of Israel and grants them God's revelation, lives out of biblical roots."[66] Matthew is engaged in a debate with other Jewish groups, but in this instance the case is advanced in a manner similar to that of other groups such as the sectaries of the Qumran scrolls or the ideas found in apocalyptic literature. The infants, the powerless ones from Matthew's viewpoint, emerge as those who are truly wise. They are the recipients of the knowledge indicating the true nature of creation and the course of human history. The consideration of the infants again appears as a significant indicator in Matt 18.[67]

As the passage builds toward its conclusion in 11:28–30 Matthew identifies Jesus himself as wisdom, not as its envoy: "Come to me, all you that are weary and are carrying heavy burdens, and I will give you rest. Take my yoke upon you, and learn from me, for I am gentle and humble in heart, and you will find rest for your souls. For my yoke is easy and my burden is light." For some commentators, the particular revelation of the previous verses coupled with the promise in this section represents a key theme of the composition.[68] References to the ease of the yoke are not uncommon in Second Temple literature. A similar emphasis is found in the poem in Ben Sira 51:13–30, especially vv. 25–26 (Hebrew): "I opened my mouth and I said, 'Acquire for yourselves wisdom without money. Bring your necks into her yoke and let your soul receive instruction. She is near for those who seek her.'"[69] Rest and joy are the result of the pursuit of wisdom in Ben Sira 6:18–37, again with a reference to "her yoke" in the Hebrew text of v. 30.[70] In rabbinic literature we find a similar argument, such as Rabbi Nechuniah ben Hakanah in m. 'Abot 3:5: "Whoever accepts 'ōl Hattôrah [the yoke of the Torah], 'ōl malkût [the yoke of the kingdom] and 'ōl derek ereṣ [the yoke of daily life] shall be removed from him." The "yoke of the kingdom" in this case refers to "the troubles suffered at the hands of those in power."[71] The rejection of the "yoke of Torah" means that these other obligations and results become operative; life is then not as "easy." Hence it is better to choose the "yoke of Torah," due to the onerous nature of the other yokes. A similar intent is apparent in m. Ber. 2:2 where it is desirable that a man first receive the "yoke of the kingdom of heaven" and then the "yoke of the commandments," that is, the acceptance of the promise of God's sovereignty precedes the obligations of the commandments. They follow as a result of promise rather than obligation.[72] At the end of the first century, the author of this composition accuses the scribes and Pharisees of imposing heavy burdens (Matt 23:4). From Matthew's standpoint the joy and the promise of the kingdom is absent from their teaching; the requirements appear arbitrary rather than presenting an invested attempt to represent the expectations and hopes of the kingdom of God.

In his study of Matt II Warren Carter has proposed a different approach to this text. It is the burden of imperial rule, the weight of the Roman Empire on the shoulders of the weary and oppressively taxed subjects who are carrying the heavy burdens.[73] In his study he identifies the passages in which the "yoke" refers to imperial rule and its implications for subject people. While Carter has contributed to the growing body of literature on the significance of empire for the study of Second Temple Judaism and of Christian origins, the references he cites to imperial rule are oblique enough in the text that they require further justification. He rejects the notion that Jesus is here speaking as wisdom in favor of the viewpoint that this is one more christological statement in the gospel in which "Jesus, the one who proclaims and demonstrates God's reign or empire, issues an invitation to those who are oppressed by Roman imperial power to encounter God's empire now in his ministry in anticipation of the time when God destroys all empires including Rome's." Such an approach does not explain the context in which it is desirable to have Jesus even identified with wisdom in the gospel's argument addressing imperial power. Such a viewpoint requires further analysis.

One other important allusion to the "yoke of wisdom" is found in 4Q421 (Ways of Righteousness[b]) 1 II, 10.[74] In this fragmentary column we find a reference to the "sage" who possesses understanding and has a role in the process of reproof. Also present is a reference, presumably to the addressee, to a man who is "'ānāyw [humble] and nəkê siklô [contrite in his insight]." This same person "seeks righteousness" and "walks in the ways of God" and "the ways of righteousness." While some suggest that this text is to be regarded as one of the rule texts rather "than a wisdom composition, this column clearly makes a connection with the vocabulary that is familiar to us from some of the sectarian compositions."[75] It is clear that the composition contains both references to wisdom and indications of sectarian connection.[76]

The "sage" refers to an office of teaching and authority in the Community Rule; it also indicates the teacher who addresses "all those who pursue righteousness" in 4Q298 (Words of the Sage to All Sons of Dawn) 1-2 I.[77] We have already pointed out above the similarity in the use of the word "righteousness" in Matthew to some of the sectarian uses of the term. In an even more fragmentary context the yoke also appears in 4Q438 (Barkhi Nafshi[e]) 3, 3: "I will bring my neck under your yoke and discipline," similar to Ben Sira 51:26. Here we find another reference to "yoke" in 5, 5, even more lacking in context. However in 4, 4 reference is made to the 'ōraḥ ḥayyîm (way of life), just as in 4Q298 1–2 I, 3, the passage already mentioned.[78] The ways of life and death constitute the center of the two small fragments of 4Q473 (The Two Ways). Within the Qumran evidence we see ample attestation of the yoke as an image of wisdom utilized in Second Temple Judaism as well as the manner in which this image was connected with the two-ways motif. While the latter is tied in many ways to Deut 27–30, the phrase "way of life" is most common in Proverbs.[79]

This path of investigation points us back to the wisdom connections evident in the Sermon on the Mount. The connection to the "way of life" and "the two ways" is most evident in Matthew 7 where the introduction to the concluding portion of the Sermon begins with the discussion of the narrow gate and the broad road, in which the narrow gate and the hard road is the one which leads to life (7:13–27); the wide gate and the easy road lead to destruction.[80] This statement leads to the warning against false prophets. They can be recognized by the fruit they produce, that is, whether they help people identify the deeds of the kingdom. If they do not help persons to understand the signs of the coming reign of God, they produce bad fruit and are fit only to be cast into a fire. If they help people see those signs and to live their lives in accordance with that knowledge, they are not false prophets and are recognized by the fruit they produce, the deeds indicating that they know of the dawning of the kingdom of God. The type of wisdom called for in Matthew 11 is of the same nature as that emphasized in the Sermon on the Mount.

Our discussion of the Sermon on the Mount began with a comparison of the macarisms of Matt 5:3–12 to 4Q525 (Beatitudes).[81] The latter is an example of a literary construction in the wisdom tradition that finds its center in Torah. In contrast to the tradition represented in that composition, Matthew finds the center of his wisdom construction to be Jesus, and those who are blessed are those who have joined the body of Jews that find in Jesus's life and teachings the expression of the will of God and accept his life and witness as evidence of the coming of the kingdom of God. This means that the author of the first gospel did not make any distinction between understanding Jesus as Torah or as wisdom. The demonstration of Jesus as the envoy of wisdom in chapter 11 is totally consistent with Jesus as the authoritative interpreter of the law in chapter 5. In 7:21–23, those who do not do the will of the Father are not recognized by the Son (of Man) in the occasion of judgment: "Go away from me, you evildoers" (literally "you who do the works of unlawfulness"). The point is clear in the final parable of the

Sermon (7:24–27), where it is the *phronimos* (wise or thoughtful man) who built his house upon the rock, while the *mōros* (foolish) built upon the sand. A similar emphasis is apparent in the eschatological chapters leading into the account of the trial, where the wise and the foolish are contrasted in the parables of both the wise and evil slaves (24:45–51) and the wise and foolish maidens (25:1–13). In both cases, the wise recognize the significance of Jesus as judge in the model of the Son of Man, a theme also apparent in the parable of the sheep and the goats at the conclusion of the chapter (25:31–46).[82] The ambiguity of Jesus as envoy of wisdom or wisdom itself in chapter 11 provides an explanation for some ambiguity in chapter 5 concerning whether Jesus replaces the law or is its authoritative interpreter. For Matthew, Jesus is the authoritative spokesperson of the will of God, and he uses a variety of literary devices and analogies from Jewish traditions and beliefs to make that point. The consistency comes from the centrality of the person of Jesus rather than any of the metaphors employed in the service of demonstrating his significance.

Having identified himself as the vehicle of wisdom, as the manner in which the will of God is made available to humankind, Matthew has Jesus conclude this discourse with the invitation to his hearers to accept "my yoke," repeated two times in these final verses. The invitation is to join those who are blessed, as in Matt 5:3–12, for it is "easy" and its burden is "light." The recognition that the kingdom of God is occurring gives rest from the oppressive powers that have and presently do dominate Jewish life at the conclusion of the first century. It is through the association with the followers of Jesus that this oppressive weight is lifted, that one can learn how to live in the midst of this imperial reality, that Jewish life is possible. In contrast to all of the other options available, promulgated by a variety of Jewish teachers and leaders, Jesus is the one who reveals the will of God for the Jewish people.

Conclusion

The claim that the will of God for the Jewish people is known only through Jesus is audacious. In advancing that claim, the author would not have been without precedent. The claims would have been familiar to those who had heard others advance options now apparent in the literature from Qumran. Perceptions of wisdom in apocalyptic literature also would have been significant, and others would have known of individuals or groups who were committed to a sectarian option that made claims for exclusive access to wisdom and knowledge the center of their Jewish life. These authors advanced the claim that their groups possessed wisdom and that the "wise" were those who affiliated with them.

An evaluation of the elements of sectarianism evident in Matthew's utilization of the wisdom tradition highlights some features different from those employed in the Sermon on the Mount. Since the element of difference concentrates on behaviors and practices, that feature is much more apparent in the Sermon than in Matthew 11. The appeal to Jesus as wisdom and as envoy of wisdom does point back to central aspects of the Beatitudes, that portion of the Sermon rooted in wisdom traditions that provides the basics of the identity upon which the resultant practices are built. The element of antagonism is apparent in the section of woes addressed to the residents of the towns of Galilee in 11:20–24, introduced by the end of v. 19, "Yet wisdom is vindicated by her deeds." Those who will not accept the words of Jesus as the authoritative statement and action of the will of God, that is, wisdom, "will be brought down to Hades," and "on the day of judgment it will be more tolerable for Tyre and Sidon [or Sodom] than for you." In the treatment of Jesus as wisdom the author of Matthew advocates an active antagonism toward those who will not accept his teaching. The element of separation is apparent in the author's justification of this viewpoint in vv. 25–27 which concludes: "All things have been handed over to me by my Father; and no one knows the Son except the Father, and no one knows the Father except the Son and anyone to whom the Son chooses to reveal him." The separation from other Jewish groups either advocating or desiring to obtain wisdom is apparent, based on the same exclusive claims already advanced in the Beatitudes. The argument that adherence to the group of the followers of Jesus is the only way to understand the will of God or to do what is pleasing to God is a sectarian claim of a nature similar to that advanced in the copies of the Community Rule or the Damascus Document. It is this same identification which permits Jesus to argue in Matt 12:42 that "something greater than Solomon is here!" Similarly in 13:54 the author has the townspeople asking, "Where did this man get this wisdom and these deeds of power?"

5 Communal Organization and Discipline

The particular attention paid to issues of communal structure and organization in the first gospel is most apparent in Matt 18:15–20. In this section we encounter the Matthean version of an interpretive tradition of Lev 19:17 (really vv. 15–18), demonstrating the nature and place of this group of the followers of Jesus within the Jewish community at the end of the first century CE. In an examination of the legal traditions of post-biblical law anchored in different viewpoints and social locations, we can find aspects of the type of Jewish life envisioned by the author of Matthew and the community that embodied this hope and expectation.

The Biblical Text and Its Immediate Successors

The interpretive tradition of the injunction to reprove one's neighbor provides a location for the examination of the Matthean text of communal discipline. It is no surprise that a general statement such as Lev 19:17 elicited a variety of readings in Judean literature of the Greek and Roman periods: "You shall not hate your kinsfolk in your heart. Reprove your kinsman but incur no guilt because of him." Within the text of the Hebrew Bible, it appears to be part of a two-verse literary unit (19:17–18) that builds toward and concludes with the well-known "golden rule": "You shall love your neighbor as yourself: I am the Lord." Intertwined with the injunction for reproof is v. 18a: "You shall not take vengeance or bear a grudge against your countrymen." Instances in which interpreters reach back to vv. 15–16 to complete their reading of these verses are also evident, so the relevant literary unit is 19:15–18. Our having identified it as a literary unit does not mean that there is a self-evident coherence among the injunctions recorded here. They do not constitute injunctions that are easily verifiable on the basis of external behavior, having as much to do with attitude as with action. The common thread of these verses is best represented by the proposal of James Kugel: "a kind of summons to go beyond merely external lawful conduct in order to purify utterly one's thoughts and deeds—the purification that is the touchstone of Levitical 'holiness.'"[1]

To understand the meaning of the phrase "You shall not hate your kinsfolk in your heart," Kugel turns to the wisdom materials rather than to comparative legal literature: "He who hates dissembles with his lips, harboring treachery within him; though he makes his voice kindly, do not trust him, for there are seven abhorrences in his heart."[2] In other words, hating kinsfolk in the heart is a problem because it is kept inside, and it is not apparent in someone's speech. Such persons are not trustworthy: they are still "harboring treachery," hence their actions and responses are unpredictable. In other words, deceit and hypocrisy are the outcomes of hatred. A similar point is evident in Prov 10:18, but there it is also connected with slander, speaking about others behind their backs: "Argue your case with your neighbor yourself, and do not disclose a secret of another, lest one who hears you exposes you to shame, and your own slander not return."[3] In this case, going directly to your neighbor may save you from public embarrassment. Spreading slander is an action whose consequences could well return to harm the perpetrator. This legislation of a paraenetic nature is deemed significant in the literature relating to identity and communal formation in the later Second Temple period.

This text is regarded as legal material in subsequent interpretation,[4] as is apparent in Ben Sira 19:13–17. The implications of this verse are obscured in the NRSV and CEB versions that translate the word *elegxon* as "question" rather than "reprove," the same Greek word employed in Matt 18:15.[5] Here the advice is similar to that of Proverbs, but the role and significance of the text as biblical law is acknowledged. Attention to the same issues is also apparent in T. Gad 4:1–3 and 6:1–5, part of the T. 12 Patr.[6] In the first reference hatred leads to someone's error being made public, with a resulting eagerness for his condemnation, punishment, and death. The text labels this as "lawlessness." In the second passage the reader is enjoined to speak peaceably to the one who sins against him or her. Forgive if the person repents, but if not, do not challenge the sinner lest you goad the person into swearing, perhaps falsely or unnecessarily, and then you also have sinned by provoking that response. The implications of Lev 19:15–18 as biblical law are being explored in these texts of the Second Temple period.

The Dead Sea Scrolls

The centrality of the laws of reproof for sectarian life are immediately evident in the central portion of the Damascus Document, CD 6:11–7:6.[7] I regard this passage as a principal ideological statement on the founding of the sectarian movement described in the various D materials. Jerome Murphy-O'Connor included this passage of precepts in a section in his identification of sources in CD, in which he referred to it as a "Memorandum," whose purpose was to remind adherents of the new covenant in the land of Damascus of the basis of their identity and what distinguished them from other Jews.[8] The development of the legislation in the Holiness Code was what Murphy-O'Connor found to be distinctive about this section. Philip Davies referred to the statements in this section as injunctions, an introduction to the halakah of Qumran, to be differentiated from specific legislation in later texts.[9] This distinction has been developed in the work of Charlotte Hempel to argue for the presence of halakah in the D materials applicable to all of Israel and to be distinguished from the specifically sectarian legislation. In this instance the passage under discussion is considered to be a series of halakic rules, specifically related to the development of subsequent legislation in the D materials.[10] It follows what Hempel characterizes as the fourth account of the origins of a movement (5:20–6:11a) in her outline of the materials. It is apparent that we are reading the texts from two different vantage points. Hempel is attempting to identify the sources of the legislation in the D materials, while I want to establish their meaning for the sectarian authors in the form found in the surviving copies, that is, their "final form." It is this form which is to be considered operative "for those who came into the new covenant in the land of Damascus."[11] Since practice, or way of life, is a fundamental question for the identity of Judeans during the late Second Temple period, it should come as no surprise that a statement of the basic legislative principles supporting the sectarian lifestyle would follow the accounts of its origins found in the first four folios of the composition.[12]

The importance of Lev 19:15–18 for the author of this section of CD is apparent. It is the basis of the communal requirement for the adherents of "the new covenant in the land of Damascus." The initial phrase in 6:20, "to love each his brother as himself," employs Lev 19:18 as an authoritative general principle to undergird the practices that follow.[13] The mandate concerning reproof, "reproving each his fellow according to the command," based on Lev 19:17, and the injunction not to bear a grudge from Lev 19:18 follow in CD 7:2. With these obvious links having been identified, other passages bear further attention. What appear to be general references now find a very specific biblical context. In CD 6:21 the injunction "to strengthen the hand of poor and needy and alien" is a sectarian interpretation of Lev 19:15: "You shall not render an unfair decision: do not favor the poor or show deference to the rich; judge your kinsman fairly."[14] While the biblical phrase speaks of impartiality in legal decisions, the sectarian text appears to emphasize support for all of the members of the "covenant." Elsewhere in CD the verb *ḥāzaq* (strengthen) is used to speak of those who "hold fast to" the sectarian commandments and statutes.[15] "To seek each the welfare of his fellow" in CD 6:21–7:1 is then the sectarian interpretation of Lev 19:16, "You shall not stand upon[16] the blood of your fellow." The author is not quoting, but very actively reading this section of Leviticus from the standpoint of the "new covenant in the land of Damascus." I employ the word "reading" at this point to keep this analysis consistent with the previous understanding of the use of Torah in the Sermon on the Mount. This is not an "interpretation" of a biblical law; it is the manner in which the sectarian author read this biblical text.

There is one phrase in this section that is not as obviously linked to Lev 19. CD 7:1–2 reads as follows: "never betraying a family member; keeping away from fornication,[17] according to the ordinance." I have elsewhere identified *zənût* (fornication/sexual impurity) as one of the central issues of sectarian self-identification addressed in CD.[18] Commandments concerning incest, divorce, polygamy, and impurity with regard to menstruation, childbirth, and related issues all come under this category. In this instance the author has integrated a major issue of sectarian identification into the biblical legislation of Lev 19:15–18; the biblical injunction "Love your neighbor as yourself" includes adhering to the sectarian interpretation of the laws of *zənût*. The same case is to be made for the final clause, "separating from all kinds of ritual impurity according to their ordinance." Purity is the other major concern of sectarian identity emphasized in the Damascus Document, central to its practice. Adherence to the sectarian commandments with regard to such central issues as fornication and purity is the way the members of the "new" covenant understand the biblical commandments.

These issues have now been integrated into an exegesis of Lev 19:15–18. Through such an approach we encounter a sectarian reading of this biblical text. Since this passage appears to be employed in a surprisingly large number of texts from Qumran, the importance of reproof in sectarian legislation is apparent.

While the term *hôkiaḥ* (reprove) is not mentioned in CD 8:4–13, the reliance on the earlier interpretation of Lev 19:15–18 is evident in the description of the traitors who rebelled and wallowed in the ways of whoredom and wicked wealth. In ll. 5–6 it is said that "each one vengefully bore a grudge against his brother, each hating his fellow, each of them kept away from nearest kin." This passage is further evidence of the importance of this tradition for the adherents of the new covenant in the land of Damascus.

Within the legal sections of the composition CD 9:2–10:3 is structured as a commentary on the biblical legislation of reproof.[19] CD 9:2–8 begins with the citation formula *'ašer 'amar* (as for that which says)[20] and then quotes Lev 19:18 with regard to taking vengeance or bearing a grudge. A commentary on the biblical verse follows, concluding with a quotation of the injunction for reproof in Lev 19:17, again introduced by the formula "as for that which says." The adherent of the covenant who out of anger or a desire to discredit presents against his fellow member a case that has not been the subject of reproof before witnesses is said to be violating Lev 19:18. This sectarian stipulation is reinforced by a quotation from Nah 1:2 concerning the same subject. Then CD 9:6 continues: "If he kept silent day by day[21] and then in anger against his fellow he spoke against him in a capital case,[22] this testifies against him that he did not fulfill the commandment of God which says to him, 'You shall reprove your fellow and not bear the sin yourself.'"[23] The subject under consideration here is much more specific and well-defined than in CD 6–7 discussed above. This passage is not justifying the use of the laws of reproof; it is dealing with one specific case.[24] This conclusion differs from the analysis of Hempel already discussed above, who characterizes this section as an example of what she terms halakah, legislation for all of Israel rather than that of a sectarian group.[25] It can be debated whether this legislation was operational in an actual sectarian organization, but I find no reason to doubt that the author(s) thought that they were dealing with issues of practice for a sectarian Jewish body.

Additional issues concerning the implementation of the laws of reproof are discussed later on the same folio, CD 9:16–10:3. This section deals with the capital crime where the violation had only one witness, that is, there is no corroborating witness. The issue of the reproof procedure with regard to a capital crime had already been raised in CD 9:6. The argument presented in this section is that conviction on a capital crime is possible if the offense has been repeated two additional times and one witness is present on each occasion.[26] Furthermore, two witnesses rather than the required three will suffice on issues of property or finance.[27] In each instance the plaintiff in the presence of the accused is to make the offense known to the *məbaqqer* (overseer), whose role is to be present and to record the occasion when the witness-plaintiff comes forward.[28] This officer was responsible for keeping a record of the public rebukes, and it seems likely that he presided over the procedures. The public nature of this event and the emphasis upon the written record are both features of this legislation which appear here for the first time in Jewish history.

The section on oaths in CD 9:8–16 appears to be of consequence for the development of our subject.[29] While the link between 1 Sam 25:26, a modified citation of which begins this section, "You may not seek a remedy under your own power," and the injunction of reproof may not be apparent, there is good evidence to suggest such a connection. That it is to be understood as a biblical quotation is evidenced by the use of the characteristic opening phrase, "as for that which says," in CD 9:8–9. In 1QS VI, 27 this same biblical passage is linked with penal procedures, and in 4Q286 the phrase "and not seek remedy" can be found in the column dealing with questions of reproof.[30] Of more importance, the introductory phrase "concerning the oath" makes sense only if it is understood to be applying to the oath of the witnesses in the cases requiring reproof discussed in the previous and presumably the following sections. There is no reason to relate 1 Sam 25:26 to the question of oaths if this is not the case. It is because of the legal requirements for a public and recorded reproof that "a man who makes someone take an oath out in the countryside and not before judges or at their bidding: such a one 'has sought a remedy under his own power.'" The author is linking 1 Sam 25:26 with the laws of reproof in Lev 19:17, presumably because of its sectarian connection with the injunction not to take vengeance. The remainder of the paragraph relates to the use of the oath in cases of missing property; anyone knowing about the missing property of an owner who has sworn a public oath attesting to its absence is himself guilty of theft if he does not come forward. Thus CD 9:2–10:3 is to be understood as one literary unit dealing with the topic of reproof.

While agreeing that the major topic is the laws of reproof, Hempel regards CD 9:16b–10:3 as one unit dealing with issues for a particular community of Israel that is not necessarily sectarian, a topic already discussed above.[31] When read from the standpoint of an address "for those who came into the new covenant in the land of Damascus," CD 9:2–10:3 is one continuous exposition on the laws of reproof.

The identification of this larger literary unit helps to clarify the breadth of the offenses covered by the laws of reproof in the Damascus Document. The designation "capital case" appears in both CD 9:6 and 9:17 in clauses where the ambiguous syntax makes it difficult to determine whether the legislation is limited to capital cases.[32] CD 9:22–10:3 applies these procedures to a broader range of cases. Issues of property are discussed in 9:10–16. Bilhah Nitzan points to the words "anything in which a man shall violate the law" in 9:16 to demonstrate the breadth of the violations covered by this procedure: "whether ... ethical, criminal, religious, or those concerning the community's discipline."[33] Capital crimes, of course, as the "worst case" scenario would be the most difficult, hence requiring the most clarity in legislative and judicial procedures.[34]

The fundamental importance of the biblical laws of reproof for the development of sectarian legislation is apparent in the other legal texts of D. We have just identified the manner in which the scriptural basis of the laws of reproof is evident in CD 6:20–7:3 and how these principles are developed in CD 9:2–10:3 as the basis for the legislation which follows in the subsequent folios. The only other evidence of the penal code in CD is the fragmentary text at 14:20–22 concerning bearing a grudge. The other D texts yield even more material; 4Q266 (D[a]) 10 I–II, 4Q267 (D[b]) 9 VI, and 4Q270 (D[e]) 7 I all attest to the presence of a penal code in the D materials.[35] Since CD 14:20 is paralleled by the opening line of the penal code in 1QS VI, 24, it seems reasonable to propose that this was the opening line for two or more versions of it.[36] The literary structure of both compositions undergirds the claim that the laws of reproof seem to have functioned as the first step in a process which leads to a more public judicial process for violations of sectarian legislation, for which the penalties were spelled out in its penal code.[37]

When we turn our attention to the S materials, the various versions of the Community Rule, the obligation of reproof is also regarded as significant.[38] The overlap with D materials on the penal code has just received mention. In the legislation listing stipulations for life within the *yaḥad* (community), 1QS V, 24–VI, 1 occupies an important place indicating a major responsibility:

> To reprove his neighbor in truth, humility and loving charity for one another. No one is to speak to a companion with anger or ill-temper or stubbornly or with a mean spirit of wickedness. He shall not hate him with his uncircumcised heart but on that day he shall reprove him so as not to incur guilt because of him. A man also shall not bring before the association[39] an issue against his neighbor without a prior rebuke before witnesses.[40]

This apparently composite document of communal legislation provides evidence for the importance Lev 19:17–18 held in the life of the sect. These lines follow the section specifying the importance of ranking in communal life based on the annual examination of both inductees and all members. In 1QS V, 20 this section begins, "When anyone enters the covenant—to live according to all these ordinances, to make common cause with the Congregation of Holiness—they shall investigate his spiritual qualities as a community, each member taking part." In other words, this process of induction into sectarian life is based on a clear commitment to their understanding of merit. This suggests that their understanding of the mandates against favoring either the poor or the rich in Lev 19:15–16 concerns not permitting anyone to advance in the hierarchy of the sect at the expense of another. Thus 1QS V, 20–VI, 1 provides the sectarian reading of Lev 19:15–18. This section follows the induction procedure outlined in 1QS V, 7b–20.[41] The laws of reproof are set within the context of a communal lifestyle with a high degree of accountability for the actions of each individual. One of the distinguishing features of this text is the role of the law of reproof as a preliminary action to a more public and presumably judicial process, a perspective already identified in CD 9:2–10:3.[42] In 1QS it appears to have been adapted to meet the needs of the *yaḥad*.[43] Other texts from the Qumran corpus also attest to its significant role in the maintenance of communal life.

The fragmentary remains of a covenantal ceremony can be found in 4Q286–290 (4QBerakhot[a-e]). Included in these fragments is a description of some laws of reproof containing many similarities to those already described.[44] Nitzan rightly suggests that the literary structure of the extant portion of the laws of reproof can be divided into two sections. Lines 1–4a of her reconstructed text present the interpretation of Lev 19:17–18 as under-

stood by this sectarian author. If this is correct, the remainder of the reconstructed text develops the manner in which these requirements functioned
within the sectarian community. It is important to note that both 1QS V,
24–VI, 2 and CD 9:2–10:3, discussed above, are followed by a description of
the sectarian leadership structure. In 4QBerakhot the role of the *məbaqqer*
(overseer) in the process of reproof follows the opening exegetical explanation.[45] Thus the literary structure, at least at the level of content, resembles
1QS and CD on this point. However, this text provides an understanding
of the purpose of the procedures not available in the copies of these other
two compositions:

> [And whoever] erred while returning [to the truth], he will reprove him
> [according to] their [commandments] and will have mercy [upon him if he
> si]ns. And no [man] will bear a grud[ge against his fellow from one day] to
> [the nex]t. [He will] not [hate him in his heart and (so) will incur] n[o guilt
> because of him.][46]

The case here is limited. The law is applied to the person who is returning "to the truth." Whether this means returning to sectarian life or to the
requirements which the person violated within the sectarian community is
not clear. In any case, the person has made this commitment and then sins,
whether unintentionally or deliberately is not specified. It is in this instance
that the obligation of reproof is brought to bear, but with the exercise of
mercy.[47] In other words, the role of reproof is to aid the person's reintegration into full sectarian participation. Fulfilling this obligation is evidence
that the sectarian does not bear a grudge or hate his erring neighbor in his
heart. The sectarian then has incurred no guilt if the erring member is not
successful in the reintegration process.

The appearance of the word *'ānaš* (punish) in l. 8 of Nitzan's reconstruction of this section of 4QBerakhot also signals the beginning of a penal
code, as in the instances cited above. The remaining lines resemble the code
of 1QS VI, 24–VII, 25, as well as the fragments of 4Q266 (D[a]) 10 I–II,
4Q267 (D[b]) 9 VI and 4Q270 (D[c]) 7 I, all of which emphasize the treatment
of fellow members of the sect. This is a rather amazing parallel, pointing
to both the importance and consistency of the laws of reproof within various descriptions of the sectarian social structures, presumably at different
times and places. Noteworthy throughout the Qumran literature discussed
up to this point is the educational, or perhaps more accurately formative,
function of the injunctions related to reproof. It could be argued that this

role is central in the development of a "sectarian lifestyle." This purpose is specified in CD 15:13–15, 20:1–8; 1QS VIII, 16b–19; and 4Q286 14.[48] CD 20:3 spells out this responsibility concerning the erring member: "According to his offense shall men of knowledge reprove him until the day when he will again stand in the formation of the men of holy perfection."[49] The sectarian membership is not to lose sight of the basic function of reproof.

Conclusive evidence of the use of the laws of reproof within the sectarian social structure is found in 4Q477 (Rebukes Reported by the Overseer).[50] These fragments contain the phrases 'anšê hayyaḥad (people of the community) and [m]aḥănê Harabbîm (camps of the Many),[51] thereby indicating its usage within the sectarian social structure. In the first fragment the line "to make their offenses be remembered" points to the purpose of this text. Offenses recorded within the text include "doing evil" in some manner which concerns the "many," since this is the word which begins the next line. Attributed to one Joḥanan is the charge that he is "short tempered" and probably that he possessed a "haughty spirit."[52] When we come to Ḥananiah Notos we learn that he "disturbed the spirit of the community" and that he mixed something (la'areb, the object is missing from the fragment). The issue of "mixing" is mentioned in both the Temple Scroll and 4QMMT.[53] Either Ḥananiah or someone missing from the fragments is then charged, "He also loves his near kin," presumably because of the failure to reprove him.[54] In CD 7:1 this injunction is found in the context of the discussion concerning reproof discussed above. Finally Ḥananiah ben Sim[on] is charged, "[Al]so he loves the fair [neck]," reconstructed on the basis of CD 1:18–19 and alluding to Hos 10:11. We do find in 4Q421 (Ways of Righteousness[b]) 1a II–b, 11, which betrays evidence of sectarian composition, that the function of reproof is related to the duties of the sage.

The Qumran texts also provide evidence that the sectarian adoption of reproof as a central feature of their penal code arose from a broader interest in the practice. This is attested in the fragments of non-sectarian texts from the corpus. 4Q372 (Narrative and Poetic Composition[b]) 1, 27–28 does not describe sectarian or group behavior, but reproof as an act of God is found in a passage based upon the sin-exile-return pattern of Second Temple literature, in this case possibly forming an anti-Samaritan polemic.[55] This idea also is present in a number of the wisdom texts, not surprisingly since it receives frequent mention in Proverbs.[56]

The centrality of the laws of reproof as an instrument for communal discipline is evident throughout the sectarian compositions from Qumran.

Also apparent is the redemptive purpose that was envisioned for these procedures in the maintenance of the sectarian communities with regard to the treatment of erring individuals. Due to lack of evidence, we do not know the extent to which these procedures were successful in accomplishing this purpose. The extant literary record does point to the many and diverse types of compositions in which its importance to communal life was highlighted and advocated. That evidence suggests that the practices are an established part of sectarian life in Jewish communities of the first century. This would have included the Jewish community or communities in which the gospel of Matthew was written and read.

Reproof in the Gospel of Matthew

While Matt 18:15–18 is sometimes interpreted within the context of an intra-Christian debate, on the assumption that it reflects tensions over issues of legalism within the early Christian community, interpreters also look to rabbinic literature for an explanation of the passage.[57] The ongoing significance of reproof in the rabbinic tradition is amply attested, as found in summary form in the later composition 'Abot R. Nat. A 29: "He [Rabbi Simeon ben Eleazar] used to say: If among your colleagues there are some who reprove you and others who praise you, love him who reproves you and hate him who praises you; because it is the one who reproves you that leads you to the life of the world to come, while he who praises you drives you out of the world."[58] Interest in the topic, with a focus on its purpose and the motivations of its practitioners, can be found in a number of talmudic passages.[59] For example, in b. Tamid 28a: "It has been taught: Rabbi says: Which is a right way that a man should choose? Let him love reproof, since as long as there is reproof in the world ease of mind comes to the world, good and blessing come to the world, and evil departs from the world, as it says. But to them that are reproved shall come delight; and a good blessing shall come upon them." The text continues by noting that whoever reproves lišmāh (with a pure motive) is considered to be in the "lot of the Holy One, Blessed be He," that is, a place in the inner circle of the righteous in heaven.

In b. Šabb. 119b the failure to reprove is one of the reasons debated by the rabbis as the cause for the destruction of Jerusalem. In a reading of Lam 1:6 they consider the problem to be shutting eyes to evil. Turning to b. 'Arak. 16b, we find more attention paid to the attitudes of both those who give and receive reproof. For example, the person offering the charge is not to do so in a manner that would result in public humiliation, a repeated concern in talmudic texts. These talmudic passages, however, do not express an interest in the outline of specific procedures, as encountered in the Qumran texts or Matthew. Davies and Allison note y. Yoma 45c: "Samuel said, 'Whoever sins against his brother, he must say to him, I have sinned against you. If he hears it, it is well. If not, let him bring others, and let him appease him before them.'" However, this is not actually a case of reproof since, as they note, it is the offender who initiates the contact in this case. While the question of witnesses is a considerable one in the talmudic tradition, it is not explicitly connected with the injunction for reproof in these texts.

Similarities between the Matthean passages and the material in 1QS and CD were recognized quite early in the process of analyzing the Qumran materials.[60] With the publication of the additional fragments from Cave 4 the significance of the exegetical tradition of Lev 19:15–18 in the Qumran texts became even more apparent. It is clearly demonstrable from the above survey that Matt 18:15–17 is closely related to the texts from Qumran. The use of kinship language is already rooted in the biblical text and is one explanation for its importance in the procedural considerations of the sectarian legislation. A similar usage can be demonstrated in Matthew, where extensive use is made of this kinship language.[61] While the procedure in CD 9 starts out at a different point, the steps spelled out in Matt 18:15–18 are remarkably similar to those of 1QS V, 24—VI, 1.[62] Here the member of the community who saw, or perhaps was victim of, the offense is enjoined to approach the offender privately. A potential reason for this action can be noted in T. Gad 4:1–3, discussed above, where it is suggested that broader dissemination of the information about someone's error could result in a quick desire for judgment, punishment, and death.[63] After this step, the similarities are rather apparent.

As in both CD 9:3 and 1QS VI, 1 the next step recorded in Matt 18:16 concerns the necessity of witnesses. Both traditions have at this point integrated Deut 19:15 into their interpretation of Lev 19:17–18. All three texts point to the necessity for the reproof to be stated in the presence of witnesses. Not only do these texts agree concerning this step in the process, they also share the same exegetical support for its justification. Furthermore, both traditions interpret Deut 19:15 to apply to the necessity for witnesses to the act of reproof, not to the original offensive act which necessitated a response.[64] Such an interpretation is not self-evident from the biblical text. There is a remarkable convergence of the Qumran evidence and Matthew at this point, not only in the practice but also in the treatment of the biblical tradition supporting it.

The next step involves an appeal to the assembly, in CD 9:4 to the *zəqenîm* (elders) of the "new covenant in the land of Damascus," in 1QS VI, 1 to the *rabbîm* (many), and in Matt 18:17 to the *ekklēsia* (assembly). The only other place where the last term is found in the gospel literature is Matt 16:19. "Church," the usual translation of this term in Matthew, is not a term which adequately conveys its meaning in a first-century Jewish context. It is used in the LXX to translate the Hebrew *qāhāl*, with reference to an "assembly."[65] In other words it is the equivalent of the *yaḥad* or the *rabbîm* in the Qumran texts, the term used in those texts to refer to the collective identity of the group. The assembly of the community is the final authority in all three cases. The similarity, however, also breaks down at this point. The focus of the legislation in CD is to assure proper procedure prior to the hearing of the case before the assembly. The formality of this process is emphasized by the description of the role of the *məbaqqer* in CD 9:18 and the records of reproof in 4Q477. The connection of the penal code with this process also emphasizes the formal and final decisions of the assembly.[66] The Matthean legislation and 1QS, in contrast, emphasize the earlier stages in the process, the personal appeal in the first instance and then the presence of two or three other members of the sect as witnesses. In Matthew the appeal to the assembly is described as significant only after the failure of these other steps. We have to remember that the sectarian texts also contain reminders of the educational function of reproof with regard to its erring members, cited in passages such as CD 15:13–15, 20:1–8; 1QS VIII, 16b–19; and 4QBer[a] 14.

So the author of the first gospel used one of the synonyms for "assembly" to designate the sectarian body that claimed to be followers of Jesus, thereby distinguishing them within the Jewish community. This negates the common distinction between "church" and "synagogue" as an appropriate description of these entities in Matthew, as well as the distinction between the individual congregation of Matt 18:17 and the universal church of Matt 16:18.[67] The *ekklēsia* was not the opponent of another religious body in the Jewish community known as the synagogue; it was the term chosen to represent the collectivity of one of the deviant groups found within that community whose central communal organization was the synagogue. This collectivity was composed of the followers of Jesus.

The Synagogue

The LXX provides us with another translation of *qāhāl* that is significant for the study of Matthew. *Sunagōgē* is employed in the LXX for both *qāhāl* and *'edāh*, the two terms designating the "company" or "congregation" of Israel in the Hebrew Bible.[68] The evidence from Judea and Galilee, both archaeological and literary, points clearly to the synagogue as a village-based community structure with both religious and communal dimensions, the latter more explicitly apparent in the first century. The origin and development of this structure that became a pillar of Jewish life are hotly contested issues in the study of Jewish history. Its nature and shape at the end of the first century CE are obscure, shrouded in a lack of evidence. Within traditional Jewish belief, the roots of the synagogue were frequently attributed to Moses, in conjunction with his reading of the law, or even to the patriarchs.[69] It has been commonplace to find the origins of the synagogue in the responses to the destruction of the temple in the sixth century BCE or in the program of communal reform and rebuilding attributed to Ezra and Nehemiah, particularly the reading of the Torah and covenant renewal of Neh 8–10.[70] More recently the complex nature of the question has been readily acknowledged.

The difficulty in determining the nature of this institution is apparent already when identifying the terminology to be employed in the discussion.[71] In the Greek literature of the diaspora the most common term employed is *proseuchē* (house of prayer), well attested in Philo and in the inscriptions and papyri from Egypt.[72] The three references to this term employed by Josephus to describe installations in Palestine are found in *Vita*, there designating a public building in Tiberias in which Jews met for deliberations, in this case about Josephus's leadership of the resistance forces.[73] In the Qumran corpus, the reference in CD 11:22 to the *bêt hištaḥăwût* (house of prostration) suggests some similarity to the "house of prayer" in the Greek materials.[74] The term usually translated as "synagogue" in the New Testament has a limited number of appearances in Josephus, but appears in inscriptions from Palestine.[75] Of some significance is the Theodotus inscription from Jerusalem, presumably to be dated to the first century CE.[76] The rabbinic materials use the term *bêt hakkəneset* (house of meeting), *kənîštāʿ* in Aramaic. There are also a number of other terms with very limited attestation that may be references to a similar phenomenon, if not to some form of the institution.[77] It is striking that the NT evidence with regard to terminology resembles the Greek terms primarily employed in Palestine. This is also the terminology found in the works of Justin Martyr in the mid-second century CE.[78] This usage is supported by the references to the *archisunagōgos* (head of the synagogue) in the Theodotus inscription, the New Testament, and Justin Martyr as well. This terminological discussion illustrates the complications regarding the issue of origins. An exploration of the origins of this institution is a necessary prelude to a discussion of its nature and function in Palestinian Judaism in the first century CE.

There are two dominant views in the contemporary literature on the topic.[79] Donald Binder understands the synagogue, in its origin and form, to be heavily influenced by the Jerusalem temple. Its architecture, its functions, its officials, its liturgy, and its sanctity find their origins in the temple. In other words, the first-century synagogue was considered a religious institution, while also carrying out communal functions.[80] Paul Flesher sees the temple as central to synagogue development as well, but the temple and synagogue were religious institutions in opposition to one another.[81] The synagogue began as an institution of the diaspora in Egypt, and when it was imported to Palestine, the two entities represented different forms of Judaism. Only synagogues of the diaspora such as that represented by the Theodotus inscription were present in Jerusalem and Judea, hence the literary and archaeological evidence for it is found primarily only in Galilee. Its origin as an institution removed from the temple resulted in its formation in geographical areas removed from the temple, thereby reflecting a history disassociated from and in tension with the form of Judaism that found its center in temple life. The religious function of the synagogue receives priority in hypotheses where the temple is the primary referent.[82]

In contrast Lee Levine sees this institution as the result of a gradual evolution during the Hellenistic and Roman periods from activities that were characteristic of the city gate in earlier eras. This development is not to be linked with any particular identifiable crisis such as the Maccabean revolt or the destruction in 70 CE. He also can find no evidence to support the view that it possessed a particular religious or halakic status as an institution.[83] Noting the lack of substantive evidence concerning the question of origins, he proposes that we look backward from the later periods when more is known to see what hints we can identify about its functions in the earlier literature. The first-century evidence, admittedly also limited and somewhat obscure, points to an entity that served as a center for a variety of religious and communal functions.[84] That broader non-sacral role he identifies with the city gate.[85] We already have noted the public reading of the law and covenant renewal ceremony described in Neh 8–10, an activity carried out in that venue. With the changing functions of the city gate in the Hellenistic and Roman periods, its public role as a place of gathering diminished as it took on increasing military and especially imperial functions. Note the manner in which successive emperors rebuilt or expanded city gates so as to leave their dominant imprint upon all those who entered the gates of the city. It is during this time that urbanization is identified as one of the prominent characteristics of life in the eastern portions of the Roman Empire. In the parade of successive empires, it could be argued that Jews lost control of the city gate, both within the diaspora, where the city gate was not in the province of Jewish control, and within Palestine, where imperial expressions of dominance were an expected architectural feature of the city gate. The loss of that space for public assembly as the nucleus of communal life is identified by Levine as the contributing factor that permitted the synagogue to develop as a center for Jewish life in the latter period of the Second Temple.

Other hypotheses too numerous to mention, much less evaluate, would include the proposals of Ellis Rivkin,[86] Steven Fine,[87] and Howard Clark Kee.[88] Closely related to the work of Lee Levine is the investigation of the archaeological evidence by Peter Richardson. He finds the closest architectural analogues among the structures of the *collegia* that were adapted for a variety of functions of both a social and religious nature.[89] This identification is possible on the basis of the use of the term in Roman documents referring to the Jewish community and the identified functions of the synagogue as a social and religious institution. Levine suggests that "the synagogue's agenda was far more comprehensive than any analogous Greco-Roman institution," thereby limiting the possibilities for too close an identification.[90] Less convincing is the critique of Runesson, who laments the failure to include "specifically liturgical criteria in the discussion."[91] In the identification of the functions of the synagogue at the conclusion of the first century, Richardson and Levine both emphasize its communal nature in their attempts to explain the archaeological evidence.[92]

A very limited number of archaeological sites in Israel/Palestine is considered to contain evidence of synagogues dated to the first century CE. With the exception of the small amount of Tannaitic literature related to the events at Yavneh discussed in Chapter 1 above, the period between the revolts yields very limited evidence concerning institutional developments within Judaism, and almost no archaeological material concerning the synagogue impels examination within that fifty-year span. Hence the archaeological evidence bearing upon the question of the nature of the synagogue in Galilee at the end of the first century CE is derived from the pre-70 attestations. Up to the beginning of the twenty-first century, only four sites had been identified by archaeologists as relevant for consideration: Gamla, Herodium, Masada, and Migdal.[93] The evidence at the last site was problematic in its interpretation, so frequently only three sites were considered.[94] However a new discovery at a different site at Magdala (Migdal) has again made that location a potential site as a first-century synagogue.[95] Since only preliminary reports are so far available, definitive evaluation of the data has not been possible even though the first-century claim appears warranted.[96] Other sites also come into consideration.

Ehud Netzer identified an edifice from the first century BCE or earlier on the eastern side of the Hasmonean and Herodian palaces at Jericho as a synagogue, making the claim that it is the oldest synagogue found in Israel.[97] While Binder and Runesson tend to argue for Netzer's identification,[98] this claim has been contested by Zvi Ma'oz and is considered to be lacking in convincing evidence by Lee Levine.[99] Recent discoveries at Modein and Kiryat Sefer also merit attention. In the excavation of Modein, the village to which Mattathias fled with his sons after the repressive measures of Antiochus IV were instituted (1 Macc 2:1) and regarded as the home of the Hasmoneans, the remains of a synagogue were found along with other evidence of Hasmonean-era habitation. With the earliest evidence of settlement dating to the Persian period, the major occupation layer attested is from the Roman period. While some evidence for a public building that may have been a synagogue predates the Roman period, the main phase for the synagogue at this location begins during the Herodian period and continues until the Bar Kokhba revolt.[100] A hall measuring ten by twelve meters with two rows of four columns each in front of stepped benches demonstrates a rather typical pattern for these first-century edifices. If the Hasmonean-era structure could be identified more definitively as a synagogue, it would be the oldest exemplar in Israel. Nearby in the modern town of Kiryat Sefer are the remains of another village dating to Hasmonean times. A smaller square structure of 9.6 meters on each side, with a raised area on three sides presumably for benches and two rows of four columns each are also found in this structure.[101] Another public building in the same vicinity at Ḥorvat Etri was found in excavations from

1999–2000, a structure thirteen by seven meters with the entry along one of the long walls, hence a broadhouse-type synagogue, according to the excavators. Three large columns across the hall supported the roof. A stepped pool identified as a mikveh was located near the entrance. The column arrangement does not match the other synagogues, and the edifice does not have permanent benches like the others. Slightly later in construction than those already described, it is difficult to establish with any certainty that this was a synagogue.[102]

What is notable about these structures from the first century is their simple construction and shape, lacking for the most part in ornamentation or cult symbolism.[103] The recently discovered inscription of a menorah on a stone from the synagogue at Migdal could be the exception. The well-known mosaics with symbols such as the Torah shrine, the incense shovel, the menorah, the shofar, the *lûlab* (palm branch), and the *'etrōg* (citron) are characteristic of those structures dated at their earliest to the third or early fourth centuries CE, apparently indicative of a growing explicit religious identification for these institutions.[104] In the first century, however, the evidence in Palestine points much more clearly to a village-based community structure with both religious and communal dimensions, the latter more explicitly apparent.[105] Not surprisingly diaspora synagogues give more evidence of the religious nature, presumably a more necessary element for Jewish identity outside of Israel. Rather than an explicitly religious identity, the evidence increasingly points to the synagogue as a central structure, and perhaps institution, for the village-based Jewish society of the late Roman period, but already present in the first century CE.[106] The square formation of many of these structures with benches on three or four sides, or even rectangular configurations still emphasizing the center rather than one end with a stage or platform for performance or lecture, appear to emphasize the communal functions of these buildings. Perhaps the ambiguity of the designation of the term *sunagōgē* itself with regard to both the assembly and the building offers evidence supporting this proposal concerning the nature of this first-century institution. Since these synagogues, with the possible exception of Gamla, were not necessarily destroyed in the Jewish War of 70 and since new models are not apparent until at least the third century CE, they are the best exemplars available for determining the nature of the synagogue in Galilee at the conclusion of the first century.

This archaeological evidence coincides with the literary evidence already discussed. The *ekklēsia* was a term used to designate the assembly of the followers of Jesus. The synagogue was the central communal institution of the village or town. These are not competing religious bodies. The *ekklēsia* designates this particular sectarian group within the town, and as such it represented and lived out a different set of Jewish practices than either the majority culture of the community or of competing sectarian organizations. That divergent set of practices can be demonstrated in the contrasting procedures of communal discipline.

The Literary Context of Matthew 18

Matthew 18 constitutes a redactional unity with a limited amount of material found in the synoptic parallels.[107] Matthew 18:15–20 is surrounded by material which emphasizes inclusion and forgiveness. Verses 6–9 concentrate on care for "the little ones" and causing offense, the latter a concern already noted in the discussion of Matt 5:29–30 above.[108] In the discussion of this earlier passage it was apparent that maintenance of the sectarian community is the major issue, and the "offense" is those actions or ideas that would detract from or be in opposition to sectarian life, that is, adultery. Whether the warning is against those external ideas, experiences, or items that could appear attractive or whether it concerns persons within the sect that propose deviant ideas or activities is not made clear. It is probably both. It certainly includes yielding to the temptation to indulge in those activities not permitted by Jewish law as interpreted by this community of the followers of Jesus. A similar case can be made for 18:8–9. Davies and Allison express a certain puzzlement regarding the disruptive presence of those two verses, since v. 10 could follow directly upon v. 7 in this chapter.[109] However, the injunction against causing one of these little ones who believe in Jesus to sin (vv. 6–7) calls for the same action as any stumbling block that stands in the way of the full participation in the sectarian way of life. These verses set the context for understanding the parable of the lost sheep and the procedures of vv. 15–20. The real concern is to deal with those who encourage other sect members toward deviant beliefs or actions. The interpretation of the action of the shepherd in 18:12–13 by the author of Matthew is made clear in 18:14, "So it is not the will of your Father in heaven that one of these little ones should be lost." Again the concern is the violation of the expectations of the sectarian community and a disruption of its life.[110] However, now the focus is explicitly on the person who causes offense, who through word or example leads "these little ones" to violate sectarian norms and expectations.

Further substantiation for such a reading of Matt 18:6 can be found in the phrase "these little ones who believe in me." In both Chapters 3 and 4 above, we have treated statements about the centrality of Jesus as affirmations of the central tenets of the Jewish sect formed by his followers in Galilee. The statement in v. 6 is the equivalent of the use of the phrase in 5:11: "Blessed are you when people revile you and persecute you and utter all kinds of evil against you *for my sake.*" Sectarian life was centered in the belief that Jesus was both spokesperson and agent of the will of God at that time in human history. That is what "the little ones" believe and have signed up for. At the beginning of the next pericope, the story of the lost sheep, we are told in v. 10 regarding the little ones that "in heaven their angels continually see the face of my Father in heaven." Through their participation in and allegiance to this group they have access to the Divine that transcends time and space, history and physical life. Elsewhere it is the "pure in heart," one of the other descriptors of the sectarians in the Beatitudes, who will see God (5:3). Outside of the references in 18:6, 10, and 14, the other occurrence of the "little ones" is found in 10:42: "Whoever gives even a cup of cold water to one of these little ones in the name of a disciple—truly I tell you, none of these will lose their reward." Here at the conclusion of the missionary discourse in 10:40–11:1 is the place in the composition where the authority of Jesus is extended to the twelve disciples: "Whoever welcomes you welcomes me, and whoever welcomes me welcomes the one who sent me." The authoritative status of the sect as the representative and agent of the will of God is being substantiated in this portrait of an expanding circle of authority and power. A similar evaluation can be found in Matt 25:31–46, in which acts performed on behalf of "one of the least of these my brothers, you did it to me" (vv. 40, 45). Of course, this latter text engages the question of how to judge those outside of the sect in light of a universal and imminent judgment. The "least" and the "little" are the same as the "meek," the "poor," and the "humble" in the beatitudes of the Sermon on the Mount. All are adjectives referring to the membership of this sectarian body of persons in the Jewish community who believed God had chosen to intervene in human history through the life and death of Jesus Christ. The maintenance of the integrity of this community which constituted the future of the Jewish people and the world was a serious task. The nature of its activities in which it incarnated the will of God in its life was a weighty responsibility. Of course, the reaction of the remainder of the world to this incarnation was an equally serious matter. In chapter 18 the concern is the manner in which the community incorporates the will of God into its life.

Matthew 18:10–14 reflects concern for the lost sheep who went astray. We have already mentioned the little ones whose "angels continually see the face of my Father in heaven." Significantly the author of the first gospel describes this single sheep using the verb *planaō* (go astray) rather than *apolumi* (lose), as in Luke 15:4.[111] Elsewhere in Matthew this term appears only at 22:29 and 24:4, 5, 11, 24. This latter chapter is the "little apocalypse" in which the warning is against false messiahs and prophets who would "lead astray" or "deceive." In other words, the term used to describe the lost sheep in the passive voice suggests "the one who is led astray." Erring members of the sect and their reincorporation into full participation in communal life are the concern of this parable in Matthew. On the other side, following the section on communal discipline we find an explicit discussion of the meaning of forgiveness for the adherents of the Matthean group, including the question about the number of times forgiveness is required and the parable of the unforgiving servant.[112] The meaning of the communal legislation for the Matthean group can only be determined within this context. Sectarian life is a very complicated social enterprise. The maintenance of group solidarity, a task that includes dealing with those people and forces that undercut group adherence while reinforcing and supporting those devoted and expectant members, is a delicate process, the execution of which largely determines the nature and tenor of the communal body. Matthew 18 spells out the attitude, procedure, and rationale for this endeavor.

What then is the meaning of the second half of the passage under consideration, Matt 18:18–20? "Truly I tell you, whatever you bind on earth will be bound in heaven and whatever you loose on earth will be loosed in heaven." This wording also appears in Matt 16:18–20, in this case in the singular and addressed to Peter. This is the only other place in the gospel where, as already mentioned, we also find the term *ekklēsia*. In this passage Peter is given the keys to the kingdom of heaven. There appear to be two primary interpretations given for the meaning of the binding and loosing in these two passages: it is either a mandate to provide authoritative legislation regarding issues pertaining to the life of the Jewish group addressed in the book, or it gives to Peter the authority to admit and exclude people from the group, presumably including reinstatement.[113] To understand the meaning of the phrase we need to examine the imagery which lies behind it. Regarding the keys of the kingdom, J. Andrew Overman has pointed to passages such as 2 Bar. 10:18 in post-70 Jewish literature in which the priests are to give up the keys of the temple because of their failure to exercise proper stewardship of their divinely appointed trust: "You, priests, take the keys of the sanctuary, and cast them to the highest heaven, and give them to the Lord and say, 'Guard your house yourself, because, behold, we have been found to be false stewards.'"[114] This apocalyptic critique of the Second Temple priesthood is accompanied by descriptions of a glorious heavenly temple in other apocalyptic compositions that in some instances is held out as a future expectation. Nickelsburg has pointed to parallels between 1 En. 12–16, T. Levi 2–7, and this commissioning story to demonstrate the priestly connections of the Matthean account.[115] Furthermore we find in the Qumran materials the hope for a more glorious and perfect future temple fit for divine habitation and the accompanying purity legislation that spells out the requirements of those preparing to be in the divine presence.[116] The sectarian community incorporated aspects of this future temple and its requirements into their communal life. The significance of this line of argumentation for the meaning of the binding and loosing texts in Matthew is then clear. For these followers of Jesus the possibility of a more suitable and glorious location for the presence of the Divine rests with the life and teaching of Jesus Christ. Living the Jewish life he taught is the manner in which participation in the divine presence is possible. Thus the delegation of authority to the assembly of the followers of Jesus in Matt 16:18–19 (through Peter) and in 18:18–20 reflects their understanding of the central role and responsibility they hold with regard to a Jewish future. They are in charge of interpreting what God wants from humankind. In later rabbinic traditions we read of discussions concerning how many persons are required to be present during the study of Torah for the Šəkīnāh (Divine Presence) to rest among them.[117] In rabbinic traditions this can indicate both a certain level of authority and also reward. The ongoing presence of Jesus assures the continuing role of the Divine in the life of the Matthean group (Matt 1:23; 28:20).

Conclusion

The role of reproof within the formal legal structures specified in the texts from Qumran has been outlined above. The text 1QS V, 25–VI, 1 situates the injunction to reprove within the context of the lifestyle expectations of the sect and sets forth its importance in the communal procedures for addressing wrongs within the group. In CD 9 we noted the manner in which the injunction to reprove is integrated into a discussion of the issue of the number of witnesses required for conviction. In this instance, Lev 19:17–18 is dealt with as a literary unit; hence reproof is related to the commandments not to take vengeance or bear a grudge. As noted, this text moves the discussion into the more serious infractions regarding crimes that involve capital punishment. The serious nature of this penal code means that the analysis of Moshe Weinfeld must be called into question when he proposes the following conclusions concerning this text: "As in other issues, this issue also deviates from legal, formalistic wording and passes into moral sermonizing."[118] While this conclusion might be drawn by comparison with materials in the Iobacchi codes, the above analysis of this interpretive tradition suggests otherwise. Given the manner in which this issue appears in a variety of sectarian compositions, its importance for group functioning is not to be underestimated. The sectarians place it within the tradition of the interpretation of biblical law. Of greatest significance is the fact that it is part of a penal code attested rather broadly in Jewish life prior to Matthew.

An examination of the Matthean code within the context of the history which has been sketched above helps to clarify its intent and purpose. A comparison of Matt 18:15–20 with the range of perspectives and roles regarding reproof in the Qumran documents demonstrates that it is closest to the legislation in 1QS where the adherent is charged with the obligation "to reprove his neighbor in truth, humility and loving charity for one another. No one is to speak to a companion with anger or ill-temper or stubbornly or with a mean spirit of wickedness" (1QS V, 24–26).[119] The motivation behind these prescriptions seems to be to set a tone of care and respect within the sect with regard to errant behavior. The tone is already apparent in Matt 18:4–5: the person who is humble "like this little child" is greatest in the kingdom of heaven. More to the point, this demonstrates the type of interaction that appears to be intended in Matt 18:15: "If your brother sins, go and point it out when the two of you are alone. If he listens to you, you have regained your brother."[120] Of some significance here is the omission of two words: "If your brother sins *against you*," in the oldest major MSS of this text.[121] A sectarian reading of this text, supported by 1QS V, 24–VI, 1, would indicate that the legislative tradition of reproof applies to the range of expectations of the behavior of sectarians and not the question of the offense against a fellow sect member, even though that is not ruled out. In both instances the initial approach is to be private, with the intent of giving the offending sectarian the benefit of the doubt with regard to the nature of the offense or the possibility of changed behavior. Mercy in the act of reproof is also advocated in the passage cited above from 4Q286.[122] In the Community Rule this is followed by the statement "A man also shall not bring before the association an issue against his neighbor without a prior rebuke before witnesses." Both the sectarians of the Community Rule and Matthew have a similar set of procedures concerning how an infraction is dealt with at the communal level. In both instances it first involves an appearance before witnesses before the matter is brought before the entire group.

The purpose of the legislation in CD 9 appears to be more legalistic, that is, interested in the development of a strict legal code by which the Qumran group could regulate acts of perceived deviance among its membership. The formational function of reproof (noted in CD 15:13–15, 20:3–8; 1QS VIII, 16b–19; and 4QBer[a] 14) would have served an important purpose for both sectarian groups. The followers of Jesus associated with the gospel of Matthew were defining their behavior within the sectarian traditions known from other groups in the Second Temple period.

Understanding the procedures for the appeal of grievances within the context of an emphasis on "brotherly" relationships has been noted in studies of the social world of Matthew, including references to the repetition of brotherhood language throughout the work, especially in the Sermon on the Mount and chapter 18.[123] The explanation for this emphasis in studies of the social history of Matthew "is that Matthew has shaped and constructed this traditional material in such a way as to provide instruction for his community about dealing with dissension and erring members.... The whole of chap. 18 ... aims at dealing with the problem of division within the community."[124] This perception appears to be rooted in the earlier redaction critical work which argued that Matthew's use of the law had a two-fold purpose: to describe the relationship of the Matthean community to Judaism; and to counter antinomian tendencies within the Christian movement. Here we propose a different option for understanding this material.

This passage deals with the problems attendant this new sectarian option within the Jewish community as the sect struggles to identify itself and present a holistic alternative to the other perceptions of Judaism in that community all of which it judges to be inadequate, hence further away from carrying out the will of God for God's people. Since boundary marking mechanisms have been established earlier in the composition, the focus of this section is on communal maintenance. In the sociological analysis of sect formation, this section highlights the element of difference. There is a very distinctive treatment of communal discipline within this section that is based on the values of the sect, but which appears also to have been drawn from earlier traditions of sectarian life available in first-century Judea, and perhaps more broadly. The element of separation is assumed in this treatment, even though it is not highlighted within the text. In this case the similarities of the procedures in the Matthean text to those from earlier sectarian compositions suggest the deliberate location of the Matthean community within that sectarian tradition. In this case the element of separation is apparent in this identification with earlier sectarian procedures, how earlier groups had attempted to maintain their own separation. This Matthean sect has utilized those earlier traditions in the service of its own maintenance, the formation and retention of its membership.

6 Jesus and His Opponents

As the story develops, the strife between Jesus and his opponents escalates. These conflicts come to a climax in Matt 23 and 26–27. As Mark Allan Powell reminds us, conflict is a necessary part of any good story.[1] In this case it is apparent by comparison with complementary versions of the same story in the other gospels that the level of conflict is most pronounced in Matthew. The significance of this characteristic requires exploration and explanation if we are to grasp the import of this writer's message for the followers of Jesus and the members of the Jewish community of which they were a part.

An outline of the contents of the first gospel receiving widespread acceptance among Matthean scholars remains an elusive goal; however it is an issue that impacts upon our understanding of this section of the text.[2] The pentateuchal structure of earlier scholarship finds an eschatological discourse with a focus on judgment beginning at Matt 19:1, with a transition to a concluding section at 26:1. In this case the diatribes of chapter 23 are seen as a different literary section of the composition from the trial and crucifixion of chapters 26–27. While also admitting the impossibility of identifying a discernible coherent structure for the composition as a whole, Craig Evans has in his outline entitled the final section "The Rejection and Vindication of the Messiah," beginning at 21:1, "When they had come near Jerusalem."[3] While I do not regard Evans's heading as an appropriate description of its content, the turn toward Jerusalem is a good point of transition for this section of the text, including chapters 23 and 26–27. The departure from Galilee is noted at 19:1, a significant transition, but 21:1 marks the shift to the final conflicts, the climax, of the composition. It is in this section that the depiction of the forces at work in this first-century

Jewish community coalesces in a comprehensive portrayal of the social world reflecting the perspective of these followers of Jesus.

The Emerging Conflict

The initial escalation of the conflict is identified by Jesus's dramatic entry into Jerusalem upon a donkey, which throws the whole city into turmoil (Matt 21:1–11). In the narrative the whole city, including both the Jewish and the Roman leadership, is put on notice through the reaction of the crowds to this entrance. This is followed immediately by the entry into the temple and the conflicts with the money-changers and those who sold doves. Following this, Jesus departs to Bethany for the night, providing a context for the irrational cursing of the fig tree. While the author does not include the confounding line found in Mark 11:13, "for it was not the season for figs," the account still bears evidence of an impulsive, angry response. The tree withers immediately and will never again be able to produce figs. While Matt 21:21–22 relates the incident to faith, picking up the theme of the faith to move mountains also found in 17:20, it is doubtful that faith here refers to a simple dogmatic assertion of the power of God. Matthew here is rather referring to the belief that there is an unprecedented action in human history, certainly the history of Israel, presently under way inaugurated through the life and death of Jesus Christ. Faith has to do with believing that this is the case and trusting that the proper way to live as a good Israelite at the present time is to follow his teachings. The cursing of the fig tree, then, indicates that the traditional authorities of the Jewish community no longer have sway in light of these unfolding events, even though they continue to attempt to exert their power. The story follows the controversy with the chief priests and scribes in the temple described only in Matt 21:14–16, resulting from the overturning of the tables, curing the blind and lame in the temple, and the cries of exaltation by the children. It precedes the return to the temple when his authority is questioned by the chief priests and elders of the people (21:23–27).

A series of parables set in the temple and addressed to the chief priests and the Pharisees focus on either the temple or these leadership bodies (Matt 21:45). Included are the parables of the two sons, the wicked tenants, and the wedding banquet (21:28–22:14). In subsequent questioning, the Sadducees also are brought into the picture, rounding out the composite portrait of the leadership structures of the Jewish community prior to and after the destruction of the temple. Some of these questions, such as the payment of taxes to Caesar, the husbands in the resurrection, and the greatest commandment, followed by the contest between Jesus and the Pharisees concerning the nature of the messiah as David's son, appear to be attempts to trick or stump the authoritative teacher. In all cases Matthew has Jesus emerge victorious in this contest of wills. Of course this portrait only makes sense if we understand it to be a composite resulting from a combination of story time and real time. In this case "story time" refers to the chronology of the events outlined in the first gospel, with a historical setting in Jerusalem during the time that prefects were appointed as governors over Judea, prior to the destruction of the temple. The storyteller is narrating from the vantage point of a Jewish community in Galilee a few decades after the destruction of the temple and the stationing of a Roman legion in Jerusalem to control events. External evidence attesting to the actual structure of Jewish communities at the end of the first century in which the gospel of Matthew would have been composed and read is so limited that it is impossible to establish with any level of certainty what it would have been. Internal evidence certainly points to the priority of the Pharisees in the world of Matthew. Presumably the Sadducees also were present. The chief priests and the scribes are primary in the prior account in Mark, and presumably the chief priests would have been the dominant players at the actual time of the crucifixion. All are present in Matthew's description of the events leading up to the execution of Jesus. This victorious encounter leads into the denunciation of the scribes and Pharisees in Matt 23.

To determine the context of chapter 23 we need to examine Matt 24–25, the apocalyptic chapters. This section begins with the prediction of the destruction of the temple (24:1–2), followed by the construction of an eschatological scenario beginning with the desolating sacrilege of Daniel. While we might presume that the sole interest of the author was in the chronology of the scenario in Daniel, that seems to be an unreliable interpretation of the manner in which first-century authors utilized inherited apocalyptic material. It is much more likely that we find in Matthew a perception that the events in the temple from 66–70 were similar to those under Antiochus Epiphanes in 167–164 BCE, a presumption of an analogous state of affairs. Only a very particular group of the faithful or pious would survive this onslaught, as described in Dan 12:1–12. The coming of the Son of Man suggests the same background for this section of the first gospel. More specifically, what the followers of Jesus are to expect, how they should react, and what they are to do are then spelled out in the remainder of these two chapters prior to the return of the chief priests and elders of the people into the story (Matt 26:3–5). Crucial for the account of the trial is the prediction of the destruction of the temple, even though now it is coupled with the accusation against Jesus, charging him with making the statement "I am able to destroy the temple of God, and to build it in three days" (26:61).

Those scholars who have examined and acknowledged the manner in which apocalyptic literature, or at least apocalyptic eschatology, is an important influence in the gospel of Matthew point to the centrality of the temple in chapters 24 and 25. In the initial monograph where David Sim highlights this aspect of the first gospel, he notes the debate regarding the extent to which the destruction of the temple is the central theme of the section he entitles "The Apocalyptic Discourse."[4] Grant Macaskill suggests that the destruction of the temple dominates this section, but then outlines the material on the basis of the two questions of the disciples in Matt 24:3: "When will this be? And what will be the sign of your coming and of the end of the age?" While some scholars have highlighted the two questions as two separate issues to be addressed, Macaskill points to a reading which sees the destruction of Jerusalem and the fall of the temple as part of an eschatological scenario that also includes the enthronement of the Son of Man and a final judgment.[5] While the coming of the Son of Man in judgment in 24:30–31 points back to Dan 7:13–14, 26–27, and Matt 24:29 places that event in the context of the eschatological expectations of Hebrew prophecy, the reference to the desolating sacrilege of Matt 24:15 explicitly mentions Daniel.[6] We are reminded of the importance of the book of Daniel to first-century Palestinian Jews.[7] The destruction of the temple is an integral event in a number of Second Temple apocalyptic scenarios.[8] While in story time this section in Matthew is predictive, in real time the story is explaining to its readers that they are in the midst of these eschatological events. This is not simply predictive as we might expect from the perspective of a linear projection; the book of Daniel provides the template whereby these followers of Jesus can understand what is happening at present. Just as in Daniel where the desolation of the temple and a judgment under the authority of the Son of Man will result in the exaltation of the "wise," thus will be the fate of these followers of Jesus who endure an analogous set of events. So why place the chapter on the scribes and Pharisees, found in neither Mark nor Luke, into the midst of this account?

The Diatribe of Matthew 23

Matthew 23 makes a rather surprising appearance in the development of the first gospel, particularly if one assumes that the author is following the outline of Mark. This account appears in the context of the encounters in the temple and is followed by attention to the fate of the temple and the consequent implications for first-century Jewish life. Matthew demonstrates more interest in the other identified Jewish groups than any of the other gospels. The Sadducees appear seven times in Matthew, but only once in both Mark and Luke. There are twenty-eight references to the Pharisees in the first gospel, only twenty in Luke, and eleven in the more abbreviated Mark. In a comparison of the synoptic gospels, it is apparent that Matthew in this section provides a more extensive treatment of the scribes, the Pharisees, and the Sadducees than is found in parallel synoptic accounts. Mark 12:38–40 criticizes only the scribes for the behavior attributed to the Pharisees in Matthew. In this instance the same can be said for Luke 20:45–47. The long diatribe directed against "the scribes and Pharisees, hypocrites" is found only in the first gospel and represents the distinctive approach of that author to other Jewish groups. Lucan parallels to many of the sayings suggest they were drawn from Q, but there is no evidence of a literary and rhetorical structure such as that found in Matthew.

The sectarian nature of the first gospel is evident throughout the argument of this chapter. Matthew is directing his message against other Jewish groups with whom the followers of Jesus would have been in competition. Two of those groups identified in Matthew, as well as in other Jewish evidence from the first century, are the Pharisees and Sadducees. These groups are brought into this account to align them with the chief priests and the leaders of the people held responsible by the author for failing in their responsibilities as leaders of Israel and, very particularly, for the death of Jesus. So the author of the first gospel marginalizes his immediate opponents by bringing them into the circle of the Jewish authorities and leaders who are held responsible for the destruction of the temple by some groups in the Jewish community. Clearly they are incapable of providing good leadership for the Jewish community. They do not have the insight to chart out the pathway for Jews after the destruction of the temple, nor do they understand the significance of the destruction of the temple for present developments in Jewish history. The scribes, the Pharisees, the Sadducees, the chief priests, and the elders of the people all are inadequate for that task. Only the followers of Jesus have the knowledge that will permit Jews to truly understand the will of God at the present time. The prominence of chapter 23 in this argument suggests that from the standpoint of the author the Pharisees are significant opponents. It may be that they constituted the opponents closest to the viewpoints of the followers of Jesus, hence providing the greatest opposition. This text suggests that they also carried some weight in the Jewish community, but given the paucity of evidence available about the nature of governance and leadership at the time, such a conclusion is less than certain.

Matthew 23 consists of three literary sections, vv. 1–12, 13–36, and 37–39;[9] the latter section should extend to 24:2.[10] If the woes of 23:13–36 are to be understood as a contrast to the blessings of 5:3–10 (see below), then to conceive of 23:1–12 in relationship to the position of Jesus in 5:1–2 does not demand a great leap of the imagination. In fact, many commentators cite 23:2 as evidence for the seated position described in Matt 5:1 as the particular venue of an authoritative teacher. While we know of archaeological evidence of a seat of honor in the synagogue in the archaeological remains of fourth- and fifth-century synagogues such as those at Chorazin and Tiberias, the nature of the reference in Matthew is less than clear.[11] Even if there was no "seat of Moses" in the first-century meeting hall, as seems probable, the portrayal of the scribes and Pharisees as having assumed a role as the authoritative interpreters of Torah is evident. This of course reflects the vantage point of the author of Matthew.

The "heavy burdens" of Matt 23:4 suggest a contrast with the yoke of 11:28–30, even though the latter passage is in tension with the preferred narrow way of 7:13–14 at the conclusion of the Sermon on the Mount. This is a complicated juxtaposition in which, on the one hand, the demands of the scribes and Pharisees are portrayed as heavy and burdensome in contrast to the easy yoke and light burden of 11:30; and on the other, the claims attributed to Jesus by the author are in tension with the expectations placed in Jesus's mouth in the Sermon on the Mount. The statement concerning the "heavy burdens" follows immediately after the charge about the disjunction between the teachings and the actions of the scribes and Pharisees, thereby setting up the subsequent references to them as hypocrites (23:2–3). Assuming that such a perspective applies to this verse as well, the problem is not simply the heavy burdens, it is their unwillingness to provide assistance in their alleviation. Their arrogant and self-serving manner does nothing toward that end, while Jesus in 11:29 is gentle, humble in heart, and provides rest for their souls.[12] That the yoke is then easy and the burden light is an outcome of the acceptance of the yoke, a familiar theme from other Second Temple literature as well and applied in a variety of circumstances.[13] This same message is apparent in the rigorous demands of the Sermon on the Mount; Matt 6:25–34 addresses the issue of anxiety about the demands of daily life, presumably due to the uncertain status of Jews throughout the Roman Empire, the oppressive nature of Roman rule in first-century Judea and Galilee, and the pressures on Jewish communities and their leadership throughout this period. This follows the earlier discussion of prayer and fasting that focuses upon the activities of the hypocrites (Matt 6:1–18). From a Matthean perspective, this relief from the burdens is apparent in the activities of Jesus noted in Matt 11:4–6, which is produced as evidence of the beginning of the reign of God he announced in 4:17 and apparent in 4:23–27. Life for most people in the Roman Empire was difficult. The best way for Jews to live within that environment was the issue for these various Jewish groups. The author of Matthew believed that the sectarian group composed of the followers of Jesus had provided the answer to that question; it was evident in their founder's proclamation and exemplified in his life and death.

Such an analysis provides an apparent context for the next section, Matt 23:5–7, which constitutes a related set of charges already leveled in 6:2–6 concerning the desire for public recognition and accolades as the primary motivation of these Jewish leaders. Within the Sermon on the Mount this already is set in contrast to the features of the sectarian identity spelled out in the Beatitudes. Here it is followed by the contrasting rationale of servanthood and humility in 23:8–12, echoes of 10:24–25 and 20:25–28, expected of the followers of Jesus. The diatribe against the religious leadership of the Jewish community is based in the sectarian identity established in the first major discourse of the composition, the Sermon on the Mount.

The use of the term "hypocrite" is striking in the "woes" section of the composition, Matt 23:13–36, and is also apparent in the Sermon on the Mount. The only other reference to the term in Matthew is 15:7 // Mark 7:6. That the term is more broadly attested in the literature of the time is apparent in its usage in Luke 12:56 and 15:13, without synoptic parallels, and in other materials.[14] The Matthean references do emerge as important both for their prominence and for the connection between the Sermon on the Mount and this diatribe. The charges against the scribes and Pharisees in Matt 23:2–11, the same people referred to as hypocrites in the following list of woes, bear a remarkable similarity to the portrayal of the hypocrites in Matthew 6:2, 5, and 16 with regard to prayer and fasting. These "actors," the original meaning of the term, pose as the representatives of the will of God, but they do not live and act as though this were true. This sectarian labeling of an influential leading group of the local Jewish community is an attempt to undercut their legitimacy and authority. The identity formation of the Sermon on the Mount establishes the basis of their own legitimacy and authority, then begins to undercut the authority and legitimacy of the group they perceive to be their major opponents. Here in Matt 23 the case is made in a much more vigorous manner. The legitimacy and authority of the scribes and Pharisees are totally undercut in this diatribe on the charge of hypocrisy. While the sociological elements of difference and separation are apparent in the Sermon on the Mount, the element of antagonism is now very evident in this demonstration of the tension between the group envisioned by the author and the Jewish socio-cultural environment in which this sect is located. This tension is heightened as the narrative prepares the way for the climax of the conflict and the ultimate act of the betrayal of the will of God, that is, the death of Jesus.

There are a total of seven woes in Matt 23, two less than the number of blessings found in Matt 5:3–12.[15] Since Matt 5:11–12 has a different structure from the earlier section, it is more accurately understood as a literary structure of 8 + 1 macarisms. A related structure of 4 + 1 is evident in 4Q525 (Beatitudes) 2 II.[16] In both cases, the first eight (or four) macarisms demonstrate a rather clear consistent literary pattern followed by one extended literary construction, apparently as a conclusion. In both cases the potentially negative consequences for those accepting the obligations attached to the initial blessings are developed. In 4Q525 2 II, 3–6 we read about times of trial, distress, and terror; in Matt 5:11–12, of persons who will revile, persecute, and make false accusations. In Matt 23:13–36 the literary pattern of the first six woes is not as consistent, particularly in the length of each strophe, but the concluding section is the one in which the rhetoric of accusation and condemnation reaches its climax, with the accusations that the scribes and Pharisees are the descendants of those who murdered the prophets; they are snakes, a brood of vipers, and they are the ones who will kill, crucify, and flog the prophets, sages, and scribes who will be sent by Jesus (23:29–36). These are the ones who carry out the activities against the members of the sect in 5:11–12. In the social world of Matthew, those who are blessed will be flogged and persecuted; those who carry out these activities are their opponents, hence they are also against the will of God. This contrast was already employed as an interpretive lens for viewing Israelite history in Deut 27–30, which concludes with a description of the two ways of life and death for Israel (30:15–20). The particular formulation of this choice by the author of Matthew, implicit in the sections just discussed, can be seen in more explicit form in the framework for the conclusion of the Sermon on the Mount provided by Matt 7:13–14; the narrow gate and difficult path leads to life, while the wide gate and the easy road leads to death. Within the first gospel the scribes and Pharisees are the facilitators of the latter option, not unlike the "seekers of smooth things," who are described in CD 1:18; 1QH^a X, 17, 34; and other texts from Qumran. Two-ways imagery can be found throughout the literature of the Second Temple era.[17] At the conclusion of the Sermon on the Mount, the two-ways imagery is employed to demonstrate the sociological element of separation necessary to sectarian identity. The choice proposed here is between the scribes and Pharisees and the followers of Jesus; Jesus is life and the Pharisees are death. Separation from the latter group is of utmost concern to Matthew. It is reinforced in Matt 5:11–12 and 23:29–36 by condemning the measures this group will take against the well-being of the sect and its members. Tension is more evident in the latter passage, with the sociological element of antagonism evident in the sectarian attitudes which here find expression.

Such a choice is evident in the opening lines of each section. In Matt 5:3 the kingdom of heaven belongs to the poor in spirit; in 23:13 the scribes and Pharisees lock people out of the kingdom of heaven.[18] They do not enter into the kingdom themselves and prohibit access to those who desire to do so. The Matthean viewpoint is reinforced in 5:20, just before the antitheses, by reminding the sectarian followers of Jesus that they will not enter the kingdom of heaven unless their righteousness exceeds that of the scribes and Pharisees. The point has already been made in 5:10 that those who are persecuted for the sake of righteousness are blessed, for the kingdom of heaven is theirs. The centrality of the kingdom of heaven as a frame for the Beatitudes, hence the interpretive context for the Sermon on the Mount, and its centrality for the entire first gospel has already been discussed above.[19]

The "children of hell" in Matt 23:15, who result from the proselytization efforts of the scribes and Pharisees, are the polar contrast to those who "will be called children of God" in Matt 5:9. This sole reference to a possible missionizing emphasis on the part of the scribes and Pharisees casts the hypothesis of such a venture in doubt. While there is evidence of gentile interest in Judaism, including both a limited number of proselytes and others who are described with various adjectives, this does not constitute an indication of substantial missionary activity on the part of the scribes and Pharisees. The name "god-fearer" attached to this group in earlier studies has not proved to be an indication of a distinct status within the social or religious communities of Jews in the Roman period. It seems more likely that this reference suggests efforts on the part of groups within Jewish communities, here the scribes and Pharisees, to move gentiles with a variety of attachments to the Jewish community into full status, that is, to make them proselytes. From the standpoint of Matthew they are being given an incorrect understanding of what it means to be a full participant in the people of Israel, hence they are being made "children of hell" rather than being brought closer to the kingdom of heaven. For these sectarians, the scribes and the Pharisees are misleading them about the way of life and the future of the Jewish people. In this passage, to "cross land and sea" suggests extensive efforts to turn these attached persons into proselytes, rather than an indication of extensive missionary travel. In the competition (i.e., conflict) among various Jewish groups at the end of the first century, proselytes will have come into consideration. This would have been a particular issue in the communities of Galilee which had both Jewish and non-Jewish populations. The level of antagonism evident in this woe suggests that the Matthean community viewed this as an area of intense conflict.[20]

The issue of oaths is addressed in both sections of Matthew. In 23: 16–22 the author castigates the attitudes the scribes and Pharisees bring to their oaths, perhaps suggesting an argument over the distinction between binding and non-binding oaths.[21] Matthew 5:33–36 forbids the swearing of all oaths. The similarity in language of the references "whoever swears by heaven swears by the throne of God" (23:22) and "Do not swear at all, either by heaven, for it is the throne of God" (5:34) is striking. Both point back to Isa 66:1, "The heaven is my throne and the earth is my footstool." In this highly contested area of discussion in Second Temple literature regarding the nature of oaths and their validity, the sectarian author certainly casts doubt on the validity of the oaths sworn in the temple, presumably because of the hierarchy's manipulation of their own commitments. The ambiguities in this legislation of the Second Temple era are apparent.

Debate about major and minor commandments, one way of framing the issue in Matt 23:23–24, is evident from the book of Matthew itself. The question of the greatest commandment has just been addressed in 22:34–40. The significance of all the law has been asserted by Jesus in 5:18–19. Similar debates pervade rabbinic literature.[22] For example, in the debate concerning whether the positive or negative commandments carry greater weight we find rabbinic reflections on how various prophets understood the essence of the law. Included in their discussions is the significance of Mic 6:8 (the basis for the assertion in Matt 23:23), "He has told you, O man, what is good, / And what the Lord requires of you: / Only to do justice / And to love goodness, / And to walk modestly with your God."[23] In some rabbinic discussions the relative weight of the laws was evaluated by comparing the severity of the punishment for violation.[24] The tithing of dill and cumin are mentioned in Tannaitic law, but not mint.[25] The well-known reply of Hillel regarding the essence of the law when asked to explain it to a proselyte is sometimes regarded as a saying closer to the time of Jesus: "What is hateful to you, do not do to your neighbor."[26] However that may be more reflective of a Tannaitic tradition within the rabbinic corpus than evidence of a first-century debate.[27] Of course, that particular injunction framed in the positive, as in Lev 19:18, is also found in the Sermon on the Mount (Matt 7:12). That the author here frames the question as an actual debate about the essence of the law is frequently overlooked: "It is these you ought to have practiced without neglecting the others." In Matt 23:24 we find an allusion to a legal debate, "You strain out a gnat but swallow a camel." CD 12:11–13 suggests that the "swarming things" of Lev 11:9–12 include the larvae of bees that are found in liquid, even though the biblical text appears to suggest only the "swarming things" in water are prohibited for human consumption. The remainder of the legislation in Lev 11 provides the basis for discussions of some complexity in rabbinic law. Later rabbinic evidence suggests a controversy over whether liquids such as wine and vinegar need to be strained in order to remove these insects. The rabbis permitted the consumption of land-based insects that were found in water and did not require the straining of liquids (t. Ter. 7:11; b. Ḥul. 66b–67a). Whether the Pharisees of that time had such a prohibition is impossible to determine. This could well be an instance in which Matthew is in conflict with the legal teachings of some other Jewish sectarian groups.[28] There is no negation of the law here, nor in Matt 5:18–19. In this case that debate is represented as one between the followers of Jesus and the Pharisees. There is no hint of a debate concerning the validity of the law or even of its leniency. The essence of the law was an important issue for any group claiming to be the best representative of the will of God for the Jewish people.

The same case can be made for the following passages: Matt 23:25–26 and 27–28. That vv. 25–26 actually are not about the cleanliness of dishes is apparent when the inside is "full of greed and self-indulgence." The same principle is to be found in rabbinic literature.[29] Intention is a major issue discussed by the rabbis with regard to the fulfillment of the law.[30] For example, all the sacrifices, whether cattle, birds, or grain, are equal as long as those making the offering have directed their minds to heaven.[31] In a discussion regarding whether the amount of Torah study is sufficient to ward off evil and illness, Rabbi Joḥanan reminds Rabbi Eleazar of this same principle.[32] This same topic continues into the next woe. However here there are certain Matthean indicators that conclude the argument. While the use of the term "righteous" (Matt 23:28) here appears to convey the broader meaning found throughout the Hebrew Bible, it also points to the term "righteousness" as it is used in a very particular manner to convey the understanding of the will of God these sectarian adherents attributed to Jesus.[33] That these Pharisees are full of hypocrisy is the charge throughout the chapter. That charge here is linked with the word "lawless" (23:28), a charge employed by Jewish groups in the denigration of their opponents already in the books of the Maccabees and continued in the first gospel.[34] The sectarians are those whose righteousness exceeds that of the scribes and Pharisees (5:20), while the hypocrites are those who are "workers of lawlessness" (7:23); "So you also on the outside look righteous to others, but inside you are full of hypocrisy and lawlessness" (23:28). While we have three woes that reflect the discussion of issues possibly common to all Jewish groups as evidenced in their appearance in the later texts of rabbinic literature, the argument concludes with the polemical barbs that redirect the readers back to the primary topic, the Pharisees. In the Sermon on the Mount we find an outline, an agenda, for those Jewish followers who believed that Jesus was the authoritative spokesperson for the will of God. In chapter 23 the opponents are described as the antithesis of those followers. In sociological terms, the tension of the group with its socio-cultural environment reflects not only the elements of separation and difference, but also a distinct antagonism.

The extended conclusion that constitutes the final woe builds upon the previous verses. Having characterized his opponents as whitewashed tombs, Jesus now advances to the charge that they murdered the prophets (Matt 23:29–36). A comparison with the Beatitudes is again instructive. The additional extended macarism (5:11–12) follows and elaborates on 5:10 and spells out in more concrete detail the author's understanding of the implications of belonging to this group of the followers of Jesus. The kingdom of heaven belongs to the "poor in spirit" (v. 3) who are "persecuted for the sake of righteousness" (v. 10). The repetition of the topic of righteousness to designate the will of God as understood by the sectarians has just been noted. Those who follow this Jewish way of life will be reviled and persecuted, just as the prophets were before them (5:11–12). As the charges in chapter 23 build toward a climax the countercharge emerges, that the sectarian followers of Jesus will go out as "prophets, sages, and scribes, some of whom you will kill and crucify, some you will flog in your synagogues and pursue from town to town" (23:34). This follows the charge that they incriminate themselves when they say that they would not have shed the blood of the prophets, as their ancestors had done. If this is a reference to 1 Kgs 18:4, 13 and 19:14, which seems quite possible, then the Pharisees are aligned with the apostate reign of Ahab and Jezebel, the former being the son of Omri and regarded as the worst king of the Northern Kingdom by the Deuteronomistic historian, even though archaeological evidence suggests that he was a quite wealthy ruler of a powerful state. The Matthean author places the followers of Jesus in the tradition of Elijah, the prophetic opponent of Ahab. This is a rather effective framing of the conflict in the Jewish community, with the Pharisees as the oppressive "other" of the biblical tradition.

Flogging in the synagogue here designates an open public context, the town forum or square, and not necessarily a specifically religious environment.[35] While it is very difficult to determine the social context, we see in m. Mak. 3:12 the reference to *ḥazzan hakkəneset* (superintendent of the synagogue) as the official charged with implementing the decisions of the court. Specific details regarding the whip and the activity are detailed in the Mishnah. While it is doubtful that this legislation was available and carried out at the conclusion of the first century CE, the role of the superintendent is described already in texts delineating temple procedures, suggesting that the position was known in the Second Temple.[36] The rabbinic descriptions of this position are concerned more with the liturgical functioning of both synagogue and temple than with the very particular role of the execution of this punishment. The references to persecution in the first gospel tell us more about the self-understanding of this body of followers than it does about their actual experiences in the Jewish community. From their sectarian perspective they are a marginalized body experiencing the consequences of that status. Their opponents, the Pharisees, are portrayed as their opposite, even bearing responsibility for their treatment within the Jewish community.

At the height of this invective, Matthew accuses the opponents of the followers of Jesus of being guilty of shedding all of the innocent blood upon the earth from Abel (see Gen 4:10) to Zechariah, presumably the son of the priest Jehoiada (2 Chr 24:20–22), even though the "son of Berachiah" describes the prophet Zechariah (Zech 1:1, 7). Whether the former is a direct allusion to 1 En. 22:7 could be questioned, but there does seem to be some similarity in the use of the figure, since "it is widely assumed that vv. 5–7 depict Abel as the prototype of the martyred righteous."[37] The "persecuted righteous" of 1 Enoch have already been discussed above and are prominent in the Epistle of Enoch (1 En. 92–105). While the acceptability and popularity of the message of the prophets is a constant issue throughout the Hebrew Bible, the question has a different cast by the time of the composition of Matthew. What this portrayal demonstrates is that Matthew employed literary imagery and theology already familiar from apocalyptic literature to describe the life and teachings of Jesus as they were understood at the conclusion of the first century by his followers and to depict their understanding of their place in Jewish communal life. The relationship of apocalyptic ideology and imagery to sectarianism is amply demonstrated in the Qumran corpus.

This section concludes with the lament for Jerusalem and the forecast of the destruction of the temple. It constitutes the rhetorical conclusion to the escalating argument advanced throughout the chapter. Of course, the murder of Zechariah already mentioned in Matt 23:35 is actually described as a stoning in 2 Chr 24:20–22, as here in v. 37. Stoning was the mode of execution mandated in Deut 17:2–7 for idolaters. We also note the mandate of death for false prophets in Deut 13:2–6 and 18:20–22. Aware of biblical law, Matthew reverses the argument suggesting that those killed are actually the righteous whom God will deliver at the time of judgment. Those engaged in the killing are the opponents rather than the proponents of the will of God. This same contrast is evident in the next phrase, *ēthelēsa* (I wished) versus *ouk ēthelēsate* (you did not wish), the contrast in person of the two verbs representing the two groups envisioned by the author. "To gather" (*episunagein*) may point to the eschatological hope identified in

Matt 24:30–31 as well as in the final verses of the composition (28:16–20). Both the vindication of Jerusalem and the ingathering of the nations are envisioned in Isaiah 66. The use of the first person in this instance suggests the possibility of the voice of wisdom, as in Matt 11:28–30. While Luz legitimately rejects an attribution of the two verses in their totality to wisdom, the question beginning *posakis* (how often), suggesting repeated appeals over an extended period of time, points to something beyond a simple appeal by Jesus.[38] The connection of wisdom and the Son of Man is already established in our treatment of Matt 11:19–24 above. The rejection of wisdom is part of that discussion.[39] Refuge under the wings of the Lord is a repeated reference in the Hebrew Bible, especially the Psalms.[40] Just as the residents of Chorazin and Bethsaida were accused of rejecting the deeds (and message) of Jesus (Matt 11:20–21) with the result that they would not fare well on the day of judgment, Jerusalem had not responded to the wisdom of Jesus, the anointed spokesperson for the will of God to whom as Son of Man authority would be given in judgment. The protection offered to those who gather under the wings was not available to those who did not accept the message, hence their destruction that could not be averted, "your house is left to you, desolate" (23:38). This prediction is made very explicit in Matt 24:2, the concluding verse of the section, "not one stone will be left . . ."

This prediction of the destruction of the temple, in story time, points the reader in real time to the recent destruction. Familiarity for many modern readers permits us to gloss over the audacious nature of the claim made in these verses. Matthew 23:13–36 has implicated the intellectual, cultural, and religious leadership including Matthew's contemporaries in a concerted attempt to oppose the will of God at this crucial time in human history. In the next section covering the trial and crucifixion, the political leadership will be added to the configuration of the opponents. This opposition to the recognition of the manner in which God has appointed an authoritative spokesperson through whom the next stages in human history will be advanced results in the destruction of the temple. While the significance of Jesus for human history is made apparent through the utilization of the imagery of the "Son of Man," here the reader is reminded of that claim in 23:35, "Blessed in the one who comes in the name of the Lord." For the first-century sectarian, the argument is that the destruction of the temple is evidence that the leadership of Israel has rejected the will of God. This Jewish minority group with a sectarian orientation based upon apocalyptic rhetoric understood all of human history to be centered on their own existence, a rather remarkable viewpoint. What is less clear is that in making that claim they understood their own *ekklēsia* to be the successor to the temple.[41] While some have found support for such a claim in the evidence from the sectarian compositions at Qumran, especially the Community Rule, it is not clear that such an interpretation is warranted either for those texts or for Matthew.[42] This argument has also been advanced on the basis of parallels from the rabbinic corpus. While isolated parallels can be cited, such an approach to the rabbinic conceptualization of the temple is also inadequate.[43] The centrality of the temple for Israelite life and the interpretation of its destruction does not necessarily have to be tied to some argument for its replacement, but might rather speak to its continuing importance, even when it is not present. Its role in the ideologies of survival after the destruction is a significant issue.

The question of the disciples in Matt 24:3 follows directly from Jesus's statement concerning the temple in v. 2 and explicitly ties the remainder of the chapter to it. In this private conversation with the disciples, the meaning of the destruction of the temple is explored within the apocalyptic context. The specific implications of this understanding of the destruction of the temple for first-century Jews, including the followers of Jesus, are developed in Matt 25, following the injunctions and the parable in 24:36–51.

Noteworthy in this section is the attention again given to wisdom. The audacious claim that the wisdom of God rested exclusively with Jesus has been advanced above on the basis of the reading of the Sermon on the Mount and Matt 11. Sectarian claims of exclusive access to wisdom were evident among some other groups in Second Temple Judaism as well. The Matthean claim finds further development in this final crucial build-up to the climactic story of the gospel. The eschatological significance of the destruction of the temple linked with the enthronement of the Son of Man is now illustrated in a series of parables. The emphasis in the first two parables is on "the faithful and wise [*phronimos*] slave" in 24:45 and the contrast between the "foolish" and the "*phronimoi* [wise]" bridesmaids of 25:2.[44] Such an allusion points us back to 7:24–27, the "*andri phronimō* [wise man]" who built his house upon the rock, the parable that concludes the Sermon on the Mount and is employed to point to the "uniquely legitimate" nature of this sectarian group. To be wise means not only to do what Jesus says, it is to understand the eschatological significance of the present time, paying attention to what God intends for the created order and its human inhabitants as explained by the authoritative spokesperson Jesus Christ, and as it is unfolding with the destruction of the temple and the inauguration of the judgment with the enthronement of Jesus Christ as the Son of Man.

To be wise is to be like the sages of Daniel and Enoch, to possess the understanding of the "wise" of Dan 11:33, 35; 12:3, 10, hence also to bear the consequences of the acceptance of that wisdom, the persecution outlined in Matt 24:9–14 and earlier in the composition. Note the similarity of the anticipated experience of the followers of Jesus to that of the wise in Dan 11:32–35, where "for some days, however, they shall fall by sword and flame, and suffer captivity and plunder. . . . Some of the wise shall fall . . . until the time of the end." Then "Michael, the great prince, the protector of your people" shall arise, hence "those who are wise shall shine like the brightness of the sky, and those who lead many to righteousness, like the stars forever and ever" (Dan 12:3). With the explicit mention of Daniel in Matt 24:15 and the enthronement scene of 24:29–30, the wisdom associated with the apocalyptic worldview of Daniel is summoned to the fore. Daniel's interpretation of the persecutions of Antiochus IV Epiphanes and his defilement of the temple provide the interpretive lens whereby the destruction of the temple by the troops of Titus and Vespasian is to be understood.

The survival of Israel, or perhaps more adequately stated, the nature of the Israel that will survive the destruction, is what is at stake in this discussion. In the ambiguity of the two centuries of Jewish existence since the Maccabean revolt and the composition of the latter portions of Daniel, the Jewish experience had become much more complicated. That certainly will have been true at the end of the first century CE. At least this is the picture which emerges in the literary evidence, particularly Josephus and certain apocalyptic writings such as the Testament of Abraham, 2 Baruch, and 4 Ezra. Hence the injunctions to watchfulness in Matt 24:36–44 and the two parables of 24:45–51 and 25:1–13. According to this apocalyptic scenario, only those who accept the wisdom of Jesus and understand his appointment as Son of Man will survive the outcome of the events that are being unleashed in human history. In Matthew's portrayal Jesus, who has been the authoritative spokesperson for the will of God, now also becomes the judge and the criterion by which people, or at least Israel, will be judged. This is clear in 24:9, 35 and in the development of the Son of Man in that same chapter (24:27–31, 36–44). It is brought to a dramatic climax in the judgment scene of the sheep and goats (24:31–46).[45] In this case, Jesus identifies with "the least of these, my brothers," and uses the treatment of them by the nations as the criterion for judgment. For the followers of Jesus in Galilee toward the end of the first century, this means that their belonging to the *ekklēsia* (community) associated with Jesus is necessary for their own survival and that of Israel. Knowing this is essential for the salvation of Israel.

As the story moves toward the climax of the conflict, the sociological element of antagonism is much more prominent in the rhetoric of the sectarian author as found in Matt 23 and 24–25. This is an indication that the element of antagonism is an integral part of the sectarian self-understanding advanced by the author of the first gospel. This high level of tension with its socio-cultural environment demonstrates how the author understood the sect's location within the Jewish community. The difference in practice and behavior has been established earlier in the composition, particularly in the Sermon on the Mount. The element of separation also is integral to the sectarian identity formation evident in those three chapters. Separation is also at the heart of the treatment of wisdom in the first gospel, with Jesus portrayed as both envoy and personification of wisdom, each in different portions of the text. While betraying evidence of a dependency on the earlier treatment of issues of discipline in sectarian groups such as those portrayed in the Dead Sea Scrolls, Matthew's portrayal of the practices prescribed for this sectarian group of the followers of Jesus is advanced as a description of the difference in its treatment from other Jewish groups. That different treatment again highlights its separation and in this case serves a purpose in the maintenance of that separation. The tendency of the author to portray this sect as uniquely legitimate with established boundaries in the Jewish community is evident throughout the composition. With the higher level of antagonism advanced in these chapters, the level of tension is demonstrated in a more vigorous and forthright manner. Significant evidence of all three elements of sect formation are amply represented in the text of Matthew and its rhetorical development by the time the reader reaches the portrayal of the trial and execution.

The Trial and the Crucifixion

The analyses of trial procedures and the execution of the death penalty, especially crucifixion, in the eastern Roman Empire have amply demonstrated the ultimate Roman responsibility for the death of Jesus.[46] Prior to the Roman conquest, the Hasmonean rulers had capital punishment within their jurisdiction. The best-known example of crucifixion is attributed to

Alexander Jannaeus (103–76 BCE), whom Josephus tells us crucified eight hundred men along with their wives and children.[47] The reference to crucifixion points to the "lion of wrath" in 4Q169 (pNahum) 3–4 I, 7, who is implicated in the death of the "seekers of smooth things," presumably the Pharisees, since he had "hung people alive in earlier times." According to 11Q19 (Temple Scroll) LXIV, 6–13, the person who betrays Israel to a foreign power or who defects to a foreign nation to avoid capital punishment is to be punished by "hanging on a tree," the penalty designated in Deut 21:22–23. The victim is not to be left on the tree overnight since he is considered cursed by God and thus defiles the land. The legislation of these Qumran texts is rooted in the Hasmonean era. Herod the Great also possessed that power, and there is abundant evidence that he used it. After Herod's death, however, capital punishment was in the hands of the Roman governors and their appointees.

The Roman crucifixion was explicitly regarded as a spectacle for deterrence, hence reserved for those regarded as insurrectionists by Roman officials and carried out along public thoroughfares visible to the local native populations. It is in this context that the inscription "This is Jesus, the king of the Jews" is to be understood.[48] Much more doubtful is the actual use of the rabbinic legislation regarding capital punishment within Jewish communities of the late Roman period; even less likely is the possibility that this legislation would illustrate the actual practice of Jewish officials in the first century CE.[49] Of particular significance is the limited role of the rabbinic movement within the Jewish communities of Galilee before the fourth century CE.[50] The procedures spelled out in m. Sanhedrin related to capital cases may never have been utilized in actual cases and certainly cannot be summoned as evidence of procedures in capital cases in the first century CE. The limited evidence concerning the death of Jesus indicates that ultimate responsibility for his death, and presumably the actual execution, would have rested in the hands of the Roman prefect and his soldiers.

Such an overview of the Roman occupation finds substantiation in the limited evidence available concerning Pilate as prefect of Judea.[51] Josephus, who gives no evidence of being a great fan of the Roman governors sent to Judea, lists some incidents documenting his impression of Pilate's governorship. The first event concerns the introduction of the bust of Emperor Tiberius on the military standards of the troops stationed in Jerusalem. This led to Jewish dissent due to the introduction of human images into Jerusalem. After a sit-in at his residence in Caesarea and an action of passive resistance when ordered to disperse, Pilate was forced to relent and retract his orders to the troops.[52] A second incident, which Josephus lists as occurring later, concerns the use of funds from the temple treasury to construct an aqueduct supplying Jerusalem with water. This inspired an assembly of "tens of thousands" of men objecting to this plan. Placing soldiers in civilian dress and armed with cudgels around the crowd, Pilate ordered the protesters to be beaten, and in the process many were killed.[53] When Philo recounts the appeal of Agrippa I to Gaius to dissuade him from erecting a statue in the temple in Jerusalem, he cites the case of Pilate, who attempted to erect some honorary shields dedicated to Tiberius in the palace of Herod in Jerusalem. This action elicited such a response that the locals appealed to Tiberius, and he ordered the shields removed and placed in the temple to Augustus at Caesarea Maritima. Philo refers to the corruption, rapine, acts of insolence, murder, cruelty, and "most grievous inhumanity" of Pilate.[54] We also note in Luke 13:1 that Pilate is said to have mixed the blood of Galileans with their sacrifices, whatever that may mean.[55] There is no evidence external to the New Testament for the hypothesis that Pilate would have been a reluctant participant in the execution of a Jew charged with insurrection.[56]

The two events recorded in *Antiquities* are followed by Josephus's description of the execution of Jesus, the *Testimonium Flavianum*.[57] This passage has been reworked by later Christian copyists, with a voluminous literature debating the original reading. That the passage has a historical kernel is most likely; that a good deal of the material has been added by later Christian editors is also certain. That Pilate "had condemned him to be crucified" can be regarded as part of Josephus's original attestation since it appears as the third incident in a record of the prefect's activities that Josephus wanted to bring to the attention of his Roman readers. The possibility that he was "accused by the men of highest standing amongst us" is more debatable.[58] Even if original, it certainly does not support the gospel portrait of formal hearings before the high priest or a Sanhedrin.

To capture the particularities of the portrayal in Matthew, some comparison with Mark is helpful. Some features of the Marcan account are apparent. The trial and death of Jesus are the consequence of reactions to his claims for authority as well as his statements on the abuse of religious and political power. The ironic portrayal of Jesus as a religious and political threat to the welfare of the Roman state and the province of Judea, while in the process of being exalted as Son of Man to judge the world, is integral to Mark's portrayal of the significance of Jesus. The arbitrary nature of the proceedings against Jesus and the decision for execution are an integral part of this portrait. In Mark both the council of the high priest and the Roman governor are implicated in the execution of this man who is not a threat to their power, but who is savior of the world, a role these judges are incapable of understanding or appreciating. This figure needs to suffer the rejection and persecution of the political and religious authorities in the process of taking his place and assuming his authority as judge.[59] We may assume that the account of the trial and crucifixion in Mark was already extant and utilized in the composition of the first gospel.

A distinctive feature of the Matthean account is the extensive attention to the figure of Judas. In the initial mention of Judas in connection with the trial we already find the motive attributed to him by Matthew, that is, money (Matt 26:14–16).[60] The account is straight-forward, leaving little ambiguity in its depiction, and follows immediately upon the story of the anointing of Jesus by the woman at Bethany, in which money also was an issue (26:6–13). The announcement of the betrayal at the Passover meal follows almost immediately thereafter (26:20–29). While the narrative sequence is the same as in Mark, the portrayal of Judas in Matthew is enhanced with the addition of 26:25: "Judas, who betrayed him, said, 'Surely not I, Teacher.'[61] He replied, 'You have said so.'" While the distinguishing characteristic of Judas at this point in the story in Mark is that he is one of the twelve (Mark 14:20), in Matthew the betrayal takes on an intense personal focus. The addition of the account of the suicide of Judas rounds out this portrait (Matt 27:3–10).[62] It is explained on the basis of the somewhat incomprehensible condemnation of the Israelite leadership found in Zech 11:12–14, incorrectly ascribed to Jeremiah by Matthew.[63] Characteristic of Matthean style, this is considered a fulfillment text in Matt 27:9. In other words, the betrayal of Judas is also linked to the condemnation of the priests and the destruction of the temple. This portrayal finds explanation in a sectarian analysis that recognizes the significance of the individual in a dualistic conception of the universe. Judas's betrayal has tragic consequences for his own life, as well as for that of the body of disciples and the fate of their leader. We recall the conclusion of the procedures on communal discipline: the person who refuses to listen is "to be to you as a Gentile and a tax collector" (18:17).

In the development of Jewish sectarianism of the Second Temple era, biblical law related to the treatment of gentiles is frequently applied to those Jews who do not subscribe to the perspectives and practices of the particular Jewish sect making those determinations. While in Mark we might understand the betrayal in the context of the divinized figure of Jesus, for the readers and hearers of the first gospel Judas also becomes the example of the person who betrays the group for purposes of personal welfare or greed. This is the first characteristic of those under the authority of the Angel of Darkness in 1QS IV, 9. Of course this is from the perspective of the Jesus group and not of the betrayer. This portrayal may have nothing to do with the actual motivations of Judas, the historical figure. From the standpoint of the Jewish followers of Jesus, Judas acted in a manner that was contrary to the will of God, not accepting the particular manifestation of the divine will that was being enacted through the person of Jesus Christ and his followers. The personal consequence of this stance for Judas was suicide. For Matthew this is related to the national disaster of the destruction of the temple.

Immediately following the suicide of Judas we find the beginning of the trial scenes with Pilate. While the account in Matthew follows the outline of the Marcan story, significant additional elements shape the reader's understanding of this event. While the initial handing off to Pilate by the high priest is similar in the two accounts, the account of Barabbas includes the significant insertion of the dream of Pilate's wife, "Have nothing to do with that righteous man" (Matt 27:19). The shifting of responsibility for the crucifixion away from Pilate and onto the Jewish leadership is already under way in this account. The wife of Pilate warns against an action of capital punishment, but the chief priests and the elders convince the people to ask for the release of Barabbas, and twice they cry out for the crucifixion of Jesus.

Then comes the scene which has played such an important role throughout history in defining Christian perceptions of Pilate and in developing the antisemitism that has plagued Christian history (Matt 27:24–26). First, Pilate washes his hands, declaring his own innocence "of this man's blood." To this the people respond, "His blood be upon us and on our children." Responsibility for the death of Jesus has been shifted to the Jewish leadership by the author of the first gospel.[64] In this account they are the ones charged with whipping up the crowds, who are portrayed as rather powerless pawns manipulated into taking responsibility for the death.[65] Already in Mark responsibility for the death of Jesus is ascribed to the chief priests, the elders, the scribes, and the whole council. As already pointed out above, the Pharisees and the Sadducees are made part of this scenario in the chapters leading into the trial. The Sadducees are part of the temple conflict in Matt 22:23 and 34, leading into the diatribe of Matthew 23. The Pharisees again receive mention in 27:62, implicated in the plot to declare the resurrection a hoax. The sectarian author has expanded the scope of the leadership circles to include those groups who presumably were of influence in the post-70 Jewish community of which the Matthean group was a part. These groups, especially the Pharisees, who have been portrayed as the source of the conflict throughout the gospel, now are complicit in the execution. In this narrative the conflict has escalated to the point that all of the competing leadership structures of the Jewish community have been demonstrated to be opponents of the will of God. Only this sectarian group knows what God wants of God's people and understands the true nature of the universe and the present time in world history, hence the future for the Jewish community. Such a conclusion is of consequence for how the sect understood the place of the Jewish community within the context of the Roman Empire.

The perception of Roman rule after the destruction of the temple, and even responsibility for the destruction of the temple, is a very complex question in the Jewish world of the last three decades of the first century. Accounts centering on two events are particularly illustrative. The first is the appearance of Josephus in Galilee before Vespasian, after the fall of Jotapata, when he predicted the latter's rise to emperor (*B.J.* 3.392–408). In Josephus's account this is the initial event that leads to his own later life in Rome and his Flavian sponsorship. Ultimately he blames the destruction of the temple on the Jewish revolutionary groups. Describing in summary fashion the order to have the entire city and temple razed to the ground, Josephus concludes, "Such was the end to which the frenzy of revolutionaries brought Jerusalem, that splendid city of world-wide renown" (*B.J.* 7.4). This has been the thesis developed throughout his vivid description of the various rebel groups during the war with Rome. At the time of the surrender of Simon ben Giora, one of the revolutionary leaders, Josephus opines, "Thus was Simon, in retribution for his cruelty to his fellow-citizens, whom he had mercilessly tyrannized, delivered by God into the hands of his deadliest enemies" (*B.J.* 7.32–33). When listing the false prophecies which led the people astray and resulted in even more murder at the hands of the Romans, Josephus indicates that these prophets had misinterpreted oracles and prophecies as signs of God's deliverance, while they actually indicated the fall of the temple and the victory of the Romans (*B.J.* 6.283–315).

Included was the prophecy from the sacred scriptures that "one from their own country would become ruler of the world." Josephus indicates that this actually pointed to Vespasian, who was declared emperor while on Judean soil, rather than to any Jewish redeemer figure.[66] For Josephus, God had acted through the hands of the Romans, and their victory was God's will.

One of the major myths of rabbinic origins has some similarities to the account of Josephus. This is the story of the founding of the rabbinic academy at Yavneh (also called Jamnia).[67] While appearing in multiple versions in talmudic literature, the common element is that Johanan ben Zakkai was carried secretly out of Jerusalem by his disciples in a coffin and is brought to appear before Vespasian. Thereupon he declared that Vespasian would be made king. In gratitude either for his advocacy of surrender to the Roman forces or for his prophecy, Vespasian gave him, at his request, Yavneh as a place to teach disciples and establish a house of study, thereby beginning (or continuing) the chain of tradition after the destruction of the temple.[68] What is evident from these accounts, that of Josephus from the same period as the composition of Matthew and the other from later traditions about that era, is that Jews took responsibility for what clearly was a Roman action or said that it was carried out according to the will of God. These traditions reflect a Palestinian context, as also does Matthew.

Attention to biblical law is apparent in the mention of the two witnesses that finally come forward in Matt 26:60, even though many false witnesses were available. This satisfies the requirement of Deut 19:15 considered basic to biblical and talmudic law. More problematic in the scholarly literature is the question of whether the reference to the destruction of the temple in 26:61 is based upon sayings of the biblical prophets, such as Jer 26:11. In this instance the reference to destruction is linked to the threat on the prophet's life.[69] Since all three references (Matt 24:2; 26:61; 27:40) are also found in Mark (13:2; 14:58; 15:29), they do not reflect a particular Matthean usage.

The culpability of the Roman imperial system for the fate of Jesus is apparent in its last appearance in the story, found only in Matthew among the canonical gospels (27:62–66; 28:11–15). While some scholars maintain that the guards assigned to the chief priests mentioned by Pilate (27:65) could have been Jews, this appears doubtful since it is the chief priests who, after the resurrection is reported to them, tell the soldiers that they will address any concerns should a report reach the governor that the soldiers had been asleep on their watch (28:13–14). This would have been of concern only to Roman soldiers in a direct chain of command to the governor.[70] The story itself serves the function of providing additional evidence of Jesus's resurrection, in this case by functionaries within the Roman system. The account concludes with the much-debated reference "and this story is still told among the Jews to this day" (28:15). This is the only appearance of the term *Ioudaioi* in the first gospel and is often interpreted as referring to the Jewish community in contrast to those persons associated with Jesus. Such a reading is doubtful. It is certainly more likely, particularly within the arguments advanced in this volume, that the "Jews" or "Judeans" are a reference to the entire community of which the followers of Jesus are a part.[71] In other words, Matthew tells his readers that everybody has heard this rumor, but you, that is, the followers addressed in this book, are the only ones who know the true story. The Roman guards have been placed in the position of authenticating the resurrection of Jesus by the storyteller.

The attention paid to the full account of the splitting of the curtain of the temple (Matt 27:51–53) has not received adequate attention in most treatments.[72] Symbolic references to the destruction of the temple are to be found elsewhere in apocalyptic literature, and this account is in continuity with those claims. Well-known are the references in the Animal Apocalypse of 1 En. 90:28–36 and in the Apocalypse of Weeks where the house is destroyed in the sixth week (1 En. 93:8), after which an eternal temple will be built in the eighth week (1 En. 91:13).[73] Commentators debate whether the temple curtain here is the inner veil that covered the Holy of Holies or the outer division between the temple and the forecourt. If it is an action related to the statements attributed to Jesus about the destruction of the temple (Matt 24:21; 26:61; 27:40), then it would be a reference to the entrance to the outer court, and this seems more likely in the apocalyptic context of Matthew.[74] Others have suggested it is the veil before the Holy of Holies and represents the opening of the presence of the Lord, a theological reading in which, "by his sacrificial death, Jesus obviates the sacrifices and priesthood, making available to all people a new, bold, unrestricted access into God's very presence."[75] Such an interpretation presumes the existence of a more advanced "Christian" understanding of the first gospel than is justified based upon the evidence currently available. The interpretation advanced here is consistent with the apocalyptic context of these verses.

References to earthquakes are to be found in Matt 24:7 and 28:2, in addition to 27:51 and 54. While earthquake activity in the Levant receives regular mention throughout recorded history, apocalyptic literature includes it in descriptions of the massive upheavals within the natural world that accompany eschatological events.[76] The massive disruption of the natural world is apparent in apocalyptic literature.[77] This context also explains the reference to the rocks being split. Whether this is an allusion to the fissures in the rock formations that appear as the result of earthquakes or a more general description of the rupture of the natural world is hard to determine. Frequently cited is the reference to the splitting of the Mount of Olives in Zech 14:4, followed by the mention of the earthquake in 14:5.[78] Nahum 1: 5–6 mentions the breaking of rocks into pieces, and T. Levi 4:1 includes the rocks being split in a listing of occurrences in the natural world at the time of the eschaton.

Within this description in Matthew we find the reference "The tombs also were opened, and the bodies of many of the *hagiōn* [holy ones][79] who had fallen asleep were raised" (27:52). Mention of an earthquake again in 28:2 when an angel of the Lord appears to Mary Magdalene and the other Mary also concerns a resurrection appearance. Matthew places these references to resurrection within an apocalyptic setting. Such a context provides the best explanation for the elusive statement in 27:53, "*After his resurrection*, they came out of the tombs and entered the holy city and appeared to many."[80] Davies and Allison regard it as an early gloss not reflected in the manuscript traditions.[81] The passage raises questions concerning whether there were others who were resurrected prior to Jesus. Or, did these holy ones remain in the open tombs until after Jesus's resurrection, a haunting visual picture?[82] Any description of resurrected bodies is of course hypothetical. The speculation concerning whether the resurrected bodies waited to enter the city from the time of Jesus's death until after his resurrection is unhelpful for understanding the meaning of the passage. The setting for the resurrection of Jesus here is found much more explicitly in an apocalyptic setting. Both references to the quaking of the earth in the context of resurrection appear only in Matthew among the synoptic accounts. The similarity of the two descriptions is more striking than the sequence of their occurrences. The author saw in the death of Jesus an event of cosmic proportions and utilized this imagery to describe events of such consequence.[83] I am not convinced that we can find any evidence in the text that the author considered this a problem.

By the time of the composition of Matthew, resurrection had become a way of describing what happens after death for some—probably many— Jews, regarded as a belief of the Pharisees in both the New Testament and the descriptions of Josephus.[84] In the Hebrew Bible it appears in a fully developed form in Dan 12:2–3 and is pointed to in Isa 26:19 and Ezek 37: 7–14.[85] Here we find the author of Matthew summoning multiple images from Second Temple Judaism to describe the significance of Jesus. In Matt 26:63–64, the Son of Man, exalted to the right hand of God, is identified with the anointed one, the Son of God. This portrayal of the Son of Man summons to mind Dan 7:13, perhaps also vv. 21–22 and 27. This constitutes the conclusion of the first apocalypse in that biblical book, a sequence of judgment and victory. The vision of the resurrected in Dan 12:2–3 holds the same place in the fourth and final apocalypse of that composition. In both cases these events result from divine intervention that is beyond or constitutes the end of normal human experience and history.

This is where Matthew places Jesus. What this means for the two references under consideration at this point is that we need to read them in the context of the resurrection accounts that are informed by the apocalyptic scenario. In this case the "holy ones" are raised, with Jesus being the first. Here the holy man who is raised appears to his disciples and close companions, while others who are raised go into the holy city and appear to many. This is a sign of the beginning of a time of divine intervention, witnessed to by the presence of Jesus among those who have chosen to follow him.

Conclusion

This is the manner in which those sectarian followers of Jesus understood their role in history and how they identified their own time and experience. In this sectarian reading of an apocalyptic perspective, the figure of Jesus is evidence of divine intervention in the life and fate of Israel. Both the death of Jesus and the destruction of the temple are evidence of the pivotal significance of the era in which these disciples live. Only the followers of Jesus have been given the wisdom to understand the nature of the present age and the contemporary struggles of Israel. They recognize the challenges before Israel at the end of the first century and are in conflict with the political and religious leadership of Israel concerning how to respond. From the perspective of these sectarians, Israel is heading into a time of judgment rather than deliverance because of its failure to understand what God wants of Israel at the present time. The end result is that the followers of Jesus are in deep conflict with the remainder of Israel, even if the present oppressive power is that of the Romans. From an apocalyptic perspective shared by the sect, Roman power is only transitory. The future of the world rests with an Israel that understands the will of God as it has been made known to this body of the followers of Jesus.

It was already demonstrated that the level of tension between this sectarian portrayal and its socio-cultural environment was highest as this narrative approached the climax of the conflict. The sociological element of antagonism was much more pronounced in Matt 21–25 just before the account of the trial and execution. The earlier portions of the composition had demonstrated the level of separation and difference the author expected of this sect in comparison to the remainder of the Jewish community. The tendency of the author to portray this sect as uniquely legitimate within the Jewish community is evident throughout the composition. With all of the religious, cultural, and political leadership of the Jewish community made complicit in the execution of Jesus, the sectarians are brought to understand their unique place in the Jewish community. The level of tension reaches its highest point with the death of Jesus, their founder (and savior). While the sectarians understand that they constitute the only hope for the survival of the Jewish community, the antagonism of the remainder of the Jewish community brings the story to its climax and conclusion. The references to resurrection confirm their unique legitimacy within the Jewish community. For Matthew there is no other group that understands what God wants from and for the Jewish people at the end of the first century.

7 Commissioning the Sect

The final paragraph of the book of Matthew has frequently served as the essential statement of the purpose of the first gospel for many interpreters. It has been argued that this passage is based upon the commissioning of Joshua (Deut 31:23; Josh 1:1–9), thereby confirming the picture of Jesus as the new Moses.[1] Most frequently Matt 28:16–20 has been juxtaposed with Matt 10:5–6 to describe the interpretive trajectory of the overall argument of the composition: "Go therefore, and make disciples of all nations" versus "Go nowhere among the Gentiles."[2] In some cases, the latter passage is attributed to the historical Jesus, the former to the author of the first gospel, thereby reflecting christological developments within the first-century Christian community. Other interpreters place these two references within the context of the development of salvation history, with the latter passage indicating the mission to Israel. With the rejection of this message by the Jewish leadership, and ultimately the people as developed in the trial scene, Matthew justifies a turn to the gentile mission in this dramatic conclusion to the account. There is, however, no basis within the text for reading them as contradictory—that is, no evidence that Matthew considered them to be so. If these two passages are read from a sectarian perspective within the context of other Jewish literature from the Second Temple era, it is much more plausible to understand them as a consistent statement about the manner in which this first-century Jewish community understood the significance of Jesus Christ for the future of the Jewish people and the world.

"Go Rather to the Lost Sheep of the House of Israel"

The initial commissioning of the twelve in Matt 10:5–6 opens with the injunction "Go nowhere among the Gentiles, and enter no town of the Samaritans, but go rather to the lost sheep of the house of Israel." A preferable translation, "Do not go on the way to the Gentiles,"[3] suggests the road leading to a gentile city,[4] an exhortation to the disciples not to extend their mission to the non-gentile areas.[5] This commission follows the development of Jesus's healing and teaching ministry in chapters 8–9, concluding with the summation in 9:35–37 and the lament "The harvest is plentiful, but the laborers are few; therefore ask the Lord of the harvest to send out laborers into his harvest." In chapter 10 the disciples are commissioned to engage in the teaching and healing ministry of Jesus described in chapters 8–9, including the details about the nature of their itinerant lifestyle and the challenges they will face.

The injunction regarding the Samaritans is arresting, the only mention of that group in the composition. From Josephus we know that Alexander the Great had already settled Macedonian colonists in the city of Samaria at the end of the fourth century BCE. After its destruction by John Hyrcanus around 111/110 BCE, Herod the Great reconstructed it as one of his showpieces, renamed it Sebaste, and constructed a massive temple to Augustus as its center. In other words, Herod understood the area to be one in which he was not impelled to cater to Jewish sensibilities with regard to the temple. This is one of the cities attacked by Jewish rebels in the lead-up to the Jewish war with Rome and was a source for Roman troops during the war and prior to it, beginning from the time of Herod.[6] We will not recount here the complicated historical issues attending the development of the group called Samaritans.[7] Their temple on Mount Gerizim at Shechem in close proximity to Samaria-Sebaste was destroyed by John Hyrcanus as well, and this constituted a significant breach between Samaritans and Jews. Vespasian did quell an attempted revolt by them at the time of the Jewish war with Rome.[8] They most likely constitute a different and independent tradition of Israel going back at least to the immediate post-exilic period. In other words, they are neither Jewish nor gentile in first-century parlance, but rather a third category. It would not have been out of character for a Jewish author such as Matthew at the end of the first century to regard Samaria as "on the way to the Gentiles." They were outside the purview of the primary interest of this sectarian author, who did not consider them to be within the scope of "the lost sheep of the house of Israel."

This phrase points to the critique of the Jewish leadership groups that pervades the entire composition. The climax of this critique is apparent in the description of the trial and the chapters leading up to it.[9] However it pervades the entire composition and is certainly integral to the arguments of the Sermon on the Mount and present in particular in the summation that provides the context for this commissioning, describing the people as "harassed and helpless, like sheep without a shepherd" (Matt 9:36).[10] This metaphor has already been employed in the Hebrew Bible (e.g., Num 27:17; 1 Kgs 22:17; Zech 10:20; and developed in Ezek 34). Of significance for our purposes is its use in the Animal Apocalypse of 1 En. 89:59–90:19 in its portrayal of the tragic consequences of the leadership of the Second Temple era.[11] This is a common indictment in Jewish apocalyptic literature and is consistent with the manner in which its portrayal is developed in Chapter 6 above. The context for what is to be proclaimed to the lost sheep of the house of Judah is evident in the next verse, "The kingdom of heaven has come near" (Matt 10:7). A new era has dawned, and it is that occurrence which ties this mission with the concluding verses of the composition.

All the Nations

It is this same mission that is described in the final commissioning injunction of Matthew. We recall Saldarini's analysis, discussed above in Chapter 2, which reached the following conclusion: "In Matthew's version of a reformed Judaism, gentiles are peripheral, but firmly present."[12] Similarly Overman: "One sees very little evidence of Gentiles (non-Jews) in the Matthean community."[13] While this conclusion is consistent with a sectarian approach and does find support in the evidence advanced, the gentile references and the conclusion of the gospel require more attention. The problem is not resolved by Foster, who argues that the growing emphasis on mission and the gentiles in the latter portion of the work is the result of the Matthean community having totally broken from the synagogue, by which he means the majority group of the first-century Jewish community, and having become an independent entity.[14] A sectarian analysis rather demonstrates that the final commission is a reference to the same mission as Matt 10:5–6 and that the gentiles have an integral place in the apocalyptic eschatology of the Jewish world in which Matthew and that community resided.

In both cases the injunction begins with the verb *poreuomai* (go), also the first word in the following verse detailing the mission (Matt 10:7). As

in the latter verse, in 28:19 the verb is in participial form followed by the
imperative, in this case *poreuthentes oun mathēteusate panta ta ethnē* (going
therefore make disciples of all nations [my translation]). The translation of
the last term, the LXX equivalent of the Hebrew *gôy*, has been a continuing
source of debate. A significant usage of the phrase *panta ta ethnē* is apparent at the conclusion of Isaiah (LXX Isa 61:11, 66:18). The particular phrase
is more prominent throughout the LXX than its Hebrew equivalent in the
MT and seems to be used in many instances to designate the non-Israelite
world.[15] The argument for the use of Isaiah at this point as a reference by
Matthew rests on the ubiquitous and significant use of the book in the first
gospel, as well as throughout Second Temple and other early Christian literature, including the literature of Qumran.[16] For Matt 28:16–20, the use of
the phrase at the center of the eschatological vision of Isaiah is important.
In the passages from Isaiah both the MT and LXX suggest "nations" as the
more appropriate translation. In this case, I would contend that this is also
the case for the conclusion of Matthew.

While the literary structure in which these two texts (Isa 61:11, 66:18)
are found is the source of continuing debate, many scholars now share the
viewpoint that Isa 60–62 forms the core of Trito-Isaiah (Isaiah 56–66).[17]
Issues such as the correct chapter division for this section, or even whether
it can be distinguished as the product of a separate author, are not particularly significant for the reading of the section employed in this study, that
is, this section may be a continuation of Deutero-Isaiah.[18] In this vindication, even exaltation, of Jerusalem we find a focus on the return of the
exiles and the recognition of the God of Israel by the nations and their
kings, either by travel to Jerusalem or the sending of goods, clearly some
of them for the temple. This recognition is an integral part of the return of
the exiles; that is, there is no distinction in this vision between the nations
and the dispersed Israelites, even though the latter tend to be the focus of
attention. Furthermore both Israel and the nations are responsible to this
God for their actions and equally subject to sanction for disobedience. In
this sense this God of the eschatological vision at the conclusion of Isaiah
can be understood as universal, that is, God of both Israel and the nations.
However to label such a reading of this section of Isaiah as universalistic in
the popular sense of the term may be simplistic and may miss the potential
it holds for a reading of the conclusion of Matthew more consonant with
the trajectory within Second Temple Judaism developed in this study.

Of particular relevance is the adoption of the term "exclusive inclusivity" advanced by Dalit Rom-Shiloni in a volume of that name to describe the ideology of Deutero-Isaiah and Zech 1–8.[19] The overall argument advanced in the work is to describe the victory of the repatriated exiles over the native Judeans who did not experience deportation. It is the identity formed in exile that becomes the dominant ideology advanced in the literature that shapes the identity of Judah throughout the Second Temple period.[20] This exclusivist identity first appears in the hierocratic descriptions of Ezekiel, also foundational for Ezra-Nehemiah, and then in the more nuanced picture of Deutero-Isaiah and Zech 1–8, especially 8:20–23.[21] In Isa 56:3, 6–8 we find reference to "the foreigner joined to the Lord."[22] Through active service in the community of Israel performing the same duties as lay Israelites, these foreigners are incorporated into the people of God. Foreigners are an integral part of the description of the faithful returnees as they gather in Jerusalem at the point of its vindication (Isa 60; 66:20). Both their return and the rebuilding are assisted by foreign rulers who recognize the activity of God in the restoration of Jerusalem. "All the nations" need to meet the same criteria as those Israelites who will benefit from God's saving activity. This is not universalism but rather an exclusivism redefined, an exclusive inclusivity.[23]

In this case Matt 10:5–6 and 28:19–20 are both references to the same eschatological vision that is now in the process of execution. The "lost sheep of the house of Israel" need to hear that the kingdom of God has approached, and the signs of that occurrence need to be pointed out to them (10:6–8). It is urgent that Israel understand what is currently happening in its midst. However all the world needs to hear about the dramatic changes in human history presently under way and be provided with the opportunity to join this reform movement at the center of these dramatic developments in Israel (28:19–20). Within the scope of Matthew's apocalyptic perspective, this eschatological vision provides the basis for the different aspects of this injunction for the community that has been formed in the name of its founder.[24]

The presence of this vision in other texts of the Second Temple era is documented in Terence Donaldson's collection of texts on Jewish patterns of universalism.[25] In 1 En. 90:30–38 "all the animals on earth and all the birds of heaven were falling down and worshipping the sheep and making petition of them and obeying them in everything." In Sib. Or. 3 we find repeated references to the end-times and the gentiles: "Again, we encounter a pattern in which descriptions of end-times bliss (702–31, 741–61, 767–95) alternate with exhortations addressed to Gentiles (732–40, 762–66)."[26] Nickelsburg makes mention of 1 En. 10:21, 91:14, 100:6, and 104:12–105:2 in pointing to the "universalistic" aspect of this seer's vision.[27] The complicated nature of that return, as presented in Isaiah and Zechariah, leaves a good deal of ambiguity with regard to the precise nature of the meaning of the treatment of the gentiles in these later texts. The gathering of the nations to Jerusalem (or Mount Zion) is amply attested (Pss. Sol. 17:31; 4 Ezra 13:31; 2 Bar. 71:1). The widespread expectation that the gentiles will turn to the God of Israel at the end of days pervades this literature.

What is instructive in Donaldson's approach to the materials from Qumran is that he turns to the treatment of both Hebrew terms *gôy* and *gēr* to complete his examination of the subject.[28] Both terms are necessary to fill out the picture of the treatment of gentiles in those texts, even though it is not possible to construct one holistic portrait encompassing all of the evidence. He notes the overall negative treatment of the gentiles in this literature in his brief examination of the Treatise on the Two Spirits (1QS III, 13—IV, 26).[29] In this rationale for a sectarian viewpoint written to teach the children of righteousness about the history of humankind, they are taught that the universe is composed of children of righteousness and children of iniquity, each existing in realms controlled by the Prince of Light and the Angel of Darkness, respectively. In this case there is no distinction between Jew and gentile; the former who have not "volunteered" to join the children of light are the children of iniquity, as is the remainder of humankind. These texts suggest that the gentiles are not really a major concern; the fate of the cosmos does not rest in their hands. What is clear is that the basic affiliations which undergird human civilization have been reordered. As noted by Schiffman, the biblical texts that speak of the nations as enemies of Israel are understood by sectarian authors to be opponents of the sect.[30] In other words the nations do not hold a very significant place in this ideological map of the world; the primary division is between members of the sect and those who are not. However this is not the entire case.

In the War Scroll, the conflict between the Sons of Light and the Sons of Darkness is carried out for the ultimate purpose of the defeat (and destruction) of the *gôyîm*. In this composition they also are considered to be the *kitîyîm* whose equivalence to the Sons of Darkness is established in the opening lines of the composition.[31] They most likely designate the Seleucids in 1QM, the Romans in 1QpHab and 1QpNah.[32] However the traditional enemies of Israel such as Edom, Moab, the Ammonites, Philistia, and others also are named.[33] We note of course in these texts and elsewhere that Israel is not reduced to being a synonym for the sect the Sons of Light, but rather retains its full identity, presumably ethnic in the Second Temple era.[34] The most likely explanation is that the sect is a specific construction designed for life as a Jew in the present evil age prior to the eschaton.

Within the sectarian literature from Qumran there is no necessary reason for assuming that it is possible to conflate the views from these and other assorted texts into one monolithic viewpoint. They are discrete compositions, presumably with distinct social settings related to their composition; this is certainly true of 1QS and 1QM and their multiple MSS.[35] However we also have ample evidence of overlap, such as the similarities in wording of the penal code found in the S and D compositions. In the case of 1QM, the similarities with 1QSa (the Rule of the Congregation, also called the Eschatological Rule) have been the subject of observation and study. It is not necessary to probe the details of the connection. What is of significance for this argument is the observation that members of the sect who copied 1QS saw fit to attach 1QSa and 1QSb to that composition, presumably considering it important for sectarian life. This is one piece of evidence pointing to the significance of eschatological compositions such as 1QM for sectarians who were related to the communal life described in 1QS and presumably to its various versions.

The other term Donaldson identifies in his consideration of universalism is gēr. This term for the resident alien in the Hebrew Bible comes to mean "proselyte" in rabbinic literature and is on the way to that meaning in Second Temple literature. Such an interpretation is well-attested at the end of the Second Temple period and important for evaluating Matthew's stance on this question.[36] While it is translated as "sojourner" or "resident alien" in the Hebrew Bible, Jokiranta points out that it already is in transition from designating a class in need of protection to a group that also has obligations; that is, there is some integration into religious life, hence the beginning of a move toward Jewish ethnic identity.[37] Whether the references in the Qumran texts represent the "resident alien" of the Hebrew Bible or the later "proselyte" is a matter of dispute. There certainly are instances where these texts rely on and/or imitate biblical law and in some cases extend it. Whatever the intended meaning of the reference, it seems doubtful that it refers specifically to converts to the sect.[38] In some cases it is an extension of the biblical law.

When we look at the evidence from Qumran we find fourteen appearances of the term. The most significant set of references in sectarian literature is found in CD. In 6:21 the sectarian is to grasp the hand of the *gēr* along with *'anî wĕbyôn* (the poor and the needy), included with widows and orphans as the objects of oppression by those who steal from the wealth of the temple. More complicated is CD 14:4, 6, in which the *gēr* is listed fourth in the hierarchy of the camp after the priests, Levites, and Israelites.[39] This passage is noteworthy for the distinctive status allotted to the *gēr*, fully included but in a particular place within the ranking. In the fragmentary text of 4Q279 5, 6 "the fourth lot [*gôral*] is for the *gērîm*." While the term *gôral* is not used in the D MSS, it is central to the ranking of the sectarian membership as it is depicted in the S MSS. A related picture is to be found in the non-sectarian 11Q19 (Temple Scroll) XL, 6, wherein the third courtyard is designated "for their daughters and for the *gērîm* that are born." Noteworthy similarities in stances on issues of biblical law in CD and the Temple Scroll have been observed.[40] Also apparent is the inclusion of the term in 4Q169 (pNahum) 3–4 II, 9 within the listing of persons who have been led astray by false teaching including "kings, princes, priests, the people, and attached *gērîm*." This rather interesting listing of the opponents of the sect who lead Israel astray includes *gērîm*, indicating their acceptance within the broader Jewish community. In 4Q174 (Florilegium) II, 4 the *gēr* is mentioned along with the foreigner and after the Ammonite, the Moabite, and the *mamzer* (bastard). The context for interpretation is missing from some of the more fragmentary texts.[41]

While the usage of the term to designate "resident alien" in some instances and "proselyte" in others is clear—though there are some passages which are hard to determine—the best translation may not be the most significant finding from this survey. It is likely that the majority of the instances should be translated "proselyte," as proposed by Donaldson. But rather than constituting evidence of their presence within any of the sectarian communities, these texts provide clear confirmation that they were a part of Jewish life at the time that the texts were composed in the first and second centuries BCE.[42] A non-sectarian text, 4Q423 (Instruction[g]) 5, 4, illustrates such a usage: "[He will jud]ge all of them with truth, he will visit fathers and sons, [proselyt]es along with all of the native born." In this case the term is presumably used to designate the all-inclusive scope of the judgment.[43] The Temple Scroll and Instruction provide evidence of the early and broad usage of the term in Second Temple Jewish life presumably to designate the "proselyte." At this point the "resident alien" would only make sense as an archaism. Within the sectarian texts there is no clear stated interest in the *gēr* beyond the issues related to resolving their status as an identifiable part of Israel, as is the case with women, children, and others. It is not a term used to designate the adherents of the sect or its inductees.

In the evidence from Qumran we encounter two distinct phenomena with regard to the treatment of the gentiles. The *gôyim* and the *kitîyîm* represent the oppressive external nations, the Seleucids and the Romans, in a manner familiar to us from the apocalyptic traditions. As in Dan 2:46–49, 3:24–30, 4:28–34, and 6:22–29, there are eschatological scenarios in which these foreign rulers recognize the ultimate power of the God of Israel and in some instances are converted to the worship of this god. More frequently they acknowledge this God's power. The evidence concerning the *gēr* is an acknowledgment of the presence of proselytes within the Jewish communities of the second and first centuries BCE. Since this was the case, their presence was one of the liminal categories which required sectarian legislation.

The Nations in Matthew

A similar case is apparent in the text of Matthew. Many interpreters find the apparently anomalous inclusion of Tamar, Rahab, Ruth, and the wife of Uriah in the opening genealogy to be the first evidence of Matthew's particular interest in the gentile mission.[44] This is not consistent with the portrayal of Mary, to whom this listing would seem to point. Rather the point would seem to be their susceptibility to accusation and suspicion from others in Israel juxtaposed with their importance in its history.[45] The recognition of Jesus by "wise men from the east" in Matt 2:1–12 points to the importance of non-Israelite attestation of divine activity. In the account of the healing of the centurion's servant, presumably a non-Israelite, we find a reference to the vision like that found in Isaiah: "Many will come from east and west and will eat with Abraham and Isaac and Jacob in the kingdom of heaven" (Matt 8:5–13). The people of Nineveh and the queen of the South are non-Israelites who are in the position to judge the lawless leadership because of their repentance and recognition of the God of Israel (Matt 12:38–42). With parallels in Luke, these instances are likely drawn from the Q source.

A similar point is apparent in the story of the Canaanite woman (Matt 15:21–28), with a parallel only in Mark, presumably its source. If there is a debate about the significance of a mission to the gentiles in the first gospel, it is to be found in this story when Jesus repeats his earlier statement, "I was sent only to the lost sheep of the house of Israel" (15:24). As in 10:6, the response is addressed to the disciples, who have in this instance asked him to send the woman away (15:23). Matthew has this response directed to the disciples in both 10:6 and 15:24; that is, it explicitly addresses the adherents of the sect composed of the followers of Jesus. In the use of this phrase the sectarian objective is reaffirmed; the reform (or restoration?) of Israel is at stake.[46] Noteworthy also is the use of the label "Canaanite" to designate the woman who is referred to as Syro-Phoenician in Mark, in both cases designated as taking place in the region of Tyre and Sidon. While there is evidence of some use of the term "Canaanite" to designate the Phoenicians of the eastern Mediterranean coast, since it reflects their origins,[47] the employment of the more common biblical term may reflect the sectarian orientation of the author.[48] "Canaanite" is a clearer designation of the historical enemies of Israel in the Hebrew Bible and continues to receive mention in the reworked biblical texts of the Second Temple era.[49] It is possible to understand the region of Tyre and Sidon, as approached from Galilee, to be an area of conflict. I would characterize it as the unruliness that results from the lack of strong local administrative and judicatory institutions rather than the clash of military forces.[50] The conflict between Israel and the nations continues in the apocalyptically oriented perspectives of the Second Temple period dominated by the realities of imperial rule in the Greek and early Roman eras.

From a sectarian perspective as it is portrayed in the evidence from Qumran, the lot of Jews who do not accept the sectarian viewpoint are regarded as non-Jews with regard to the eschatological future. From a halakic standpoint, the distinction between Jews and non-Jews is retained; however the expected manner in which the Jewish life is to be lived is available through the teachings and lifestyle of the sect.[51] The affirmation of the Canaanite woman then is analogous to the recognition of the God of Israel by the Babylonian rulers in texts such as Dan 2:46–49, 3:24–30, 4:28–34, and 6:22–29. In this case the truth of the claim of the Jesus group is upheld when Jesus points to the woman's faith. The primary concern of the sectarian author is that Jews live according to what God finds pleasing, what this God wants Israel to do and be. Matthew's portrayal of Jesus's lament over the failure of leadership and lack of vision in the Jewish community and the enormous obstacle this poses for the development of a broader understanding of the significant events presently transforming Jewish—and by implication world—history is the concern of the story. This sectarian community believed in a reformed Israel that would be of a significantly different nature. That is where the divine favor now rests. The story does not point to a distinctively gentile mission, but it ultimately has cosmic implications. While the subsequent verses reporting extensive healing activity would appear to be directed to the people of Israel, the concluding phrase is significant, "And they praised the God of Israel" (Matt 15:31), as the Canaanite woman presumably had. The confession of the centurion in Matt 27:54 can be viewed in the same perspective.

The nations receive mention in the most explicitly apocalyptic section as well as elsewhere in the first gospel.[52] The birth pangs of the end of the age, when nation will rise up against nation and kingdom against kingdom and there will be famine and earthquakes, is also the time when "they will hand you over to be tortured and will put you to death, and you will be hated by all nations [*pantōn tōn ethnōn*] because of my name" (Matt 24:9). The last phrase reminds the reader of the last beatitude wherein the disciples are told that they can expect to be reviled, persecuted, and spoken evil of "on account of me" (5:11). In this sectarian interpretation, that is, that full knowledge of the present situation of Israel rests with the sect, the mistreatment is expected to come from the native Jewish leadership rather than from the nations. Just prior to the apocalyptic vision of Matt 24, Jesus tells the scribes and Pharisees in the conclusion of his diatribe that they will kill and crucify some of those he will send, will flog them in their synagogues, and will pursue them from town to town (Matt 23:34). The proclamation of the vision and its realization can be expected to encounter resistance and rejection by both Israel and the nations, in the same manner in which its all-inclusive nature is addressed to and holds out promise for both. The comprehensive aspect of this vision is apparent in Matt 24:14, "The good news of the kingdom will be proclaimed throughout the world, as a testimony to all the nations [*pasin tois ethnesin*], and then the end will come." This is followed by the great judgment scene when *panta ta ethnē* (all the nations) will be gathered before the Son of Man and be judged according to their actions, that is, the manner in which they treated him and his representatives (Matt 25:31). Proclamation to and judgment of all of the world is integral to the entire book of Matthew. That this viewpoint is in direct continuity with eschatological expectations found in Jewish apocalyptic literature, and already present in earlier eschatology, rather than a distinct innovation in Jewish thinking at the conclusion of the first century CE is the inevitable conclusion when the question of the gentiles is approached from a sectarian perspective.[53]

Making Disciples

The disciples are to go, "baptizing them in the name of the Father and of the Son and of the Holy Spirit" (Matt 28:19).[54] Already attested in the letters of Paul, baptism is a rite of initiation whose direct origin is obscure and the subject of continuing debate. While it apparently is rooted in the practice of immersion integral to the biblical purity laws, the origins of the manner of its formulation within the Jesus movement are unknown. Since it is amply attested in NT literature composed prior to Matthew, and since we cannot identify a usage particular to this composition, we will not dwell on it. It is the clearest initiation rite attested in the early Christian materials, the rite that marks enrollment in the sect of Jews who were followers of Jesus. Here it is presented without detail and appears to be assumed, even though it is modeled in the account of Jesus's baptism by John the Baptist in Matt 3:13–17. Sectarian induction also would appear to be implied in the use of the imperative, *mathēteusate* (make disciples). With the exception of Acts 14:21, this verb only appears in Matthew.[55] Our English translations of these two verses tend to obscure the use of the verb: "Therefore every scribe who has been *trained as a disciple* for the kingdom of heaven" (Matt 13:52);[56] "a rich man from Arimathea, named Joseph, who also was a disciple of Jesus" (27:57). In the first instance we find emphasis on the teaching of a sectarian, as in 28:20. The second reference indicates that Joseph of Arimathea was not simply a distant admirer of Jesus; he was a member of the group, that is, he had already become a disciple. Matthew claims him as a member of the sect of the followers of Jesus, in contrast to Mark 15:43 and Luke 23:50–51, where he is a member of the council seeking the kingdom of God. That such an option would have been present in Matthew's literary imagination points to the diversity of representation among the Jewish adherents of the Jesus group at the time of the first gospel's composition. The injunction "to make disciples" receives specification here in the conclusion by the central role of teaching the inductees and the manner of address, that is, in the name of the Father and the Son and the Holy Spirit. Of course, teaching is necessary for a group who are considered to be "wise."

While there has been a good deal of debate about whether the author was invoking a triadic phrase representing the theology of the author or whether the phrase was already in use as a baptismal formula,[57] some recent commentators suggest other options.[58] Father, Son, and Holy Spirit are present in the first gospel in a significant way, with Jesus portrayed as Son, both Son of God and the Son of Man. A divine spirit is central to the story of Jesus's baptism (Matt 3:16) and the ensuing account of the temptations (4:1). When the disciples are commissioned to go out and are brought before governors and kings, they do not have to worry about what they will say, "for the Spirit of your Father [is] speaking through you" (10:20). In the quotation of Isa 42:1 in Matt 12:18, "I will put my Spirit upon him," we again find the spirit of the Divine represented. Repeated references to a divine spirit, the Spirit of God, Holy Spirit, are scattered throughout the composition. Representations of the presence and power of the God of Israel are developed in the portrayal of the figure of Jesus and of other divine activity through the Spirit of God.

Apocalyptic literature has been examined for the background of this triadic formula. The most interesting proposal was advanced by Jane Schaberg. It is in Daniel 7 that she identifies a triad—the Ancient of Days, one like a son of man (or "human being"), and the angels—that ultimately leads to the Matthean phrase.[59] The development of the imagery of Daniel 7 in apocalyptic literature and throughout the New Testament provides the links between the texts. The direct link she proposes is questionable. However Schaberg uses the method of comparative midrash to come to her conclusion. In this case the manner in which she collects the material for the triad related to God and the divine realm in Daniel is somewhat similar to the process just described for Matthew. In both cases the authority given by the Divine to one like a son of man is a crucial link, and the exercise of that power is assisted by the angels or the Spirit of God. However there is no other instance in Matthew where this triadic formula finds mention. Hence it should not be considered a central affirmation but rather a convenient concluding summary of the portrayal of divine activity in the text.

This connection finds support in Matt 28:18: "All authority on heaven and on earth has been given to me." Recent commentators have found this to be rooted in the portrayal of the son of man as initially depicted in Daniel 7, in particular LXX Dan 7:13–14.[60] This connection is clear in the apocalyptic chapter, Matt 24:30–31, where the Son of Man comes with power and great glory, again in the judgment scene at 25:31, and in Jesus's response to the high priest at the trial in 26:64. This figure is designated in a similar manner in the Book of Parables of 1 Enoch.[61] The description even includes the very important reference for the Matthean context, to be "the light to the nations."[62] The Son of Man is a very powerful image in apocalyptic literature, which Matthew employs to demonstrate the divine authority and power that has been ascribed to the now resurrected figure of Jesus. The angels are accompanying the figure of the Son of Man in these passages from the first gospel. This authority has already been distributed in an interesting manner throughout the gospel. After all, the statement in 28:18 is not a new revelation at this point but a theme that has been developed in various ways and stated throughout, hence rather constituting a final summation. In addition to the authority attached to the figure of Jesus through the use of the titles "Son of God" and "Son of Man," and in the ascription of authority to his teaching (7:29) and his healing (9:8), the disciples are given authority over unclean spirits (10:1).

This authoritative figure stands behind the injunction "Go, make disciples" (Matt 28:19). As the followers assembled in Galilee go about making known the dramatic events under way, they are to teach these inductees "to obey everything that I have commanded you." Within the debates about the meaning of the last four verses of this gospel, these words have not received the attention they deserve. Some commentators acknowledge passages from the Hebrew Bible which express a similar sentiment, such as Exod 7:2 and Deut 1:3 and 6:1.[63] Hagner appears to be closer to the matter at hand when he proposes that the passage points back to Matt 5:19, while noting the many instances in which the author describes Jesus as teaching.[64] As was developed in Chapters 3 and 4 above, Jesus as portrayed in the first gospel is not just any teacher but rather is portrayed as the authoritative teacher and interpreter of the scriptures of first-century Judaism. The arguments developed in the antitheses of 5:21–48 do not rest on the superior intellect of the teacher; they are based in his authority. Similarly Jesus is not simply the source of superior wisdom, but rather is the only place where true wisdom is to be found. The sectarian claim that a person needs to join the followers of Jesus in order to understand what is under way and to live in this particular time period in harmony with the divine will is the argument made in these closing verses. That way of life has been outlined in this biography of the founder and in the accounts of his teaching and actions.

That the author of the first gospel now wants readers to understand themselves as custodians of this authority is apparent not solely from this verse in the conclusion of the composition. It has already been made clear that this authority rests with the community that has been formed in his name: "whatever you bind on earth will be bound in heaven, and whatever you loose on earth will be loosed in heaven" (Matt 16:19; 18:18).[65] First ascribed to Peter, here described as the foundation of this assembly of his followers, and then to the assembly, charged with the responsibility for its own maintenance and discipline, the applicable understandings of biblical law were now the responsibility of the followers.[66] This is the equivalent of what in later Jewish literature came to be regarded as halakah. The followers have been entrusted with the care of "everything that I have commanded you." This injunction in the conclusion then is not some dramatic new mandate given to his followers at the point of some new mission; it is the summation of what has been advanced throughout the composition and constitutes instruction for those who accept this revelation. At the center of the concern behind this mandate was the maintenance of the sectarian community that had been formed around the name of its founder.

The injunction in Matt 28:19–20 concludes with the promise of the divine presence. As frequently recognized, this conclusion along with the naming of the baby as Emmanuel, the Aramaic of "God with us," in 1:23 brackets the entire biography. In between we find the various ways in which the author develops the portrait of the divinized human figure of Jesus. By the end of the biography the reader understands how the promise in Matt 1:23 is possible and how Jesus can be understood to be the person selected by God to unveil and preside over the climactic events in human history. The reader also understands how it is through this human being that it is possible to speak of the divine presence that will remain until the completion of history. As in Matt 28:20, "I am with you always," this divine presence is shared with the followers, most apparently in 18:20: "For where two or three are gathered in my name, I am there among them."[67] The readers expect to find evidence of the continuing divine presence within the assembly of the followers of Jesus. It is in this assembly that they expect to gain an authoritative understanding of what God wills for the future of Israel and what that means for their collective life, that is, to become wise. The final summation constitutes the theological justification of their sectarian identity.

This divine presence is assured "until the end of the age" (Matt 28:20). It is most likely that this phrase again points to the apocalyptic nature of the composition, here resembling Dan 12:13 (Theodotion): "But you, go your way and rest; you shall rise for your reward at the end of the days."[68]

While the evidence for dependence upon this text is not clear, the apocalyptic conclusion of both compositions is evident. Of equal significance is the fact that references to the end of the age are also to be found within Matthew.[69] The gospel concludes on this note, consistent with the way in which this theme has been developed throughout the composition.

These closing verses provide a summary of the way forward for those followers of Jesus who believe that God has initiated a series of events through Jesus Christ that turn the tide of world history toward its end. The manner in which Jews are to live during this period is based upon the teachings of Jesus, as told in the gospel of Matthew. The evidence supporting this view of history is apparent in the divinization of Jesus, in the manner in which God has designated him as the authoritative spokesperson and interpreter of the divine will as well as in his designation as authoritative judge. His resurrection is an indication that these final events are being set in motion. So the concluding injunction of the first gospel to its sectarian adherents is to pay attention to what they teach and how they live.

Conclusion

The eschatological vision undergirding the first gospel is summarized in the last four verses of this sectarian composition. The only viable vision of a Jewish future is advanced throughout Matthew, and here its propagation is made the responsibility of the adherents of the Jewish sect composed of the followers of Jesus Christ. Its role as a Jewish reform group has explicitly been made clear in the first commissioning account in Matt 10:5–6; its broader significance is reiterated and acknowledged in Matt 15:24. This summation places the role of this sectarian group within the vision of exclusive inclusivity described in the final chapters of Isaiah. Foreigners are an integral part of the description of the faithful returnees as they gather in Jerusalem (Isa 60; 66:20) and recognize the activity of God in its restoration. "All the nations" need to meet the same criteria as those Israelites who will benefit from God's saving activity. This is not universalism but rather an exclusivism redefined. According to Matthew, the work of the sect originates within the failings of the Jewish leadership of the late Second Temple era, and its goal is a renewed Israel.

The consequences of this call for renewal have global implications. While the "nations" in this text represent the imperial powers, the oppressive weight of Roman rule is not the focus of sectarian interest. While

Matthew seems to be aware of this reality, the focus is on "the lost sheep of the house of Israel." The sectarian perspective of the work focuses on the life of the Jewish community within that empire rather than the empire itself. This sect also lives with the hope and imminent expectation that the "nations" will come to recognize the might of the God of Israel as the eschaton approaches. It is within that context that the sect is sent out to proclaim that the kingdom of God has drawn near, evident throughout the gospel in the mighty acts performed by and in the name of Jesus as well as in the authority of his teaching. That authority is now resident in the sect that bears his name. It is with this sect that the fate of the Jewish people now rests. The universal significance of the manner in which God has placed the fate of the Jewish people in the hands of the sect is to be explained to all the nations so that they also can understand what the future holds in store.

The final commission summarizes the sectarian identity that coincides with the sociological definition of sect utilized in this study.[70] It is developed throughout the work as "a voluntary association of protest" whose mission is clearly identified in this conclusion. The "boundary marking mechanisms" are evident in the claim that "all authority in heaven and on earth has been given to me" (Matt 28:18), given the manner in which that authority has been described and used throughout the remainder of the composition. The social differentiation found in that definition is implicit in the claim for authority.

This summation also can be understood within the context of the three elements of sect formation developed by Stark and Bainbridge.[71] The element of difference is evident throughout the work, developed most explicitly in the Sermon on the Mount. The extent and importance of the difference is reiterated in the concluding summary when the disciples are enjoined to "teach them everything that I have commanded you" (Matt 28:10). There is a Jewish way of life based upon what is pleasing to God, and that way of life is now the programmatic agenda of this sect. This different way of being Jewish is to be taught to all who are interested. The subcultural deviance of the group is evident in its behaviors and practices. The element of separation is apparent in the exclusive claim for authority: "All authority in heaven and upon earth has been given to me" (28:18). This element finds expression in the treatment of wisdom in the first gospel and in its understanding of communal discipline.[72] As already noted, this authority now rests only with the sect. No other group within the Jewish community adequately or correctly understands the will of God. The narrative has developed a distinctive identity for the sect in which it is able "to distinguish between its own members and those otherwise normally regarded as belonging to the same national or religious identity."

The element of antagonism is not explicit in this summation because it follows the narrative climax in which all of the elements of the Jewish leadership groups had coalesced in opposition to Jesus and were in collusion to effect his execution. The narrative of antagonism is a theme developed throughout the composition. It begins to build with a higher level of intensity with the turn to Jerusalem in Matt 21:1. This portrayal shows the antagonism toward Jesus from the scribes, the Pharisees, the Sadducees, the chief priests, the elders, and the council, that is, all of the spiritual, intellectual, and political leadership of the Jewish community. Finally the people are indicted, clearly because of its leadership. Since the sectarian interest is to differentiate itself from "those normally regarded as belonging to the same national or religious entity," the Roman officials come off with less responsibility for the execution.[73] A sectarian author is not primarily interested in letting them off the hook but rather in keeping the focus on the Jewish leadership, who is the primary "other" of the sect. From a sectarian perspective, it is the leadership of the Jewish community that has led to the present situation for the Jews within the Roman Empire. The execution also represents the place of the sect vis-à-vis the other segments of the Jewish community at the end of the first century CE. The apocalyptic eschatology in these last eight chapters of the composition demonstrates the victory of God in the life of the sect. While the present situation of the sect appears to be one of persecution, torture, and hatred, their ultimate vindication is clear. The antagonism of the remainder of the Jewish community toward the sect is seen as self-evident by Matthew. The projection of this antagonism onto sectarian life demonstrates the antagonism of this sectarian author toward the remainder of the Jewish community. In this context the historical apocalypse of Matt 24 permits the reader to understand the transitory nature of their present experience, a situation which will be reversed by divine activity.

The portrayal of the historical reversal prior to the execution permits the resurrection to be understood as the beginning of this divine activity. This resurrection is present in the opening of the tombs in Matt 27:52–53 as well as in the resurrection appearances of Jesus. While earlier in the gospel divine activity had been portrayed in the teaching, healing, and other miracles of Jesus and in the commissioning of the disciples in Matt 10:7–8 to "cure the sick, raise the dead, cleanse the lepers, cast out demons," in the summary conclusion they are sent out to make disciples, baptize, and teach. The cycle of events projected in the apocalyptic scenario has begun, and it is necessary that the world know this. The divine favor rests with those who choose to join the sect of the followers of Jesus. It will endure until the Roman Empire is destroyed and the Jewish people live according to the way of life of the sect formed in the name of Jesus Christ. Until then, "I am with you always, to the end of the age" (Matt 28:20). Until the projected massive upheaval in human history, the will of God is reflected in the teachings and lifestyle of the sect. This is knowledge that has global consequences and needs to be made known among all of the nations.

Conclusion

The gospel of Matthew is distinguished among the writings of the New Testament by notable similarities to other sectarian literature composed by Jews of the Second Temple era. This "most Jewish" gospel was regarded for a good deal of its history as a work originally composed in either Hebrew or Aramaic, a distinctive characteristic that gave it a certain authority and caused it to be regarded as the first gospel. With the advent of modern critical study and the widely accepted hypothesis of the priority of Mark, the particular Jewish nature of this gospel required a different explanation. An alternate rationale emerged with the wider utilization of the methodologies of the social sciences in biblical studies coupled with an altered historiography of Jewish life during the Roman period in greater Syria, especially Galilee. This historiography was influenced extensively by the archaeological work in Galilee that began in the early 1970s and the adoption of more critical approaches to the evaluation of the historical evidence.

The importance of sectarianism for the late Second Temple era became evident with the discovery of the Dead Sea Scrolls from the area of Qumran in 1947.[1] Debates about the history of groups associated with those compositions, the archaeological site, and ancillary evidence from Greek and Latin sources continue to this day. The use of sociological methodologies in the examination of this evidence has been one attempt to understand the extent, role, and function of sectarian groups from that time period. The sociological characteristics of new religious movements identified by Stark and Bainbridge are significant for the study of this phenomenon in the Second Temple era. Their work focused on the level of tension of the sect with the socio-cultural environment within which it is located and the tendency to view itself as uniquely legitimate or to establish boundaries against another.[2] While there are a number of scholars of Jewish history of the early and middle Roman periods who propose similar or related definitions, in this study I adopted that of Albert Baumgarten: "a voluntary association of protest, which utilizes boundary marking mechanisms—the social means of differentiating between insiders and outsiders—to distinguish between its own members and those otherwise normally regarded as belonging to the same national or religious entity."[3] This definition emphasizes the opposition of these groups to prevailing views, a feature shared among the majority of the definitions proposed. The significance of the inclusion of boundary marking mechanisms in the definition is that it provides the basis for an analysis from the sectarian perspective. The sect is evaluated upon the basis of its own claims regarding its relationship to the larger socio-cultural environment rather than upon the basis of claims made by the dominant body regarding a group it considers deviant. From a methodological standpoint this is important in the study of Matthew in part because of the difficulties involved in defining the character of that dominant body at the end of the first century CE. More specifically, the reader of the gospel of Matthew might get the impression that the Pharisees actually were in control of the Jewish community at the time in which this gospel was composed, hence in the leadership of the dominant body. Other evidence suggesting that this would have been the case is rather limited. A sectarian analysis focuses on the manner in which Matthew proposed that the followers of Jesus addressed in the composition should differentiate themselves from the remainder of the Jewish community and the rationale for acting in this manner. In this case being able to define the dominant community is not so significant a factor in sectarian analysis.

Such an approach to the study of the Second Temple era permits sectarian analysis to be employed in a more discriminating manner than frequently has been the case. The sociological category "sect" is an attempt to describe the response of certain new religious movements to the society in which they originated and existed. It is not a valid method for constructing the shape of the society as a whole. But it can be demonstrated to be a category that fits the descriptions of Jewish life in the Rules texts and certain other compositions from the Qumran corpus. The argument of this volume is that this is also the case for the gospel of Matthew.

For the study of the first gospel, the texts from Qumran provide evidence not only of a similar social structure whose legislative and communal dimensions receive extensive treatment in the sectarian Rules. In the preceding chapters of this volume, specific intersections with that sectarian material have been demonstrated. This is most apparent in the Sermon on the Mount, the first and most prominent section of major paraenetic material in Matthew, in which intersection with specific legislation in the Rules text is apparent as well as similarities in the treatment of law and the utilization of Torah. The authority of the sect for the lifestyle of its adherents is apparent in both; the authorization processes betray distinct similarities. Closely related is the ubiquitous appearance of sectarian wisdom in both bodies of literature demonstrating the manner in which sectarian membership was necessary for the acquisition of knowledge and developing the ability and the perspective of a "wise" person. The manner in which knowledge is exclusively related to the person and teaching of Jesus in Matthew and the role of his person and teaching in the education and development of the lives of his followers as assumed in the text is remarkably similar to the manner in which truth and knowledge rest exclusively with the sectarian membership as outlined in the Rules texts from Qumran. As outlined there, the acquisition of this knowledge and truth is possible only within the sect. That both bodies of literature appear within the context of Jewish apocalypticism of the late Second Temple era should not escape notice.

This sectarian reading of the first gospel is advanced as an alternate *Jewish* identity; it is proposed as one manner in which the adherent could live as a Jew at the conclusion of the first century CE. This could be said of a number of Jewish compositions of the era which demonstrate an affinity with Jewish apocalypticism. Stanton argued that such a sectarian analysis permits one to understand the manner in which these followers of Jesus were able to establish an identity independent of the Jewish community as a whole, which he described as a painful separation from the parent body.[4] However as noted, a sectarian reading permits us only to identify the parent body as it is understood within the text of the first gospel, and it is not clear that a "parent body" for a Jewish community in southern Syria/Galilee can be identified in any clear manner at the end of the first century. There is no clear evidence in this composition of a *move away* from the Jewish community; it is rather *within* the Jewish community that such a sectarian reading finds explanation. Such a reading does not lend itself to an attempt to place Matthew on a "parting of the ways" spectrum as an initial level of analysis. This would appear to be the issue with which Stanton was grappling. He certainly is not alone in bringing such an orientation to the text.[5]

The sectarian reading proposed in this volume suggests that the significant question being addressed by Matthew is "Where does this group of the followers of Jesus fit within the Jewish community?" What happens with the response to that question in subsequent Christian treatment is a topic worthy of investigation, but not one that the author of the first gospel addressed. A most interesting proposal on the fate of a "Matthean community" which has not received adequate attention is that advanced by Sim, suggesting that it was alienated from the broader Christian movement and its viewpoints regarded as irrelevant.[6] This conclusion is based upon his development of a sectarian reading of the first gospel.

What also is apparent is that Jewish sects emerged within the context of the Greek and Roman Empires, in which voluntary associations played an increasingly important role in the maintenance of the social structure of the society. While there appears to be some convergence between the advance of the role of Torah and the growth in power of the Hasmonean state, Weinfeld and Gillihan have demonstrated the similarities between the sectarian structures in the Rules texts from Qumran and the emergent voluntary structures in Greek and then Roman society. This is particularly the case in the Roman world as the influence of the communal civic structures of the forum and related institutions gave way to greater imperial control. Within the Jewish world, sectarian groups provided an alternative identity and ideology to the Roman imperial world. More importantly they were the source of an alternate identity and ideology to the Jewish social structure, which was perceived in some instances as both failing and corrupt. At the same time, Jewish sectarian groups will have been recognizable along with other voluntary associations within the multicultural communities of greater Syria and Galilee inhabited by Jew, Greek, and other local ethnicities.

The Sermon on the Mount provides the best example of a sectarian Jewish text found in the NT gospels.[7] It can be located within the development of the wisdom traditions attested in Second Temple Jewish literature as demonstrated in the initial macarisms with which it opens and in the two-ways traditions in its conclusion. Specific vocabulary used for the description—or identification—of the body of followers of Jesus in the Beatitudes is also used to refer to the sectarians in some of the texts from Qumran. The sectarian identification of the followers of Jesus is most evident in the apparent replacement of the law with Jesus as the central point of reference, demanding exclusive allegiance in Matt 5:11–12 and the only final point of authority in 5:17–20. Such an argument is advanced within the late Second Temple Jewish world in which Torah is to be identified more clearly by its association with a revelation to Moses than the specific words it becomes identified with in the later Masoretic tradition. The central sectarian values of righteousness and perfection are attested in 5:20 and 5:48. Within the context of the Sermon, it is Jesus's authoritative response in each of the six antitheses that reinforces the sectarian understanding of its unique place among the Jewish people and its particular responsibility with regard to the kingdom of God, an outline for and an assurance of the Jewish future.

The identification of Jesus with wisdom, presumed in the Sermon on the Mount, is most evident in Matt 11.[8] Earlier arguments both for and against a wisdom Christology were inadequate attempts to penetrate the dynamic of the portrayal of wisdom in the first gospel. The complex nature of this presentation in Matthew is more apparent after the extensive research and discussion impelled by the discovery of the wisdom texts among the Dead Sea Scrolls. It is then possible to see that Jesus is treated as wisdom in the first gospel and also as its envoy. This apparent inconsistency finds resolution in the advancement of a sectarian identity with Jesus at its center and as its founder. It is this identity which is affirmed as the source of the acts of power to be conveyed to John the Baptist in 11:5 and the subsequent macarism of 11:6, the latter with echoes of 5:11–12 and more direct references to 24:10 and 26:31–33. The rejection of wisdom, known from Second Temple literature, provides the context for 11:16–24, including the failure to recognize the acts of power detailed in 11:5. Jesus and the sect comprising his followers is the exclusive provenance of wisdom in 11:25–27. The correlation of wisdom and Torah in some texts of the Second Temple era here identified with Jesus makes it necessary to understand the Sermon on the Mount in the light of this portrayal. In some instances wisdom as portrayed in works such as 1 En. 42 fills out its portrait in Matt 11. The sapiential context and its relation to revelation is an integral part of Matthew's portrayal of Jesus, as it is in so many other Jewish texts of the Second Temple and middle Roman periods.

Similarities to the communal structures and practices attested in the Rules texts from Qumran is most evident in Matt 18:15–20.[9] While there is a significant interpretive history of Lev 19:15–18 to be found throughout the immediate post-biblical and into the later rabbinic literature, the particular Matthean formulation is most similar to that attested in the Rules texts and some related compositions among the scrolls. These procedures and related legislation such as the penal codes figured prominently in the lives of sectarians related to the Qumran scrolls. A clear comparison of the various sectarian practices and supporting ideologies of the Qumran compositions with those of the Matthean legislation provides a window into respective sectarian self-understandings.

The narrative of the story displays a higher level of tension as it begins with the approach to Jerusalem in Matt 21:1.[10] Having differentiated the practices and ideology of the sect from its Jewish competitors and the dominant culture of that community in earlier portions of the composition, the story now shifts into a more direct portrayal of the antagonism between Jesus and his opponents. The verbal contests of Matt 21 and 22 bring the chief priests, the elders, and the Sadducees into the picture along with the primary opponent, the Pharisees. The tension between Jesus and the Pharisees escalates with his diatribe of Matt 23. These conflicts are the manner in which Matthew has chosen to articulate his understanding of the relationship between the sectarian followers of Jesus and the remainder of the Jewish community, including the various segments and leadership groups within it. In the case of Matt 23 we find the Pharisees depicted as the counterexample to the followers of Jesus whose sectarian practices and rationale have been advanced in the Sermon on the Mount. As this diatribe comes to a conclusion, it focuses more directly on the fall of the temple and the destruction of Jerusalem, the center of attention in Matt 24–25 with its apocalyptic sections. The various segments of the leadership of the Jewish community now are the objects of the antagonism of the Matthean sect as the narrative continues into the trial and execution. By means of this literary development, all of the segments of Jewish leadership are implicated in the trial and death, in contrast to the other synoptic accounts where only the chief priests and the elders are present. In Matthew the trial and execution demonstrate the high level of tension between the sect and its co-religionists. Due to their sectarian sensibilities, their primary interest is in the Jewish leadership, which in the definition of sectarianism employed in this study represents "those otherwise normally regarded as belonging to the same national or religious entity."[11] The author wants these sectarian followers of Jesus to understand that it is these "other" Jews who are responsible for the death. The Romans are not the primary perpetrators; the Roman military and administrative structures are not the primary opponents who challenge the existence and welfare of the Matthean sect in the Jewish communities where they live. This is more pro-sectarian than it is explicitly pro-Roman.

The apparent emphasis on the gentiles in Matt 28:16–20 serves as a description of the primary purpose of the first gospel for many commentators. The juxtaposition of the commissioning of the disciples to "go nowhere among the Gentiles" in Matt 10:5–6 with "Go therefore and make disciples of all nations" in Matt 28:19 then constitutes the central interpretive problem of the work.[12] A sectarian analysis suggests that 28:16–20 is a summary of the position of the sect that has been developed throughout the composition, hence a final statement on the place of the sect in Jewish life and history. In the apocalyptic outlook developed particularly in the latter portion of this sectarian composition, the sect constitutes the expression and practice of the Jewish community that represents the will of God. It is a sectarian position on the ultimate outcome of human history. All will come to recognize the God of Israel. It is that God whose will for humankind finds expression in the life of the sect. As human history is hurtling toward its conclusion, the membership of the sect is called upon to teach all the nations, including non-sectarian Israel, the Jewish way of life that this god finds pleasing. This mandate includes "all the nations" but is not universal in the conventional manner in which that term is understood today. It rather is an expression of the "exclusive inclusivity" that constitutes the vision of the future already known in the prophetic writings such as Second Isaiah.

Perhaps the most apt manner for describing the first gospel in terms of its literary genre is to suggest that it is a sectarian narrative. The life of Jesus functions to provide a model and rationale for the development of a sectarian expression of Judaism and guidance for problems that arise in such a quest. This sect does fit within the definition proposed by Baumgarten and repeated at the beginning of this chapter in that the life of Jesus provides a model for "a voluntary association of protest."[13] In the teaching attributed to its founder, we find in the Sermon on the Mount and other texts clear markers distinguishing the followers of Jesus from their co-religionists. This definition had its basis in the sociological work of Stark and Bainbridge, who noted the high level of tension between the sect and its socio-cultural environment in their observations of modern religious movements. In the study of sect formations they noted three elements they could identify. The two elements of separation and difference are identified throughout the narrative of Matthew in the figure and, more particularly, the teachings of Jesus. In his words are found those defining actions and practices that distinguish his followers from the remainder of the Jewish community. The structure of this sectarian community suggests some level of separation, most evident in the communal discipline texts of Matt 18. Both difference and separation are behind the purpose of the concluding injunction, "teaching them to obey everything that I have commanded you." Both separation and difference are evident in the claims for Jesus as the authoritative teacher and the exclusive source of wisdom. Within this narrative the third element, antagonism, escalates throughout the story and reaches its climax with the trial and execution. The denunciation of the Jewish leadership is an integral part of the antagonism demonstrated by the sect. As with other sectarian movements, the self-perception of the sect is that the situation is very dire; the future of the Jewish people and even the fate of the world are at stake. The will of God in this situation can be known only through this sectarian option.

Notes

Introduction

1. See the discussion by Shaye Cohen, *Beginnings of Jewishness*, 25–106; Cohen, *Significance of Yavneh*, ix–x.

Chapter 1. Matthew and the First-Century Jewish World

1. A. Baumgarten, *Flourishing of Jewish Sects*, 1–28.
2. For the sake of economy I will throughout this book use the name "Matthew" to designate the gospel of Matthew and/or its author. The reader should not assume that with this designation I am making any statement about authorship. Where it is not evident from context that I am rather alluding to the person Matthew, named a disciple in the first gospel, I will indicate so in the text.
3. Mason, *Josephus, Judea*, 141-84; Mason, "Ancient Jews"; A.-J. Levine, "Jesus in Jewish-Christian," 179–82; Reinhartz, "Vanishing Jew"; Reinhartz, "Snared by Words?"
4. Cohen, *Beginnings of Jewishness*, 71–106.
5. Mason, "Jews, Judaeans,"; Mason, "Ancient Jews"; Boyarin, *Border Lines*, 151–226; Boyarin, "Rethinking Jewish Christianity."
6. D. R. Schwartz, "'Judaean' or 'Jew?'" 13–14, n. 18. See also D. R. Schwartz, "Judeans, Jews."
7. S. Schwartz, "How Many Judaisms?" 235.
8. See Chapter 3, nn. 90–94, below.
9. L. I. Levine, *Ancient Synagogue*, 75.
10. Eusebius, *Hist. eccl.* 3.39.16. This is the extent of the quotation in Eusebius, here translated in Koester, *Introduction*, 2:172. On the dating of Papias, see Davies and Allison, *Matthew*, 1.128–29. For an appraisal of the various proposals related to this quotation, see Kümmel, *Introduction*, 120–21.
11. The term is used for pronouncements attributed to God in the New Testament: Acts 7:38; Rom 3:2; Heb 5:12; 1 Pet 4:11.
12. Note the extensive evaluation by Davies and Allison, *Matthew*, 1.7–17; Luz, *Matthew*, 1.46–47.

13. Eusebius, *Hist. eccl.* 6.25.4. Translation is from Stanton, *Gospel*, 114–15. Note also the attribution to Clement by Eusebius (*Hist. eccl.* 6.14.5). In *Hist. eccl.* 6.36.2 Eusebius credits Origen with the authorship of twenty-five volumes on Matthew. Only a portion of these have survived. Concerning these texts, see Howard, *Hebrew Gospel*, 157–60.

14. Eusebius, *Hist. eccl.* 5.8.2.

15. Jerome, *Vir. Ill.* 3. This is an important piece of evidence accepted by Viviano for his argument that Caesarea Maritima was the locale for the composition of Matthew ("Where Written?" 542–46).

16. Note that Eusebius advances the view that Matthew was directed to Jewish followers before the apostle himself, assumed to be the author of this gospel, embarked on the gentile mission (*Hist. eccl.* 3.24.6). For a survey and collection of the impact of the first gospel on the early Christian writers, see the volumes by Massaux, *Influence of the Gospel*.

17. Sim, *Gospel of Matthew*, 289–97.

18. Note the listing in Luz, *Matthew*, 1.56–57; Sim, "Reconstructing," 20.

19. Witherington, *Matthew*, 25–28. While this site would be of some interest in our quest due to its Galilean provenance, the name in Matthew is derived largely from the Marcan source. It is used four times in Matthew compared to three times in Mark. Only in Matt 11:23 is it used in a context that does not follow directly from the Marcan source; in this context its use is analogous to Chorazin and Bethsaida.

20. Bacon, *Studies*, 15–23; Kennard, "Place of Origin"; Osborne, "Provenance." But note the caution on the use of Edessa by Russell, "Avoiding the Lure."

21. Hagner, *Matthew*, 1.lxxv; Carter, *Matthew and Empire*, 35–53; Luz, *Matthew*, 1.56–58; Keener, *Socio-rhetorical Commentary*, 41–42; Sim, "Reconstructing," 19–25; Konradt, *Israel, Church, and the Gentiles*, 366.

22. Overman, *Matthew's Gospel*, 159; Overman, *Church and Community*, 16–19; Gale, *Redefining Ancient Borders*, 41–63; Runesson, "Rethinking," 106–7.

23. A. Segal, "Matthew's Jewish Voice," 26–27.

24. F. Grant, *The Gospels*, 140–41.

25. This claim needs to be qualified with the admission that the linguistic environment of first-century Judea and Galilee remains a complicated issue, still contentious in modern scholarship. For a discussion of these issues bearing on the language usage of the synoptic gospels, see Notley, Turnage, and Becker, *Jesus' Last Week*; Buth and Notley, *Language Environment*.

26. Howard, *Hebrew Gospel*, 190–234; Howard, "Shem-Tob's Hebrew Matthew." His original argument (*Gospel of Matthew*, 181–226) that this text represents a later version of an independent Hebrew text of Matthew from the second to the fourth centuries CE has faced considerable criticism, and he modified his own opinion in the revised version. See William Horbury in Davies and Allison, *Matthew*, 3.729–38; Luz, *Matthew*, 1.60.

27. Luz, *Matthew*, 1.60. Hans-Martin Schenke considers the possibility that it is a Coptic translation of an earlier Hebrew or Aramaic version completely different from the canonical text (*Matthäus Evangelium*).
28. Recent surveys of this research include the following: Hezser, *Jewish Literacy*, 227–50, Hezser, "Jewish Literacy"; Gale, *Redefining Ancient Boundaries*, 49–52; Smelik, "Languages of Roman Palestine."
29. Josephus, *B.J.* 1.20, 617–40.
30. Josephus, *B.J.* 2.40–79.
31. Josephus, *B.J.* 3.7, 29
32. Aland, *Synopsis*, 49.
33. Zangenberg, "Region in Transition," 10.
34. Andrade, *Syrian Identity*, 96–97.
35. Andrade, *Syrian Identity*, 113–15, 126–36.
36. Andrade, *Syrian Identity*, 128–241.
37. S. Schwartz, *Imperialism and Jewish Society*, 103–10.
38. S. Schwartz, *Imperialism and Jewish Society*, 129–61.
39. Schürer-Vermes, 1.531–34.
40. The term *polis* is found twenty-seven times in Matthew, while only eight times in Mark. This is in contrast to the term *komē*, usually translated "village," which appears four times in Matthew, seven times in Mark. While the term appears frequently in Luke as well, this has no bearing on the present discussion since we assume an urban locus for that composition. Matthew does not always make a strict distinction between it and *komē* (Davies and Allison, *Matthew*, 1.274). See also Strathman, "πολις," 530, for the same point; Overman, *Matthew's Gospel*, 159. Josephus appears to understand the same distinction in *Vita* 235.
41. Matt 22:7. This passage is most often understood, presumably correctly, to be a reference to the destruction of the Jerusalem temple by the Romans.
42. On the "synagogue," see below in Chapter 5.
43. Hagner questions this conclusion, arguing that Matthew could have been written after Mark but before the destruction of the temple. He also advances other considerations that would point to a pre-destruction date (*Matthew*, 1.lxxiii–lxxiv).
44. Schoedel, *Ignatius of Antioch*, 92, cites the Ascension of Isaiah as significant.
45. Schoedel, *Ignatius of Antioch*, 222.
46. See Chapter 3 below.
47. Attributed to Koester by Schoedel, *Ignatius of Antioch*, 222.
48. Sim, "Reconstructing," 17–18.
49. The initial debate proposed either the traditional date prior to 117 CE or after 160 CE. However in a rather interesting argument in which he also summarizes the earlier debates, Barnes proposes a mediating position of about 140 CE ("The Date of Ignatius"). A recent apology for the traditional position is found in the work of Brent, *Ignatius of Antioch*.

50. This argument is contra Luz, who argues for the use of Matthew in 1 Pet 5:13 and a date not much after 80 (Luz, *Matthew*, 1.58).
51. J. Collins, *Apocalyptic Imagination*, 195–225.
52. Danby, *Mishnah*, 446, n. 5.
53. Schürer-Vermes, 2:323–24, 388.
54. Josephus, *B.J.* 1.110–13. Josephus does not name the eight hundred captives killed by Jannaeus as Pharisees, even though this is assumed by many scholars (*B.J.* 1.97).
55. Josephus, *A.J.* 13.288–98 (cf. *B.J.* 1.67–69). See E. P. Sanders, *Judaism*, 381. In b. Qidd. 66a a description of a similar event is attributed to Jannaeus. See Neusner, *From Politics to Piety*, 59–60.
56. E. P. Sanders, *Judaism*, 389–90. He notes that in Josephus, *A.J.* 13.288, the assumption behind the text appears to be that the monarchy and the high priesthood are separate, a possibility during the time of Herod rather than the Hasmoneans.
57. Josephus, *A.J.* 13:171–72.
58. For a reading of Josephus highlighting the role of the Pharisees during this period, see Rivkin, *Hidden Revolution*, 35–50.
59. Neusner, *From Politics to Piety*, 66. With the mention of Aristobulus, he is referring to the son of Salome Alexandra to whom the opponents of the Pharisees fled for refuge during her reign and to the military campaign he launched against his mother and brother Hyrcanus II (Josephus, *A.J.* 17.32–45).
60. E. P. Sanders, *Judaism*, 387, 412. He also thinks they may have had substantive control before Hyrcanus I and during the period of Hyrcanus II (p. 535, n. 54), i.e., in the later Hasmonean era moving into the Herodian period.
61. E. P. Sanders, *Judaism*, 388.
62. Stemberger, *Jewish Contemporaries*, 24–28. Note also the treatment of Matthew by Pickup, "Matthew's and Mark's Pharisees." While in his conclusion, Pickup suggests the treatment in the two works is similar, in his analysis he often refers to the manner in which Matthew highlights the role of the Pharisees in comparison to Mark.
63. The evidence from the gospels places the disputes of Jesus and the Pharisees for the most part in Galilee (Stemberger, *Jewish Contemporaries*, 117–18). The extent to which these disputes are more extensive and play a greater role in Matthew suggests the significance of the Galilean provenance for the gospel.
64. This is also the argument of M. Smith, "Palestinian Judaism," 77.
65. A. Segal, "Matthew's Jewish Voice," 26–27.
66. Sim, *Gospel of Matthew*, 60–62. Admitting the lack of evidence, he suggests that the interrelated nature of the Jewish community in Judea, Galilee, and the diaspora makes widespread knowledge of the Pharisees a more likely option. He cites as evidence the statement by Paul in Phil 3:5, "As to the law, a Pharisee," without any explanation addressed to his diaspora audience. A summary of the scholarship on the issue is that of Overman, "Kata Nomon Pharisaios." A

recent proposal of some significance is that of Cover, "*Paulus als Yischmaelit?*" I thank my colleague Ryan Schellenberg for drawing these articles to my attention.

67. Stemberger, *Jewish Contemporaries*, 141–42.

68. Stemberger, *Jewish Contemporaries*, 24–28.

69. Saldarini, *Pharisees, Scribes*, 156, 175, 291–92; Stemberger, *Jewish Contemporaries*, 21–23, 28–31.

70. Matt 22:45.

71. For a more detailed treatment of Matt 23 and the trial, see Chapter 6 below.

72. The connection between the Pharisees and the chief priests is also made throughout the gospel of John (7:32, 45; 11:47, 57; 18:3). In this case they share jurisdiction over the police forces with the chief priests (Stemberger, *Jewish Contemporaries*, 34–37).

73. Josephus, *B.J.* 2.411; *Vita* 20–23, 196–97.

74. Josephus, *Vita* 191; *B.J.* 4.159.

75. Runesson, "Rethinking," 115.

76. McGuire, *Religion*, 150–62. While aware that these sociological categories had their origins in the development of analytical tools for predominantly Christian societies, McGuire clarifies the manner in which they can be utilized for the examination of other religious contexts.

77. Niebuhr, *Social Sources of Denominationalism*, 21–25. For him, this was not a positive description since "they represent the accommodation of religion to the caste system." Furthermore, "denominationalism thus represents the moral failure of Christianity."

78. Josephus, *A.J.* 13.171–73.

79. Josephus, *B.J.* 2.165; also *A.J.* 18.16.

80. Matt 22:23; Mark 12:18; Luke 20:27; Acts 23:8.

81. Josephus, *A.J.* 13.288–98 (cf. *B.J.* 1.67–69).

82. Matt 3:7; 16:1–12.

83. In some MSS this last issue is attributed to a Galilean *min* (heretic) rather than to a Sadducee. On these texts, see Stemberger, *Jewish Contemporaries*, 45–50.

84. In some MSS this is ascribed to a *min* (heretic). See Schürer-Vermes, 2.384–86.

85. M. Ḥag. 2:4.

86. M. Mak. 1:6.

87. This is a very complicated issue throughout Jewish law; here see m. Parah 3:3, 7.

88. Schiffman, "Halakhic Letter," 64–73.

89. Some of these stances are attributed to an even less attested group, the Boethusians, as well. While outside the context of the concerns in this book, we note that those issues and stances continue to reassert themselves in later Jewish texts.

90. Lightstone, "Pharisees and Sadducees," 285–86.

91. Stemberger lists this and some additional texts among his "unusable and questionable texts" (*Jewish Contemporaries*, 40–45).

92. Matt 5:20; 12:38; 15:1; 23:2, 13, 15, 23, 25, 27, 29.
93. Saldarini, *Pharisees, Scribes*, 163–65.
94. Matt 9:11 (Mark 2:16); Matt 9:34, 12:24 (Mark 3:22); Matt 21:45 (Mark 11:27, 12:12 [cf. Matt 21:23]); Matt 22:34 (Mark 12:28).
95. "Scribes" in Mark (22) versus Matt (23); "Pharisees" in Mark (12) versus Matt (29).
96. Mark 11:18 (no parallel in Matt); 11:27 (Matt 21:23); 14:1 (Matt 26:3); 14:43 (Matt 26:47); 14:53 (Matt 26:57—has scribes); 15:1 (Matt 27:1); 15:31 (Matt 27:41—has scribes).
97. Cook, *Mark's Treatment*.
98. The professional role of scribes has become clearer with further examination of the role of written texts and levels of literacy in Second Temple Judaism: Jaffee, *Torah in the Mouth*; Hezser, *Jewish Literacy*; Schniedewind, *How the Bible Became a Book*; Carr, *Origins*; Horsley, *Scribes, Visionaries*.
99. Saldarini, *Pharisees, Scribes*, 241–76. For a description of them as intellectual "retainers," as advisors and administrators in the temple-state of second-century BCE Judea, see Horsley, *Scribes, Visionaries*, 193–203 (a summary of the volume as a whole). He suggests that there were no more than a few dozen persons in this category at that time (201). See also his *Revolt of the Scribes*, 9–17.
100. For a discussion of Matt 23 and the trial, see Chapter 6 below.
101. E. P. Sanders, *Judaism*, 402.
102. Josephus, *A.J.* 17.42.
103. Josephus, *A.J.* 18.20; cf. Philo, *Prob.* 75.
104. E. P. Sanders, *Judaism*, 47 (see also 11–12). He develops his understanding of what this entailed in *Judaism*, 47–303. He is already referring to "a common, underlying feature" of Judaism in the Second Temple period in *Jewish Law*, 359–60, n. 6.
105. Josephus, *C. Ap.* 2.108. The organization into four tribes in this description appears to reflect Ezra 2:36 and Neh 7:39; however elsewhere he refers to the twenty-four priestly courses (*A.J.* 7.363–67), which coincides with the descriptions outlined in rabbinic literature. Josephus bases this on the descriptions in 1 Chr 23—24, in which the author lists thirty-eight thousand Levites.
106. Grabbe, *Judaism*, 2.538.
107. L. I. Levine notes the explicit temple symbolism of the synagogue mosaics at Beth Shean and Sepphoris as well as the relationship of the depiction of Torah shrines to temple imagery (*Visual Judaism*, 337–41).
108. L. I. Levine, *Visual Judaism*, 260–79.
109. L. I. Levine, *Rabbinic Class*, 171–73; Miller, "Priests, Purities," 375–402; Fraade, *Legal Fictions*, 523–54.
110. Grabbe concludes that the Jewish experience prior to 70 CE is centered in the priesthood and cult rather than on the synagogue (*Judaism*, 2.538–45). A more extensive discussion of the synagogue is found in Chapter 5 below.
111. E. P. Sanders, *Judaism*, 77–118, 170–89.

112. We will examine in more detail the nature of Jewish law at the conclusion of the first century CE in Chapter 3 below.

113. A fuller discussion of first-century sectarianism is found in Chapter 2.

114. The term *rabbi* is found in Matt 23:7, 8; 26:25, 49. The argument that these references only designate the word "teacher" in Hebrew and not members of the specific group that emerges later in Jewish history follows from the discussion in the next section.

115. E. P. Sanders, *Judaism*, 412. Sanders already in earlier work had pointed out the difficulties involved in developing an understanding of this relationship (*Paul and Palestinian Judaism*, 60–62).

116. Deines, "'Judaism' and 'Common Judaism,'" 503–4; Deines, "Pharisees."

117. Cohen, "Significance of Yavneh," 38.

118. Sievers, "Who Were the Pharisees?" 137–55.

119. Acts 5:34–39; 22:3.

120. Josephus, *Vita* 191–92. Note also Stemberger, *Jewish Contemporaries*, 39.

121. 'Abot de Rabbi Nathan in its final form is a later composition based upon m. 'Abot and is included in collections of the "Minor Tractates" of the Babylonian Talmud. It is found in two versions, A and B, but may include some traditions older than those found in m. 'Abot, which itself is considered to be a late addition to the Mishnah.

122. Boyarin, "*Diadoche* of the Rabbis"; Tropper, "Tractate *Avot*."

123. M. Stern, "Period of Second Temple," 234–38, 319–30. Note the argument for this position advanced by Rivkin, "Defining the Pharisees," 214–20.

124. In addition to the major reference in m. Yad. 4:6–8 discussed above, we also find them referred to in m. Ḥag. 2:7; m. Soṭah 3:4; m. Ṭehar. 4:12.

125. Stemberger, *Jewish Contemporaries*, 50–64; the only reference to the Pharisees is in t. Ḥag. 3:35.

126. The Tosefta and the Palestinian Talmud are considered to be closer to the earlier Palestinian traditions, hence the historical suspicion when relying on the evidence in the Babylonian Talmud.

127. Cohen, "Rabbi." Note also his earlier condensation of his argument, "Place of the Rabbi."

128. Cohen, "Place of the Rabbi," 159–60.

129. Lapin, "Rabbinic Movement," 206. See also Himmelfarb, *Kingdom of Priests*, 165–66.

130. Hezser, *Social Structure*, 55–68.

131. Mark 9:5; 11:21; 14:45; John 1:38, 49; 3:2, 26; 4:21; 6:25; 9:2; 11:8 (also *rabbouni* in Mark 10:51 and John 20:16).

132. Matt 23:7, 8; 26:25, 49. The last reference is the only one that designates Jesus, and this is by Judas in the garden. Hezser (*Social Structure*, 56) does not deal with the other references on this point, since they do not have parallels with Mark, which would provide more potential evidence for their pre-70 usage.

133. Hezser, *Social Structure*, 60–61. The address to Jesus as *kurie* (lord) may be the translation or equivalent of *mārî*.

134. A few exceptions are listed by Hezser, *Social Structure*, 63, n. 54.

135. Hezser, *Social Structure*, 62–64.

136. Josephus, *Vita* 1–12. His Galilean command is of course a major subject in *B.J.* 2.568–3.442 and throughout *Vita*.

137. Josephus, *Vita* 197.

138. S. Schwartz, *Josephus*, 197–200, 209–16; Meier, *Marginal Jew*, 301–5; Grey, "Jewish Priests," 158–62.

139. Grey, "Jewish Priests," 84–151. He provides a nuanced description of the relationship of priests and sages after 70 and throughout the second century, indicating points of competition with some priests or priestly families while also providing evidence of priests within the rabbinic movement and the similarity of functions of both ("Jewish Priests," 152–237).

140. Hezser, *Social Structure*, 70. In his study of Josephus, the presence of the "priestly rabbis" had already been identified by S. Schwartz, *Josephus*, 96–107, 219–21. See also Grey, "Jewish Priests," 92–97. Citing Hezser, Grey notes that the priestly sages seem to have avoided Joḥanan ben Zakkai but are found to be affiliated with Gamaliel II ("Jewish Priests," 220).

141. Cohen, "Judaean Legal Tradition," 131–33. His major argument in this article, however, is to demonstrate that while the mishnaic sages inherited laws from various sources known from the Second Temple era, "they did not inherit the modes of argumentation, the dominant concerns, the logic, and the rhetoric that would come to characterize the Mishnah" (p. 140). In other words, the innovative nature of this literature created by this new group is more significant for the identification of its distinctive character than noting what it preserved.

142. Cohen, "Significance of Yavneh."

143. Its significance is still cited in recent Matthean studies: Boxall, *Discovering Matthew*, 63–68, 73–74, 104.

144. W. D. Davies, *Setting of the Sermon*. See the evaluation of this work in Chapter 3 below.

145. Lewis, "Jabneh?" 125–32; repr. in Leiman, *Canon and Masora*, 254–61. Lewis updates his work in "Jamnia after Forty Years" and "Jamnia Revisited."

146. Hezser, *Social Structure*, 68. She notes that parallels in y. Ber. 4:1 (7d) and y. Taan. 4:1 (67d) provide the same explanation of the vineyard in Yavneh, but do not make the connection with the Sanhedrin.

147. This concerns the appointment of Rabbi Eleazar ben Azariah as head of the academy at Yavneh, even if it was only temporary.

148. Meyers and Chancey, *Alexander to Constantine*, 162, n. 52, citing Peter Schäfer.

149. Tropper, "Tractate *Avot*," 170.

Chapter 2. Matthew within Jewish Sectarianism

1. Kingsbury, "Conclusion," 264–65, for this summary of conclusions in the conference volume edited by Balch, *Social History*. Here are listed only those features of relevance for this discussion. Note that Kingsbury was identifying points of an apparent consensus among these presentations on social history and not necessarily his acceptance of these points. The list of presenters and participants was much more extensive than is represented in the published essays.

2. Bultmann, *History*.

3. See my comments in "Sectarian Form," 340–42.

4. The classic study for redaction criticism of Matthew is by Bornkamm, Barth, and Held, *Tradition and Interpretation*.

5. Kingsbury, *Matthew as Story*. The impact of Jack Dean Kingsbury's work is apparent in a long list of doctoral students who worked under him and developed this aspect considerably. See, e.g., Powell, *What Is Narrative Criticism?*; Powell, "Narrative Criticism."

6. For a summary of methods employed in the study of Matthew, see Powell, *Methods*, which includes his own article, "Literary Approaches and the Gospel of Matthew," 44–82.

7. The remarkable exception was W. D. Davies, *Setting of the Sermon*.

8. Overman, *Matthew's Gospel*. A subsequent volume provided a more comprehensive treatment of the entire content of the first gospel but did not add substantive material to the methodological discussion: Overman, *Church and Community*.

9. Overman, *Matthew's Gospel*, 159.

10. This was one of the major critiques of Philip Esler in his review of *Matthew's Gospel* by Overman.

11. Overman, *Matthew's Gospel*, 155. Other studies seem to hold this same viewpoint: Stambaugh and Balch, *New Testament*, 103; White, "Crisis Management," 238–40. The latter is based on White's earlier discussion, "Shifting Sectarian Boundaries."

12. Saldarini, *Matthew's Christian-Jewish Community*, 84–123; they are listed on pp. 88–90. See also Saldarini, "Gospel of Matthew."

13. Esler, *First Christians*. Note also Holmberg and Winninge, eds., *Identity Formation*; Tucker and Baker, eds., *Clark Handbook*. In social psychology, the concept of social identity goes back to the work of Tajfel and Turner: Tajfel and Turner, eds., *Differentiation Between Social Groups*; Tajfel, *Human Groups and Social Categories*; Turner, *Rediscovering the Social Group*. Two volumes of essays building on this theoretical work are Robinson, ed., *Social Groups and Identities*; and Worchel et al., eds., *Social Identity*. For the impact on New Testament studies see Holmberg and Winninge, eds., *Identity Formation*.

14. Saldarini, *Matthew's Christian-Jewish Community*, 89.

15. Esler, "Jesus and the Reduction: Good Samaritan," 328; in an abridged form, "Jesus and the Reduction," 186–87.

16. Saldarini, *Matthew's Christian-Jewish Community*, 108. This is the methodology of his conference paper, "Gospel of Matthew." The more recent study of Stark and Bainbridge does not add to this theoretical discussion since it concentrates on the manner in which religion acts as an integrating factor with regard to varieties of deviant behaviors in modern Western societies (*Religion, Deviance*).

17. Saldarini, "Gospel of Matthew," 48–50.

18. Saldarini, *Matthew's Christian-Jewish Community*, 109. He also notes that it is related to what a society fears.

19. Saldarini, *Matthew's Christian-Jewish Community*, 58–61, 78–81.

20. Saldarini, *Matthew's Christian-Jewish Community*, 83.

21. See Chapter 7 below for a fuller discussion of this issue.

22. Sim, "Gospel of Matthew"; Runesson, "Rethinking," 101–6.

23. Sim, *Gospel of Matthew and Christian Judaism*. Note the update on his views in "Reconstructing"; Sim, "Matthew: The Current State."

24. Arlo Nau labels the evidence cited by Sim for a response to Paul within the text of Matthew as "oblique" (review of *Gospel of Matthew and Christian Judaism*, by Sim).

25. Note the article by Harrington, "Paul and Matthew," 25–26. In the words of reviewer Scott McKnight, "Or, more likely, was there not a little more Torah in Paul than Sim allows?"

26. Stanton, *Gospel*, 85–107.

27. Stanton, *Gospel*, 102. While not stressing the sectarian nature of the gospel, Freyne notes the primacy of the teaching role in this work which contains rites for admission and expulsion similar to Qumran and other sectarian halakah ("Vilifying the Other," 120–21).

28. Stanton, *Gospel*, 106.

29. The second section of Stanton's book (*Gospel*) is entitled "The Parting of the Ways" (113–281), in which he attempts to determine the crucial issues which defined the Matthean community.

30. Foster, *Community, Law and Mission*, 253.

31. Foster, *Community, Law and Mission*, 212.

32. Foster, *Community, Law and Mission*, 80–217.

33. Foster, *Community, Law and Mission*, 218–52.

34. Runesson, "Rethinking"; Runesson, "Behind the Gospel of Matthew."

35. Bauckham, ed., *Gospels for All Christians*.

36. Runesson, "Rethinking," 95, n. 1.

37. Runesson bases his sociological categories upon McGuire, *Religion*, 150–62. While I am less certain about the category of denomination, the lower level of tension is an apt observation. See Chapter 1 above.

38. See Chapter 5 below for a further discussion of the synagogue. In that discussion I will note what I consider to be the lack of evidence for the "association" type of synagogue.

39. See my analysis of the earlier literature on this subject in "Sectarian Form of Antitheses," 338–42, 357–63. A more comprehensive discussion can be found in the following article, from which this discussion is adapted with permission: Kampen, "The Books of the Maccabees and Sectarianism."

40. Johnson, "On Church and Sect"; Johnson, "Church and Sect Revisited."

41. Wilson, *Magic and the Millennium*; Wilson, *Social Dimensions of Sectarianism*.

42. Wilson, *Magic and the Millennium*, 18–28.

43. See Luomanen, "Sociology of Sectarianism," 120; Wassen and Jokiranta, "Groups in Tension," 208. But note the employment of his spectrum in Jokiranta, "Learning from Sectarian Responses."

44. See also Jokiranta, *Social Identity*, 17–76.

45. A. Baumgarten, *Flourishing of Jewish Sects*, 7.

46. White, "Shifting Sectarian Boundaries," 14.

47. Cohen, *Maccabees to Mishnah*, 125.

48. Jokiranta, "Sectarianism." See also Nickelsburg, *Ancient Judaism*, 181–82 and the notes to that discussion.

49. Jokiranta, "Sectarianism," 228–30, 236–39.

50. Stark and Bainbridge, *Future of Religion*, 49–67.

51. Jokiranta, "Social-Scientific Approaches," 250.

52. Stark and Bainbridge, *Future of Religion*, 66.

53. This chronology is accepted by Dimant, "Qumran Sectarian Literature," 542–47.

54. Josephus, *A.J.* 13.171–72; Vermes, *Complete Dead Sea Scrolls*, 61–62. This leads Cross to posit that the Wicked Priest, the opponent of the Teacher of Righteousness, would be Jonathan or his brother Simon (Cross, *Ancient Library* [3rd ed.], 105–17). The passage is considered as not very significant for the study of the origin of the sects by Sievers, *The Hasmoneans*, 86.

55. This observation coheres with the historical premise of the work of A. Baumgarten, *Flourishing*.

56. Stone, "Book of Enoch"; Stone, *Scriptures, Sects*, 27–47.

57. Nickelsburg, "Enoch, First Book of," 515–16; Nickelsburg, *1 Enoch 1*, 169–71, 230–31, 238–47; Dimant, "Qumran Sectarian Literature," 542–50.

58. García Martínez, "Origins of Qumran"; Boccaccini, *Beyond the Essene Hypothesis*. For another proposal, see Charlesworth, "Origin and Subsequent History."

59. See also CD 12:22–23.

60. The efforts to interpret this text within the context of a celibate movement are misguided: Wassen, *Women*, 122–28; J. Collins, *Beyond the Qumran Community*, 31–33.

61. J. Collins, *Beyond the Qumran Community*, 150–51.

62. Pliny the Elder, *Nat.* 5.17.4. See also one other later reference attributed to Dio Chrysostom by Synesisus of Cyrene in *Dio* 3.2.

63. Philo, *Prob.*, 76. The frequent translation of the latter term (*anomia*) as "un-godliness," while an attempt to convey the significance of the term for first-century Jews, obscures its significance.

64. Philo, *Hypoth.*, 11.1.

65. Josephus, *B.J.* 2.124 (my translation).

66. Note the evaluation of Bauckham, "Early Jerusalem Church," 66–73.

67. J. Collins, *Beyond the Qumran Community*, 12–51.

68. J. Collins, *Beyond the Qumran Community*, 208.

69. Schofield, *From Qumran to* Yaḥad, 7.

70. Schofield, *From Qumran to* Yaḥad, 189.

71. Weinfeld, *Organizational Pattern*, 51–57.

72. Gillihan, *Civic Ideology*.

73. Gillihan, *Civic Ideology*, 75–78, 505–6.

74. Gillihan, *Civic Ideology*, 95–132.

75. Gillihan, *Civic Ideology*, 508.

76. This material is charted in Gillihan, *Civic Ideology*, 509, 514–24. The work of Gillihan places into a different perspective the objections by Philip Harland to the employment of sectarian analysis in the study of the Christian and Jewish institutions of late antiquity (Harland, *Associations, Synagogues*; Harland, *Dynamics of Identity*; also valuable is the collection of Ascough, Harland, and Kloppenborg, eds., *Associations*). In his far-reaching and thorough studies of associations in the Greek and Roman worlds, Harland poses associations as an alternative model to the employment of sectarian analysis for the social scientific study of Judean and Christian groups in antiquity (Harland, *Associations, Synagogues*, 182–212). A few observations about his studies are in order. First, he concentrates on the Pauline and epistolary literature in his studies, with some attention to Revelation. The evidence in the gospels receives little attention, and the literature on social history and social science related to the gospel of Matthew is not mentioned. Second, the focus of a good deal of the attention is on diaspora synagogues and Christian identity throughout Asia Minor. So it is not clear that his critique applies to an analysis of Matthew viewed as a production of Palestinian Jews within southern Syria-Galilee. Harland's objections concern those attempts to classify most early Christian groups as sectarian and not to the use of the classification (*Associations, Synagogues*, 191–92). Gillihan permits us to understand that sects arose as one type of voluntary association within the Jewish world.

77. A. Baumgarten, *Flourishing of Jewish Sects*, 7.

78. Jokiranta, "Sectarianism," 228–30, 236–39.

79. Stark and Bainbridge, *Future of Religion*, 49–67.

80. The beginning of 4Q259 (S^e) coincides with 1QS V, 1, hence would be missing the covenant renewal ceremony.

81. Dimant, "The Volunteers."

82. CD 9:2, 12; 10:6; 13:14; 14:2; 15:1–9; 16:1, 12; 19:13–16; 20:12, 25, 29.

83. Wassen and Jokiranta, "Groups in Tension," 210–25.

84. Scott, "Sectarian Truth"; Kampen, "Wisdom in Deuterocanonical," 107–10. See also Chapter 4 below.

85. Cohen, "Significance of Yavneh," 27–53.

86. S. Schwartz, *Ancient Jews from Alexander*, 111.

87. Goodman, *State and Society*, xii-xiii. He cites two earlier articles, "Sadducees and Essenes," and "Function of *Minim.*"

88. Burns, "Essene Sectarianism."

89. Magness, "Sectarianism before and after." In need of further discussion is the claim that the archaeological evidence of purity issues such as mikvehs and stone vessels after 70 CE is evidence of continuing sectarianism.

90. Himmelfarb, *Kingdom of Priests*, 175.

91. Himmelfarb, *Kingdom of Priests*, 175, 233, nn. 78, 79. See Boyarin, *Border Lines*.

92. Note the manner in which this material is collected by Broshi, "Anti-Qumranic Polemics."

93. In m. Ḥag. 2:8 this view is initially attributed to the House of Shammai in contrast to the House of Hillel, even though it is also ascribed to an anonymous body ("the words of them") at the end of the mishnah.

94. See also Wacholder, *Dawn of Qumran*, 160–67; Burns, "Essene Sectarianism," 262–63. The texts of the Sadducees and the Boethusians are dealt with together in Regev, "Priests All the Same?" 161.

95. Mayo, "Role of the *Birkath Haminim.*" It is regarded as one of the actions taken at Jamnia by W. D. Davies, *Setting of the Sermon*, 275–79. On the evaluation of the rabbinic evidence relating to the context of this debate, see "The Rabbis" in Chapter 1 above.

96. The arguments of Joel Marcus for an earlier dating of the *birkat hamminim* rely heavily upon an analysis of the implications of this reference: Marcus, "Birkat Ha-Minim Revisited"; Marcus, "A Jewish-Christian *'Amidah*?" In his analysis he assumes a simple correlation between the Pharisees attested in NT sources and the Rabbis, a hypothesis that is not sustainable.

97. That this may refer to sectarians related to the Qumran texts is suggested by Boyarin, *Border Lines*, 67–73. He argues that this cannot refer to Christianity, as is frequently assumed. See also Teppler, *Birkat haMinim*; Van der Horst, "Birkat Ha-Minim." Note also the argument that this charge against opponents begins with the Essenes advanced by David Flusser, "4QMMT."

98. Frankfurter, "Jews or Not?" 403.

99. Frankfurter, "Jews or Not?" 411.

100. The most extensive evaluation of this category is found in Becker and Reed, eds., *Ways That Never Parted*.

101. The evidence about these groups in the writings of the church fathers (i.e., they are all male in this collection) has been gathered by Klijn and Reinink, *Patristic Evidence*. For this reference, see Irenaeus, *Haer.* I.26.2 (Klijn and Reinink,

105); Hippolytus, *Haer.*, Prol. VII.34.2 (Klijn and Reinink, 113); X.22.1 (Klijn and Reinink, 121); Origen, *Hom. luc.* III.5 (Klijn and Reinink, 127).

102. Epiphanius, *Pan.* 30.18.7–9.

103. Epiphanius, *Pan.* 30.2.2–6.

104. Jerome, *Comm. Isa.* 1, 3 (Klijn and Reinink, *Patristic Evidence*, 219).

105. Fitzmyer, "Qumran Scrolls, Ebionites."

106. Reeves, "'Elchasaite' Sanhedrin"; Reeves, *Heralds*, 42–64. I here extract only a few highlights from his more elaborate argumentation.

107. Eusebius, *Hist. eccl.* 6.16.3.

108. Reeves, *Heralds*, 44.

109. Irenaeus, *Haer.* I.26.2; III.11.7 (Klijn and Reinink, *Patristic Evidence*, 105).

110. Epiphanius, *Pan.* 28.5.1 (Klijn and Reinink, *Patristic Evidence*, 165).

111. Epiphanius, *Pan.* 30.3.7 (Klijn and Reinink, *Patristic Evidence*, 179).

112. Epiphanius, *Pan.* 30.13.2 (Klijn and Reinink, *Patristic Evidence*, 179).

113. Eusebius, *Hist. eccl.* III.27.4 (Klijn and Reinink, *Patristic Evidence*, 141, and see also pp. 30–31).

114. Regev, "Wealth and Sectarianism"; Regev, "Were the Early Christians Sectarians?" Luomanen, "Sociology of Sectarianism," does focus specifically upon Matthew, but also understands it to be more aligned with the other early Christian texts rather than those compositions which help us understand the Jewish community of the first century. Thus his sociological analysis also comes to the conclusion that the community associated with Matthew should be regarded as a cult.

Chapter 3. The Polemic of the Sermon on the Mount

1. Bauman, *Modern Quest*; Betz, *Sermon on the Mount*, 5–44; Greenman, Larsen, and Spencer, eds., *Sermon on the Mount*.

2. Luz, *Matthew*, 1.168–69.

3. Stanton, *Gospel*, 290–91.

4. Luz, *Matthew*, 1.216; Luther, *Antinomerdisputation*, 3.2 WA 39/1, 351.

5. Luz, *Matthew*, 1.229, n. 25; Calvin, *Inst.* 2.8.7.

6. Luz, *Matthew*, 1.216.

7. Weiss, *Jesus' Proclamation*.

8. Schweitzer, *Quest of the Historical Jesus*.

9. W. D. Davies, *Setting*. This work already received mention in the discussion of Yavneh in Chapter 1.

10. W. D. Davies, *Setting*, 315.

11. W. D. Davies, *Setting*, 235. He mentions 5:13–15, 22b, 34, 43ff., 48 and 19:21 as examples (W. D. Davies, *Setting*, 252).

12. Schubert, "Sermon on the Mount," 118–28.

13. For a critique of this method in the study of Matthew, see Kampen, "Sectarian Form," 340–42.

14. W. D. Davies, *Setting*, 315.

15. For a summary of the discussion of structure, see Evans, *Matthew*, 8–10. The significance of the five discourses and the outline of the gospel of Mark are better explanations for the structure than the influential tripartite structure proposed by Kingsbury (*Matthew: Structure*, 7–25) and developed in subsequent publications as well as by his students. This structure overlooks the significance of unique features of the first gospel such as the Sermon on the Mount, thereby failing to provide an adequate explanation for its particular argumentation within a Jewish context.

16. Matt 4:23–5:2 is treated as a distinct literary unit by Davies and Allison, *Matthew*, 1.410–28.

17. On the use of the figure of Moses as having multiple motivations in this composition, see Allison, *New Moses*, 91–92. Note the neglect of the first gospel in the study of Lierman, *New Testament Moses*. He argues that Allison is simply using a Mosaic typology, hence engaged in a different task than the portrayal of the figure of Moses (p. 17). As a result, the treatment of Moses in any of the synoptic gospels does not receive adequate attention.

18. Luz, *Matthew*, 1.181.

19. Allison, *New Moses*, 140–96.

20. Josephus, *A.J.* 2.210–16. Note the listing of connections in Allison, *New Moses*, 140–65. See also Luz, *Matthew*, 1.104–5, 119–20.

21. Luz, *Matthew*, 1.151. A similar reference can be found in the portrayal of the time that Elijah spent on Mount Horeb (1 Kgs 19:8; Allison, *New Moses*, 166–69).

22. See also Num 27:12–14; Deut 3:27; 32:48–52; Allison, *New Moses*, 170–72.

23. Luz, *Matthew*, 1.182; Hagner, *Matthew*, 1.84–86.

24. See Allison, *New Moses*, 175–79.

25. The definitive statement of Keener that they stood for reading Torah and sat for interpreting it appears to rely too heavily upon Luke 4:16, 20 (*Socio-rhetorical Commentary*, 164).

26. Lierman, *New Testament Moses*, 153–55.

27. Macaskill, *Revealed Wisdom*, 126–31.

28. 4Q525 1, 1–3. For detailed treatment of 4Q525, including translation and bibliography, see Kampen, *Wisdom Literature*, 307–40.

29. MS A. For Hebrew text, see Beentjes, *Ben Sira in Hebrew*, 43. Translation is mine.

30. Kampen, *Wisdom Literature*, 317.

31. This reconstruction is based upon Ps 24:4–6, which refers to "clean hands and pure hearts" in v. 4. This is in contrast to the reconstructions, "Blessed is he who speaks truth," proposed by Puech (see n. 34 below) on the basis of Ps. 15:2–3, or "Blessed is he who speaks," proposed by Charlesworth on the basis of Pss 1:1 and 15:3 (Charlesworth, "Qumran Beatitudes," 18, n. 16).

32. The use of the term "macarism" is based upon the Greek *makarios* rather than the Latin term *beatitudo* (blessedness, happiness), rendered as the plural adjective *beati* in the text of Matthew.

33. Brooke, *Scrolls and New Testament*, 221.

34. Puech, "4Q525," 89–105; Puech, "Collection," 356–61.

35. The parallel in this structure argues against the suggestion of Evans that this might be the tenth beatitude, corresponding to the Mosaic pattern of the ten commandments (*Matthew*, 109).

36. Whether this verbal usage is related to the term *hagu*, *hagy*, or *haguy* in D, 1QSa, and 4Q417 (Instruction) is another issue.

37. Kampen, *Wisdom Literature*, 250–69.

38. Goff, *Discerning Wisdom*, 134–35.

39. Kampen, *Wisdom Literature*, 252. A similar viewpoint regarding the text is advanced by Goff (*Discerning Wisdom*, 123–24), who regards it as "roughly contemporary" with Ben Sira and Instruction, but who also says it could be from the first century BCE.

40. Macaskill, *Revealed Wisdom*, 204–7. He includes a discussion of the macarism in 2 En. 42:6–14.

41. This intersection was explored in Wright and Wills, eds., *Conflicted Boundaries*.

42. Note the preference for the use of the term "correlated" or "congruous" rather than "identified" by Goering, *Wisdom's Root*, 8–9.

43. Kampen, "Wisdom in Deuterocanonical," 107–10. The subject of Jesus and wisdom in Matthew is explored more fully in Chapter 4 below.

44. Note particularly Brooke, *Scrolls and New Testament*, 224–33.

45. Flusser, "Blessed Are the Poor"; Flusser, "Some Notes," 115–25. In his article, of course, he used citations from an older version of 1QHᵃ, hence different numbering.

46. Stegemann with Schuller, *Qumran Cave 1: III*, 281. I have followed the translation of Schuller and Newsom in that volume, except that I translated the Hebrew *nekeh ruaḥ* as "broken in spirit" rather than "contrite in spirit."

47. Note also Evans, *Matthew*, 103–6.

48. 4Q171 (Pesher Psalms) 1–10 II, 10.

49. 4Q171 (Pesher Psalms) 1–10 III, 10. The term for "poor" in these two passages is *'ebyônîm*, discussed above in Chapter 2 with regard to the Ebionites.

50. Brooke, *Scrolls and New Testament*, 225.

51. Evans, *Matthew*, 106. My reading is more in line with that of Davies and Allison, when they understand "righteousness" in this verse to point to "the right conduct which God requires" (*Matthew*, 1.452–53).

52. NRSV. Later in the same chapter it is "the abundance of your heart and your mercy" that is withheld from Israel when it strays (Isa 63:15).

53. The phrases *rōb raḥămîm* and *hāmôn raḥămîm* are included in these numbers as well as reconstructions, which in this case I consider fairly reliable since it

is the final edited version of the text from Stegemann with Schuller, *Qumran Cave 1: III*, 40.

54. See also Davies and Allison, *Matthew*, 1.454–55. It is not clear, however, from the arguments in this study that these texts on mercy could have been directed against "the rabbinate of his time."

55. Goldin, *Fathers*, 32–35.

56. Schecter, *Aspects of Rabbinic Theology*, 201–2, 215–16, 239–40, 322–24; Urbach, *The Sages*, 1.330–33, 448–61.

57. The stress on purity and impurity (clean vs. unclean) in these texts in contrast to a comparative lack of mention of sin, iniquity, and forgiveness more prominently featured in the later work of the rabbis is noted by Wacholder, *Dawn of Qumran*, 12.

58. This development has been explained as the integration of the ideas of ritual and moral impurity into a single concept of defilement by Klawans, *Impurity and Sin*, 48–52, 72–75, 90. This also provides the basis for the monograph by Werrett, *Ritual Purity*, 293–300.

59. Evans notes its distinctive nature (*Matthew*,107); see also Hagner,*Matthew*, 1.94.

60. M.'Abot 1:12 (see also 1:18). "Making peace between a man and his neighbor" is one of the activities which a person enjoys in this world as well as giving the individual capital in the world to come (m. Peah 1:1). The traditions of Rabban Johanan ben Zakkai are discussed in Chapter 1 above.

61. The contradiction is noted by Davies and Allison (*Matthew*, 1.457–58), who do not see the theme of peace as prominent in the first gospel. They list the contrast between these texts as one of a number of inconsistencies found in the composition.

62. Luz, *Matthew*, 1.199. Note his analysis of the term in his section on style in the introduction (*Matthew*, 1.28).

63. Luz, *Matthew*, 3.153–54.

64. This is included as one of the Matthean terms of redactional significance by Luz, *Matthew*, 1.34. See Matt 4:12; 5:25; 10:4, 17, 19, 21; 11:27; 17:22; 18:34; 20:18, 19; 24:9, 10; 25:14, 20, 22; 26:2, 15, 16, 21, 23, 24, 25, 45, 46, 48; 27:2, 3, 4, 18, 26.

65. Luz, *Matthew*, 1.28.

66. A. Baumgarten, *Flourishing of Jewish Sects*, 7. See the discussion in Chapter 2 above.

67. Nickelsburg, *1 Enoch 1*, 2–5, 63–68, 119; Macaskill, *Revealed Wisdom*, 54–56.

68. The imperial context and its implications for life in Judea as reflected in the apocalyptic literature produced in reaction to it has been developed in a significant analysis by Portier-Young, *Apocalypse against Empire*.

69. 1 En. 104:1–2.

70. 1 En. 103:9–10.

71. Portier-Young, *Apocalypse against Empire*, 313–81.

72. J. Collins, *Daniel*, 66–68; Portier-Young, *Apocalypse against Empire*, 254–76.

73. CD 1:21.
74. Stegemann with Schuller, *Qumran Cave 1: III*, 95. See the comments on the "poor in spirit" with reference to Matt 5:3 above.
75. Knibb, "Teacher of Righteousness," 290.
76. Newsom, *Self as Symbolic Space*, 232–53, 274–75, 293–300.
77. C. R. Moss, *Ancient Christian Martyrdom*, 77–78.
78. Schürer-Vermes, 3.77–78, 122.
79. That the designation of "christian" in the decree of Nero is actually an anachronistic description of Tacitus reflecting his own perceptions around 115 CE is argued by C. R. Moss, *Myth of Persecution*, 138–39.
80. That we really do not know how any of the apostles died is reinforced by C. R. Moss, *Myth of Persecution*, 134–38.
81. C. R. Moss, *Ancient Christian Martyrdom*, 49–50.
82. A. Collins, *Crisis and Catharsis*, 69–73, 111–16; Duff, *Who Rides the Beast*, 6–10; Pagels, *Revelations*, 46.
83. Portions of the next two sections of this chapter are based in part upon my article "Sectarian Form."
84. Luz, *Matthew*, 1.173, 210.
85. Note that the argument for a series of inclusios that form a ring around the Sermon as well as explain its literary structure begins with the identification of Matt 4:23 with 9:35 (Luz, *Matthew*, 1.166). It seems much more likely that 9:35 is part of the prelude to the discourse on the commissioning of the disciples in Matthew in the same manner as 4:23 is to the Sermon. While 5:21–48 and 6:19–7:11 are of roughly equal length, the same cannot be said of all of the other sections that constitute this ring structure. The connection between this section of Matthew 4 and Matthew 10 is also identified by Davies and Allison (*A Shorter Commentary*, 60–61).
86. This is termed the "preface" by Luz, *Matthew*, 1.210–25; he called it the "preamble" in his earlier edition (*Matthew 1–7*, 255–73). The latter term was also used by Davies and Allison, while characterizing its intent as the prevention of a misunderstanding of the material to follow (*Matthew: Shorter Commentary*, 72–73). They use the term *prokatalepsis* in the earlier commentary (*Matthew*, 1.481–82).
87. Note an illustration of this problem in the introduction to the article by Westerholm, "Law in the NT." The issue and its problematic nature were placed at the center of NT studies by the landmark work of E. P. Sanders, *Paul and Palestinian Judaism*.
88. The specific nature of the debate regarding the law is overlooked by Witherington, *Matthew*, 114, 125–29. While his emphasis on wisdom is to be commended, the relationship between wisdom and law in Second Temple Judaism bears more consideration.
89. Note attempts to overcome this problem, such as the two-volume set of essays edited by Carson, O'Brien, and Seifrid, eds., *Justification and Variegated No-*

mism. The extent to which debates about the law are driven by perceptions of the issues in Paul is evident in a volume such as this.

90. Cohen, *From Maccabees to Mishnah*, 53–55.

91. S. Schwartz, "How Many Judaisms?" 128–30, quote from 130.

92. M. 'Abot 1:1–2. This is not to be interpreted as evidence that the concept was already present among the Pharisees or circles of sages in the Second Temple era. For an exposition on the rabbinic understanding of this concept, see Urbach, *The Sages*, 1.286–314.

93. Tso, *Ethics in Qumran Community*, 76–87. For a summary, see Najman, "Torah and Tradition," 1316–17.

94. The following material on this topic is adapted from my article "'Torah' and Authority," 231–54, and is used with permission.

95. Davies and Allison, *Matthew*, 1.481–82.

96. This phrase also appears in 1 Macc 3:6.

97. The only other place where the term appears in the gospels is Mark 15:28, presumably a later reading.

98. Delitzsch, *Hebrew New Testament*, 7–8; Howard, *Hebrew Gospel*, 16.

99. Luz, *Matthew*, 3.193–94.

100. E.g., Davies and Allison, *Matthew*, 3.343; Evans, *Matthew*, 404.

101. Knibb, *Qumran Community*, 94–103. There is extensive debate about this passage and its relationship to dualism in other sectarian compositions in Qumran, summarized by Frey, "Recent Perspectives." For an extensive evaluation of dualism in the Qumran texts, see Xeravits, *Dualism in Qumran*.

102. These are central to the hypotheses of historical development posited by both García Martínez ("Origins of the Qumran Movement") and Boccaccini (*Beyond the Essene Hypothesis*).

103. 1 Macc 2:44; 3:5, 6, 20; 7:5; 9:23, 58, 69; 10:61; 11:25; 14:14.

104. The complex role of Torah in Second Temple Jewish life is developed by S. Schwartz, *Imperialism*, 49–99.

105. Najman, *Seconding Sinai*, 1–40. Contra Levinson, *Deuteronomy and Hermeneutics*.

106. The phrase "Torah of Moses" is used here for conceptual clarity. The phrase *tôrat Môšeh* is not found in the Pentateuch and appears a limited number of times in the Hebrew Bible.

107. Grossman, "Beyond the Hand," 298–301.

108. D. Schwartz, "Special People," 50–56. In this instance, he cites 4QMMT C 9–11.

109. See Kampen, "'Torah' and Authority," 237–40.

110. Kampen, "'Torah' and Authority," 240–54.

111. This subject is treated in greater detail in Kampen, "'Righteousness' in Matthew."

112. It is found only in Luke 1:75; John 16:8, 10. Even the adjective "righteous" is found more often in Matthew than in the other gospels; it is relatively absent from Mark and John. See also Evans, "Fulfilling the Law."

113. Overman, *Matthew's Gospel*, 93–94.

114. Hill, "Dikaioi"; J. Baumgarten, "Heavenly Tribunal."

115. Przybylski, *Righteousness*, 85–87. Davies and Allison note the connection of the verse with both the sixth antithesis and the section as a whole (*Matthew*, 1.560). We note that the "righteousness" theme continues in the next verse (Matt 6:1).

116. Daube, *New Testament*, 63–66. An earlier and more extensive version of this argument in found in Kampen, "Sectarian Form."

117. Tannehill, *Sword of His Mouth*, 67–77.

118. Daube, *New Testament*, 55–62. Daube did note, however, that Matthew had altered the form to suit his own purposes.

119. Daube, *New Testament*, 58.

120. Similarly unconvincing is the attempt to fit what he considers to be issues of halakah into the Hellenistic genre of the epitome by Betz, "Sermon on the Mount/Plain," 1107–8. He regards the Sermon on the Mount as an independent Jewish Christian composition from the middle of the first century CE in conflict with both Pharisaic Judaism and gentile Christianity, but which does not reflect the viewpoint of the author of this gospel, whose perspective is to be seen in Matt 28:18–20. See Betz, *Essays*, 19–22. For a critique of his perspective, see Stanton, "Origin and Purpose," 181–92. Note Daube's rejection of the possibility of Greek antecedents (*New Testament*, 66).

121. Rivkin (*Hidden Revolution*, 138–39) has noted the manner in which this and other disputes center on the question of law or halakah.

122. 11Q19 (Temple Scroll[a]) LXI, 11–12; Jub. 4:31–32 (cf. 21:19–20).

123. I have omitted, because it is irrelevant to the point being made, a discussion of the fact that these Zadokite charges are found in a document which is assumed to be Pharisaic.

124. This means examples of *egō de legō* (but I say) from rabbinic literature cited by M. Smith (*Tannaitic Parallels*, 28–29) are not significant for developing an understanding of the Matthean text and may simply be an example of "parallelomania."

125. The exception is m. Yad. 4:6, in which Johanan ben Zakkai is engaged in the debate. However, here he is cited as an outsider to the Zadokite-Pharisee interaction.

126. Some later versions read *ṣadûqî* (Zadokite or Sadducean) rather than *mîn* (heretic).

127. This translation is from Goldin, *Fathers*, 39. Note the discussion of this passage in Chapter 1 above.

128. I identify the content in the central core of this document as legal rather than halakic literature, not to remove it from consideration as a product of Jewish literary creativity during the Second Temple era but to limit the former term to the material it originally designated, the legal rulings of the rabbis and the literature which discussed it. The identification of the rulings of MMT with

sections of CD legislation that she regards as non-sectarian, as proposed by Hempel (*Qumran Rule Texts*, 173–86), may have some merit, but her labeling of this material as halakic to designate all non-sectarian legislation reflects a distinctive use of the term.

129. Qimron and Strugnell, *Qumran Cave 4: V*, 147.

130. Note the discussion of the literature on the identification of the first, second, and third persons in MMT by Reinhartz, "We, You, They."

131. Hempel ("Context of 4QMMT") argues that there is no evidence of an actual separation. I think this is incorrect. In her denial Hempel links too closely the possibility of separation with the types of sectarian communities envisioned in the S and D materials.

132. See the description of the Judean legal materials as witnessed in the Mishnah by Cohen, "Judaean Legal Tradition." Both priestly law and "common practice" are significant categories for the basis of mishnaic law. This also is the argument developed by E. P. Sanders, *Judaism*. On MMT, see Fraade, *Legal Fictions*, 69–91; Hempel, *Qumran Rule Texts*, 173–86.

133. This is the setting in which the Sermon is placed as well by Betz, *Essays*, 92. Betz is also aware of and notes its polemical setting.

134. Fraade has demonstrated the manner in which this is consistent with sectarian formulations (*Legal Fictions*, 69–91). Hempel argues for the manner in which the sectarian provisions of D materials are additions to this basis (*Qumran Rule Texts*, 173–86).

135. Guelich, *Sermon on the Mount*, 180–81; Gundry, *Literary and Theological Art*, 83. Note also Davies and Allison, *Matthew*, 1.507; Luz, *Matthew*, 1.228. This is rejected by Hare, *Matthew*, 50. See also Kingsbury, "Place, Structure and Meaning," 131–41. On p. 139 he suggests the thrust of this passage is that Matthew is pitting the authority of Jesus against that of Moses. This seems good but its implications require further development.

136. The most common form used elsewhere in the gospel is *rhēthen* (that which was spoken), the participle.

137. See Wacholder, *Dawn of Qumran*, 1–32.

138. Allen, *Critical and Exegetical Commentary*, 47. Note also Albright and Mann, *Matthew*, 60.

139. Bornkamm, Barth, and Held, eds., *Tradition and Interpretation*, 93. Note also Str-B 1.253–54.

140. Schubert, "Sermon on the Mount." He lists CD 8:4; it should read 1:4. *Ri'šōnim* is a more likely reading than *laqqadmōnim* employed in the Delitsch translation or recorded in the later text published by Howard, *Primitive Hebrew Text*, 18.

141. CD 1:16; 3:10; 4:6, 8; (6:2?); 8:17; 19:29; 20:8, 31.

142. 1QS IX, 10. This general usage is also to be found in rabbinic literature. Note the references to the "first mishnah" in m. Ketub. 5:3; m. Naz. 6:1; m. Giṭ. 5:6;

m. Sanh. 3:4; m. 'Ed. 7:2. These references are found in W. D. Davies, *Setting*, 267.

143. VanderKam, *Book of Jubilees*, 1.6.

144. Charles, "Jubilees," 11.

145. Najman, *Seconding Sinai*, 43–50; Crawford, *Rewriting Scripture*, 62.

146. Davies and Allison, *Matthew*, 1.511; Hagner, *Matthew*, 1.115. Evans suggests it may also have included subsequent oral traditions (*Matthew*, 121).

147. Schiffman, *Halakhah at Qumran*, 22–76.

148. This ideology is not confined to Qumran sectarians in Second Temple Judaism; however it does receive great emphasis in that literature. Along with many others I reject any reading of *tois archaiois* as an instrumental dative. This is also rejected by Guelich, *Sermon on the Mount*, 179; and Gundry, *Literary and Theological Art*, 84. The "first" here are those spoken to, not the speakers.

149. It must be noted, of course, that the rabbis can speak of *ḥasidim hāri'šōnim* and *zəqenim hāri'šōnim*. See my discussion in *Hasideans and Origin*, 187–207.

150. Daube, *New Testament*, 57–58. Albright and Mann follow his interpretation; *Matthew*, cix.

151. That the formulation of the antitheses is the responsibility of the gospel writer is documented very well in Gundry, *Literary and Theological Art*, 82–84, as well as in his subsequent commentary on each section. This is contra Davies and Allison, *Matthew*, 1.504–5, where one can find a discussion of the relevant literature. See also Strecker, *Sermon on the Mount*, 63.

152. Exod 20:13 // Deut 5:17.

153. Daube, *New Testament*, 56; Gundry, *Literary and Theological Art*, 84; Davies and Allison, *Matthew*, 1.511; Basser, *Mind Behind the Gospels*, 132.

154. Note that Davies and Allison, *Matthew*, 1.510, also entertains a connection of these verses in Matthew to the biblical story of Cain; however, without reference to the story in Jubilees.

155. The principle of a "measure for measure" punishment is also employed in Jub. 48:14, justifying the drowning of the Egyptians. See Segal, *Book of Jubilees*, 222–23, n. 52. For additional references to this idea see Kugel, *Traditions of the Bible*, 507–9.

156. Jub. 7:20–33.

157. Jub. 6:8; 11:2–6; 21:6–20.

158. Jub. 15:26; 16:9; 20:4–5; 30:7–10; 33:10–17; 11Q19 (Temple Scroll^a) XXXV, 6–7; LI, 16–18; LV, 15–21; LXIV, 7–9, 9–13; LXVI, 1–3.

159. My translation.

160. Albright and Mann, *Matthew*, 61; Gundry, *Literary and Theological Art*, 85; Allen, *Critical and Exegetical Commentary*, 47; Lambrecht, *Sermon on the Mount*, 91; Evans, *Matthew*, 122.

161. The necessity of dealing with the phrase in both instances in a similar manner is noted by Davies and Allison, *Matthew*, 1.512.

162. Hempel, "Penal Code."

163. Allen, *Critical and Exegetical Commentary*, 49; Albright and Mann, *Matthew*, 62.

164. This view was reasserted and developed by E. P. Sanders, *Judaism*, 47–278. Evaluations of this perspective are to be found in McCready and Reinhartz, *Common Judaism*, and Udoh, *Redefining First-Century Identities*. On the temple in Qumran texts, see Kampen, "Significance of the Temple," 185–97.

165. 11Q19 (Temple Scroll[a]) LVII, 11–15. For a discussion see Yadin, *Temple Scroll*, 1.349–53.

166. 11Q19 (Temple Scroll[a]) LI, 11–18; Yadin, *Temple Scroll*, 1.383–85.

167. 11Q19 (Temple Scroll[a]) LIV, 6–13; Yadin, *Temple Scroll*, 1.373–82.

168. This possibility is presented by Davies and Allison, *Matthew*, 1.523.

169. Jub. 20:3. Following VanderKam's translation at this point, I adopt the terms "sexual impurity" and "sexual offense" to render the Hebrew *zǝnût* and the Greek *porneia*.

170. Kampen, "Matthean Divorce Texts," 161.

171. Meier, *Matthew*, 52.

172. Note my earlier paper, "Matthean Divorce Texts," portions of which are utilized here with permission.

173. Gundry, *Literary and Theological Art*, 90; Davies and Allison, *Matthew*, 1.528–31. On Deut 24:1, see Tigay, *Deuteronomy*, 221.

174. See also Fitzmyer, "Matthean Divorce Texts," 203.

175. See my analysis of these in Kampen, "Matthean Divorce Texts," 151–60.

176. Kampen, "Matthean Divorce Texts," 161.

177. Evans, *Matthew*, 123. The italics and the inclusion of the Greek term are mine.

178. Evans, *Matthew*, 127.

179. Philo, *Spec. Laws* 2.2. See also *Decal.* 84.1.

180. Ben Sira 23:9–11.

181. Josephus, *B.J.* 2.135.

182. Josephus, *B.J.* 1.139.

183. Davies and Allison, *Matthew*, 1.533.

184. Note that the LXX of Deut 23:22 also contains a form of the verb *apodidōmi*.

185. The validity of the various formulas for the swearing of oaths is also the subject of debate in the rabbinic tradition; e.g., m. Ned. 1:3; m. Sanh. 3:2; m. Šeb. 4:13.

186. The author returns to the subject of swearing in Matt 23:16–22. Note the discussion in Chapter 6 below. The polemic of Matt 23 shows evidence of connection with portions of the Sermon in addition to the Beatitudes.

187. 2 En. 49:1–2. We do find debates in rabbinic literature as to whether "Yes, Yes" and "No, No" have the force of oaths (b. Sanh. 36a). See the discussion in Montefiore, *Rabbinic Literature*, 48–50. Josephus seems to have understood the Essenes to have had a viewpoint similar to Matthew (*B.J.* 2.135). See also Vahrenhoerst, "The Presence and Absence," 367–70.

188. This is also portrayed in Isa 60.

189. Yadin, *Temple Scroll*, 2.275–78.

190. Daube, *New Testament*, 255–59. He argues that "life for life" is not included here in Matthew since in the rabbinic tradition this phrase was divorced from the others in Deut 19:21 because they applied to monetary compensation. See also Montefiore, *Synoptic Gospels*, 2.69–76; Montefiore, *Rabbinic Literature*, 50–59.

191. The same principle is employed with regard to the death of the Egyptians in Jub. 48:14.

192. Note this also seems to be implied concerning the Boethusians in Meg. Ta'an. 4. On this passage, see Wacholder, *Dawn of Qumran*, 164. For a listing of capital offenses in these two compositions, see Wacholder, *Dawn of Qumran*, 51–52.

193. My translation.

194. The same phrase is found at 11Q19 (Temple Scroll[a]) LIV, 17, taken from Deut 13:6; and 11Q19 (Temple Scroll[a]) LVI, 10, from Deut 17:12.

195. 1QS I, 18, 24; II, 5, 19; III, 20, 21, 23; X, 2; CD 4:13, 15; 5:18; 8:2; 12:2; 16:5; 19:14; also 12 times in 1QH, 14 times in 1QM, as well as in other texts.

196. Carter, *Matthew and the Margins*, 150–54.

197. See Chapter 1 above.

198. Evans, *Matthew*, 133–34.

199. Davies and Allison, *Matthew*, 1.550.

200. See also 1QS I, 4.

201. 1QS I, 3–4. The addressee is frequently considered to be the *maskil* (sage).

202. Similar sentiments are found in CD 8:16–18 (cf. 19:30–31).

203. 1QS IX, 21, cf. IX, 16.

204. 1QS IV, 1. Hatred is also mentioned in this dualistic context in 1QS IV, 24 and lies behind the hymn in 1QS X, 17–21. See also CD 2:13, 15. The only place where hatred of one's fellow is mentioned in a negative way is in CD 8:6 (19:18), where it applies to relationships within the group. This is also the focus of 1QS V, 26.

205. Since gentiles are used as a negative in Matt 5:47, I suspect that the primary concern of this writer was the Jewish community. This holds true for most of the gospel; however the conclusion requires explanation. See Chapter 7 below for a discussion of "gentile" in Matthew.

206. Davies and Allison, *Matthew*, 1.560.

207. Davies and Allison, *Matthew*, 1.561–63. For the listing of texts, see Abegg, Bowley, and Cook, *Dead Sea Scrolls Concordance*, 1.2.764–65. For its significance as a sectarian term, see Strawn with Rietz, "(More) Sectarian Terminology," 53–64.

Chapter 4. Sectarian Wisdom

1. Matt. 11:19; 12:42; 13:54.

2. Matt 11:25; 23:34.

3. Suggs, *Wisdom, Christology, and Law*. At the same time, Felix Christ argued that wisdom was central to Matthew, Luke, and Q (*Jesus Sophia*). This era of research is evaluated by Johnson, "Reflections on Wisdom."

4. Deutsch, *Lady Wisdom*, 1.

5. Saldarini, *Matthew's Christian-Jewish Community*, 183–84.

6. Boring, "The Gospel of Matthew," 269, 275.

7. Pregeant, *Matthew*, 80–82.

8. Davies and Allison, *Matthew*, 2.264–65, 272–73.

9. Kampen, "Diverse Aspects"; Kampen, *Wisdom Literature*, 1–4.

10. J. Sanders, *Psalms Scroll*, 69.

11. Attributed to J. Sanders in Worrell, "Concepts of Wisdom," 115.

12. Burrows, *Dead Sea Scrolls*, 252–60. Manual of Discipline is the earlier name used for the Community Rule.

13. Burrows, "Discipline Manual," 168–71 (quote from p. 168); cf. Dupont-Sommer, *Dead Sea Scrolls*, 42, 65, n. 1. DCD is now abbreviated as CD and refers to the Damascus Document.

14. W. D. Davies, "Knowledge," 135.

15. *Da'at* is also the primary term for the employment of *epistēmē* and *synesis* in the Greek versions.

16. For an overview of this question, see Wright and Wills, *Conflicted Boundaries*.

17. Goff, *4QInstruction*. See also Goff, *Discerning Wisdom*, 9–68; Kampen, *Wisdom Literature*, 36–190.

18. Strugnell and Harrington, *Qumran Cave 4: XXIV*, 1–2, 501; Tigchelaar, *To Increase Learning*, 15–17, 167–69. A few additional fragments have been identified and are included in Kampen, *Wisdom Literature*, 38–40; Goff, *4QInstruction*, 1–7.

19. Strugnell and Harrington, *Qumran Cave 4: XXIV*, 36. The fact that two copies were rolled in reverse manner, with the beginning in the inside of the scroll, suggests active usage at the time of the Roman siege in 68 CE (Elgvin, "An Analysis," 13–14).

20. Strugnell and Harrington, *Qumran Cave 4: XXIV*, 22.

21. Note the summaries in Goff, *Discerning Wisdom*, 65–67; Kampen, *Wisdom Literature*, 40–44; Goff, *4QInstruction*, 27–29. I am not convinced by Goff's suggestion in the latter work that the later chronology for the archeological site proposed by Jodi Magness would make a later date of composition possible. This argument implies too direct a connection between the sectarian development of the site and the date of this work.

22. Elgvin, "Priestly Sages," 83–84.

23. Nickelsburg dates the Book of the Watchers (1–36) and the majority of the Animal Apocalypse (85–90) to the period of the Diadochoi, 323–301 BCE (*1 Enoch 1*, 25–26, 427–28). A third or second century BCE date is also posited for the Book of the Luminaries (Nickelsburg and VanderKam, *1 Enoch 2*, 339–45).

24. A version of this table is also found in my article "Wisdom in Deuterocanonical," 108.

25. All statistics in this paper for the Hebrew Bible are based upon Even-Shoshan, *A New Concordance*.

26. All statistics for the Qumran corpus are based upon Abegg, Bowley, and Cook, *Dead Sea Scrolls Concordance*, 1.1 and 1.2.

27. The texts identified are the Cave 1 texts, 1QH, 1QS, 1QM, and 1QpHab along with CD as well as the other MSS from the remainder of the corpus that are identified with these compositions. The specific MSS included are 4Q255–64, 266–73, 427–32, and 491–96.

28. Burrows, "Discipline Manual," 168–71; cf. Dupont-Sommer, *Dead Sea Scrolls*, 42, 65, n. 1.

29. W. D. Davies, "Knowledge."

30. I note that this examination is by way of illustration rather than providing an extensive study of the issues. The list of terms is not exhaustive. For example, in her list of terms related to knowledge in the Thanksgiving Hymns, Newsom would also include *raz* (mystery) and *maḥšābāh* (thought, plan, intention) (*Self as Symbolic Space*, 209). This investigation also only includes nominal forms, a distinct limitation for a comprehensive viewpoint.

31. The statistics for 1QHᵃ are from Stegemann with Schuller, *Qumran Cave 1: III*, 40. This volume was not used for the cumulative statistics from Qumran and the sectarian texts compiled in the *Dead Sea Scrolls Concordance*. See n. 26 above.

32. 1Q27; 4Q299–300; 4Q301(?). See Kampen, *Wisdom Literature*, 191–96.

33. For a survey of these issues, see Kampen, "Diverse Aspects," 211–23; Harrington, *Wisdom Texts from Qumran*, 75–80; Goff, *Discerning Wisdom*, 6–8. On the variety of terms used in the Thanksgiving Hymns, see Newsom, *Self as Symbolic Space*, 209.

34. This is evident in the discussion of Essene theology by Hengel, *Judaism and Hellenism*, 1.218–24.

35. 1QS III, 13–17. Translation is from Wise, Abegg, and Cook, *Dead Sea Scrolls*, 120. This section is sometimes regarded as an independent earlier composition incorporated into the Community Rule. Even if this is the case, it is a good statement of sectarian ideology.

36. 1QS IV, 18–20.

37. 1QS IV, 22.

38. 1QS IV, 26.

39. 1QHᵃ V, 30–31. Translation altered for consistency of usage in the Hebrew terms in this volume.

40. 1QHᵃ XIX, 12–13.

41. CD 1:1. Translation altered for consistency of usage in the Hebrew terms in this volume.

42. CD 2:14. See Kampen, "Diverse Aspects," 218–20.

43. This summary follows my discussion in *Wisdom Literature*, 25–28.

44. Newsom, "Sage in the Literature of Qumran," 373–82; see p. 375.

45. 1QS IX, 17–18. On the development of the use of this term within the compositional history of the S documents, see Hempel, "Maskil(im) and Rabbim," 133–56.

46. See Newsom, *Self as Symbolic Space*, 277–86. The term also is significant in 4Q298 (Words of the Maskil to All Sons of Dawn) 1–2 I, 1; 4Q400–6 (Songs of the Sabbath Sacrifice); and 4Q510–11 (Songs of the Sage).

47. Strugnell, "Smaller Hebrew Wisdom Texts," 43–44.

48. Some basic viewpoints concerning this development have been sketched in my article "Diverse Aspects."

49. Dunn, *Christology in the Making*, 197–98.

50. Luz, *Matthew*, 2.149; cf. 17–18, 28. While he disregards the evidence of 1 Enoch as significant for Jewish listeners (p. 17), I would argue that it is precisely in circles such as those related to compositions such as this one that the gospel of Matthew was composed and read/heard. For a longer discussion of the term, see Davies and Allison, *Matthew*, 2.43–53.

51. My translation amended, *Wisdom Literature*, 94, with commentary on 94–102. Portions are reconstructed on the basis of parallel copies. For a summary of the literature on this text and an analysis, see Goff, *4QInstruction*, 137–72. His analysis unduly stresses the relationship to creation at the expense of the relationship to the formation of an ethic in this passage.

52. Evans, *Matthew*, 232, who sees Matt 11:1 as the conclusion of the previous section. Certainly it is transitional, but the connection with 11:20 is clear.

53. Macaskill, *Revealed Wisdom*, 144.

54. The location of this city remains a point of debate. See Parsenios, "Beth-Saida," 445–46. See also Arav and Freund, *Bethsaida*; Bockmuehl, "Simon Peter and Bethsaida."

55. Note the manner in which Matt 10:1 and 11:1 designate the intervening material specifically directed to the twelve.

56. Nickelsburg and VanderKam, *1 Enoch 2*, 138–41. Note also the discussion of the withdrawal of Lady Wisdom in Deutsch, *Lady Wisdom*, 18–19, 52–53.

57. See Chapter 1 above.

58. According to the decrees recorded by Josephus: *A.J.* 14.190–210.

59. Josephus, *B.J.* 1.422.

60. Luz, *Matthew*, 2.153.

61. Evans, *Matthew*, 242–43.

62. E.g., Prov 1:4(2), 22(2), 32.

63. Contra Luz, *Mattthew*, 2.163–64.

64. Deutsch, *Lady Wisdom*, 57.

65. See Chapter 3, "The Beatitudes," above.

66. Luz, *Matthew*, 2.164.

67. See Chapter 5 below.

68. For Deutsch, it represents a combination of the two major themes of revelation and discipleship (*Lady Wisdom*, 57). See also Lybaek, *New and Old*, 149.
69. My translation.
70. Genizah Ms. A (Beentjes, *Ben Sira*, 29).
71. Danby, *The Mishnah*, 45.
72. See also Schechter, *Aspects of Rabbinic Theology*, 66–67, 70–72, 100–4.
73. Carter, *Matthew and Empire*, 108–29. For quote see 112.
74. Portions of the column are reconstructed from parallels in 4Q420 (Ways of Righteousness[a]) 1a II-b. See Elgvin, 188–90; Kampen, *Wisdom Literature*, 293–95.
75. See the summary of the issue in Kampen, *Wisdom Literature*, 286–88.
76. Note the similarities of 4Q421 1 I to 1QS I.
77. On this text, see the discussion in Hempel, *Qumran Rule Texts*, 169–70.
78. This is based upon a reliable reconstruction from the parallel passage in 4Q437 (Barki Nafshi[d]) 4a II, 4.
79. Prov 2:19; 5:6; 10:17; 15:24.
80. For other examples of the two ways, see Nickelsburg, *1 Enoch 1*, 454–56; Evans, *Matthew*, 171–73.
81. See Chapter 3 above.
82. Macaskill, *Revealed Wisdom*, 180.

Chapter 5. Communal Organization and Discipline

1. Kugel, "Hidden Hatred," 44–45.
2. Prov 26:24–25 (transl. by Kugel, "Hidden Hatred," 45).
3. Kugel, "Hidden Hatred," 46 (also Kugel's translation).
4. The following examples are drawn from Kugel, "Hidden Hatred," 49–52; Kugel, *Traditions*, 752–58.
5. In the NRSV this is translated "point out the fault"; in CEB, "correct."
6. The date of this text is a matter of debate. See Kugel, "Hidden Hatred"; Kugel, *Traditions*, 946–47. For an emphasis on the second-century CE authorship as a Christian composition, see Kugler, *Testaments*, 31–38; Kugler, "Patriarchs, Testaments," 1031–33. I am inclined to accept Kugel's argument regarding these passages that they seem to be preliminary to the usages of the passage developed in the sectarian texts from Qumran.
7. Portions of this and the following sections of this chapter are adapted from Kampen, "Social World," 158–74. This material is used by permission of Bloomsbury Publishing.
8. Murphy-O'Connor, "Literary Analysis," 216–20. CD 6:11–7:4 is characterized as "le petite code des douze préceptes" by Denis, *Les thèmes de connaissance*, 124.
9. P. Davies, *Damascus Covenant*, 125–42; P. Davies, *Behind the Essenes*, 47–48.
10. Hempel, *Laws of Damascus Document*, 15–26; Hempel, "Damascus Document and 4QMMT," 80–84.

11. This latter description also appears only at CD 8:21 // 19:33; cf. CD 20:12. Much more common throughout the D materials is the term "covenant" without the adjective "new" and lacking the geographical descriptor.

12. Since Damascus Document A and B are copies of medieval MSS found in the Ben Ezra synagogue in Cairo, they have been written on bound folios rather than scrolls. This accounts for the different numbering system used in references to the text.

13. The alteration in CD 6:20 to 'aḥîḥû (your brother) from the biblical re'ăka (your neighbor) of Lev 19:18 is noted by Ginzberg, *Unknown Jewish Sect*, 202–3. He explains this as an obvious attempt to emphasize the sectarian theology of the author.

14. In his commentary, Schechter points to Ezek 16:49 (*Documents of Jewish Sectaries*, xxxix [71]). The author of CD appears to be utilizing Ezekiel's interpretation of Lev 19:15.

15. CD 3:12, 20; 7:13; 8:2; 19:14; 20:27; cf. Rabin, *Zadokite Documents*, 25.

16. NJPS here has "profit by." I have rendered a more literal translation.

17. That the Hebrew word here is meant to be understood as zənût is already identified by Schechter, *Documents of Jewish Sectaries*, xxxix (71). The Cairo Genizah text has an additional *waw*, hence zônôt, which is a doubtful reading.

18. See Chapter 3 above; Kampen, "Matthean Divorce Texts," 152–59.

19. Schiffman, *Sectarian Law*, 89–90. In this instance he notes, "The requirement of reproof is exegetically derived," with regard to this passage. In the Qumran texts there is evidence of reading and rereading of biblical legislation, already discussed above in Chapter 3. Commentary on biblical texts including biblical legislation is also common. On the significance of this genre, see Bockmuehl, "Dead Sea Scrolls."

20. My translation.

21. See Schiffman, *Sectarian Law*, 91.

22. Schiffman (*Sectarian Law*, 92) asks whether the intent of the passage is to limit it to capital cases.

23. My translation.

24. This approach recasts the argument of Schiffman, who suggests that this text is "the full explanation of the Qumran law of reproof as a requisite for punishment" (*Sectarian Law*, 93). I am less convinced of the implied chronological relationship between the sections in his claim that CD 7:2–3 "is worded so as to constitute a direct reference to the law of CDC 9:2–8" (p. 93). CDC is an older form of the abbreviation for CD.

25. Hempel, *Laws of Damascus Document*, 32–34.

26. While the extent to which this legislation differed from the rabbinic materials has been noted, there is some disagreement about the particulars of this text, particularly on the number and nature of the witnesses: B. A. Levine, "Damascus Document IX," 195–96; Neusner, "Testimony of Two Witness"; Schiffman, "Qumran Law of Testimony"; Schiffman, *Sectarian Law*, 73–88.

27. Schiffman, *Sectarian Law*, 96.

28. Hempel, "Who Rebukes?"; contra Eshel ("4Q477," 111–12) who seems to argue that the overseer is the one who carries out the public rebuke.

29. While Schiffman is correct in pointing to the literary unity of CD 9:10–23, the section should be viewed as one unit on the law of reproof rather than testimony (*Sectarian Law*, 95).

30. Nitzan, "Laws of Reproof,"160. Note also the further discussion of this text below.

31. Hempel, *Laws of Damascus Document*, 91–100. See discussion of her work above.

32. Schiffman, *Sectarian Law*, 92.

33. Nitzan, "Laws of Reproof," 156.

34. Ginzberg, *Unknown Jewish Sect*, 41; Schiffman, *Sectarian Law*, 92.

35. See J. Baumgarten, "Cave 4 Versions"; J. Baumgarten, *Damascus Document*, 72–75, 110–11, 162–66.

36. J. Baumgarten, *Damascus Document*, 72–73.

37. Schiffman, *Sectarian Law*, 94–96; Schiffman, "Reproof as a Requisite"; Nitzan, "Laws of Reproof," 157.

38. On the literary relationship and historical development of the S and D materials, see Kampen, "'Torah' and Authority," 240–42.

39. This is my attempt to provide an English equivalent for *rabbim* (many) which is probably quite close to a synonym for *yaḥad* in this document, even though the latter is the more specific term which I assume was used to designate the sectarian body. See the comment by Eshel, "4Q477," 121.

40. For this translation I utilized the text of Eshel, "4Q477," 118.

41. Kampen, "'Torah' and Authority," 240, 244.

42. Kugel, "Hidden Hatred"; Nitzan, "Laws of Reproof," 150.

43. The term *hayyaḥad* appears in CD 20:1, 14, 32.

44. Nitzan, "Laws of Reproof," 158–63; Nitzan, "286. 4QBerakhotᵃ," 40–48.

45. This term is reconstructed by Nitzan at this point and not present in the fragments. While one cannot be certain about this reconstruction, the presence of the phrases "men of the community," "discipline him in all," and "reproving him in the presence of witnesses" attest to the general subject discussed in these lines.

46. This is based upon the reconstruction of Nitzan and her translation ("286. 4QBerakhotᵃ," 46–47). See also Nitzan, "Laws of Reproof," 159–60.

47. Note also CD 13:17–19 // 4Q266 9 III, 6–10, cited in Kister, "Divorce, Reproof," 220.

48. Nitzan, "Laws of Reproof," 157. Note the error in the citation of 1QS.

49. Schiffman, *Sectarian Law*, 170.

50. Eshel, "477." See also Eshel, "4Q477"; Hempel, "Who Rebukes?"

51. 4Q477 2 I (my translation).

52. Since there is a lacuna between the first and second charges, it is difficult to say with certainty that the latter offense should be attributed to Joḥanan, even though it seems most likely.

53. The importance of this issue in Qumran literature is amply documented. In 11QT XXXV, 12 and XXXVII, 11, the term is used to maintain the separation of the priests and their sacrifices from the remainder of the Israelites. In 4Q397 (MMT[d]) IV (frag. 14–21), 7–8, those who indicate that "we have separated ourselves from the multitude of the p[eople]" also distinguished themselves from "being mixed in these matters" (my translation), apparently with regard to defilement and impurity. It is used with regard to contact with expelled members in 1QS VII, 24–25.

54. There is good evidence to support the proposal that *š.y.r* in Qumran orthography refers to *šəʾēr*, thereby referring to "near kin," also alluded to in CD 7:1, 8:6, and 19:19.

55. Schuller and Bernstein, "372." See also Kister, "Divorce, Reproof," 222–23; Thiessen, "4Q372 1."

56. 4Q299 (Mysteries[a]) 7, 5 // 4Q300 (Mysteries[b]) 7, 2; 4Q418 (Instruction[d]) 222, 3; 4Q525 (Beatitudes) 5, 10; 13, 3.

57. Relevant texts are cited by Davies and Allison, *Matthew*, 2.786–91; Hagner, *Matthew*, 2.531–33.

58. Translation adapted from Cashdan, "Abot d'Rabbi Nathan," 1.139 (chap. 29).

59. Str-B, 1.787–90. Note the comments on that treatment by Montefiore, *Rabbinic Literature*, 264–66. See also Davies and Allison, *Matthew* 2.784–85; Basser and Cohen, *Gospel of Matthew*, 468–74.

60. Brownlee, *Dead Sea Manual*; Schubert, "Sermon on the Mount," 126; Johnson, "Manual of Discipline," 139; Stendahl, "Matthew," 789.

61. Saldarini, *Matthew's Christian-Jewish Community*, 91–93.

62. Knibb, *Qumran Community*, 115.

63. Kugel, "Hidden Hatred," 55.

64. Davies and Allison, *Matthew* 2.784–85; Hagner, *Matthew*, 2.532.

65. Kampen, *Hasideans*, 82–87. Note Davies and Allison, *Matthew* 2.785: "The local community is here meant, not the church universal."

66. The obligatory and formal nature of the laws of reproof in CD 9:28 is also emphasized by P. Davies, *Damascus Covenant*, 132.

67. The latter is found recently again in Weren, "Ideal Community," 178–79.

68. Kampen, *Hasideans*, 81–85.

69. Runesson, *Origins*, 73–87; Levine, *Ancient Synagogue*, 21–26.

70. Y. Meg. 4, 1 (75a); b. Meg. 3a; b. B. Qam. 82a. E.g., Tadmor, "Period of First Temple," 173; Rabinowitz, "Synagogue."

71. Hachlili, *Ancient Synagogues*, 7–13. Stuart Miller recognized this in his attempt to correlate the talmudic evidence with the archaeological record, "Number of Synagogues."

72. Levine, *Ancient Synagogue*, 82–91. On these terms, see also Bloedhorn and Huttenmeister, "Synagogue," 268–70.

73. *Vita* 277, 280, 293. For discussion, see L. I. Levine, *Ancient Synagogue*, 52–54.

74. L. I. Levine, *Ancient Synagogue*, 64–65.

75. Josephus, *B.J.* 2.285, 289 (Caesarea); 7.44 (Antioch); Josephus, *A.J.* 19.300, 305 (2) (Dor).

76. L. I. Levine, *Ancient Synagogue*, 57–59; Runesson, *Origins*, 226–31. The objection to the first century dating of this inscription is outlined by Kee, "First Century C.E. Synagogue," 7–26. Note the detailed analysis in support of a first century date by Kloppenborg, "Dating Theodotus," 243–80.

77. Runesson, *Origins*, 170–74.

78. This material is collected in Runesson, Binder, and Olsson, *Ancient Synagogue*, 267–73.

79. Hachlili, *Ancient Synagogues*, 5–6, 13–16.

80. Binder, *Temple Courts*, 204–26, 477–93. Note the proposal by James F. Strange that the peculiar placement of the columns in front of the benches in most of these structures is an imitation of the temple structure ("Ancient Texts," 44).

81. Flesher, "Palestinian Synagogues," 27–39.

82. Note the response to Binder and Flesher by L. I. Levine, "Synagogue," 524–25.

83. L. I. Levine, *Ancient Synagogue*, 45–45; L. I. Levine, "Synagogue," 522–25. For a discussion of this question in rabbinic literature, see also Cohen, "Temple and Synagogue." L. I. Levine does note the case for Torah reading in first-century synagogues, even though this is not connected with the temple: "First-Century C.E. Synagogue"; L. I. Levine, *Ancient Synagogue*, 38–42.

84. L. I. Levine, *Ancient Synagogue*, 28–44; L. I. Levine, "Synagogue," 522–24.

85. Note that Binder (*Temple Courts*, 211–26) indicates agreement on the importance of the city gate. However his argument for the cultic significance of the city gate provides a very different understanding of its structure and functions. As outlined by Runesson (*Ancient Synagogue*, 95–97), the description of Binder's work as complementary to that of L. I. Levine in identifying the primacy of the city gate to the development of the synagogue suggests more agreement than is warranted.

86. Rivkin, "Nonexistence of the Synagogue"; Rivkin, "Defining Pharisees"; Rivkin, *A Hidden Revolution*.

87. Fine, *This Holy Place*.

88. Kee, "First-Century C.E. Synagogue." See also his earlier essay, "Transformation of the Synagogue."

89. Richardson, "Early Synagogues"; Richardson, "Architectural Case." A revised copy of these articles is now available in Richardson, *Building Jewish*, 111–33, 207–21.

90. L. I. Levine, "Synagogue," 524.

91. Runesson, *Origins*, 131.

92. Richardson does not accept L. I. Levine's hypothesis regarding the origins of the synagogue in the city gate, noting that there is no archaeological evidence of transitional structures between the two constructions (review of L. I. Levine, *Ancient* Synagogue, 362).

93. Strange, "Ancient Texts."

94. L. I. Levine, *Ancient Synagogue*, 71–72; Hachlili, *Ancient Synagogues*, 37.

95. Avshalom-Gorni, "Migdal," 121; Avshalom-Gorni and Najjar, "Migdal"; Corbett, "New Synagogue Excavations," 52–59; Hachlili, *Ancient Synagogues*, 33–34, 40–41; Aviam, "Decorated Stone."

96. Private communications from Jodi Magness and Lee I. Levine.

97. Netzer, "Synagogue from Hasmonean Period"; Netzer, *Hasmonean and Herodian Palaces*, 2.159–92; Hachlili, *Ancient Synagogues*, 28–30.

98. Runesson, *Origins*, 181–82, 359; Runesson, Binder, and Olsson, *Ancient Synagogue*, 40–42.

99. Ma'oz, "Synagogue That Never Existed"; L. I. Levine, *Ancient Synagogue*, 72–74; Hachlili, *Ancient Synagogues*, 28–30.

100. Weksler-Bdolah, Onn, and Rapuano, "Hasmonean Village of Modi'in"; L. I. Levine, *Ancient Synagogue*, 70; Runesson, Binder, and Olsson, *Ancient Synagogue*, 57–58; Hachlili, *Ancient Synagogues*, 34–35.

101. Magen, Zionit, and Sirkis, "Qiryat Sefer"; L. I. Levine, *Ancient Synagogue*, 69; Runesson, Binder, and Olsson, *Ancient Synagogue*, 65–66; Hachlili, *Ancient Synagogues*, 34–36.

102. Zissu and Ganor, "Ḥorvat 'Etri"; Ma'oz, "Zissu and Ganor's Article"; L. I. Levine, *Ancient Synagogue*, 74; Runesson, Binder, and Olsson, *Ancient Synagogue*, 36–38.

103. Strange, "Ancient Texts"; L. I. Levine, "First-Century C.E. Synagogue"; Hachlili, *Ancient Synagogues*, 39–45.

104. On the variety of interpretive possibilities for these representations and the enhanced religious dimension of the institution in this period, see L. I. Levine, *Ancient Synagogue*, 230–42; L. I. Levine, *Visual Judaism*, 53–58. See also Hachlili, *Ancient Synagogues*, 39–42, 285–338.

105. The local nature of the synagogue as to architecture and function is emphasized in the conclusion of his article on the first-century synagogue by L. I. Levine, "First-Century C.E. Synagogue," 19–21. This is also noted by E. P. Sanders, "Common Judaism," 12–13; Hachlili, "Synagogues," 30–38, 65.

106. See Chapter 3 above.

107. Overman, *Matthew's Gospel*, 101; M. Davies, *Matthew*, 129. A thorough analysis of the community discipline passage within the context of the remainder of the chapter is that of Konradt, "'Whoever humbles himself. . . .'"

108. See Chapter 1 above.

109. Davies and Allison, *Matthew*, 2.764–65.

110. The only major difference between 5:29–30 and 18:8–9 is the inclusion of the phrase "to enter into life," found only in the latter passage (Hagner, *Matthew*, 2.523).

111. Overman, *Matthew's Gospel*, 101.

112. Overman, *Matthew's Gospel*, 102–3; Saldarini, *Matthew's Christian-Jewish Community*, 92; M. Davies, *Matthew*, 129.

113. Nickelsburg, "Enoch, Levi, and Peter," 594. A variety of interpretations are listed in Davies and Allison, *Matthew*, 2.635–41.
114. Overman, *Matthew's Gospel*, 20–21: 2 Bar. 10:18; 4 Bar. 4:4 (Jeremiah casts the keys toward the sun); 'Abot R. Nat. A 4
115. Nickelsburg, "Enoch, Levi, and Peter," 590–600.
116. Kampen, "Reexamination," 48–50.
117. M. 'Abot 3:2 suggests that two who are speaking words of Torah between them are the beneficiaries of the Šǝkīnāh's presence, or even one who sits and occupies himself with the law. The conclusion is similar in 3:7, but the discussion starts with ten and works down to one. The interest in the requirements that will assure the presence of God is an ongoing concern among religious Jews throughout these times.
118. Weinfeld, *Organizational Pattern*, 40.
119. For this translation see n. 40 above.
120. My translation.
121. Both Hagner (*Matthew*, 2.259) and Luz (*Matthew*, 3.448) attest to the lack of definitive evidence for its omission or inclusion. See Metzger, *Textual Commentary*, 45.
122. Nitzan, "286. 4QBerakhotᵃ," 46–47.
123. Forkman, *Limits of Religious Community*, 123; Overman, *Matthew's Gospel*, 102–3; Saldarini, *Matthew's Christian-Jewish Community*, 92.
124. Overman, *Matthew's Gospel*, 101.

Chapter 6. Jesus and His Opponents

1. Powell, "Plot and Subplots"; Powell, ed., *Methods*, 44–82.
2. Davies and Allison, *Matthew*, 1.58–72; Hagner, *Matthew*, 1.l–liii.
3. Evans, *Matthew*, 10.
4. Sim, *Apocalyptic Eschatology*, 156–69.
5. Macaskill, *Revealed Wisdom*, 161–74.
6. Dan 9:27; 11:31; 12:11.
7. We note the extensive use of Daniel already in the Dead Sea Scrolls: Flint, "Daniel Tradition," 329–67. For the New Testament, note the following articles in the same volume: Evans, "Daniel in the New Testament" and Dunn, "Danielic Son of Man."
8. 1 En. 90:28–36; 93:8; 2 Bar. 32:2–4; Apoc. Ab. 27:3–5; 4 Ezra 10:21–23; Sib. Or. 5:398–413.
9. Davies and Allison, *Matthew*, 3.257–58. I include Matt 23:34–36 in the woes section since it continues the topic already begun in vv. 29–33, the last of the woes. However it also is a transition to the section on Jerusalem, 23:37–24:2, as noted by Hagner (*Matthew*, 2.673–78), who refers to it as an "Appendix to the Seventh Woe."
10. Luz, *Matthew*, 3.92–93.

11. Evans, *Matthew*, 388. Literary allusions include Pesiq. Rab Kah. 1.7; Exod Rab. 43.4 (on Exod 32:22); Song Rab. 1:3 §1; Esth Rab 1.11 (on Esth 1:2).

12. Luz, *Matthew*, 3.102.

13. See the discussion of the yoke in Chapter 4 above.

14. On the term, see Luz, *Matthew*, 1.300; 3.115–16; Evans, *Matthew*, 140.

15. This number does not include Matt 23:14, not mentioned in the best MSS. The connections between Matt 23 and the remainder of the first gospel are noted by Freyne, "Vilifying the Other," 137–39, 143.

16. Brooke, *Dead Sea Scrolls*, 221–24; Kampen, *Wisdom Literature*, 210–12. See the discussion in Chapter 3 above.

17. See the summary in Kampen, *Wisdom Literature*, 287–88.

18. See Hood, "Matthew 23–25," 540–42.

19. See Chapter 3 above.

20. McKnight, *Light among the Gentiles*, 106–8; Luz, *Matthew*, 3.117–18; Donaldson, *Judaism and the Gentiles*, 412–20, 445–47; Burns, "God-fearers," 681–82.

21. Davies and Allison, *Saint Matthew*, 3.290–93.

22. The similarity between the position of Jesus in these verses and the later rabbis is apparent in the extended discussion of the question in rabbinic literature by Urbach, *The Sages*, 1.342–65.

23. B. Mak. 23b–24a.

24. Note for example the list of crimes yielding *kārēt* (excommunication or divine punishment) in m. Ker. 1. Debate about rewards for observance of commandments also is evident. This would seem to be behind the debate in b. Bik. 39b, where the observance of the commandment to honor one's parents (Deut 5:16) is the same as for the dismissal of the nest (Deut 22:6–7).

25. In m. Ma'aś. 4:5 there is disagreement regarding whether all of the dill plant has to be tithed or only the seeds. M. Demai 2:1 lists cumin among the products that must be tithed, even if imported. Mint is not mentioned in rabbinic law regarding tithes.

26. B. Šabb. 31a.

27. Alexander, "Jesus and Golden Rule," 363–88. However note the argument by D. Schwartz, "Hillel and Scripture," arguing that the authoritative declarations of Hillel precede the development of the rabbinic exegetical tradition.

28. Magness provides a good discussion of the biblical and rabbinic legislation (*Stone and Dung*, 74–80).

29. B. Ber. 28a; b. Yoma 72b. See Evans, *Matthew*, 395.

30. Urbach, *The Sages*, 1.393–99.

31. M. Menaḥ. 13:11.

32. B. Šabb. 5b. See also b. Ber. 17a.

33. See the discussion of righteousness in Matthew in Chapter 3 above.

34. See the discussion of *anomia* (lawless) in Chapter 3 above.

35. See the discussion of the synagogue in Chapter 5 above.

36. M. Šabb. 1:3; m. Yoma 7:1; m. Soṭah 7:7–8, 9:15; t. Sukkah 4:6, 11; t. Taʻan. 1:14. In the temple, m. Sukkah 4:4; m. Tamid 5:3. See Safrai, "The Synagogue," 935–36, 940–42; Schürer-Vermes, 2.418, 438; L. I. Levine, *Ancient Synagogue*, 435–42; Hachlili, *Ancient Synagogues*, 17–19. It is interesting to note that the reference to the synagogue in this passage is only found in the title of the *ḥazzan*. The remainder of the tractate refers to actions taken by the *bêt dîn* (court). So there is no reference here to activity within the synagogue.

37. Nickelsburg, *1 Enoch 1*, 306; see also Luz, *Matthew*, 3.154. On 1 En. 22:7 see Wacker, *Weltordnung und Gericht*, 181–82.

38. Luz, *Matthew*, 3.159–61.

39. See Chapter 4 above. See Bar 3:9–4:4; 1 En. 42, perhaps in contrast to Ben Sira 24:7–11, where the "beloved city" is the resting place given by the creator and Jerusalem is the domain awarded to wisdom.

40. Ruth 2:12; Pss 36:8; 57:2; 61:5; 63:8; 91:5. It is no surprise that this image appears later in rabbinic literature with regard to the proselyte who is to be brought under the wings of the *Šəkînāh* (e.g., Lev. Rab. on 1:2). The image is also employed in Lev Rab. on 19:23.

41. Davies and Allison, *Matthew* 3.336.

42. These viewpoints are summarized in Kampen, "Significance of the Temple."

43. Klawans, *Purity, Sacrifice, and Temple*, 175–254.

44. Macaskill, *Revealed Wisdom*, 180.

45. This is already clear in the Sermon on the Mount (Matt 5:11; 7:21–27) and in the declarations on wisdom (Matt 11:27). The treatment of the "little ones" in Matt 18:6, 10, and 14 raises similar issues. See Chapters 3, 4, and 5 above.

46. Rivkin, *What Crucified Jesus?*; Crossan, *Historical Jesus*, 354–94; Crossan, *Who Killed Jesus?*; Horsley, "Death of Jesus"; McLaren, "Exploring the Execution"; Dunn, *Jesus Remembered*, 784–85; Cook, "Jewish Jurisprudence"; Clabeaux, "Why Was Jesus Executed?"

47. Josephus, *B.J.* 1.97; Josephus, *A.J.* 13.380. These are often considered to be Pharisees. See Schürer-Vermes, 1.221–24.

48. Matt 27:37. In Mark 15:26 it is recorded as "The king of the Jews."

49. Stemberger, "Dating Rabbinic Traditions," 79–96.

50. Harries, "Creating Legal Space"; Harries, "Courts and the Judicial System"; Lapin, *The Rabbis as Romans*, 98–125.

51. Bond, *Pontius Pilate*, 49–93.

52. Josephus, *B.J.* 2.169–74; Josephus, *A.J.* 18.55–59.

53. Josephus, *B.J.* 2.175–77; Josephus, *A.J.* 18.60–62. The estimates of numbers of participants tends to be quite exaggerated.

54. Philo, *Legat.* 299–305. See Bond, *Pontius Pilate*, 24–48.

55. For discussion and literature, see Bond, *Pontius Pilate*.

56. Sloyan, *Jesus on Trial*, 16–28; Skinner, *Trial Narratives*, 13–22.

57. Josephus, *A.J.* 18.63–64.

58. McLaren, "Exploring the Execution," 14–15. For the earlier bibliography and discussion of this passage, see Feldman, *Josephus*, 9.48–51.

59. Skinner, *Trial Narratives*, 33–51.

60. Overman, *Church and Community*, 361.

61. This is the more accurate translation of the Greek term *rabbi*, since the formal title was not yet in use in the first century.

62. His death is recounted in a different manner by the author of Luke in Acts 1:16–20.

63. Sloyan, *Jesus on Trial*, 62.

64. A. J. Levine, "Matthew, Mark, and Luke," 91–92; Donaldson, *Jews and Anti-Judaism*, 30–54.

65. I fail to find the account of Warren Carter convincing in which he posits that Pilate is in control of this scene and manipulating the entire sequence of events (*Pontius Pilate*, 82–98). Equally unconvincing is the argument that the issue is Jerusalem versus Galilee (France, "Matthew and Jerusalem"). The emphasis on the leadership is demonstrated in an important manner by Gurtner, "Matthew's Theology of Temple."

66. Rajak, *Josephus: Historian*, 185–95.

67. See the discussion of these traditions in Lapin, "Origins and Development," 207–12.

68. B. Git. 56a–b; 'Abot R. Nat. A 4.

69. Davies and Allison, *Matthew*, 3.335; Sloyan, *Jesus on Trial*, 60. I am not convinced that the use of the term *dynamai* (be able) presents less of a threat than the simple future of Mark 14:58 (Skinner, *Trial Narratives*, 57).

70. Hagner, 2.863; Luz, *Matthew*, 3.588; Evans, *Matthew*, 474.

71. Overman, *Church and Community*, 401.

72. Matt 27:51–53 // Mark 15:38 // Luke 23:45b. While there is some difference in detail between Gurtner's account and mine, in both cases our reading of the text reflects an apocalyptic setting and reaches similar conclusions (Gurtner, *Torn Veil*).

73. See also 2 Bar. 32:2–4; Apoc. Ab. 27:3–5; 4 Ezra 10:21–23; Sib. Or. 5:398–413.

74. Davies and Allison, *Matthew*, 3.629–32.

75. Hagner, *Matthew*, 2.849.

76. Isa 24:19; 29:6; Jer 10:10; Amos 8:8; Zech 14:5; 4 Ezra 3:18; 9:3; 2 Bar. 27:7; 70:8; 1 En. 57:2.

77. 1 En. 18:12–16; 21:1–10; 83:3–4, 7; 2 Bar. 70:8. While the last reference is ostensibly to the flood, we see the resulting redemption also described in cosmic terms (1 En. 83:11). See Davies and Allison, *Matthew*, 3.340–41.

78. Davies and Allison, *Matthew*, 3.632; Hagner, *Matthew*, 2.849.

79. My translation of this term.

80. Italics are mine.

81. Davies and Allison, *Matthew*, 3.634.

82. Hagner, *Matthew*, 2.850.

83. Evans (*Matthew*, 466) regards it as a scribal supplement, probably inspired by Matt 28:2.

84. In the New Testament, the denial of the resurrection is explicitly attributed to the Sadducees (Matt 22:23 // Mark 12:18 // Luke 20:27). For the latter, see Josephus, *B.J.* 2.163; 3.374; Josephus, *C. Ap.* 2.218. This idea also forms the centerpiece of the iconic accounts of martyrdom in 2 Macc 6:18–7:40.

85. On this development, see Levenson, *Resurrection and Restoration*. On all aspects of this topic, see A. Segal, *Life after Death*.

Chapter 7. Commissioning the Sect

1. Allison, *New Moses*, 262–66. This portrait has already been discussed above in Chapter 3.

2. Luz, *Matthew*, 2.72–75; Sim, "Matthew: The Current State of Research," 41–43.

3. Translation of Luz, *Matthew*, 2.73.

4. Davies and Allison, *Matthew*, 2.165.

5. A. J. Levine, *Social and Ethnic Dimensions*, 52–57.

6. For a summary of this evidence, see Schürer-Vermes, 2.160–64.

7. Zsengellér, ed., *Samaria*; Pummer, *The Samaritans*.

8. Anderson, "Samaritans."

9. See Chapter 6 above. While a good piece of research, I do not find convincing the argument of Willitts that this is a reference to the remnants of the former Northern Kingdom of Israel located in Galilee and its environs (*Messianic Shepherd King*, 181–219).

10. Evans, *Matthew*, 212.

11. Nickelsburg, *1 Enoch 1*, 387–401.

12. Saldarini, *Matthew's Christian-Jewish Community*, 83.

13. Overman, *Matthew's Gospel*, 157. This is also the conclusion of Konradt, *Israel, Church, and the Gentiles*, 365–67.

14. Foster, *Community, Law and Mission*.

15. Donaldson, *Judaism and the Gentiles*, 19–20; Karrer, "Licht über dem Galiläa," 51.

16. Flint, "Interpretation of Scriptural Isaiah"; Flint, "Interpreting the Poetry."

17. Blenkinsopp, *Isaiah 56–66*, 207; but note Seitz, "The Book of Isaiah 40–66," 504–5.

18. Paul, *Isaiah 40–66*, 5–12; Rom-Shiloni, *Exclusive Inclusivity*, 121. Note also the collection of essays: Tiemeyer and Barstad, eds., *Continuity and Discontinuity*.

19. Rom-Shiloni, *Exclusive Inclusivity*.

20. See also D. Smith, *Religion of the Landless*, 14–16, 56–65.

21. Rom-Shiloni, *Exclusive Inclusivity*, 59–61, 121–24. C. M. Moss (*Zechariah Tradition*, 20, 93) misses the opportunity to develop this aspect of the use of Zechariah.

22. Rom-Shiloni, *Exclusive Inclusivity*, 122–23. The distinctive nature of this appeal is also noted by Paul, *Isaiah 40–66*, 19.

23. It is this dimension of the argument that is missing in Fuller, *Restoration of Israel*, 111–48.

24. Overman, *Church and Community*, 404–11.

25. Donaldson, *Judaism and the Gentiles*, 499–513.

26. Donaldson, *Judaism and the Gentiles*, 117–23, see 122 for quote. The numbers are references to the texts collected in the volume.

27. Nickelsburg, "Revealed Wisdom," 76–77; Nickelsburg, *1 Enoch 1*, 54, 428.

28. Donaldson, *Judaism and the Gentiles*, 195–215. Note also the treatment of 1QS V, 3–6 in Jokiranta, "Conceptualizing *Ger*," 672.

29. Donaldson, *Judaism and the Gentiles*, 195–96.

30. Schiffman, *Qumran and Jerusalem*, 353–80.

31. 1QM I, 1–2.

32. Schultz, *Conquering*, 127–58, 393–94.

33. 1QM I, 1–2; II, 10–16.

34. Schultz, *Conquering*, 365; Donaldson, *Judaism and the Gentiles*, 196; J. Collins, *Scriptures and Sectarianism*, 180.

35. Schultz, *Conquering*, 366–90; Schofield, *From Qumran to the* Yaḥad, 69–130; J. Collins, *Beyond the Qumran Community*, 60–68.

36. Well-known is the appearance of the term *prosēlutos* in the charges against the Pharisees in Matt 23:15.

37. Jokiranta, "Conceptualizing *Ger*," 661–64.

38. P. Davies, "The 'Damascus' Sect," 74–75. See the response in Donaldson, *Judaism and the Gentiles*, 204.

39. The parallel text of 4Q267 9 VI, 8 only includes the second reference in l. 6.

40. Wacholder, *Dawn of Qumran*, 101–35. The literary connections are significant even if the argument for Zadok as the Teacher of Righteousness cannot be sustained.

41. 4Q159 (Ordinances[a]) 2–4, 1; 4Q307 (Text Mentioning Temple) 1, 6; 4Q377 (apocPent. B) 1 I, 6; 4Q498 (papSap/Hymn) 7, 1; 4Q520 (papUnclassifed Frgs.) 45, 3.

42. See Donaldson, *Judaism and the Gentiles*, 215. In contrast to Donaldson, I do not find a basis for determining whether they were hypothetical or real. The hypothetical or real nature of the Qumran legislation is a problem for the interpretation of many of these texts.

43. Goff, *4QInstruction*, 304.

44. Luz, *Matthew*, 1.83–85.

45. Evans, *Matthew*, 35–36.

46. This approach stands in stark contrast to Philip Esler, who applies an ethnic identity to his analysis: "Matthew is writing for a group or groups of Christ-followers that embrace Judean and non-Judean members sharing a new trans-ethnic, superordinate group identity in-Christ" ("Judaean Ethnic Identity," 208).

47. Luz, *Matthew*, 2.338; Schmitz, "Canaan (Place)"; Dearman, "Canaan, Canaanites."

48. Davies and Allison, *Matthew*, 2.547; Evans, *Matthew*, 303.

49. 4Q377 (apocPent. B) 1 I, 8; 4Q522 (Prophecy of Joshua) 3, 2; 9 II, 9; 11Q19 (T^a) LXII, 14; PAM 43.692 85, 1.

50. Carter, *Matthew and the Margins*, 321–25. My portrayal of the administration of the area is to be found in Chapter 1 above.

51. Schiffman, *Qumran and Jerusalem*, 353–80.

52. Already discussed in Chapter 6 above.

53. This is in contrast to the conclusions of Freyne's otherwise very insightful study (*Jesus Movement*, 306–10). A similar lack is to be found in the good work of Runesson, *Divine Wrath and Salvation*, 343–433 (this volume appeared late in the revision process of this manuscript, precluding a detailed discussion of its very thorough analysis of many of the same issues covered in the present volume). A similar problem is evident in the work of Konradt, *Israel, Church, and the Gentiles*. In a careful discussion of the nature of a transition to the gentiles, he finds it resolved on the basis of Christology and ecclesiology.

54. In the following evaluation of Matt 28:19, I have retained the capitalization of the NRSV when quoting that text. But since I regard them as descriptors rather than formal titles in my treatment of this text, they are not capitalized in the remainder of this discussion.

55. Evans, *Matthew*, 887.

56. Translation is mine.

57. Hagner, *Matthew*, 2.887–88; Evans, *Matthew*, 485–86.

58. Davies and Allison, *Matthew*, 3.684–86. See also Dunn, *Christology*, 49.

59. Schaberg, *Father, Son*, 183–87.

60. Schaberg, *Father, Son*, 111–221; Hagner, *Matthew*, 2.886; Davies and Allison, *Matthew*, 3.682–83; Evans, *Matthew*, 483.

61. 1 En. 48; 52:4, etc. Note also the essays by Macaskill, "Matthew and *Parables*," and Walck, *Parables of Enoch*."

62. 1 En. 48:4, cf. Isa 42:6; 49:6. See Walck, *Son of Man*, 89–91.

63. Davies and Allison, *Matthew*, 3.686; Evans, *Matthew*, 483.

64. Hagner, *Matthew*, 2.886.

65. See Chapter 5 above.

66. Luz, *Matthew*, 3.633–34.

67. Hagner, *Matthew*, 2.888; Davies and Allison, *Matthew*, 3.686.

68. Evans, *Matthew*, 486. Also Davies and Allison, *Matthew*, 3.686.

69. Matt 13:39–40, 49; 24:3; Hagner, *Matthew*, 2.889.

70. The sociological definition is that of Albert Baumgarten discussed in Chapter 2 above.

71. Note the description and treatment of these three elements in Chapter 2 above.

72. See Chapters 4 and 5 above. This element is also evident in the Sermon on the Mount, as treated in Chapter 3 above.

73. A. Baumgarten, *Flourishing of Jewish Sects*, 7. See Chapter 6 above.

Conclusion

1. See Chapter 2 above.
2. Stark and Bainbridge, *Future of Religion*, 49–67; Jokiranta, "Sectarianism," 228–30, 236–39.
3. A. Baumgarten, *Flourishing of Jewish Sects*, 7.
4. See Chapter 2.
5. See the discussions in Chapters 1 and 2 above.
6. Sim, *Apocalyptic Eschatology*, 210–21.
7. This argument is developed in Chapter 3 above.
8. See Chapter 4 above.
9. See Chapter 5 above.
10. See Chapter 6 above.
11. A. Baumgarten, *Flourishing of Jewish Sects*, 7.
12. See Chapter 7 above.
13. This topic receives extensive treatment in Chapter 2 above.

Bibliography

Abegg, Martin G., James E. Bowley, and Edward M. Cook. *The Dead Sea Scrolls Concordance.* 5 vols. Leiden: Brill, 2003–15.

Aland, Kurt, ed. *Synopsis of the Four Gospels.* 9th ed. Stuttgart: German Bible Society, 1989.

Albright, W. F., and C. S. Mann. *Matthew: A New Translation with Introduction and Commentary.* AB 26. Garden City: Doubleday, 1971.

Alexander, P. S. "Jesus and the Golden Rule." Pp. 363–88 in *Hillel and Jesus: Comparative Studies of Two Major Religious Leaders.* Edited by James H. Charlesworth and Loren L. Johns. Minneapolis: Fortress, 1997.

Allen, Willoughby C. *A Critical and Exegetical Commentary on the Gospel According to St. Matthew.* 3rd ed. ICC. Edinburgh: T & T Clark, 1912.

Allison, Dale C., Jr. *The New Moses: A Matthean Typology.* Minneapolis: Fortress, 1993.

Anderson, Robert T. "Samaritans." *NIDB* 5.75–82.

Andrade, Nathanael J. *Syrian Identity in the Greco-Roman World.* New York: Cambridge University Press, 2013.

Arav, Rami, and Richard A. Freund. *Bethsaida Excavations Project Reports and Contextual Studies.* Kirksville, Mo.: Thomas Jefferson University Press, 1995.

Ascough, Richard S., Philip A. Harland, and John S. Kloppenborg. *Associations in the Greco-Roman World: A Sourcebook.* Waco, Tex.: Baylor University Press, 2012.

Aviam, Mordechai. "The Decorated Stone from the Synagogue at Migdal: A Holistic Interpretation and a Glimpse into the Life of Galilean Jews at the Time of Jesus." *NT* 55 (2013): 205–20.

Avshalom-Gorni, Dina. "Migdal." *Hadashot Arkheologiyot* 121 (2009). http://www.hadashot-esi.org.il/report_detail_eng.aspx?id=1236&mag_id=115.

Avshalom-Gorni, Dina, and Arfan Najjar. "Migdal," *Hadashot Arkheologiyot* 125 (2013). http://www.hadashot-esi.org.il/report_detail_eng.aspx?id=2304&mag_id=120.

Bacon, Benjamin W. *Studies in Matthew.* New York: H. Holt, 1930.

Balch, David L., ed. *Social History of the Matthean Community: Cross-Disciplinary Approaches.* Minneapolis: Fortress, 1991.

Barnes, Timothy D. "The Date of Ignatius." *ExpTim* 120 (2008): 119–30.

Barth, Gerhard. "Matthew's Understanding of the Law." Pp. 58–164 in *Tradition and Interpretation in Matthew*. Edited by Günther Bornkamm, Gerhard Barth, and Heinz Joachim Held. Translated by Perry Scott. NTL. Philadelphia: Westminster, 1963.

Basser, Herbert. *The Mind Behind the Gospels: A Commentary to Matthew 1–14*. Boston: Academic Studies Press, 2009.

Basser, Herbert, and Marsha B. Cohen. *The Gospel of Matthew and Judaic Traditions: A Relevance-Based Commentary*. Brill Reference Library of Judaism 46. Leiden: Brill, 2015.

Bauckham, Richard. "The Early Jerusalem Church, Qumran, and the Essenes." Pp. 63–89 in *The Dead Sea Scrolls as Background to Postbiblical Judaism and Early Christianity: Papers from an International Conference at St. Andrews in 2001*. Edited by James R. Davila. STDJ 46. Leiden: Brill, 2003.

———, ed. *The Gospels for All Christians: Rethinking the Gospel Audiences*. Grand Rapids: Eerdmans, 1998.

Bauman, Clarence. *The Sermon on the Mount: The Modern Quest for Its Meaning*. Macon: Mercer University Press, 1990.

Baumgarten, Albert I. *The Flourishing of Jewish Sects in the Maccabean Era: An Interpretation*. JSJSup 55. Leiden: Brill, 1997.

Baumgarten, Joseph M. "The Cave 4 Versions of the Qumran Penal Code." *JJS* 43 (1992): 268–76.

———. "The Heavenly Tribunal and the Personification of Sedeq in Jewish Apocalyptic." *ANRW* 19.1.219–39.

———. *Qumran Cave 4: XIII. The Damascus Document: 4Q266–273*. DJD 18. Oxford: Clarendon, 1996.

Becker, Adam H., and Annette Yoshiko Reed, eds. *The Ways That Never Parted: Jews and Christians in Late Antiquity and the Early Middle Ages*. Minneapolis: Fortress, 2007.

Beentjes, Pancratius C. *The Book of Ben Sira in Hebrew*. VTSup 68. Atlanta: SBL, 2006.

Betz, Hans Dieter. *Essays on the Sermon on the Mount*. Translated by L. L. Welborn. Philadelphia: Fortress, 1985.

———. *The Sermon on the Mount: A Commentary on the Sermon on the Mount, including the Sermon on the Plain (Matthew 5:3–7:27 and Luke 6:20–49)*. Hermeneia. Minneapolis: Fortress, 1995.

———. "Sermon on the Mount/Plain." *ABD* 5.1106–12.

Binder, Donald D. *Into the Temple Courts: The Place of the Synagogues in the Second Temple Period*. SBLDS 169. Atlanta: SBL, 1999.

Blenkinsopp, Joseph. *Isaiah 56–66: A New Translation and Commentary*. AB 19B. New York: Doubleday, 2003.

Bloedhorn, Hans, and Gil Hüttenmeister. "The Synagogue." *CHJ* 3.267–95.

Boccaccini, Gabriele. *Beyond the Essene Hypothesis: The Parting of the Ways between Qumran and Enochic Judaism.* Grand Rapids: Eerdmans, 1998.

Bockmuehl, Markus. "The Dead Sea Scrolls and the Origins of Biblical Commentary." Pp. 3–29 in *Text, Thought, and Practice in Qumran and Early Christianity.* Edited by Ruth A. Clements and Daniel R. Schwartz. Leiden: Brill, 2009.

———. "Simon Peter and Bethsaida." Pp. 54–91 in *The Missions of James, Peter, and Paul: Tensions in Early Christianity.* Edited by B. Chilton and C. Evans. NovTSup 115. Leiden: Brill, 2005.

Bond, Helen K. *Pontius Pilate in History and Interpretation.* SNTSMS 100. Cambridge: Cambridge University Press, 1998.

Boring, M. Eugene. "The Gospel of Matthew." *NIB* 8.89–505.

Bornkamm, Günther, Gerhard Barth, and Heinz Joachim Held. *Tradition and Interpretation in Matthew.* Translated by Percy Scott. NTL. Philadelphia: Westminster, 1963.

Boxall, Ian. *Discovering Matthew: Content, Interpretation, Reception.* Grand Rapids: Eerdmans, 2015.

Boyarin, Daniel. *Border Lines: The Partition of Judaeo-Christianity.* Philadelphia: University of Pennsylvania Press, 2004.

———. "The *Diadoche* of the Rabbis; or, Judah the Patriarch at Yavneh." Pp. 285–318 in *Jewish Culture and Society Under the Christian Roman Empire.* Edited by Richard Kalmin and Seth Schwartz. Interdisciplinary Studies in Ancient Culture and Religion 3. Leuven: Peeters, 2003.

———. "Rethinking Jewish Christianity; An Argument for Dismantling a Dubious Category (to which is appended a correction to my *Border Lines*)." *JQR* 99 (2009): 7–36.

Brent, Allen. *Ignatius of Antioch: A Martyr Bishop and the Origin of the Episcopacy.* London: Continuum, 2007.

Brooke, George J. *The Dead Sea Scrolls and the New Testament.* Minneapolis: Fortress, 2005.

Broshi, Magen. "Anti-Qumranic Polemics in the Talmud." Pp. 589–600 in vol. 2 of *The Madrid Qumran Congress: Proceedings of the International Congress on the Dead Sea Scrolls, Madrid, 18–21 March 1991.* Edited by Julio Trebolle Barrera and Luis Vegas Montaner. 2 vols. STDJ 11. Leiden: Brill, 1992.

———. "Essene Gate." *EDSS* 1.261–62.

Brownlee, W. H. *The Dead Sea Manual of Discipline: Translation and Notes.* BASORSup 10–12. New Haven: ASOR, 1951.

Bultmann, Rudolf. *History of the Synoptic Tradition.* Translated by J. Marsh. Oxford: Blackwell, 1972.

Burns, Joshua Ezra. "Essene Sectarianism and Social Differentiation in Judaea after 70 C.E." *HTR* 99 (2006): 247–74.

———. "God-fearers." *EDEJ* 681–82.

Burrows, Millar. *The Dead Sea Scrolls.* New York: Viking, 1955.

———. "The Discipline Manual of the Judaean Covenanters." *Oudtestamentische Studiën* 8 (1950): 156–92.

Buth, Randall, and R. Steven Notley, eds. *The Language Environment of First Century Judaea.* Vol. 2 of *Jerusalem Studies in the Synoptic Gospels.* Leiden: Brill, 2014.

Carr, David M. *Writing on the Tablet of the Heart: Origins of Scripture and Literature.* Oxford: Oxford University Press, 2005.

Carson, D. A., Peter T. O'Brien, and Mark A. Seifrid, eds. *Justification and Variegated Nomism: The Complexities of Second Temple Judaism.* 2 vols. WUNT 2:140, 181. Tübingen: Mohr Siebeck; Grand Rapids: Baker Academic, 2001, 2004.

Carter, Warren. "Matthew and Empire." *USQR* 59, no. 3–4 (2005): 86–91.

———. *Matthew and Empire: Initial Explorations.* Harrisburg, Pa.: Trinity Press International, 2001.

———. *Matthew and the Margins: A Sociopolitical and Religious Reading.* Maryknoll, N.Y.: Orbis, 2000.

———. *Pontius Pilate: Portraits of a Roman Governor.* Collegeville: Liturgical Press, 2003.

Cashdan, Eli. "'Abot d'Rabbi Nathan." Pp. 1–210 in *The Minor Tractates of the Talmud.* Edited by A. Cohen. 2 vols. London: Soncino, 1963.

Charles, R. H., revised by C. Rabin, "Jubilees." Pp. 1–140 in *The Apocryphal Old Testament.* Edited by H. F. D. Sparks. Oxford: Clarendon, 1984.

Charlesworth, James H. "The Origin and Subsequent History of the Authors of the Dead Sea Scrolls: Four Transitional Phases Among the Qumran Essenes." *RevQ* 10 (1980): 213–33.

———. "The Qumran Beatitudes (4Q525) and the New Testament (MT 5:3–11; LK 6:20–26)." *RHPR* 80 (2000): 13–35.

Chester, Andrew. "The Parting of the Ways: Eschatology and Messianic Hope." Pp. 239–313 in *Jews and Christians: The Parting of the Ways, A.D. 70–135. The Second Durham-Tübingen Research Symposium on Earliest Christianity and Judaism (Durham, September, 1989).* Edited by James D. G. Dunn. WUNT 66. Tübingen: J.C.B. Mohr (Paul Siebeck), 1992.

Christ, Felix. *Jesus Sophia: Die Sophia-Christologie bei den Synoptikern.* ATANT 57. Zürich: Zwingli-Verlag, 1970.

Clabeaux, John. "Why Was Jesus Executed? History and Faith." Pp. 27–40 in *Pondering the Passion: What's at Stake for Christians and Jews.* Edited by Philip Cunningham. Lanham: Sheed and Ward, 2004.

Cohen, Shaye J. D. *The Beginnings of Jewishness: Boundaries, Varieties, Uncertainties.* Berkeley: University of California Press, 1999.

———. *From the Maccabees to the Mishnah.* 3rd ed. Louisville: Westminster John Knox Press, 2014.

———. "The Judaean Legal Tradition and the *Halakhah* of the Mishnah." Pp. 121–43 in *The Cambridge Companion to the Talmud and Rabbinic Literature.* Edited by Charlotte Elisheva Fonrobert and Martin S. Jaffee. Cambridge: Cambridge University Press, 2007.

———. "The Place of the Rabbi in Jewish Society of the Second Century." Pp. 157–73 in *The Galilee in Late Antiquity*. Edited by Lee I. Levine. New York: Jewish Theological Seminary, 1992.

———. "The Rabbi in Second Century Jewish Society." *CHJ* 3.922–90.

———. *The Significance of Yavneh and Other Essays in Jewish Hellenism*. TSAJ 136. Tübingen: Mohr Siebeck, 2010.

———. "The Significance of Yavneh: Pharisees, Rabbis, and the End of Jewish Sectarianism." *HUCA* 55 (1984): 27–53; republished, pp. 44–70 in Cohen, *Significance of Yavneh*.

———. "The Temple and the Synagogue." *CHJ* 3.298–325.

Collins, Adela Yarbro. *Crisis and Catharsis: The Power of the Apocalypse*. Philadelphia: Westminster, 1984.

Collins, John J. *The Apocalyptic Imagination: An Introduction to Jewish Apocalyptic Literature*. 3rd ed. Grand Rapids: Eerdmans, 2016.

———. *Beyond the Qumran Community: The Sectarian Movement of the Dead Sea Scrolls*. Grand Rapids: Eerdmans, 2010.

———. *Daniel*. Hermeneia. Minneapolis: Fortress, 1993.

———. *The Invention of Judaism: Torah and Jewish Identity from Deuteronomy to Paul*. Oakland: University of California, 2017.

———. *Scriptures and Sectarianism: Essays on the Dead Sea Scrolls*. WUNT 332. Tübingen: Mohr Siebeck, 2014.

Cook, Michael J. *Mark's Treatment of the Jewish Leaders*. NovTSup 51. Leiden: Brill, 1978.

———. "The Problem of Jewish Jurisprudence and the Trial of Jesus." Pp. 13–25 in *Pondering the Passion: What's at Stake for Christians and Jews*. Edited by Philip Cunningham. Lanham: Sheed and Ward, 2004.

Corbett, Joey. "New Synagogue Excavations in Israel and Beyond." *BAR* 37, no. 4 (2011): 52–59.

Cover, Michael Benjamin. "*Paulus als Yischmaelit?* The Personification of Scripture as Interpretive Authority in Paul and the School of Rabbi Ishmael." *JBL* 135 (2016): 617–37.

Crawford, Sidnie White. *Rewriting Scripture in Second Temple Times*. Studies in the Dead Sea Scrolls and Related Literature. Grand Rapids: Eerdmans, 2008.

Cross, Frank Moore. *The Ancient Library of Qumran*. 3rd ed. Minneapolis: Fortress, 1995.

Crossan, John Dominic. *The Historical Jesus: The Life of a Mediterranean Jewish Peasant*. San Francisco: HarperCollins, 1992.

———. *Who Killed Jesus? Exposing the Roots of Anti-Semitism in the Gospel Story of the Death of Jesus*. San Francisco: HarperSanFrancisco, 1995.

Danby, Herbert, trans. *The Mishnah*. Oxford: Clarendon Press, 1933.

Daube, David. *The New Testament and Rabbinic Judaism*. London: Athlone Press, 1956.

Davies, Margaret. *Matthew*. Sheffield: JSOT Press, 1993.

Davies, Philip R. *Behind the Essenes: History and Ideology in the Dead Sea Scrolls.* BJS 94. Atlanta: Scholars Press, 1987.

———. *The Damascus Covenant: An Interpretation of the "Damascus Document."* JSOTSup 25. Sheffield: JSOT Press, 1983.

———. "The 'Damascus' Sect and Judaism." Pp. 70–84 in *Pursuing the Text: Studies in Honor of Ben Zion Wacholder on the Occasion of His Seventieth Birthday.* Edited by John C. Reeves and John Kampen. JSOTSup 184. Sheffield: Sheffield Academic Press, 1994.

Davies, W. D. "'Knowledge' in the Dead Sea Scrolls and Matthew 11:25–30." *HTR* 46 (1953): 113–39.

———. *The Setting of the Sermon on the Mount.* London: Cambridge University Press, 1964.

Davies, W. D., and Dale C. Allison, Jr. *A Critical and Exegetical Commentary on the Gospel According to Saint Matthew.* 3 vols. Edinburgh: T & T Clark, 1988–97.

———. *Matthew: A Shorter Commentary.* London: T & T Clark, 2004.

Dearman, J. Andrew. "Canaan, Canaanites." *NIDB* 1.532–35.

Deines, Roland. "Pharisees." *EDEJ* 1061–63.

———. "The Pharisees between 'Judaism' and 'Common Judaism.'" Pp. 443–504 in *Justification and Variegated Nomism.* Vol. 1, *The Complexities of Second Temple Judaism.* Edited by D. A. Carson, Peter T. O'Brien, and Mark A. Seifrid. WUNT 140. Tübingen: Mohr Siebeck, 2001.

Delitzsch, Franz. *The Hebrew New Testament.* Leipzig: Dörffling & Franke, 1883.

Denis, Albert-Marie. *Les thèmes de connaissance dans le Document de Damas.* Studia Hellenistica 15. Louvain: Publications Universitaires de Louvain, 1967.

Deutsch, Celia M. *Lady Wisdom, Jesus, and the Sages: Metaphor and Social Context in Matthew's Gospel.* Valley Forge: Trinity Press International, 1996.

De Vaux, Roland. *Archaeology and the Dead Sea Scrolls.* Rev. ed. London: University Press, 1973.

Dimant, Devorah. "Qumran Sectarian Literature." Pp. 483–550 in *Jewish Writings of the Second Temple Period: Apocrypha, Pseudepigrapha, Qumran Sectarian Writings, Philo, Josephus.* Edited by Michael E. Stone. CRINT 2.2. Assen: Van Gorcum; Philadelphia: Fortress, 1984.

———. "The Volunteers in the Rule of the Community: A Biblical Notion in Sectarian Garb." *RevQ* 23 (2007): 233–45.

Donaldson, Terence L. *Jews and Anti-Judaism in the New Testament: Decision Points and Divergent Interpretations.* London: SPCK; Waco, Tex.: Baylor University Press, 2010.

———. *Judaism and the Gentiles: Jewish Patterns of Universalism (to 135 CE).* Waco, Tex.: Baylor, 2007.

Duff, Paul B. *Who Rides the Beast: Prophetic Rivalry and the Rhetoric of Crisis in the Churches of the Apocalypse.* Oxford: Oxford University Press, 2001.

Dunn, James D. G. *Christology in the Making: A New Testament Inquiry into the Origins of the Doctrine of Incarnation.* 2nd ed. Grand Rapids: Eerdmans, 1996.

————. "The Danielic Son of Man in the New Testament." Pp. 528–49 in vol. 2 of *The Book of Daniel: Composition and Reception*. Edited by John J. Collins and Peter W. Flint. 2 vols. VTSup 83. Leiden: Brill, 2001.

————. *Jesus Remembered*. Christianity in the Making 1. Grand Rapids: Eerdmans, 2003.

Dupont-Sommer, A. *The Dead Sea Scrolls: A Preliminary Survey*. Translated by E. Margaret Rowley. Oxford: Basil Blackwell, 1952.

Elgvin, Torlief. "An Analysis of *4QInstruction*." Ph.D. diss., Hebrew University, 1997.

————. "Priestly Sages? The Milieus of Origin of 4QMysteries and 4QInstruction." Pp. 67–87 in *Sapiential Perspectives: Wisdom Literature in Light of the Dead Sea Scrolls. Proceedings of the Sixth International Symposium of the Orion Center, 20–22 May, 2001*. Edited by John J. Collins, Gregory E. Sterling, and Ruth A. Clements. STDJ 51. Leiden: Brill, 2004.

Eshel, Esther. "477. Rebukes Reported by the Overseer." Pp. 474–83 in *Qumran Cave 4: XXVI. Cryptic Texts and Miscellanea, Part 1*. Edited by Stephen J. Pfann, Philip Alexander, et al. DJD 36. Oxford: Clarendon, 2000.

————. "4Q477: The Rebukes by the Overseer," *JJS* 45 (1994): 111–22.

Esler, Philip Francis. *The First Christians in Their Social Worlds: Social-Scientific Approaches to New Testament Interpretation*. London: Routledge, 1994.

————. "Jesus and the Reduction of Intergroup Conflict." Pp. 185–205 in *The Social Setting of Jesus and the Gospels*. Edited by Wolfgang Stegemann, Bruce J. Malina, and Gerd Theissen. Minneapolis: Fortress, 2002.

————. "Jesus and the Reduction of Intergroup Conflict: The Parable of the Good Samaritan in the Light of Social Identity Theory." *BibInt* 8 (2000): 325–57.

————. "Judaean Ethnic Identity and the Matthean Jesus." Pp. 194–210 in *Receptionen des Galiläers in Wissenschaft, Kirche und Gesellschaft: Festschrift für Gerd Theissen zum 70. Geburtstag*. Edited by Petra von Gemünden, David G. Horrell, and Max Küchler. SUNT 100. Göttingen: Vandenhoeck and Ruprect, 2013).

————. Review of *Matthew's Gospel and Formative Judaism: The Social World of the Matthean Community*, by J. Andrew Overman. *BibInt* 1 (1993): 255–58.

————. "The Social World of Luke-Acts: Models for Interpretation." *BibInt* 1 (1993): 255–58.

Evans, Craig A. "Daniel in the New Testament: Visions of God's Kingdom." Pp. 491–527 in vol. 2 of *The Book of Daniel: Composition and Reception*. Edited by John J. Collins and Peter W. Flint. 2 vols. VTSup 83. Leiden: Brill, 2001.

————. "Fulfilling the Law and Seeking Righteousness in Matthew and the Dead Sea Scrolls." Pp. 102–14 in *Jesus, Matthew's Gospel and Early Christianity: Studies in Memory of Graham N. Stanton*. Edited by Daniel M. Gurtner, Joel Willitts, and Richard A. Burridge. LNTS 435. London: T & T Clark, 2011.

————. *Matthew*. New Cambridge Bible Commentary. New York: Cambridge University Press, 2012.

Even-Shoshan, A. *A New Concordance of the Bible*. 4 vols. Hebrew. Jerusalem: Kiryat Sepher, 1979.

Feldman, Louis H. *Josephus.* Vol. 9. LCL. Cambridge: Harvard University Press, 1969.

Ferguson, Everett. *Baptism in the Early Church: History, Theology, and Liturgy in the First Five Centuries.* Grand Rapids: Eerdmans, 2009.

Fine, Steven. *This Holy Place: On the Sanctity of the Synagogue during the Greco-Roman Period.* Christianity and Judaism in Antiquity 11. Notre Dame: University of Notre Dame Press, 1997.

Fitzmyer, Joseph A. *Essays on the Semitic Background of the New Testament.* London: Geoffrey Chapman, 1971.

———. "The Matthean Divorce Texts and Some New Palestinian Evidence." *ThSt* 37 (1976): 197–226.

———. "The Qumran Scrolls, The Ebionites and Their Literature." Pp. 435–80 in *The Semitic Background of the New Testament.* Biblical Resource Series. Grand Rapids: Eerdmans, 1997.

Flesher, Paul V. M. "Palestinian Synagogues Before 70 C.E.: A Review of the Evidence." Pp. 27–39 in *Ancient Synagogues: Historical Analysis and Archaeological Discovery.* Edited by D. Urman and P. V. M. Flesher. StPB 47. Leiden: Brill, 1995.

Flint, Peter W. "The Daniel Tradition at Qumran." Pp. 329–67 in vol. 2 of *The Book of Daniel: Composition and Reception.* Edited by John J. Collins and Peter W. Flint. 2 vols. VTSup 83. Leiden: Brill, 2001.

———. "Interpretation of Scriptural Isaiah in the Qumran Scrolls: Quotations, Citations, Allusions, and the Form of the Scriptural Source Text." Pp. 389–406 in vol. 1 of *A Teacher for All Generations: Essays in Honor of James C. VanderKam.* Edited by Eric F. Mason et al. 2 vols. JSJSup 153. Leiden: Brill, 2012.

———. "Interpreting the Poetry of Isaiah at Qumran: Theme and Function in the Sectarian Scrolls." Pp. 161–95 in *Prayer and Poetry in the Dead Sea Scrolls and Related Literature: Essays in Honor of Eileen Schuller on the Occasion of Her 65th Birthday.* Edited by Jeremy Penner, Ken M. Penner, and Cecilia Wassen. STDJ 98. Leiden: Brill, 2012.

Flusser, David. "Blessed Are the Poor in Spirit . . ." Pp. 102–14 in *Judaism and the Origins of Christianity.* Jerusalem: Magnes Press, Hebrew University, 1988.

———. "4QMMT and the Benediction Against the *Minim.*" Pp. 70–118 in *Judaism of the Second Temple Period: Qumran and Apocalypticism.* Translated by Azzan Yadin. Grand Rapids: Eerdmans, 2007.

———. "Some Notes to the Beatitudes." Pp. 115–25 in *Judaism and the Origins of Christianity.* Jerusalem: Magnes Press, Hebrew University, 1988.

Forkman, Göran. *The Limits of Religious Community: Expulsion from the Religious Community within the Qumran Sect, within Rabbinic Judaism, and within Primitive Christianity.* Lund: Gleerup, 1972.

Foster, Paul. *Community, Law and Mission in Matthew's Gospel.* WUNT 177. Tübingen: Mohr Siebeck, 2004.

Fraade, Steven. *Legal Fictions: Studies of Law and Narrative in the Discursive Worlds of Ancient Jewish Sectarians and Sages*. JSJSup 147. Leiden: Brill, 2011.

France, R. T. "Matthew and Jerusalem." Pp. 108–27 in *Built Upon the Rock: Studies in the Gospel of Matthew*. Edited by Daniel M. Gurtner and John Nolland. Grand Rapids: Eerdmans, 2008.

Frankfurter, David. "Jews or Not? Reconstructing the 'Other' in Rev 2:9 and 3:9." *HTR* 94 (2001): 403–25.

Frey, Jörg. "Recent Perspectives on Johannine Dualism." Pg. 127–57 in *Text, Thought, and Practice in Qumran and Early Christianity: Proceedings of the Ninth International Symposium of the Orion Center for the Study of the Dead Sea Scrolls and Associated Literature, Jointly Sponsored by the Hebrew University Center for the Study of Christianity, 11—13 January, 2004*. Edited by Ruth A. Clements and Daniel R. Schwartz. STDJ 84. Leiden: Brill, 2009.

Freyne, Sean. *The Jesus Movement: Meaning and Mission*. Grand Rapids: Eerdmans, 2014.

―――. "Vilifying the Other and Defining the Self: Matthew's and John's Anti-Jewish Polemic in Focus." Pp. 117–43 in *"To See Ourselves as Others See Us": Christians, Jews, "Others" in Late Antiquity*. Edited by Jacob Neusner and Ernest S. Frerichs. Chico, Calif.: Scholars Press, 1985.

Fuller, Michael E. *The Restoration of Israel: Israel's Regathering and the Fate of the Nations in Early Jewish Literature and Luke-Acts*. BZNW 138. Berlin: De Gruyter, 2006.

Gale, Aaron M. *Redefining Ancient Boundaries: The Jewish Scribal Framework of Matthew's Gospel*. New York: T & T Clark, 2005.

Galor, Katharina, and Hanswulf Bloedhorn. *The Archaeology of Jerusalem: From the Origins to the Ottomans*. New Haven: Yale University Press, 2013.

Galor, Katharina, Jean-Baptiste Humbert, and Jürgen Zangenberg, eds. *Qumran, The Site of the Dead Sea Scrolls: Archaeological Interpretations and Debates. Proceedings of a Conference Held at Brown University, November 17–19, 2002*. STDJ 57. Leiden: Brill, 2006.

García Martínez, Florentino. "The Origins of the Qumran Movement and of the Essene Sect." Pp. 77–96 in *The People of the Dead Sea Scrolls: Their Writings, Beliefs and Practices*. Edited by Florentino García Martínez and Julio Trebolle Barrera. Translated by Wilfred G. E. Watson. Leiden: Brill, 1995.

Gillihan, Yonder Moynihan. *Civic Ideology, Organization, and Law in the Rule Scrolls: A Comparative Study of the Covenanters' Sect and Contemporary Voluntary Associations in Political Context*. Leiden: Brill, 2012.

Ginzberg, Louis. *An Unknown Jewish Sect*. New York: Jewish Theological Seminary, 1976.

Goering, Gregory Schmidt. *Wisdom's Root Revealed: Ben Sira and the Election of Israel*. JSJSup 139. Leiden: Brill, 2009.

Goff, Matthew J. *Discerning Wisdom: The Sapiential Literature of the Dead Sea Scrolls*. VTSup 116. Leiden: Brill, 2007.

————. *4QInstruction.* WLAW 2. Atlanta: SBL, 2013.

Goldin, Judah, trans. *The Fathers According to Rabbi Nathan.* New York: Schocken Books, 1974.

Goodman, Martin. "The Function of *Minim* in Early Rabbinic Judaism." Pp. 163–73 in *Judaism in the Roman World: Collected Essays.* AGJU 66. Leiden: Brill, 2007.

————. "Sadducees and Essenes after 70." Pp. 153–62 in *Judaism in the Roman World: Collected Essays.* AGJU 66. Leiden: Brill, 2007.

————. *State and Society in Roman Galilee: A.D. 132–212.* 2nd ed. Portland: Valentine Mitchell, 2000.

Grabbe, Lester L. *Judaism from Cyrus to Hadrian.* 2 vols. Minneapolis: Fortress, 1992.Grant, Frederick C. *The Gospels: Their Origin and Their Growth.* New York: Harper and Brothers, 1957.

Greenman, Jeffrey P., Timothy Larsen, and Stephen R. Spencer, eds. *The Sermon on the Mount Through the Centuries: From the Early Church to John Paul II.* Grand Rapids: Brazos, 2007.

Grey, Matthew J. "Jewish Priests and the Social History of Post-70 Palestine." Ph.D. diss., University of North Carolina at Chapel Hill, 2011.

Grossman, Maxine L. "Beyond the Hand of Moses: Discourse and Interpretive Authority." *Prooftexts* 26 (2006): 294–301.

————. "Women and Men in the Rule of the Congregation: A Feminist Critical Assessment." Pp. 229–45 in *Rediscovering the Dead Sea Scrolls: An Assessment of Old and New Approaches and Methods.* Edited by Maxine L. Grossman. Grand Rapids: Eerdmans, 2010.

Guelich, R. A. *The Sermon on the Mount.* Waco, Tex.: Word Books, 1982.

Gundry, R. H. *Matthew: A Commentary on His Literary and Theological Art.* Grand Rapids: Eerdmans, 1982.

Gurtner, Daniel. "Matthew's Theology of the Temple and the 'Parting of the Ways': Christian Origins and the First Gospel." Pp. 128–53 in *Built Upon the Rock: Studies in the Gospel of Matthew.* Edited by Daniel M. Gurtner and John Nolland. Grand Rapids: Eerdmans, 2008.

————. *The Torn Veil: Matthew's Exposition of the Death of Jesus.* SNTSMS 139. Cambridge: Cambridge University Press, 2007.

Hachlili, Rachel. *Ancient Synagogues—Archaeology and Art: New Discoveries and Current Research.* HdO 105. Leiden: Brill, 2013.

————. "Synagogues: Before and After the Roman Destruction of the Temple." *BAR* 41, no. 3 (May/June 2015): 30–38, 65.

Hagner, Donald A. *Matthew.* WBC 33A/B. 2 vols. Dallas: Word Books, 1993–95.

Hanson, Richard S. *Tyrian Influence in the Upper Galilee.* Cambridge: ASOR, 1980.

Hare, D. R. A. *Matthew.* Interpretation. Louisville: John Knox, 1993.

Harland, Philip A. *Associations, Synagogues, and Congregations: Claiming a Place in Ancient Mediterranean Society.* Minneapolis: Fortress, 2003.

————. *Dynamics of Identity in the World of the Early Christians: Associations, Judeans, and Cultural Minorities.* New York: T & T Clark, 2009.

Harries, Jill. "Courts and the Judicial System." Pp. 85–101 in *The Oxford Handbook of Jewish Daily Life in Roman Palestine*. Edited by Catherine Hezser. Oxford: Oxford University Press, 2010.

———. "Creating Legal Space: Settling Disputes in the Roman Empire." Pp. 63–81 in *Rabbinic Law in Its Roman and Near Eastern Context*. Edited by Catherine Hezser. TSAJ 97. Tübingen: Mohr Siebeck, 2003.

Harrington, Daniel J., S.J. "Paul and Matthew." Pp. 11–26 in *Matthew and His Christian Contemporaries*. Edited by David C. Sim and Boris Repschinski. LNTS 333. New York: T & T Clark International, 2008.

———. *Wisdom Texts from Qumran*. The Literature of the Dead Sea Scrolls. London: Routledge, 1996.

Hempel, Charlotte. "The Context of 4QMMT and Comfortable Theories." Pp. 275–92 in *Dead Sea Scrolls: Texts and Context*. Edited by Charlotte Hempel. STDJ 90. Leiden: Brill, 2010.

———. *The Damascus Texts*. Sheffield: Sheffield Academic, 2000.

———. "The Laws of the Damascus Document and 4QMMT." Pp. 69–84 in *The Damascus Document: A Centennial of Discovery. Proceedings of the Third International Symposium of the Orion Center for the Study of the Dead Sea Scrolls and Associated Literature, 4–8 February, 1998*. Edited by Joseph M. Baumgarten, Esther Chazon, and Avital Pinnick. STDJ 34. Leiden: Brill, 2000.

———. *The Laws of the Damascus Document: Sources, Tradition and Redaction*. STDJ 29. Leiden: Brill, 1998.

———. "Maskil(im) and Rabbim: From Daniel to Qumran." Pp. 133–56 in *Biblical Traditions in Transmission: Essays in Honour of Michael A. Knibb*. Edited by Charlotte Hempel and Judith M. Lieu. JSJSup 111. Leiden: Brill, 2006.

———. "The Penal Code Reconsidered." Pp. 337–48 in *Legal Texts and Legal Issues: Proceedings of the Second Meeting of the IOQS Cambridge 1995; Studies Presented in Honour of J. Baumgarten*. Edited by Moshe Bernstein, Florentino García Martínez, and John Kampen. STDJ 23. Leiden: Brill, 1997.

———. *The Qumran Rule Texts in Context: Collected Studies*. TSAJ 154. Tübingen: Mohr Siebeck, 2013.

———. "Who Rebukes in 4Q477?" *RevQ* 16 (1995): 655–56.

Hengel, Martin. *Judaism and Hellenism: Studies in Their Encounter in Palestine during the Early Hellenistic Period*. Translated by John Bowden. 2 vols. Philadelphia: Fortress, 1974.

Hezser, Catherine. "Jewish Literacy and Writing in Late Roman Palestine." Pp. 149–95 in *Jewish Culture and Society Under the Christian Roman Empire*. Edited by Richard Kalmin and Seth Schwartz. Interdisciplinary Studies in Ancient Culture and Religion 3. Leuven: Peeters, 2003.

———. *Jewish Literacy in Roman Palestine*. Tübingen: Mohr-Siebeck, 2001.

———. *The Social Structure of the Rabbinic Movement in Roman Palestine*. TSAJ 66. Tübingen: Mohr Siebeck, 1997.

Hill, D. "Dikaioi as a Quasi-Technical Term." *NTS* 9 (1964–65): 296–302.

Himmelfarb, Martha. *A Kingdom of Priests: Ancestry and Merit in Ancient Judaism.* Philadelphia: University of Pennsylvania Press, 2006.

Holmberg, Bengt, and Mikael Winninge, eds. *Identity Formation in the New Testament.* WUNT 227. Tübingen: Mohr Siebeck, 2008.

Hood, Jason. "Matthew 23–25: The Extent of Jesus' Fifth Discourse." *JBL* 128 (2009): 527–43.

Horsley, Richard A. "The Death of Jesus." Pp. 395–422 in *Studying the Historical Jesus: Evaluations of the State of Current Research.* Edited by Bruce Chilton and Craig A. Evans. Leiden: Brill, 1994.

———. *Revolt of the Scribes: Resistance and Apocalyptic Origins.* Minneapolis: Fortress, 2010.

———. *Scribes, Visionaries, and the Politics of Second Temple Judea.* Louisville: Westminster John Knox, 2007.

Howard, George. *The Gospel of Matthew According to a Primitive Hebrew Text.* Macon: Mercer University Press, 1987.

———. *Hebrew Gospel of Matthew.* Rev. ed. Macon: Mercer University Press, 1995.

———. "Shem-Tob's Hebrew Matthew and Early Jewish Christianity." *JSNT* 70 (1998): 3–20.

Hultgren, Stephen. *From the Damascus Covenant to the Covenant of the Community: Literary, Historical, and Theological Studies in the Dead Sea Scrolls.* STDJ 66. Leiden: Brill, 2007.

Humbert, Jean-Baptiste, and Alain Chambon. *Fouilles de Khirbet Qumrân et de Aïn Feshka.* NTOASA 1. Friburg: Éditions Universitaires; Göttingen: Vandenhoeck & Ruprecht, 1994.

———, eds. *The Excavations of Khirbet Qumran and Ain Feshka: Synthesis of Roland de Vaux's Field Notes.* Translated and revised by Stephen J. Pfann. NTOASA 1B. Friburg: Éditions Universitaires; Göttingen: Vandenhoeck & Ruprecht, 2003.

Humbert, Jean-Baptiste, and Jan Gunneweg. *Khirbet Qumrân et 'Aïn Feshka II. Études d'anthropologie, de physique et de chimie.* NTOASA 3. Friburg: Éditions Universitaires; Göttingen: Vandenhoeck & Ruprecht, 2004.

Jaffee, Martin S. *Torah in the Mouth: Writing and Oral Tradition in Palestinian Judaism, 200 BCE–400 CE.* Oxford: Oxford University Press, 2001.

Johnson, Benton. "Church and Sect Revisited." *JSSR* 10 (1971): 124–37.

———. "On Church and Sect." *ASR* 28 (1963): 539–49.

Johnson, Marshall D. "Reflections on a Wisdom Approach to Matthew's Christology." *CBQ* 36 (1974): 44–64.

Johnson, Sherman E. "The Dead Sea Manual of Discipline and the Jerusalem Church of Acts." Pp. 129–42 in *The Scrolls and the New Testament.* Edited by Krister Stendahl. New York: Harper and Bros., 1957.

Jokiranta, Jutta M. "Conceptualizing *GER* in the Dead Sea Scrolls." Pp. 659–78 in *In the Footsteps of Sherlock Holmes: Studies in the Biblical Text in Honour of Anneli Aejmalaeus.* Edited by Kristen De Troyer, T. Michael Law, and Marketta Liljeström. Leuven: Peeters, 2014.

————. "Learning from Sectarian Responses: Windows on Qumran Sects and Emerging Christian Sects." Pp. 177–209 in *Echoes from the Caves: Qumran and the New Testament*. STDJ 85. Leiden: Brill, 2009.

————. "'Sectarianism' of the Qumran 'Sect': Sociological Notes." *RevQ* 20 (2001): 223–39.

————. *Social Identity and Sectarianism in the Qumran Movement*. STDJ 105. Leiden: Brill, 2013.

————. "Social-Scientific Approaches to the Dead Sea Scrolls." Pp. 246–63 in *Rediscovering the Dead Sea Scrolls: An Assessment of Old and New Approaches and Methods*. Edited by Maxine L. Grossman. Grand Rapids: Eerdmans, 2010.

Kampen, John I. "Aspects of Wisdom in the Gospel of Matthew in Light of the New Qumran Evidence." Pp. 227–39 in *Sapiential, Liturgical and Poetical Texts from Qumran: Proceedings of the Third Meeting of the International Organization for Qumran Studies, Oslo 1998, Published in Memory of Maurice Baillet*. Edited by Daniel K. Falk, F. García Martínez, and Eileen M. Schuller. STDJ 35. Leiden: Brill, 2000.

————. "The Books of the Maccabees and Sectarianism in Second Temple Judaism." Pp. 11–30 in *The Books of the Maccabees: History, Theology, Ideology. Papers of the Second International Conference on the Deuterocanonical Books, Pápa, Hungary, 9–11 June, 2006*. Edited by Géza Xeravits and József Zsengellér. JSJSup 118. Leiden: Brill, 2007.

————. "The Diverse Aspects of Wisdom in the Qumran Texts." Pp. 211–43 in vol. 2 of *The Dead Sea Scrolls after Fifty Years: A Comprehensive Assessment*. Edited by James C. VanderKam and Peter Flint. 2 vols. Leiden: Brill, 1998.

————. *The Hasideans and the Origin of Pharisaism: A Study in 1 and 2 Maccabees*. SBLSCS 24. Atlanta: Scholars Press, 1988.

————. "The Matthean Divorce Texts Reexamined." Pp. 149–67 in *New Qumran Texts and Studies: Proceedings of the First Meeting of the International Organization for Qumran Studies, Paris 1992*. Edited by George J. Brooke and Florentino García Martínez. STDJ 15. Leiden: Brill, 1994.

————. "A Reexamination of the Relationship between Matthew 5:21–48 and the Dead Sea Scrolls." *SBL Seminar Papers* 29 (1990): 34–59.

————. "'Righteousness' in Matthew and the Legal Texts from Qumran." Pp. 461–88 in *Legal Texts and Legal Issues: Proceedings of the Second Meeting of the IOQS Cambridge 1995; Studies Presented in Honour of J. Baumgarten*. Edited by Moshe Bernstein, Florentino García Martínez, and John Kampen. STDJ 23. Leiden: Brill, 1997.

————. "The Sectarian Form of the Antitheses within the Social World of the Matthean Community." *DSD* 1 (1994): 338–63.

————. "The Significance of the Temple in the Manuscripts of the Damascus Document." Pp. 185–97 in *The Dead Sea Scrolls at Fifty: Proceedings of the 1997 Society of Biblical Literature Qumran Section Meetings*. Edited by Robert A. Kugler and Eileen M. Schuller. EJL 15. Atlanta: Scholars Press, 1999.

———. "The Social World of the Matthean Community." Pp. 158–74 in *Communal Life in the Early Church: Essays Honoring Graydon F. Snyder.* Edited by Julian V. Hills. Harrisburg, Pa.: Trinity Press International, 1998.

———. "'Torah' and Authority in the Major Sectarian Rules Texts from Qumran." Pp. 231–254 in *The Scrolls and Biblical Traditions: Proceedings of the Seventh Meeting of the IOQS in Helsinki.* Edited by George J. Brooke, Daniel K. Falk, Eibert J. C. Tigchelaar, and Molly M. Zahn. STDJ 103. Leiden: Brill, 2012.

———. "Wisdom in Deuterocanonical and Cognate Literatures." Pp. 89–120 in *Canonicity, Setting, Wisdom in the Deuterocanonicals: Papers of the Jubilee Meeting of the International Conference on the Deuterocanonical Books.* Edited by Géza G. Xeravits, József Zsengellér, and Szabo Xaver. DCLS 22. Berlin: De Gruyter, 2014.

———. *Wisdom Literature.* ECDSS. Grand Rapids: Eerdmans, 2011.

Karrer, Martin. "Licht über dem Galiläa der Völker: Die Fortschreibung von Jes 9: 1–2 in der LXX." Pp. 33–53 in *Religion, Ethnicity, and Identity in Ancient Galilee: A Region in Transition.* Edited by Jürgen Zangenberg, Harold W. Attridge, and Dale B. Martin. WUNT 210. Tübingen: Mohr Siebeck, 2007.

Kee, Howard Clark. "Defining the First Century C.E. Synagogue: Problems and Progress." Pp. 7–26 in *Evolution of the Synagogue: Problems and Progress.* Edited by Howard Clark Kee and Lynn H. Cohick. Harrisburg, Pa.: Trinity Press International, 1999.

———. "The Transformation of the Synagogue after 70 C.E.: Its Import for Early Christianity." *NTS* 36 (1990): 1–24.

Keener, Craig S. *The Gospel of Matthew: A Socio-rhetorical Commentary.* Grand Rapids: Eerdmans, 2009.

Kennard, J. Spencer. "The Place of Origin of Matthew's Gospel." *ATR* 31 (1949): 243–46.

Kingsbury, Jack Dean. "Conclusion: Analysis of a Conversation." Pp. 259–69 in *Social History of the Matthean Community: Cross-Disciplinary Approaches.* Edited by David L. Balch. Minneapolis: Fortress, 1991.

———. *Matthew as Story.* 2nd ed. Philadelphia: Fortress, 1988.

———. *Matthew: Structure, Christology, Kingdom.* Philadelphia: Fortress, 1975.

———. "The Place, Structure and Meaning of the Sermon on the Mount Within Matthew." *Int* 41 (1981): 131–41.

Kister, Menahem. "Divorce, Reproof, and Other Sayings in the Synoptic Gospels: Jesus Traditions in the Context of 'Qumranic' and Other Texts." Pp. 195–229 in *Text, Thought, and Practice in Qumran and Early Christianity: Proceedings of the Ninth International Symposium of the Orion Center for the Study of the Dead Sea Scrolls and Associated Literature, Jointly Sponsored by the Hebrew University Center for the Study of Christianity, 11–13 January, 2004.* Edited by Ruth A. Clements and Daniel R. Schwartz. STDJ 84. Leiden: Brill, 2009.

Klawans, Jonathan. *Impurity and Sin in Ancient Judaism.* New York: Oxford University Press, 2000.

———. *Purity, Sacrifice, and the Temple: Symbolism and Supersessionism in the Study of Ancient Judaism.* Oxford: Oxford University Press, 2006.

Klijn, A. F. J., and G. J. Reinink. *Patristic Evidence for Jewish-Christian Sects.* Nov TSup 36. Leiden: Brill, 1973.

Kloppenborg, John S. "Dating Theodotus (CIJ II 1404)." *JJS* 51 (2000): 243–80.

Knibb, Michael A. *The Qumran Community.* Cambridge: Cambridge University Press, 1987.

———. "Teacher of Righteousness." *EDSS* 2.918–21.

Knoppers, Gary N. *Jews and Samaritans: The Origins and History of Their Early Relations.* New York: Oxford University Press, 2013.

Koester, Helmut. *Introduction to the New Testament.* 2 vols. Philadelphia: Fortress; Berlin: De Gruyter, 1982.

Konradt, Matthias. *Israel, Church, and the Gentiles in the Gospel of Matthew.* Translated by Kathleen Ess. Baylor Mohr-Siebeck Studies in Early Christianity. Waco, Tex.: Baylor University, 2013.

———. "'Whoever Humbles Himself Like This Child . . .': The Ethical Instruction in Matthew's Community Discourse (Matt 18) and Its Narrative Setting." Pp. 105–38 in *Moral Language in the New Testament: The Interrelatedness of Language and Ethics in Early Christian Writings.* Edited by Ruben Zimmermann and Jan G. van der Watt. WUNT 296. Tübingen: Mohr Siebeck, 2010.

Kugel, James. "On Hidden Hatred and Open Reproach: Early Exegesis of Leviticus 19:17." *HTR* 80 (1987): 43–61.

———. *Traditions of the Bible: A Guide to the Bible as It Was at the Start of the Common Era.* Cambridge, Mass.: Harvard University Press, 1998.

Kugler, Robert A. "Patriarchs, Testaments of the Twelve." *EDEJ,* 1031–33.

———. *The Testaments of the Twelve Patriarchs.* Guides to Apocrypha and Pseudepigrapha. Sheffield: Sheffield Academic Press, 2001.

Kümmel, Werner Georg. *Introduction to the New Testament.* Translated by Howard Clark Kee. Nashville: Abington Press, 1996.

Lambrecht, Jan, S.J. *The Sermon on the Mount: Proclamation and Exhortation.* Good News Studies 14. Wilmington: Michael Glazier, 1986.

Lange, Nicholas de. *An Introduction to Judaism.* 2nd ed. Cambridge: Cambridge University Press, 2010.

Lapin, Hayim. "The Origins and Development of the Rabbinic Movement in the Land of Israel." *CHJ* 4.206–29.

———. *The Rabbis as Romans: The Rabbinic Movement in Palestine, 100–400 CE.* New York: Oxford University Press, 2012.

Leiman, Sid Z., ed. *The Canon and Masora of the Hebrew Bible.* New York: Ktav, 1974.

Levenson, Jon D. *Resurrection and the Restoration of Israel: The Ultimate Victory of the God of Life.* New Haven: Yale University Press, 2006.

Levine, Amy-Jill. "Jesus in Jewish-Christian Dialogue." Pp. 175–88 in *Soundings in the Religion of Jesus: Perspectives and Methods in Jewish and Christian Scholarship.*

Edited by Bruce Chilton, Jacob Neusner, and Anthony Le Donne. Minneapolis: Augsburg Fortress, 2012.

———. "Matthew, Mark, and Luke: Good News or Bad?" Pp. 77–98 in *Jesus, Judaism, and Christian Anti-Judaism: Reading the New Testament after the Holocaust.* Edited by Paula Fredriksen and Adele Reinhartz. Louisville: Westminster John Knox, 2002.

———. *The Social and Ethnic Dimensions of Matthean Salvation History: "Go Nowhere among the Gentiles" (Matt. 10:5b).* SBEC 15. Lewiston, N.Y.: Edwin Mellen, 1988.

Levine, Baruch A. "Damascus Document IX, 17–22: A New Translation and Comments." *RevQ* 8 (1973): 195–96.

Levine, Lee I. *The Ancient Synagogue: The First Thousand Years.* 2nd ed. New Haven: Yale University Press, 2005.

———. "The First-Century C.E. Synagogue in Historical Perspective." Pp. 1–24 in *The Ancient Synagogue from Its Origins until 200 C.E.: Papers Presented at an International Conference at Lund University, October 14–17, 2001.* Edited by Birger Olsson and Magnus Zetterholm. ConBNT 39. Stockholm: Almqvist & Wiksell, 2003.

———. *The Rabbinic Class of Roman Palestine in Late Antiquity.* Jerusalem: Yad Yizhaq Ben-Zvi; New York: Jewish Theological Seminary, 1989.

———. "The Synagogue." Pp. 521–44 in *The Oxford Handbook of Jewish Daily Life in Roman Palestine.* Edited by Catherine Hezser. Oxford: Oxford University Press, 2010.

———. *Visual Judaism in Late Antiquity: Historical Contexts of Jewish Art.* New Haven: Yale University Press, 2012.

Levinson, Bernard M. *Deuteronomy and the Hermeneutics of Legal Innovation.* New York: Oxford University Press, 1997.

Lewis, Jack P. "Jamnia after Forty Years." *HUCA* 70–71 (1999–2000): 233–59.

———. "Jamnia Revisited," Pp. 146–62 in *The Canon Debate.* Edited by Lee Martin McDonald and James A. Sanders. Peabody, Mass.: Hendrickson, 2002.

———. "What Do We Mean by Jabneh?" *JBR* 32 (1964): 125–32.

Lierman, John. *The New Testament Moses: Christian Perceptions of Moses and Israel in the Setting of Jewish Religion.* WUNT 173. Tübingen: Mohr Siebeck, 2004.

Lightstone, Jack. "The Pharisees and the Sadducees in the Earliest Rabbinic Sources." Pp. 255–95 in *In Quest of the Historical Pharisees.* Edited by Jacob Neusner and Bruce D. Chilton. Waco, Tex.: Baylor University Press, 2007.

Luomanen, Petri. "The 'Sociology of Sectarianism' in Matthew: Modeling the Genesis of Early Jewish and Christian Communities." Pp. 109–30 in *Fair Play: Diversity and Conflicts in Early Christianity: Essays in Honor of Heikke Räisänen.* Edited by Ismo Dundenberg, Christopher Tuckett, and Kari Syreeni. NovTSup 103. Leiden: Brill, 2002.

Luz, Ulrich. *Matthew.* Translated by James E. Crouch. 3 vols. Hermeneia. Minneapolis: Fortress, 2001–7.

————. *Matthew 1–7: A Commentary*. Translated by Wilhelm C. Linss. Minneapolis: Augsburg, 1989.

Lybaek, Lena. *New and Old in Matthew 11–13: Normativity in the Development of Three Theological Themes*. Göttingen: Vandenhoeck & Ruprecht, 2002.

Macaskill, Grant. "Matthew and the *Parables of Enoch*." Pp. 218–30 in *Parables of Enoch: A Paradigm Shift*. Edited by James H. Charlesworth and Darrell L. Bock. London: Bloomsbury, 2014.

————. *Revealed Wisdom and Inaugurated Eschatology in Ancient Judaism and Early Christianity*. JSJSup 115. Leiden: Brill, 2007.

Magen, Y., Y. Zionit, and E. Sirkis. "Qiryat Sefer: A Jewish Village and Synagogue of the Second Temple Period." *Qadmoniot* 33 (1999): 25–32 (Hebrew).

Magness, Jodi. "Sectarianism before and after 70 CE." Pp. 69–89 in *Was 70 CE a Watershed in Jewish History? On Jews and Judaism before and after the Destruction of the Second Temple*. Edited by Daniel R. Schwartz and Zeev Weiss. AGJU 78. Leiden: Brill, 2012.

————. *Stone and Dung, Oil and Spit: Jewish Daily Life in the Time of Jesus*. Grand Rapids: Eerdmans, 2012.

Ma'oz, Zvi. "Notes on B. Zissu and A. Ganor's Article in *Qadmoniot* 123—'Horvat Etri.'" *Qadmoniot* 36, no. 125 (2006): 55 (Hebrew).

————. "The Synagogue That Never Existed in the Hasmonean Palace at Jericho: Remarks Concerning an Article by E. Netzer, Y. Kalman, and R. Loris." *Qadmoniot* 32 (1999): 120–21 (Hebrew).

Marcus, Joel. "Birkat Ha-Minim Revisited." *NTS* 55 (2009): 523–51.

————. "A Jewish-Christian 'Amidah'?" *Early Christianity* 3, no. 2 (2012): 215–25.

Mason, Steve. "Ancient Jews or Judeans? Different Question, Different Answers." Pp. 11–17 in *Jew and Judean: A Marginalia Forum on Politics and Historiography in the Translation of Ancient Texts*. Edited by Timothy Michael Law and Charles Halton. The Marginalia Review of Books, August 26, 2014. https://dl.orangedox.com/yTWsrMwDFZF3fqx2kt/Jew%20and%20Judean.pdf.

————. "Jews, Judeans, Judaizing, Judaism: Problems of Categorization in Ancient History." Pp. 141–84 in *Josephus, Judea, and Christian Origins: Methods and Categories*. Peabody: Hendrickson, 2009.

Massaux, Édouard. *The Influence of the Gospel of Saint Matthew on Christian Literature before Saint Irenaeus*. Edited by Arthur J. Bellinzoni. Translated by Norman J. Belval and Suzanne Hecht. 3 vols. New Gospel Studies 5/1–3. Macon: Mercer University Press, 1990–93.

Mayo, Philip L. "The Role of the *Birkath Haminim* in Early Jewish-Christian Relations: A Re-examination of the Evidence." *BBR* 16 (2006): 325–44.

McCready, Wayne O., and Adele Reinhartz, eds. *Common Judaism: Explorations in Second Temple Judaism*. Minneapolis: Fortress, 2008.

McGuire, Meredith B. *Religion, The Social Context*. 5th ed. Belmont: Wadsworth, 2002.

McKnight, Scott. *A Light among the Gentiles: Jewish Missionary Activity in the Second Temple Period.* Minneapolis: Augsburg Fortress, 1991.

———. "Or, More Likely, Was There Not a Little More Torah in Paul Than Sim Allows?" *CBQ* 62 (2000): 375–77.

McLaren, James S. "Exploring the Execution of a Provincial: Adopting a Roman Perspective on the Death of Jesus." *ABR* 49 (2001): 5–28.

Meier, John P. *A Marginal Jew: Rethinking the Historical Jesus.* Vol. 4, *Law and Love.* New Haven: Yale University Press, 2009.

———. *Matthew.* NTM 3. Wilmington, Del.: Glazier, 1980.

Metso, Sarianna. *The Serekh Texts.* London: T & T Clark, 2007.

———. *The Textual Development of the Qumran Community Rule.* STDJ 21. Leiden: Brill, 1997.

Metzer, Bruce M. *A Textual Commentary on the Greek New Testament.* London: United Bible Societies, 1975.

Meyers, Eric M., and Mark A. Chancey. *From Alexander to Constantine: Archaeology of the Land of the Bible.* AYBRL 3. New Haven: Yale University Press, 2012.

Miller, Stuart S. "On the Number of Synagogues in the Cities of 'Ereẓ Israel." *JJS* 49 (1998): 51–66.

———. "Priests, Purities, and the Jews of Galilee." Pp. 375–402 in *Religion, Ethnicity, and Identity in Ancient Galilee.* Edited by Jürgen Zangenberg, Harold W. Attridge, and Dale B. Martin. WUNT 210. Tübingen: Mohr Siebeck, 2007.

Montefiore, C. G. *Rabbinic Literature and Gospel Teachings.* London: Macmillan, 1930.

———. *The Synoptic Gospels: Edited with an Introduction and a Commentary by C. G. Montefiore Together with a Series of Additional Notes by I. Abrahams.* 3 vols. London: Macmillan, 1909.

Moss, Candida R. *Ancient Christian Martyrdom: Diverse Practices, Theologies, and Traditions.* AYBRL. New Haven: Yale University Press, 2012.

———. *The Myth of Persecution: How Early Christians Invented a Story of Martyrdom.* New York: Harper One, 2013.

Moss, Charlene McAfee. *The Zechariah Tradition and the Gospel of Matthew.* BZNW 156. Berlin: De Gruyter, 2008.

Murphy-O'Connor, Jerome. "A Literary Analysis of Damascus Document VI, 2—VIII, 3." *RB* 78 (1971): 210–32.

Najman, Hindy J. *Seconding Sinai: The Development of Mosaic Discourse in Second Temple Judaism.* JSJSup 77. Leiden: Brill, 2003.

———. "Torah and Tradition." *EDEJ* 1316–17.

Nau, Arlo. Review of *The Gospel of Matthew and Christian Judaism: The History and Social Setting of the Matthean Community,* by David Sim. *RBL,* July 19, 2003. https://www.bookreviews.org/pdf/3532_3741.pdf.

Netzer, Ehud. *Hasmonean and Herodian Palaces at Jericho, Final Reports of the 1973–1987 Seasons.* 4 vols. Jerusalem: Israel Exploration Society, Institute of Archaeology, Hebrew University, 2001–8.

————. "A Synagogue from the Hasmonean Period Recently Exposed in the Western Plain of Jericho." *IEJ* 49 (1999): 203–21.

Neusner, Jacob. "'By the Testimony of Two Witnesses' in the Damascus Document IX, 17–22 and in Pharisaic-Rabbinic Law." *RevQ* 8, no. 2 (1972–75): 197–217.

————. *From Politics to Piety: The Emergence of Pharisaic Judaism.* Englewood Cliffs, N.J.: Prentice Hall, 1973.

Newsom, Carol A. "The Sage in the Literature of Qumran: The Functions of the Maskil." Pp. 373–82 in *The Sage in Israel and the Ancient Near East.* Edited by John G. Gammie and Leo G. Perdue. Winona Lake, Ind.: Eisenbrauns, 1990.

————. *The Self as Symbolic Space: Constructing Identity and Community at Qumran.* STDJ 52. Atlanta: SBL, 2004.

Nickelsburg, George W. E. *Ancient Judaism and Christian Origins: Diversity, Continuity, and Transformation.* Minneapolis: Fortress, 2003.

————. "Enoch, First Book of." *ABD* 2.509–16.

————. "Enoch, Levi, and Peter: Recipients of Revelation in Upper Galilee." *JBL* 100 (1981): 575–600.

————. *1 Enoch 1: A Commentary on the Book of 1 Enoch. Chapters 1–36; 81–108.* Hermeneia. Minneapolis: Fortress, 2001.

————. "Revealed Wisdom as a Criterion of Inclusion and Exclusion: From Jewish Sectarianism to Early Christianity." Pp. 73–91 in *"To See Ourselves as Others See Us": Christians, Jews, "Others" in Late Antiquity.* Edited by Jacob Neusner and Ernest S. Frerichs. Chico, Calif.: Scholars Press, 1985.

Nickelsburg, George W. E., and James C. VanderKam. *1 Enoch 2: A Commentary on the Books of 1 Enoch 37–82.* Hermeneia. Minneapolis: Fortress, 2012.

Niebuhr, H. Richard. *The Social Sources of Denominationalism.* New York: Meridian Books, 1957.

Nitzan, Bilhah. "286. 4QBerakhot^a (Pls. I–IV)." Pp. 7–48 in *Qumran Cave 4: VI. Poetical and Liturgical Texts, Part 1.* Edited by Esther Eshel, Hanan Eshel, Carol Newsom, Bilhah Nitzan, Eileen Schuller, and Ada Yardeni. DJD 11. Oxford: Clarendon Press, 1998.

————. "The Laws of Reproof in 4QBerakhot (4Q286–290) in Light of Their Parallels in the Damascus Covenant and Other Texts from Qumran." Pp. 149–65 in *Legal Texts and Legal Issues: Proceedings of the Second Meeting of the International Organisation for Qumran Studies, Cambridge, 1995: Published in Honour of Joseph M. Baumgarten.* Edited by Moshe Bernstein, Florentino García Martínez, and John Kampen. STDJ 23. Leiden: E. J. Brill, 1997.

Notley, Steven R., Marc Turnage, and Brian Becker, eds. *Jesus' Last Week.* Vol. 1 of *Jerusalem Studies in the Synoptic Gospels.* Leiden: Brill, 2006.

Osborne, Robert E. "The Provenance of Matthew's Gospel." *Studies in Religion* 3 (1973): 220–35.

Overman, J. Andrew. *Church and Community in Crisis: The Gospel According to Matthew.* The New Testament in Context. Valley Forge: Trinity International, 1996.

———. "Kata Nomon Pharisaios: A Short History of Paul's Pharisaism." Pp. 180–93 in *Pauline Conversations in Context: Essays in Honor of Calvin J. Roetzel.* Edited by Janice Capel Anderson, Philip Sellew, and Claudia Setzer. London: Sheffield Academic, 2002.

———. *Matthew's Gospel and Formative Judaism: The Social World of the Matthean Community.* Philadelphia: Fortress, 1990.

Pagels, Elaine. *Revelations: Visions, Prophecy, and Politics in the Book of Revelation.* New York: Viking, 2012.

Parsenios, George L. "Beth-Saida," *NIDB* 1.445–46.

Paul, Shalom M. *Isaiah 40–66: Translation and Commentary.* ECC. Grand Rapids: Eerdmans, 2012.

Pickup, Martin. "Matthew's and Mark's Pharisees." Pp. 67–112 in *In Quest of the Historical Pharisees.* Edited by Jacob Neusner and Bruce D. Chilton. Waco, Tex.: Baylor University Press, 2007.

Portier-Young, Anathea. *Apocalypse against Empire: Theologies of Resistance in Early Judaism.* Grand Rapids: Eerdmans, 2011.

Powell, Mark Allan, ed. *Methods for Matthew.* Cambridge: Cambridge University Press, 2009.

———. "Narrative Criticism." Pp. 240–58 in *Hearing the New Testament: Strategies for Interpretation.* Edited by Joel B. Green. 2nd ed. Grand Rapids: Eerdmans, 2010.

———. "The Plot and Subplots of Matthew's Gospel." *NTS* 38 (1992): 187–204.

———. *What Is Narrative Criticism?* Guides to Biblical Scholarship: New Testament Series. Minneapolis: Fortress, 1990.

Pregeant, Russell. *Matthew.* Chalice Commentaries for Today. St. Louis: Chalice, 2004.

Przybylski, B. *Righteousness in Matthew and His World of Thought.* SNTSMS 41. Cambridge: Cambridge University Press, 1980.

Puech, É. "The Collection of Beatitudes in Hebrew and in Greek in 4Q525 1–4 and MT 5:3–12." Pp. 353–68 in *Early Christianity in Context.* Edited by Manns Frédéric. Jerusalem: Franciscan Printing Press, 1993.

———. "4Q525 et les péricopes des Béatitudes en Ben Sira et Matthieu." *RB* 138 (1991): 90–106.

Pummer, Reinhard. *The Samaritans: A Profile.* Grand Rapids: Eerdmans, 2016.

Qimron, Elisha, and John Strugnell. *Qumran Cave 4: V. Miqṣat Ma'aśe Ha-Torah.* DJD 10. Oxford: Clarendon, 1994.

Rabin, Chaim. *The Zadokite Documents.* 2nd ed. Oxford: Clarendon, 1958.

Rabinowitz, Louis Isaac. "Synagogue: Origins and History." *EncJud* 19.353–55.

Rajak, Tessa. *Josephus: The Historian and His Society.* 2nd ed. London: Duckworth, 2002.

Reeves, John C. "The 'Elchasaite' Sanhedrin of the Cologne Mani Codex in Light of Second Temple Jewish Sources." *JJS* 42 (1991): 68–91.

———. *Heralds of That Good Realm: Syro-Mesopotamian Gnosis and Jewish Traditions.* Nag Hammadi and Manichaean Studies 41. Leiden: Brill, 1996.

Regev, Eyal. "Between Two Sects: Differentiating the Yaḥad and the Damascus Covenant." Pp. 331–49 in *The Dead Sea Scrolls: Texts and Contexts.* Edited by Charlotte Hempel. STDJ 90. Leiden: Brill, 2010.

———. "Wealth and Sectarianism: Comparing Qumranic and Early Christian Social Approaches." Pp. 211–29 in *Echoes from the Caves: Qumran and the New Testament.* Edited by Florentino García Martínez. STDJ 85. Leiden: Brill, 2009.

———. "Were the Early Christians Sectarians?" *JBL* 130 (2011): 771–93.

———. "Were the Priests All the Same? Qumranic Halakhah in Comparison with Sadducean Halakhah." *DSD* 12 (2005): 158–88.

Reinhartz, Adele. "Snared by Words? (Proverbs 6:2): On the Perils of Editing." *JBL* 135 (2016): 441–45.

———. "The Vanishing Jews of Antiquity." Pp. 5–10 in *Jew and Judean: A Marginalia Forum on Politics and Historiography in the Translation of Ancient Texts.* Edited by Timothy Michael Law and Charles Halton. The Marginalia Review of Books, August 26, 2014. https://dl.orangedox.com/yTWsrMwDFZF3fqx2kt/Jew%20and%20Judean.pdf.

———. "We, You, They: Boundary Language in 4QMMT and the New Testament Epistles." Pp. 89–105 in *Text, Thought, and Practice in Qumran and Early Christianity: Proceedings of the Ninth International Symposium of the Orion Center for the Study of the Dead Sea Scrolls and Associated Literature, Jointly Sponsored by the Hebrew University Center for the Study of Christianity, 11—13 January, 2004.* Edited by Ruth A. Clements and Daniel R. Schwartz. STDJ 84. Leiden: Brill, 2009.

Richardson, Peter. "An Architectural Case for Synagogues as Associations." Pp. 90–117 in *The Ancient Synagogue: From Its Origins until 200 C.E.* Edited by B. Olsson and M. Zetterholm. Stockholm: Almqvist & Wiksell, 2003.

———. *Building Jewish in the Roman East.* Waco, Tex.: Baylor, 2004.

———. "Early Synagogues as Collegia in the Diaspora and Palestine." Pp. 90–109 in *Voluntary Associations in the Greco-Roman World.* Edited by John S. Kloppenborg and Stephen G. Wilson. London: Routledge, 1996.

———. Review of *The Ancient Synagogue: The First Thousand Years* by Lee I. Levine. *JBL* 121 (2002): 361–64.

Rivkin, Ellis. "Ben Sira and the Nonexistence of the Synagogue: A Study in Historical Method." Pp. 320–54 in *In the Time of Harvest: Essays in Honor of Abba Hillel Silver on the Occasion of his 70th Birthday.* Edited by Daniel Jeremy Silver. New York: Macmillan, 1963.

———. "Defining the Pharisees: The Tannaitic Sources." *HUCA* 40 (1969): 205–49.

———. *A Hidden Revolution: The Pharisees' Search for the Kingdom Within.* Nashville: Abingdon, 1978.

———. *What Crucified Jesus? The Political Execution of a Charismatic.* Nashville: Abingdon, 1984.

Robbins, V. K. "Form Criticism (NT)." *ABD* 2.841–44.

Robinson, W. Peter, ed. *Social Groups and Identities: Developing the Legacy of Henri Tajfel.* International Series in Social Psychology. Oxford: Butterworth Heinemann, 1996.

Rom-Shiloni, Dalit. *Exclusive Inclusivity: Identity Conflicts between the Exiles and Those Who Remained (6th–5th Centuries BCE).* London: Bloomsbury, 2013.

Runesson, Anders. "Behind the Gospel of Matthew: Radical Pharisees in Post-War Galilee?" *CurTM* 37, no. 6 (2010): 460–71.

———. *Divine Wrath and Salvation in Matthew: The Narrative World of the First Gospel.* Minneapolis: Fortress, 2016.

———. *The Origins of the Synagogue: A Socio-historical Study.* ConBNT 37. Stockholm: Almqvist & Wiksell, 2001.

———. "Rethinking Early Jewish-Christian Relations: Matthean Community History as Pharisaic Intragroup Conflict." *JBL* 127 (2008): 95–132.

Runesson, Anders, Donald D. Binder, and Birger Olsson. *The Ancient Synagogue from Its Origins to 200 C.E.: A Sourcebook.* AJEC 72. Leiden: Brill, 2008.

Russell, Paul S. "Avoiding the Lure of Edessa: A Plea for Caution in Dating the Works of Ephraem the Syrian." Pp. 71–74 in *Papers Presented at the Fourteenth International Conference on Patristic Studies held in Oxford 2003.* Edited by F. Young, M. Edwards, and P. Parvis. StPatr 43. Leuven: Leuven University, 2006.

Safrai, S. "The Synagogue." *CRINT* 1.2:908–44.

Saldarini, Anthony J. "The Gospel of Matthew and Jewish-Christian Conflict." Pp. 38–61 in *Social History of the Matthean Community: Cross-Disciplinary Approaches.* Edited by David L. Balch. Minneapolis: Fortress, 1991.

———. *Matthew's Christian-Jewish Community.* Chicago: University of Chicago Press, 1994.

———. *Pharisees, Scribes and Sadducees in Palestinian Society: A Sociological Approach.* Wilmington, Del.: Michael Glazier, 1988.

Sanders, E. P. "Common Judaism and the Synagogue in the First Century." Pp. 1–17 in *Jews, Christians, and Polytheists in the Ancient Synagogue: Cultural Interaction during the Greco-Roman Period.* Edited by Steven Fine. London: Routledge, 1999.

———. *Jewish Law from Jesus to the Mishnah: Five Studies.* London: SCM; Philadelphia: Fortress, 1990.

———. *Judaism: Practice and Belief, 63 B.C.E.–66 C.E.* London: SCM Press; Philadelphia: Trinity Press International, 1994.

———. *Paul and Palestinian Judaism: A Comparison of Patterns of Religion.* Philadelphia: Fortress, 1977.

Sanders, J. A. *The Psalms Scroll of Qumran Cave 11 (11QPsᵃ).* DJD 4. Oxford: Clarendon, 1965.

Schaberg, Jane. *The Father, the Son and the Holy Spirit: The Triadic Phrase in Matthew 28:19b.* SBLDS 61. Chico, Calif.: Scholars Press, 1982.

Schechter, Solomon. *Aspects of Rabbinic Theology: Major Concepts of the Talmud.* New York: Schocken Books, 1961—orig. 1909.

————. *Documents of Jewish Sectaries.* Vol. 1, *Fragments of a Zadokite Work.* Library of Biblical Studies. New York: Ktav, 1970.

Schenke, Hans-Martin. *Das Matthäus-Evangelium im mittelägyptischen Dialekt des Koptischen (Codex Schøyen).* Manuscripts in the Schøyen Collection 2. Oslo: Hermes, 2001.

Schiffman, Lawrence H. *The Halakhah at Qumran.* SJLA 16. Leiden: Brill, 1975.

————. "The New Halakhic Letter (4QMMT) and the Origins of the Dead Sea Sect." *BA* 53, no. 2 (June 1990): 64–73.

————. *Qumran and Jerusalem: Studies in the Dead Sea Scrolls and the History of Judaism.* Grand Rapids: Eerdmans, 2010.

————. "The Qumran Law of Testimony." *RevQ* 8, no. 2 (1972–75): 603–12.

————. "Reproof as a Requisite for Punishment in the Law of the Dead Sea Scrolls." Pp. 59–74 in *Jewish Law Association Studies II: The Jerusalem Conference Volume.* Atlanta: Scholars Press, 1986.

————. *Sectarian Law in the Dead Sea Scrolls: Courts, Testimony and the Penal Code.* BJS 33. Chico, Calif.: Scholars Press, 1983.

Schmitz, Philip C. "Canaan (Place)." *ABD* 1.828–31.

Schniedewind, William M. *How the Bible Became a Book: The Textualization of Ancient Israel.* Cambridge: Cambridge University Press, 2004.

Schoedel, William R. *Ignatius of Antioch.* Hermeneia. Philadelphia: Fortress, 1985.

Schofield, Alison. *From Qumran to the Yaḥad: A New Paradigm of Textual Development for the Community Rule.* STDJ 77. Leiden: Brill, 2009.

Schubert, Kurt. "The Sermon on the Mount and the Qumran Texts." Pp. 118–28 in *The Scrolls and the New Testament.* Edited by Krister Stendahl. New York: Harper and Bros., 1957.

Schuller, Eileen, and Moshe Bernstein, "372. Narrative and Poetic Composition[b]." Pp. 167–78 in *Wadi Daliyeh II: The Samaria Papyri from Wadi Daliyeh; and Qumran Cave 4: XXVIII. Miscellanea, Part 2.* Edited by Douglas M. Gropp, Moshe Bernstein, Monica Brady, James Charlesworth, Peter Flint, Haggai Misgav, Stephen Pfann, Eileen Schuller, Eibert J. C. Tigchelaar, and James VanderKam. DJD 28. Oxford: Clarendon, 2001.

Schultz, Brian. *Conquering the World: The War Scroll (1QM) Reconsidered.* STDJ 76. Leiden: Brill, 2009.

Schürer, Emil. *The History of the Jewish People in the Age of Jesus Christ (175 B.C.–A.D. 135).* Revised and edited by Geza Vermes, Fergus Millar, and Martin Goodman. 4 vols. Edinburgh: T & T Clark, 1973–87. (Abbreviated as Schürer-Vermes throughout this volume.)

Schwartz, Daniel R. "Hillel and Scripture: From Authority to Exegesis." Pp. 335–62 in *Hillel and Jesus: Comparative Studies of Two Major Religious Leaders.* Edited by James H. Charlesworth and Loren L. Johns. Minneapolis: Fortress, 1997.

————. "'Judaean' or 'Jew'? How Should We Translate *ioudaios* in Josephus?" Pp. 3–27 in *Jewish Identity in the Greco-Roman World.* Edited by Jörg Frey, Daniel R. Schwartz, and Stephanie Gripentrog. AGJU 71. Leiden: Brill, 2007.

―――. "Judeans, Jews, and Their Neighbours: Jewish Identity in the Second Temple Period." Pp. 13–31 in *Between Cooperation and Hostility: Multiple Identities in Ancient Judaism and the Interaction with Foreign Powers*. Edited by Albertz Rainer and Jakob Wöhrle. JAJSup 11. Göttingen: Vandenhoeck & Ruprecht, 2013.

―――. "Special People or Special Books? On Qumran and New Testament Notions of Canon." Pp. 49–62 in *Text, Thought, and Practice in Qumran and Early Christianity: Proceedings of the Ninth International Symposium of the Orion Center for the Study of the Dead Sea Scrolls and Associated Literature, Jointly Sponsored by the Hebrew University Center for the Study of Christianity, 11–13 January, 2004*. Edited by Ruth A. Clements and Daniel R. Schwartz. STDJ 84. Leiden: Brill, 2009.

Schwartz, Seth. *The Ancient Jews from Alexander to Muhammed*. Key Themes in Ancient History. Cambridge: Cambridge University Press, 2014.

―――. "How Many Judaisms Were There? A Critique of Neusner and Smith on Definition and Mason and Boyarin on Categorization." *JAJ* 2 (2011): 208–38.

―――. *Imperialism and Jewish Society, 200 B.C.E. to 640 C.E.* Princeton: Princeton University Press, 2001.

―――. *Josephus and Judaean Politics*. Columbia Studies in the Classical Tradition 18. Leiden: Brill, 1990.

Schweitzer, Albert. *The Quest of the Historical Jesus: A Critical Study of Its Progress from Reimarus to Wrede*. New York: Macmillan, 1968.

Scott, Ian W. "Sectarian Truth: The Meaning of 'Emet in the *Community Rule*." Pp. 303–43 in *Celebrating the Dead Sea Scrolls: A Canadian Collection*. Edited by Peter W. Flint, Jean Duhaime, and Kyung S. Baek. EJL 30. Atlanta: SBL, 2011.

Segal, Alan F. *Life after Death: A History of the Afterlife in the Religions of the West*. New York: Doubleday, 2004.

―――. "Matthew's Jewish Voice." Pp. 3–37 in *Social History of the Matthean Community: Cross-Disciplinary Approaches*. Edited by David L. Balch. Minneapolis: Fortress, 1991.

Segal, Michael. *The Book of Jubilees: Rewritten Bible, Redaction, Ideology and Theology*. JSJSup 117. Leiden: Brill, 2007.

Seitz, Christopher R. "The Book of Isaiah 40–66: Introduction, Commentary, and Reflections." *NIB* 6.309–552.

Sievers, J. "Who Were the Pharisees?" Pp. 137–55 in *Hillel and Jesus: Comparisons of Two Major Religious Leaders*. Edited by James H. Charlesworth and Loren L. Johns. Minneapolis: Fortress, 1997.

Sim, David C. *Apocalyptic Eschatology in the Gospel of Matthew*. SNTSMS 88. Cambridge: Cambridge University Press, 1996.

―――. *The Gospel of Matthew and Christian Judaism: The History and Social Setting of the Matthean Community*. Edinburgh: T & T Clark, 1998.

―――. "The Gospel of Matthew and the Gentiles." *JSNT* 57 (1995): 19–48.

―――. "Matthew: The Current State of Research." Pp. 33–51 in *Mark and Matthew I: Comparative Readings; Understanding the Earliest Gospels in Their First-*

Century Settings. Edited by Eve-Marie Becker and Anders Runesson. WUNT 271. Tübingen: Mohr Siebeck, 2011.

———. "Reconstructing the Social and Religious Milieu of Matthew: Methods, Sources, and Possible Results." Pp. 13–32 in *Matthew, James, and Didache: Three Related Documents in Their Jewish and Christian Settings.* Edited by Huub van de Sandt and Jürgen K. Zangenberg. SymS 45. Atlanta: SBL, 2008.

Sivertsev, Alexei. *Households, Sects, and the Origins of Rabbinic Judaism.* JSJSup 102. Leiden: Brill, 2005.

———. "Sects and Households: Social Structure of the Proto-Sectarian Movement of Nehemiah 10 and the Dead Sea Sect." *CBQ* 67 (2005): 59–78.

Skinner, Matthew L. *The Trial Narratives: Conflict, Power, and Identity in the New Testament.* Louisville: Westminster John Knox, 2010.

Sloyan, Gerard S. *Jesus on Trial: A Study of the Gospels.* 2nd ed. Minneapolis: Fortress, 2006.

Smelik, Willem. "The Languages of Roman Palestine." Pp. 122–41 in *Oxford Handbook of Jewish Daily Life in Roman Palestine.* Edited by Catherine Hezser. Oxford: Oxford University Press, 2010.

Smith, Daniel L. *The Religion of the Landless: The Social Context of the Babylonian Empire.* Bloomington: Meyer-Stone, 1989.

Smith, Morton. "Palestinian Judaism in the First Century." Pp. 67–82 in *Israel: Its Role in Civilization.* Edited by M. Davis. New York: Jewish Theological Seminary of America/Harper & Brothers, 1956.

———. *Tannaitic Parallels to the Gospels.* JBLMS 7. Philadelphia: SBL, 1951.

Stambaugh, John E., and David L. Balch. *The New Testament in Its Social Environment.* LEC 2. Philadelphia: Westminster, 1986.

Stanton, Graham N. *A Gospel for a New People: Studies in Matthew.* Edinburgh: T & T Clark, 1992.

———. "The Origin and Purpose of Matthew's Sermon on the Mount." Pp. 181–92 in *Tradition and Interpretation in the New Testament: Essays in Honor of E. Earle Ellis for His 60th Birthday.* Edited by G. F. Hawthorne and O. Betz. Grand Rapids: Eerdmans; Tübingen: J.C.B. Mohr, 1987.

Stark, Rodney. *The Rise of Christianity: A Sociologist Reconsiders History.* Princeton: Princeton University Press, 1996.

Stark, Rodney, and William Sims Bainbridge. *The Future of Religion: Secularization, Revival and Cult Formation.* Berkeley: University of California Press, 1985.

———. *Religion, Deviance, and Social Control.* New York: Routledge, 1996.

Stegemann, Hartmut, with Eileen Schuller. *Qumran Cave 1: III. 1QHodayot^a with Incorporation of 1QHodayot^b and 4QHodayot^a-f.* DJD 40. Oxford: Clarendon, 2009.

Stemberger, Günter. "Dating Rabbinic Traditions." Pp. 79–96 in *The New Testament and Rabbinic Literature.* Edited by Reimund Bieringer. JSJSup 136. Leiden: Brill, 2010.

———. *Jewish Contemporaries of Jesus: Pharisees, Sadducees, Essenes.* Minneapolis: Fortress, 1995.

Stendahl, Krister. "Matthew." Pp. 769–98 in *Peake's Commentary on the Bible.* Edited by Matthew Black. London: Thomas Nelson & Sons, 1962.

Stern, Menahem. "The Period of the Second Temple." Pp. 185–238 in *A History of the Jewish People.* Edited by H. H. Ben-Sasson. Cambridge, Mass.: Harvard University Press, 1976.

Stone, Michael E. "The Book of Enoch and Judaism in the Third Century B.C.E." *CBQ* 40 (1978), 479–92.

———. *Scriptures, Sects and Visions: A Profile of Judaism from Ezra to the Jewish Revolts.* Philadelphia: Fortress, 1978.

Strange, James F. "Ancient Texts, Archaeology as Text, and the Problem of the First-Century Synagogue." Pp. 27–45 in *Evolution of the Synagogue: Problems and Progress.* Edited by Howard Clark Kee and Lynn H. Cohick. Harrisburg, Pa.: Trinity Press International, 1999.

Strathmann, Hermann. "πόλις κτλ." *TDNT* 6.516–35.

Strawn, Brent A., and Henry W. Morisada Rietz. "(More) Sectarian Terminology in the Songs of the Sabbath Sacrifice: The Case of *təmîmê derek.*" Pp. 53–64 in *Qumran Studies: New Approaches, New Questions.* Edited by Michael Thomas Davis and Brent A. Strawn. Grand Rapids: Eerdmans, 2007.

Strecker, G. *The Sermon on the Mount: An Exegetical Commentary.* Translated by O. C. Dean, Jr. Nashville: Abingdon, 1988.

Strugnell, John. "The Smaller Hebrew Wisdom Texts Found at Qumran: Variations, Resemblances, and Lines of Development." Pp. 31–60 in *The Wisdom Texts from Qumran and the Development of Sapiential Thought.* Edited by C. Hempel, A. Lange, and H. Lichtenberger. BETL 159. Leuven: Leuven University Press, 2002.

Strugnell, John, and Daniel J. Harrington, S.J. *Qumran Cave 4: XXIV. Sapiential Texts, Part 2. 4QInstruction (Mûsār lĕ Mēvîn): 4Q415ff.* DJD 34. Oxford: Clarendon, 1999.

Suggs, M. Jack. *Wisdom, Christology and Law in Matthew's Gospel.* Cambridge, Mass.: Harvard University Press, 1970.

Tadmor, H. "The Period of the First Temple, the Babylonian Exile and the Restoration." Pp. 91–182 in *The World History of the Jewish People.* Edited by H. H. Ben-Sasson. Cambridge, Mass.: Harvard University Press, 1976.

Tajfel, Henri. *Human Groups and Social Categories: Studies in Social Psychology.* Cambridge: Cambridge University Press, 1981.

Tajfel, Henri, and John C. Turner, eds. *Differentiation between Social Groups: Studies in the Social Psychology of Intergroup Relations.* London: Academic Press, 1978.

Tannehill, Robert C. *The Sword of His Mouth.* Philadelphia: Fortress; Missoula: Scholars Press, 1975.

Teppler, Yaakov Y. *Birkat haMinim: Jews and Christians in Conflict in the Ancient World.* Translated by Susan Weingarten. Tübingen: Mohr Siebeck, 2007.

Thiessen, Matthew. "4Q372 1 and the Continuation of Joseph's Exile." *DSD* 15 (2008): 380–95.

Tiemeyer, Lena-Sofia, and Hans M. Barstad, eds. *Continuity and Discontinuity: Chronological and Thematic Development in Isaiah 40–66.* FRLANT 255. Göttingen: Vandenhoeck & Ruprecht, 2014.

Tigay, Jeffrey H. *Deuteronomy.* JPS Torah Commentary. Philadelphia: Jewish Publication Society, 1996.

Tigchelaar, Eibert J. C. *To Increase Learning for the Understanding Ones: Reading and Reconstructing the Fragmentary Early Jewish Sapiential Text 4QInstruction.* STDJ 44. Leiden: Brill, 2001.

Tropper, Amram. "Tractate *Avot* and Early Christian Succession Lists." Pp. 159–88 in *The Ways That Never Parted: Jews and Christians in Late Antiquity and the Early Middle Ages.* Edited by Adam H. Becker and Annette Yoshiko Reed. Minneapolis: Fortress, 2007.

Tso, Marcus K. M. *Ethics in the Qumran Community: An Interdisciplinary Investigation.* Tübingen: Mohr Siebeck, 2010.

Tucker, J. Brian, and Coleman A. Baker, eds. *T & T Clark Handbook to Social Identity in the New Testament.* London: Bloomsbury, 2014.

Turner, John C. *Rediscovering the Social Group: A Self-Categorization Theory.* Oxford: Blackwell, 1987.

Udoh, Fabian E., ed. *Redefining First-Century Jewish and Christian Identities: Essays in Honor of Ed Parish Sanders.* Notre Dame: University of Notre Dame Press, 2008.

Urbach, Ephraim E. *The Sages: Their Concepts and Beliefs.* Translated by Israel Abrahams. 2 vols. Jerusalem: Magnes Press, Hebrew University, 1975.

Vahrenhoerst, Martin. "The Presence and Absence of a Prohibition of Oath in James, Matthew, and the Didache and Its Significance for Conceptualization." Pp. 361–77 in *Matthew, James, and Didache: Three Related Documents in Their Jewish and Christian Settings.* Edited by Huub van de Sandt and Jurgen K. Zangenberg. SymS 45. Atlanta: SBL, 2008.

Van der Horst, Pieter. "The Birkat Ha-Minim in Recent Research." Pp. 113–24 in *Hellenism–Judaism–Christianity: Studies in Their Interaction.* 2nd ed. Leuven: Peeters, 1998.

VanderKam, James C. *The Book of Jubilees.* 2 vols. CSCO 511. Louvain: Peeters, 1989.

Vermes, Geza. *The Complete Dead Sea Scrolls in English.* Rev. ed., 50th anniversary ed. London: Penguin Books, 2011.

Viviano, Benedict T., O.P. "Where Was the Gospel According to St. Matthew Written?" *CBQ* 41 (1979): 533–46.

Wacholder, Ben Zion. *The Dawn of Qumran: The Sectarian Torah and the Teacher of Righteousness.* HUCM. Cincinnati: Hebrew Union College Press, 1983.

Wacker, Marie-Therese. *Weltordnung und Gericht: Studien zu 1 Enoch 22.* 2nd ed. Würzburg: Echter, 1985.

Walck, Leslie W. "The *Parables of Enoch* and the Synoptic Gospels." Pp. 231–68 in *Parables of Enoch: A Paradigm Shift*. Edited by James H. Charlesworth and Darrell L. Bock. London: Bloomsbury, 2014.

———. *The Son of Man in the Parables of Enoch and in Matthew*. London: T & T Clark, 2011.

Wassen, Cecilia. *Women in the Damascus Document*. AcBib 21. Atlanta: SBL, 2005.

Wassen, Cecilia, and Jutta Jokiranta. "Groups in Tension: Sectarianism in the *Damascus Document* and the *Community Rule*." Pp 205–45 in *Sectarianism in Early Judaism: Sociological Advances*. Edited by David J. Chalcraft. London: Equinox, 2007.

Weinfeld, Moshe. *The Organizational Pattern and the Penal Code of the Qumran Sect: A Comparison with Guilds and Religious Associations of the Hellenistic-Roman Period*. NTOA 2. Freiburg: Universitätsverlag; Göttingen: Vandenhoeck & Ruprecht, 1986.

Weiss, Johannes. *Jesus' Proclamation of the Kingdom of God*. Translated by Richard H. Hiers and D. Larrimore Holland. Philadelphia: Fortress, 1971.

Weksler-Bdolah, Shlomit, Alexander Onn, and Yehuda Rapuano. "Identifying the Hasmonean Village of Modi'in." *Cathedra* 109 (2003): 69–86 (Hebrew).

Weren, Wim J. D. "The Ideal Community According to Matthew, James, and the Didache." Pp. 177–200 in *Matthew, James, and Didache: Three Related Documents in Their Jewish and Christian Settings*. Edited by Huub van de Sandt and Jürgen K. Zangenberg. SymS 45. Atlanta: SBL, 2008.

Werrett, Ian C. *Ritual Purity and the Dead Sea Scrolls*. STDJ 72. Leiden: Brill, 2007.

Westerholm, Stephen. "Law in the NT." *NIDB* 3.594–602.

White, L. Michael. "Crisis Management and Boundary Maintenance: The Social Location of the Matthean Community." Pp. 211–47 in *Social History of the Matthean Community: Cross-Disciplinary Approaches*. Edited by David L. Balch. Minneapolis: Fortress, 1991.

———. "Shifting Sectarian Boundaries in Early Judaism." *BJRL* 70 (1988): 7–24.

Willitts, Joel. *Matthew's Messianic Shepherd-King: In Search of "The Lost Sheep of The House of Israel."* BZNW 147. Berlin: De Gruyter, 2007.

Wilson, Bryan. *Magic and the Millennium: A Sociological Study of Religious Movements of Protest among Tribal and Third-World Peoples*. New York: Harper & Row, 1973.

———. *The Social Dimensions of Sectarianism: Sects and New Religious Movements in Contemporary Society*. Oxford: Clarendon, 1990.

Wise, Michael O., Martin G. Abegg, Jr., and Edward M. Cook. *The Dead Sea Scrolls: A New Translation*. Rev. ed. San Francisco: HarperSanFrancisco, 2006.

Witherington, Ben, III. *Matthew*. Smyth & Helwys Bible Commentary. Macon: Smyth & Helwys, 2006.

Worchel, Stephen J., Francisco Morales, Darío Páez, and Jean-Claude Deschamps, eds. *Social Identity: International Perspectives*. London: Sage, 1998.

Worrell, J. E. "Concepts of Wisdom in the Dead Sea Scrolls." Ph.D. diss., The Claremont Graduate School, 1968.

Wright, Benjamin G., III, and Lawrence M. Wills, eds. *Conflicted Boundaries in Wisdom and Apocalypticism.* SymS 35. Atlanta: SBL, 2005.

Xeravits, Géza. *King, Priest, Prophet: Positive Eschatological Protagonists of the Qumran Library.* STDJ 47. Leiden: Brill, 2003.

———, ed. *Dualism in Qumran.* London: T & T Clark International, 2010.

Yadin, Yigael. *The Temple Scroll.* 3 vols. Jerusalem: Israel Exploration Society, 1983.

Zangenberg, Jürgen. "A Region in Transition." Pp. 1–10 in *Religion, Ethnicity, and Identity in Ancient Galilee: A Region in Transition.* Edited by Jürgen Zangenberg, Harold W. Attridge, and Dale B. Martin. WUNT 210. Tübingen: Mohr Siebeck, 2007.

Zissu, B., and A. Ganor. "Ḥorvat 'Etri: The Ruins of a Second Temple Jewish Village on the Coast Plain." *Qadmoniot* 35, no. 123 (2002): 18–27 (Hebrew).

Zsengellér, József, ed. *Samaria, Samarians, Samaritans: Studies on Bible, History and Linguistics.* Berlin: De Gruyter, 2011.

Index of Subjects

ing the sect, 189, 192, 201–2; and communal organization and discipline, 146; in first-century Jewish world, 16–17, 19–20, 23, 32, 34, 37, 174–75, 178–79; and Jesus, 162, 175, 178–79, 182; and Jewish sectarianism, 53, 65; and Sermon on the Mount, 83, 106; and wisdom texts, 127

Sabbath, 21, 55, 61
Sabinius, 15
Sadducees: and communal organization, 9; on false witnesses, 92–93; in first-century Jewish world, 6, 19, 22–24, 26–28, 30; Jesus's conflict with, 157–58, 160–73, 177–78, 201, 208, 214n63; Jesus's resurrection denied by, 248n84; and sectarianism, 50, 60–62; and Sermon on the Mount, 93–94
sages. See ḥākāmîm
Salome Alexandra, 23, 214n59
Samaritans, 185
Sanhedrin, 33, 35–36, 174–75
Sayings Source "Q," 4, 8–9, 11–12, 38, 72, 83, 121, 160, 192
scribes: and communal organization, 9; in first-century Jewish world, 19, 22, 25, 28–30; Jesus's conflict with, 158–59, 160–73, 194, 214n63; and peacemaking, 110; role of, 216nn98,99; and Sermon on the Mount, 87, 91, 110; and wisdom texts, 126
sectarianism, 38–67; and boundary marking mechanisms, 48, 54, 66, 77–78, 81, 106, 154–55, 200, 204; cognition's role in group formation, 40; communal nature of, 83, 120, 131–55, 191, 194, 198, 210; in Dead Sea Scrolls, 49–59; definitions of, 47–49, 208; development of, 6, 46; in first-century Jewish

world, 6–37; formation of groups, 40, 49, 54, 106, 112, 155, 173, 200, 209; hierarchy in, 99, 120; and identity, 43, 125, 134, 206; membership in groups, 120, 140, 191, 205; and norms, 49, 103, 149; persecution as theme in, 57, 75, 80–85, 91, 111, 168, 172, 176, 201; after temple destruction (70 CE), 59–65; as voluntary associations of protest, 41, 48, 53–54, 66, 84–85, 200, 204–6; and wisdom texts, 113–30. See also antagonism element of sectarianism; difference element of sectarianism; separation element of sectarianism; and specific groups
self-understanding, 80, 91, 168
separation element of sectarianism: and communal organization and discipline, 155, 241n53; in Dead Sea Scrolls, 57, 58, 67; defined, 49; and Jesus, 183, 208, 210; and Sermon on the Mount, 85, 104, 106, 108, 110, 111, 112, 230n131; and wisdom texts, 130
Sepphoris, 14–15, 17, 29, 32, 35, 37, 39, 45, 216n107
Sermon on the Mount, 68–112; and antagonism element of sectarianism, 85, 106, 108, 111, 112; antitheses content in, 98–111; antitheses form in, 92–97; and apocalyptic texts, 76, 80; Beatitudes, 74–85, 90–91, 110–12, 128, 130, 150, 162–64, 168, 194, 206; and capital punishment, 92, 98–99, 106–7; and commandments, 90, 100–101, 104–5, 108; and communal organization and discipline, 110; and covenant, 79, 82, 87, 103, 105, 109; and Dead Sea Scrolls, 74, 76, 90, 96–97, 102–3, 107; and difference element of sectarianism, 85, 106, 108, 111; and eschatological discourse, 69, 71; and Essenes, 70, 94, 104, 109; and

Index of Modern Authors

294

Index of Ancient Sources

Deuterocanonical Books (Apocrypha)